# Helga

This book breaks the silence about the horrors faced by people from the Eastern states of Germany at the end of the Second World War. It is the story of a Swiss family trying to live an ordinary life in Hitler's Germany and told by Helga, the daughter.

She was born near the Lithuanian border, as a young girl met Hitler, supported her mother when the SS repeatedly searched their home and, as a medical student cared for some of the thousands of wounded soldiers returning from the Russian battlefields in cattle trucks.

Alone, she joined the refugee treks in the severe winter of 1944/45, fleeing over land and frozen lakes, chased and shot at by the Russian army. There was no food, no shelter, no warmth, only ice, wind, snow and the dead bodies of the refugees fallen by the wayside. Helga's courage helped her to survive.

Miraculously she found her family again and they lived like Gypsies in great poverty in a wooden hut on an empty army radio station without running water or sanitation before returning to Switzerland.

Helga Gerhardi

# Helga

The true story of a young woman's flight as a refugee

and how she re-united her war-scattered family

*Kind regards*

*Helga Gerhardi*

**VIRONA**
PUBLISHING

First published 1993 by Virona Publishing
24 Putnams Drive, Aston Clinton, AYLESBURY, Bucks. HP22 5HH


© Helga Gerhardi 1993


The right of Helga Gerhardi to be identified as author
of this work has been asserted by her in accordance with
the Copyright, Designs and Patents Act 1988


British Library Cataloguing-in-Publication Data.
A catalogue record for this book is
available from the British Library


ISBN 0 9521933 0 2


Typeset by Virona Publishing, Aston Clinton

# Author's Note

The book tells the story of my family and myself in Hitler's Germany before and during the war, and carries on to describe what happened to me subsequently. Being Swiss by birth, we were "foreigners", and we were sometimes made to feel this, particularly by the SS during the war.

Life in East Prussia, away from the Reich (State), was not quite the same as in the main part of Germany. The old life and the traditions, although overshadowed by Nazism, were often still in the forefront. During the war, we were all extremely conscious of the fact that we were nearer to Poland and Russia, than to France and England.

I had a very happy childhood and adolescence, until the Russians advanced into East Prussia. The journey, as a refugee, from Königsberg, in the terrible, cold winter months at the beginning of 1945, was a nightmare. Some of it can never be told. It took me years before I was even able to think about it or even talk about it, and it is only now that I can write down what happened to me and my fellow sufferers.

The war ended and, having lost everything, we lived like Gipsies, in terrible poverty, on an abandoned radio station, sleeping on palliasses. There was no sanitation, running water or heating, and very little food. I travelled from the north of Germany to the south, 800 km, with a broken bicycle, in search of my family, and even got imprisoned. In the end, our family was united, and the Swiss Embassy helped us to return to Switzerland.

I always kept a patchy diary, and was able to draw on it for many facts in this book. Occasionally I have altered a name to protect the person, if still alive - but there were so many that got killed, or gave their lives for the Vaterland, and they won't mind being mentioned.

Tilsit (Sovetsk) and Königsberg (Kaliningrad), the two places where we lived, are now Russian. Danzig (Gdansk), where my mother came from, became a Polish harbour after the war, and although it is now possible to visit these places, I have not done so. I have no desire to see our house, if not destroyed, occupied by Russian people. I like to remember it as it was.

It was my husband and my two sons, Victor and Peter, being always very interested in my past, who encouraged me to write about it. I have to thank them for the existence of the book.

Helga Gerhardi

## Acknowledgements

I would like to thank the following:

Victor, my son, who assisted in getting the book ready for print

Gill, for her encouragement and suggestions

Brett, my grandson, who drew the maps onto the computer

My husband, for all his help, understanding and patience

Dr. Hilary Johnson, who did the final editing of the book

Norrie Semple for scanning the photographs and documents

Martin Haydon for designing the cover

For my children and their children
and my husband, without whose help the publication
of this book would have remained a dream.

# CONTENTS

## PART ONE
### LIFE IN TILSIT AND KÖNIGSBERG

# PART TWO
## THE GREAT ESCAPE

# ILLUSTRATIONS

# PART ONE

LIFE IN TILSIT AND KÖNIGSBERG

# CHAPTER ONE

## My Early Years

My Grandfather, Georg Albert, was born in Switzerland on the 3rd of June 1854, in a little village called Zihlschlacht, in the Kanton of Thurgau. His parents had a small farm. He grew up knowing all about cows and milk, and how to make butter and cheese. Grandfather was one of nine children and, as he was not the eldest boy, he knew that he would not inherit the farm. Not liking the idea of working as an ordinary farmhand for his brother for the rest of his life, he decided to emigrate.

There was fertile land in the north-east of Germany and Lithuania, and a number of Swiss had emigrated, after 1870, to those districts. They worked there as "cheesemakers", on different large farms.

Grandfather joined the emigrants and, after working for a short time on a farm, he met and married grandmother, Amalie Berta Ehrenteit, then aged twenty. They settled down in Ragnit, a small town next to Tilsit, by the river Memel. Lithuania was not far away and, although the land there was more fertile, and the cows produced better milk, the grandparents preferred to stay in Germany because of the language. Grandfather spoke Swiss, a dialect of German. Through hard work, and being very frugal, *Omama* (grandmother) and *Opapa* (grandfather) got on well. They established a dairy in Ragnit and another in Tilsit.

*Opapa* concentrated on the making of cheese, and eventually made a name for himself when he won the Gold Medal for one of his cheeses at the Leipzig Fair, which he had called "Tilsiter", incorporating the name of the town where it was made. Today, Tilsiter cheese is produced in many countries, and is often sold packed in slices. In *Opapa's* day, it was shaped into a small wheel, 40 cm across, and about 10-15 cm thick, called *Brot* or *Laib* (loaf), and covered in thin mutton cloth. It was stored on boards in a cellar, and left to mature for two months or more. It was necessary to have the dampness of the cellar to help with the maturation of the cheese. The Tilsiter cheese was actually a copy of the Swiss

Emmentaler, and one could say an unsuccessful reproduction. *Opapa* wanted to produce smaller, faster maturing cheese than the Emmentaler, and without having to use a press, and the result was the new cheese.

*½ lb Butter Wrapper*

Grandmother was looking forward to children, and particularly to daughters. Unfortunately this was not to be; she had six sons: Benno in 1884, Hugo in 1886, Kurt in 1887, Paul in 1890, who died aged 17, my father, Georg Hans in 1892, and Bruno in 1895.

Over the years, *Opapa* became a very rich man. He did not believe in putting his money into banks, but kept it in gold coins in a safe. When he had too much, he bought land and property. In that way, he acquired two farms and two more dairies, which were run by managers.

My father was the only one of the boys who was interested in the dairy business. Already, as a young boy, he used to follow *Opapa* when he went around the dairy, and watch the making of the butter and cheese. It was decided that he should eventually take over the dairy management. Before that, he was sent to university in Bamberg to study commerce and banking.

When war broke out in 1914 my father had to return home, and so never finished his studies. He started in the dairy in Ragnit but after a year *Opapa* put him into the dairy in Tilsit as manager. The dairy and the large house were built at the corner of the Grabenstrasse (Ditch Street), and, together with the stables and the gated fence and shop, formed a rectangle, enclosing a cobbled yard. The house was divided into flats, which were let until my father got married, and we lived there as children.

2

The war did not affect the family much. The boys did not have to join the army, because they were Swiss. Food was needed, therefore the dairies prospered, and so did the two farms. In 1916, grandfather died suddenly and my father now had also to keep an eye on the dairy in Ragnit, which was managed by a manager appointed by grandmother. When the war ended, my father was 26 years old. Before settling down for good, he wanted to do some travelling. *Omama* agreed with him, and gave him the money to travel. The only stipulation was that my father had to spend some time at different dairies in order to see the various types of cheese or butter making. My father travelled for a year, keeping to his promise and stopping longer at some places to work for a time in several dairies. He finished up in Hamburg, working there at a large dairy, where he met my mother.

My mother was born on the 9th of January 1899 in Landau, a suburb of Danzig, the large port on the river Weichsel (Vistula) by the Baltic. My mother's father was the pork butcher in Landau. When my mother was born it was a small village, but later, when Danzig grew, it became a suburb of the city. My grandmother came from farming stock, and was very domesticated. My grandparents had three children, Erich, Trude, who died in a drowning accident aged 12 or 13, and Erna, my mother. They lived a simple life in a small community, working very hard. In the summer, *Omama* picked fruit, made jam, bottled vegetables, pickled cucumbers and made *Sauerkraut* (pickled white cabbage). In the winter, she spun wool, and knitted all the garments necessary for the family. Any spare time she had, she helped *Opapa* with his business, making sausages, pickling meat, smoking the ham, or selling in the shop.

When my mother was 14 years old, she finished with the village school but, having always been top of the class, she was encouraged by her teacher to carry on with some kind of education. She took a three year course at a commercial college in Danzig learning shorthand, typing, book-keeping and a little French and English, and then had a job in the town in a big Import/Export business. This was all very unusual, because girls in those days stayed at home and helped mothers, or, when coming from poorer families, went into service. Girls did not go out and earn money!

I am not quite sure how my mother met my father, but I think it was at a party she attended, given by her employers while she was working in Hamburg. Being in Hamburg, a long way from home, they both had a common link, coming from the East and, with their love for dancing, a

3

start was made to get acquainted. My mother said she was never quite sure how things were going, because my father also had other girl friends. Aunt Dora, with whom she lived, had a different opinion:

'Erna,' she said, 'mark my words, you have a serious admirer there. One of these days he will propose'.

But then came a crisis in my father's family, when his brother Benno lost a great deal of money through gambling, and my father returned home. He promised to write, also invited my mother to come and stay with his mother. Things were different in those days. A young girl didn't just turn up at a place after such a casual invitation, and so my mother said:

'You have got to come and fetch me, or your mother has to ask me to come. I want a proper invitation.'

My father only laughed. He wrote and told her about Benno, and also that he had to get back into the business again in Tilsit. A letter did arrive from his mother, asking my mother to come and stay with her, but my mother didn't go. Auntie Dora encouraged her; she liked my mother and had grown fond of my father, but my mother was adamant.

'It is a long journey,' she said. 'It will take two days and, in any case, why should I travel so far? Hans hasn't proposed, he is only a boy friend, and I most certainly will not go to the Lithuanian border to see a boyfriend, just because he wants me to.'

After a while, my father stopped writing. Auntie Dora blamed my mother.

'There are not many eligible men about these days,' she said. 'You have ruined your future. What do you want, somebody with no job? Hans is young, good looking, with a good business and an excellent future in front of him, and his mother has invited you.'

It wasn't easy for my mother to hear all this from her aunt, because she would have liked to go. She had fallen in love with my father, but she felt that if she did travel to Tilsit it would be like running after him, and she was too proud to do this.

And then, one day, my father just turned up at my aunt's door. He told my mother that he had come to take her back to Tilsit, so that they could get married. *Omama* told my mother later that it was my mother's refusal to come to Tilsit which helped to make up her son's mind.

'If she isn't coming here, I will go and fetch her, and marry her', he said, and that was what he did.

4

My parents got married on August 13th 1921, and, after a short honeymoon in Königsberg, the capital of East Prussia, settled down in Ragnit. The idea was that my father would run the dairy in Tilsit and Ragnit, and move later to Tilsit.

It wasn't long before my mother was involved in the business. She was good at accounts and, being able to write shorthand and type, she took over part of the correspondence and supervised the book-keeping. Living close to my father's mother, she often spent her time with her, and got very attached to her.

My sister Astra (called Sternchen by the family) was born in March 1923, a great disappointment to my father, who had hoped for a son. I was born in July the following year, and the disappointment on my father's side was even greater. Now he had two daughters, and still no son. He decided to treat me more like a son than a daughter, as it was soon realized that I was not a quiet child. I was very strong-willed, obstinate and without any fear, so it seemed. Astra was a beautiful child, with dark hair and lovely blue eyes, quiet and well behaved. I was chubby, with blue eyes and mousy coloured hair, an ordinary looking child, not ugly, not beautiful.

The following year, my parents moved to Tilsit. It was probably because of the move from Ragnit to Tilsit that my mother had a miscarriage that year and then, in 1926, my sister Christel was born.

'Three girls,' my father said, 'and still no son.'

I was two years old, and as wild, noisy and self-willed as any boy. But all was forgiven, because Christel was like a fairy doll, with lovely fair curls, small, delicate, sweet and always smiling. I became very naughty, the girl in the middle, reminding my parents of my presence, because my father adored Christel, and my mother preferred Astra. It was decided, when I was only three years old, that I had to attend the local nursery school because even the children's nurse whom my mother employed couldn't cope with me.

My brother was born in February 1928, during a very severe winter. He was a premature baby, weighing 3½ German pounds, very thin, weak and small and, to keep him warm, he was wrapped up, put into a cigar box and, every so often, put for a little while into the *Ofenröhre*. (The warm space in the tiled stove where we baked our apples). After that, we called him Apple Hans. At last my father was happy, he had a son.

It could not have been easy for my mother to cope with four children, helping in the business and doing a certain amount of entertaining. Tilsit was a small town, and all officials and business people knew one another.

My mother gave big dinners, and had coffee afternoons for the ladies, and occasionally, my parents went to a ball, sometimes in fancy dress. She had quite a bit of help at home. We had a live-in nurse, a cook, a maid to clean the house and a washerwoman. For the dinner parties, the chauffeur would dress up and help with the serving. My mother liked to be with us, but there was often no time. She had a lot of trouble with the nurses, some of them untrained. Quite a few were not capable of managing us, although their job was only to look after us.

When I was not quite six it was decided that I should go to school. I had accompanied Sternchen from time to time, and I had also grown out of the nursery school. I was a big girl for my age, often involved in fights if I didn't get my way, and the two elderly sisters who were running the nursery school couldn't cope with me any more.

It was a private school and the classes were not very big. There must have been ten classes, because I started in class 10, whilst Sternchen was already in class 9. She looked down at me, and we often wouldn't even go to school together. When we played in the playground, she pretended not to know me.

The first day at school was really grand, and I loved it. Proudly I arrived with my new satchel, slate board and chalk box, also a small sandwich for the morning break. It was fun sitting at the desk, and one could lift the lid up, or stand up, and the seat folded back. The satchel had its place under the desk lid, and the coat hung up outside the classroom in the hallway where there were hooks with animal and flower pictures. I had an elephant, and was told that I must hang up my coat there every day. Everything was so different on the first day. You were told all the time what to do, and teacher seemed to say to me more often "don't" than "do". I was quite tired by dinner time, and not all that sure that I really would like to go every day. School was from 8am until 12.30pm, a long morning, but there was no school in the afternoon. I was glad the first day was finished.

When I came out of school, I was surprised to see so many mothers waiting, a lot of them with wrapped-up things in their hands. I soon discovered what they were because there stood my mother; she had unwrapped the most enormous *Schultüte* (paper school bag) I had ever seen. It was nearly as big as I was. The *Schultüte* is given to each child on the first school-day and I had forgotten about it. It is shaped like a long big cone, hollow inside and, at the top, around the opening, is coloured paper pulled together with a ribbon. The whole shape is covered in gaily patterned paper, with pictures on it. The centre is filled with sweets and little presents.

In the afternoon, my favourite Uncle Kühl arrived, and he, too, gave me a *Schultüte*. He was not a real Uncle, but he was one of the kindest people I knew. He was a widower with no children, a dapper little man with a big round tummy like a ball. He was a business acquaintance of my father's and loved children. Over the years he used to come and see my father, but also always made a point of coming to see us. He generally wore a suit and waistcoat and had a lovely watch and chain. He would let us look into certain pockets, where we always found some little presents or sweets.

Sternchen didn't like him much; she said he smelled of beer and tobacco. Christel was shy, and Hans a little too young to have much of an opinion. I was always fascinated with his big round tummy and I would stroke it. It was a little in the way when I sat on his lap when he played with me, bouncing his knees up and down like a horse, then suddenly opening his legs so that I slid down, screaming with delight.

I enquired from my parents why Uncle had such a round tummy, and my father laughed, saying:

'He has got a balloon in it.'

That was really interesting. So, the next time he came, I banged his tummy, hoping to burst the balloon, but he only got cross with me and told me that I hurt him. Well, I had to think of something else, I was determined to burst the balloon. It would also give me more space to sit on his lap. The next time he came, I pushed a needle into his tummy. You could say the balloon went up! What a commotion, and all because I wanted to burst the balloon.

I screamed at everybody that I only wanted to burst the balloon, but I was banned from the living room and had to stay all alone for the rest of the afternoon in the nursery. After a time I was forgiven and Uncle explained that he didn't have a balloon.

After the excitement of the first day at school, and when the novelty had worn off, I didn't like school any more. I was not allowed to get up unless I asked permission, or we had our break. Then we had to draw letters. We learnt to print the alphabet first at this school. So, with chalk, we had to write on our desk again and again "A" and then "a", after that "B" and then "b" and by the time we got to "D" and "d", I thought it was silly to write this thing once like this "b" and once like this "d". I thought they should decide which way round the letter went, and give it the same sound and not different ones. In any case, I wanted to know how to read, as I had lovely story books, but could only look at the pictures. We even had to practice our letters at home on our slate, and bring this to school and, if it didn't look right, the lady teacher would wash it off with a wet sponge, and I had to dry it with my square, and write it again.

I was often in trouble when I had forgotten to wet my sponge. One could always wet it at school but most days I was lucky to reach my desk before the teacher, because there were always so many things to see on the way to school. There was no corporal punishment at this school, but naughty children had to stand in the corner. After a time, they were asked to say sorry, and allowed to sit down again. I didn't like to say sorry if I felt I wasn't in the wrong so sometimes I had to stay in the corner for a long time. If I hadn't wet my sponge I had to stand in the corner, but then I soon said sorry, because I realized it was my mistake.

One day I was late again and had forgotten to wet my sponge. I knew I would never make it to the basin in the toilet room, and get into class before the teacher so, when I saw a puddle outside the school, I quickly wet my sponge and dived through the door and into the classroom to my desk. My letters were not very well done, according to the teacher. She was cross, and took the dripping sponge (I hadn't even wrung it out in the hurry), saying:

'At least you wet your sponge.'

She rubbed all my letters off and, whilst doing so, a pungent smell came up to our noses from the sponge and slate.

'Wherever did you wet your sponge?' she said, holding it over the side of the desk and squeezing it again. The water dripping out of it had a peculiar dirty brown/yellow colour, combined with a terrible smell. Of course, she guessed where I had wet my sponge. It hadn't rained lately, but there were plenty of horses on the road!

'You dirty girl!' she scolded, 'How could you do a thing like that. I will write a letter to your father. Now, go and wash the sponge and your hands.'

The letter to my father arrived in due course but, when he told me off, I saw that he wasn't all that cross, because he had difficulties in keeping a straight face.

We moved to Königsberg when I was 7 years old. My parents felt that, with four children, there would be better opportunities for our education. Tilsit in those days didn't even have a grammar school. Königsberg was chosen because it was the capital of East Prussia and also because it had a university. It was a lovely old town, full of solidly built, imposing buildings, and a beautiful castle. The 375,000 inhabitants were very proud of their town.

*Königsberg Castle (demolished by the Russians)*

My parents had a house built on the outskirts of the town, in Ratshof, a so-called *Vorort* (suburb). The town centre could be reached from our house by tram in half an hour. It was a big house and when I arrived, I discovered that the furniture was all standing in the middle of the rooms, as my mother hadn't decided where to put things. The carpets were still rolled up, and all the linen, glasses and china were in boxes, which were now being unpacked. The garden outside was very bare and big, with builder's rubble still lying about. It was Easter time, so I had no school; in any case, I didn't know where my new school would be. The whole area was a new development because, although there were a few houses near us, there was a big field opposite, divided into allotments. Ours was a corner house, with the entrance on Metgetherstrasse, a small road leading off a bigger one. The main road, with the tramlines, was on the other side of the allotments, but we could see the road and trams very well from our house.

We had only moved a few days, when my mother stopped unpacking, and there seemed to be discussions going on between my parents. Then suddenly we were informed that we would move out and things which had been unpacked got packed again. Although the house was finished, it had not dried out sufficiently and the walls were damp. My mother refused to stay there with four children, saying that we would all be ill, so my father had to find another place, a big downstairs flat in another part of the town, and we moved there for the time being. It was in the poorer part of the town, near a Gypsy camp, and my father was the only one there who possessed a car. We were also foreigners, but this was not known at first. We looked the same and spoke the same language, so there was no need to mention it. My mother didn't like the district, and we mostly had to play indoors, as she didn't want us to mix with the "rough" children outside. She hardly communicated with the neighbours, but couldn't avoid meeting them in the shops. She often sent me to the grocer to put in an order, which he then delivered. In this way she avoided meeting the people who lived around us. This was, of course, a silly thing to do, because it made it very difficult for us children, as we were considered snobs.

Sternchen, who often copied my mother, agreed with her and would not mix with the children, not even at school. Christel was frightened of them, and Hans, who was only three years old, had no opinion. I got on alright with the local children after I had a few fights. The children played different games to the ones I had known. We had always been rather protected in Tilsit, having had a nurse to look after us, and I had been to a private nursery and main school.

Sternchen and I were sent to the local school, called *Grundschule* (primary school). Neither of us liked the school, but for different reasons. Sternchen didn't like the rough children; they made fun of her, and pulled her skirt, and the teacher didn't help her enough in the big class. We were both used to small classes and lots of attention. It was at this time that Sternchen developed a wonderful imagination as far as illnesses were concerned, which she never lost. She would have headaches, tummy upsets, breathing problems, or giddiness. As my mother believed her, she often missed school, and I had to take a note for the teacher with me. I knew it wasn't true when she said she was ill, because I would go and see her sometimes after my mother had put her back to bed in the morning, and she would laugh at me and put her tongue out and say:

'I don't have to go to school, and I won't go tomorrow either!' with the stress on "I".

My father only came home for weekends, because he spent the rest of the week in Tilsit and Ragnit at the dairies. He was very busy at this time, negotiating to buy another two small dairies in Lithuania. All I knew as a child was that my father's business was alright, that he was busy and had to travel during the week. He was always at home at the weekend. We did not miss our father all that much, but my mother did as she found it increasingly difficult to cope with us. I was very naughty, and the usual saying was:

'You wait until your father comes home at the weekend.'

When my father did come home, all my naughtiness was told, and I often received quite severe corporal punishment. I soon got frightened of my father, and didn't look forward to his homecoming at all. To cover up things, I lied, and gradually became quite good at it, even being able to convince my parents at times.

School was extremely difficult for me. Not only because of the other children, but also because of non-understanding teachers. I had started off with printed letters, and my spelling of even some complicated words was quite good. In the new school, I was expected to write in the old German writing called *Sütterlinschrift*. My parents wrote in it, and the children at this particular school had started off with it. It was only when I left school, at the age of 18, that I started to write in the so-called Latin writing, and gradually developed my own style of handwriting. I was good with numbers and sums, actually I was advanced compared with the others.

***Example of Sütterlinschrift***

I was glad to leave the school when, in the summer holiday, we moved back into our house in the Metgetherstrasse. By now it had dried out.

I was eight years old now, and Sternchen one year older. Christel was six and ready to go to school. It was very difficult for my mother to decide where to send us to school. Private schools hardly existed; in any case, there were none near us. The nearest school was only five minutes away, but a mixture of children attended there, some even from the Kapornerstrasse. The street was full of people and children, dirty houses and dirty gardens. People even lived in the cellars and, although the houses on both sides of the street were laid out in flats with small front gardens, people couldn't afford the rent, and so they sublet. One could find whole families in one room. I had no idea what communists were, but I knew they lived in the Kapornerstrasse.

My mother was afraid that when we mixed with those children, we would pick up bad language and bad habits. After a lot of deliberation a choice was made. Sternchen and Christel went to the local school, and I had to go to a different school, a more modern one, about 15 minutes by bicycle away from home. It was apparently a better school than the local one, with nicer children. It was felt that Sternchen would be alright in the local school; she never picked up any bad language at the last school. Christel definitely had to attend a school near to us. She was very delicate, small, shy and often frightened. She never played outside with the other children unless I was there.

The school I went to was named after the famous socialist leader, Friedrich Ebert. I stayed there for the next two years, and was quite happy. The teachers and the curriculum were well established, the discipline strict, and everything was orientated towards learning. When Hitler took over the government, the school became a showpiece for the new regime. An extension was built to house a large gymnasium and shower rooms, the playground was enlarged and covered with tarmac, new sports fields were created next to the school, and the old building had a face-lift to such an extent that one couldn't recognize the old school. Even the name changed, in a grand opening ceremony with a number of local top ranking Nazis present, to Adolf Hitler *Schule* (school). My parents were quite shocked but, as I was only staying there until the age of ten, it was decided not to upset me again with another change of school.

A block of flats on the other corner side of Metgetherstrasse was being built at the same time as our house, with their entrances in Wiebestrasse. Later on, the police department built a big police station next to it and took over the flats, which were then occupied by the administration staff working in the station. Our favourite play area was the allotments opposite the house, on the Vierbrüderplatz (Four brothers' place). We could only use this in the autumn, winter or early spring as most people grew vegetables and potatoes on the allotments. Some preferred flowers and tomatoes. As soon as autumn came and the last potatoes were harvested, we children would take over the empty area. There are two things I remember playing on the allotments, football, and Cowboys and Indians. Often I was the only girl amongst the crowd of boys. I came into football because they needed a goal keeper. Everybody wanted to kick the ball, nobody wanted to go into the goal.

Helma, a small tough boy with red hair and freckles, was the leader. His father was the local police chief, and his brother Uwe, also a redhead, and a year younger, was a little shy. Helma always looked after him and protected him. Helma would measure out the football pitch and mark it with stones. For goal posts, we had pieces of wood, collected from building sites or handy fathers. To get the pitch flat, the children trampled all over the area, which often was quite rough from digging up the potatoes. This could take hours, but was a lot of fun, and was the first thing I was allowed to do for the boys. Even Christel joined in if I was holding her hand. Once the ground was fairly flat, the teams were chosen, and then the game began. Often there was no referee, and the teams had only a few children on either side, but it was a game. Christel and I watched it, standing on the pavement by the allotments and, if the ball went into the road, I would kick it back.

'You are good,' Helma said to me one day 'You can join us, you can go into the goal.'

I was terribly proud and told Christel to watch. But, after a time, I got bored. The game seemed to be more in the middle of the field, with the boys pushing one another to get to the ball. There were not many rules and, in any case, who was there to uphold them? There wasn't much to do in the goal and, if I let a ball through, I got told off. In the end I told Helma if I wasn't permitted to be in the team I wouldn't go into the goal again. Helma needed me, and so it was felt it would be better to take it in turns. At least they had an extra person for the game. And then it was discovered that I could outrun them all; being so much faster, I was able to score several times. I became popular; everybody wanted me in their team. The best player and the best runner was of course Helma. He was a little shorter than myself, and three months younger than I. He was terribly jealous if I scored a goal and he didn't, because I was only a girl.

It was very fashionable at that time to read Karl May's books, and we were all enthusiastic about the different Indian tribes, and their fight against the white man. We were not interested in being Cowboys, we all wanted to be Indians. We dug a big hole on the allotments, and then steps to go into it. The earth and dirt taken out of the hole was put around the top, which gave us the feeling of being really deep in the hole. So that it wouldn't get too wet inside, we covered the top with planks, branches, boxes, anything big and, in the end, we piled the green foliage from the potatoes on to the top, and the weeds from the compost heap. This was now our wigwam, where we could sit by candlelight and discuss things, like the war against the white man. I was allowed to be a woman, the wise old woman who knew the future, the squaw.

One day Helma arrived with a pipe and some tobacco. Now we were real Indians and could smoke a peace pipe. Old Shatterhand had come to help the Mohicans (Helma was Old Shatterhand), and now we had to smoke and talk. The pipe was lit and handed around. We were sitting cross-legged on the floor on old pieces of cardboard. I didn't like the tobacco, it tasted terrible, and so I only puffed a little. Helma was the big, strong, brave white man, and smoked a lot. Suddenly he changed colour and dived outside. We could hear him retching and coughing. There was dead silence in the circle around the camp fire (a candle), and then one or two more chased outside. Nobody really mentioned it, but we all knew what had happened, and why. Gradually we became crafty, and would only puff a bit, never inhale. When the tobacco was finished, we had to find something else. We smoked all sorts of mixtures, potato foliage, dried leaves and grass, even rose leaves, dried and chopped, which were the best substitute, in our opinion. When we had nothing, we just handed the empty pipe around.

And then one day, after heavy rain and some snow, the whole contraption collapsed, and it was impossible to resurrect it. In any case, the winter had come and, as we usually had lots of snow and did sledging and skating, the interest for that particular game had gone.

In winter we had plenty of snow, so we went tobogganing. Toboggans were made in several sizes, one, two, three or four seater ones, and some had back and arm rests on one end, like an armchair, for the little children. We had several sledges. They were always brought down from the attic when the first snow came, usually in November and, by March, they were cleaned up, all metal parts were oiled, and the sledges put back into the attic. The three-seater sledge with backrest was used whilst Hans and Christel were young, but later it was replaced with a two seater one, which was the more popular. Hans and Christel would sit on the sledge, all wrapped up in blankets, and we would pull them along. We would all go for a walk on Sundays and my father would pull the sledge. Sometimes he would run and then suddenly pull the string sharply to one side, which made the sledge spin round. If this was done too sharply, the sledge would tip over, and we would all fall off, with shrieks of laughter. The weather could be bitterly cold, often 20 C below zero, and 10 C below zero was an accepted temperature in the winter.

We didn't do any skiing, because we had no decent hills, but we all had skates. We used the road to skate on, as we had no frozen lake close by, but when I got older, I used to go with Christel to the *Schlossteich* (castle lake) in the centre of the town. At night, they would sweep the marked-out area on the lake, then squirt it with water, in order to have it really smooth. The water froze overnight and looked beautiful the next day. There were benches at the side, where we could sit and put on our skates. When it was dark, usually just after 4 o'clock, they switched on big lights on the clubhouse, and also had lamps on the frozen lake. Music blared from the loudspeakers, and one could dance a waltz, or just skate along with a partner, or make a long row, holding on to the waist of the person in front, or just glide along, watching some of the experts performing in a separate enclosure.

I was never an expert, but I could skate, and got a lot of pleasure out of it, particularly as a teenager, with a boyfriend. In the summer the clubhouse was used as a restaurant, and one could also hire boats there to row around the lake. We only used the facilities in the winter, because it was quite a long way to go on the tram and in the summer there were many other interests locally, even a lake to swim in.

# CHAPTER TWO

## Changes under Hitler

Hitler came to power on the 30th of January 1933, and it was the first time that it was brought home to me that we were different, not German, but Swiss. I have never forgotten that day.

The voting on that day was only to say 'yes' or 'no' for Hitler to become chancellor of the German republic. Marshal Paul von Hindenburg remained President. If you had said 'yes' (*Ja*), you received a little pin with *Ja* formed from wire, which was pinned to the lapel. Everybody seemed to have such a pin on that day, although it was a secret ballot but, being a child, I didn't think about that.

On the day in question we had no school, because a number of schools were needed as polling stations and, as there was a lot of snow about, we went tobogganing in the morning. Fresh snow fell at dinner time but just before dark it stopped, and Christel and I decided to build a snowman on the allotment. We started with a small ball. We rolled it along, and it got bigger and bigger, and was soon big enough to form the bottom part of our snowman. A second big roll was formed in the same way and lifted on top, then a third one, but smaller, for the head. In the meantime, other children had arrived, and we were quite a crowd, all enjoying the snow. I went indoors to get the different things for the face, a carrot as nose, coal pieces for the eyes and the mouth, a stick for the cigar, an old hat and scarf, and the finished object was most attractive. Suddenly somebody said to us:

'Didn't your parents vote "*Ja*"?'

I looked around, and nearly everybody had the little "*Ja*" pins in their coat lapels, given to them by their fathers. I didn't really know what it was all about. I had thought the grown-ups had to sign some papers in the schools, that's why we had a free day, and when I asked my mother, she told me that it had nothing to do with us, because we were not German. We had been told, in a casual way, that we were Swiss, but I always thought that was only because grandfather had left his home country. I never felt any different from the other children. I didn't look any different and spoke the same language, dressed the same, went to the same school. Still, my parents didn't vote and I wasn't bothered whether I had that pin or not, so I just replied:

'My father didn't vote.'

'Why not?' said Klaus, a boy living in the police flats.

'We are not German, we are Swiss,' I replied, 'we don't vote.'

'Rubbish,' said Klaus, 'everybody votes, you either say "*Ja*" or "*Nein*" (Yes or No).'

'My father doesn't need to vote,' I replied, getting a little more agitated. I didn't like to be questioned; I wasn't quite sure what was going on. I didn't know anything about politics, I was only eight years old. My brother who had joined us in the snowman building and Christel moved a little closer to me as they felt an argument developing.

'You are all Communists!' shouted one of the children.

I had heard that the Communists lived in the Kapornerstrasse, where I had to go and take my father's collars to be washed and starched, and I wasn't allowed to hang around there, because they were bad people. Calling me a Communist was an insult, and all three of us knew that. I could see this developing into a possible fight, so I pushed Christel away, and told her to go indoors. Hans could look after himself. If he didn't want to fight, he would run home, but Christel would hang around and wait.

'I am no Communist, and neither is my father,' I said. 'You take that back, or you will be in trouble.'

'You haven't got the *Ja* pin,' called out Klaus.

'Communist, Communist, you haven't got the *Ja* pin!'

It was then repeated by the other children, and they all chanted:

'Communist, Communist, you haven't got the *Ja* pin!'

If it was the *Ja* pin they were concerned about, that was not so difficult. I would just take one away from one of them, even if it meant a fight. If I was in a temper, my fists would fly. So I just went for the loudest screaming boy, and soon had his *Ja* pin. After that, a real battle developed. We were rolling in the snow, hitting one another, throwing snowballs, pulling the *Ja* pins about, and generally making a lot of noise. My friend Helma, his brother Uwe, and one or two children I knew were on my side, but we were outnumbered and, when one of the boys started to destroy our lovely snowman, I hit him with my fists, and jumped on his back.

I don't know what would have happened, but I suddenly felt a heavy hand pulling me up, and I heard my father's voice:

'Now then, what is going on here? Why can't you all play together quietly?'

I tried to explain, but I was out of breath, and the others just stared silently at my father, some of them trying to sneak away.

'Just stay here,' called my father, 'I want to tell you something.'

There was no need for me to explain, because he had heard it already from Christel who had run indoors.

'You have all been good friends for quite a long time,' my father said, 'and, because I didn't vote, you are now going to be enemies? We are not German, but Swiss, and come from a lovely small mountainous German-speaking country and, because of that, I am not allowed to vote.

I have no right to decide how Germany is governed, because it is not my country, and this is right and proper. But, if you are worried about the *Ja* pin, they have boxes of them at the polling station and anybody can take one. If you want some, I can go and fetch them for you. You don't have to vote, you can just take a pin.'

They all looked, started fidgeting, glanced at my father, then at me, and murmured:

'Well, the pin isn't so important.' Helma then took his pin out and gave it to me.

'There,' he said, 'it is quite a nice brooch, maybe it is better for a girl than a boy,' and they all laughed.

I opened my hand, and showed them that I had two pins, and said:

'I'd better give them back,' but nobody wanted them.

It was quite dark by now, only the street lamps, and the white snow gave us some light, but we couldn't really carry on playing outside, so we just split up and went home.

'Thanks,' I said to Helma and Uwe.

They grinned conspiratorially when I passed them. Once indoors, my father said:

'I wish you wouldn't always fight. You are not a boy, you are a girl, and it is time you realized it and grew up.'

What could I say to that? For years he had tried to shape me into a boy but once Hans was born it wasn't necessary any more.

Things changed in the country after that. A number of changes didn't affect us, we only heard about them. It was probably the fact that East Prussia was cut off from Germany by the Polish Corridor, and we lived so far away from the main capital, Berlin. We practically lived in the wilderness, where foxes and wolves said goodnight to one another. Hitler carried out the so-called Nazi revolution. All public positions were only to be filled with Aryans, non Jews. I hadn't heard the word Aryans before, but we were soon enlightened at school.

Hitler declared that the National Socialist Party was the only legal party in the state. Racial laws were passed against the Jews, and the churches in Germany were nationalized. Everybody had to pay a church tax but, if you didn't want to pay it, you could sign a declaration that you were a *Freidenker* (free thinker), and didn't believe in the church. Some people did this, many only to save themselves some money. In industry, strikes and lockouts were forbidden because from now on all Germans would march forth together. Now that Hitler was in power, and in order to please the army, he cleaned up the Nazi party, getting rid of the bully boys from the street-fighting days of the depression.

On the night of June 30th 1934, Hitler carried out the so-called Great Blood Purge, or "the night of the long knives". The *Sturmabteilung* (storm troopers), together with prominent party men and rivals to Hitler were rounded up and shot, including General Schleicher, the former chancellor, and his wife. Hitler could now tell the army that the party was clear of radical influences, which they had found so distasteful.

At the age of ten in 1934 I changed school for the last time, and went to the grammar school.

Children don't usually know what they want to do later in life, but I had already decided to become a doctor. I was fascinated with ailments and the different parts of the body. My mother had a very big, thick book which dealt with *Naturheilkunde* (Nature healing), and in it were drawings and photographs of the parts of the body. In front of the book was a nude figure of a man, and another one of a woman, in colour, which could be taken to pieces. One folded the different layers of the body, made in thin coloured cardboard, either to the side or to the top, starting with the skin of arms and legs, exposing the muscles and bones, then folding back the skin of the body exposing the lungs and the heart and other organs. My mother had shown the book to me once, but then locked it up again, probably thinking I was too young for some of the pictures. I soon found out where she kept the key and, when she was not at home, I would get the book out and look at it. Christel knew about it and used to keep a look-out for my mother's possible return. The book was a fund of information for us for years! So there was no question on my part as to which Grammar School I had to attend.

*Hufen, State High School*

*School Flag*

The nearest school to us was a twenty minute tram ride away, or one could cycle; to walk took three-quarters of an hour. The school was excellent, and very popular, situated in the district of the so-called better class people away from the centre of the town. The district was called Hufen, and the school took its name from it: *Staatliches Hufen-Oberlüzeum Königsberg Pr.* (Hufen, State High School, Königsberg Pr. (Prussia)). Unfortunately, there were not enough places for all the girls that applied to go there, so the director set an examination paper, taking only enough girls to fill two classes. I passed, but Sternchen did not, and my mother was quite shocked. My father could not give her any advice, as he was away. So my mother talked to the headmaster of the Middle School, being determined to get us both into the same school. The headmaster reassured her, saying that if I wanted to go to university, I could probably change to

21

the Grammar School after six years, before they started with Latin. This was only taught in the last three years in the Grammar School. With that, my mother had us both registered for the Middle School.

My father returned at the weekend and when he heard what had happened he was furious. It was one of the few times that he stood up for me. It didn't matter whether I wanted to study medicine or not, (he actually didn't agree with it, saying that girls never finish anything, but get married), I had passed the examination, and had every right to go to the first chosen school. It wasn't right for my mother to hold me back because of Sternchen. My father went to see the schools and the headmasters on the Monday, and the result was that I went to the Grammar School, and Sternchen to the Middle School.

By the time everything was sorted out, I had already missed a few days of school, and it might sound silly, but these few days made a difference, in that I never really had a special friend in the class and also I lagged behind academically straight away, particularly in French, a completely new subject.

All pupils had to enter the school by the side door, through which one came into a small hall, completely laid out with a thick brush-like mat let into the floor. Here we had to clean our shoes thoroughly before entering through another door, part of a glass partition, into the lower corridor.

After entering the school through the glass partition, one walked up the staircase on the right to the different floors with the classrooms, or straight on into the big gymnasium, with a good selection of apparatus. Leading off the gymnasium were two large changing rooms, another room where chairs were kept, a First Aid room with a bed, washbasin and a medicine cupboard, and a large double door behind, which was a passageway, and another door opening on to the playground.

The school was very well equipped. We had laboratories for chemistry and physics, with the appropriate apparatus for experiments, a biology room, with plenty of coloured books, stuffed birds and animals, dried branches, leaves and feathers, jars of preserved specimens, like frogs, tadpoles, mice and some fish. There was a big, light room for painting and drawing, and a needlework room containing three sewing machines.

Chairs were put out in the gymnasium for parents days, school theatre performances, some prize-givings, and when Hitler made a speech to his Fatherland. It was obligatory to listen to these speeches in all schools and at home. To make this possible, everybody had to have a radio, and people who could not afford one were given a *Volksradio* (People's Radio) free. This was a cheap radio with only one programme, tuned in to the local station which, of course, always transmitted Hitler's speeches and announcements. At other times, one got the local news on this radio, children's programmes, and music from the Königsberger *Rundfunk*. Schools were supplied with loudspeakers, so that they, too, could organise a general get-together and listen to Hitler's or sometimes Goebbels' speeches.

The persecution of the Jewish people started in earnest after General Hindenburg's death in 1934, and the NS (National Socialists) had seized power. Most German people were tricked into believing that National Socialism was a movement based on virtues and values, whereas, in reality it embodied evil. The people in Königsberg were inspired, manipulated and seduced by National Socialism. We were taught at school, and it was hammered home in the newspapers, that the Jews were the cause of all Germany's misfortune. We had a small picture book in the school library, written by an 18-year-old girl, in which were the words (I quote from memory):

*Trau keinem Fuchs auf grüner Heid* (Trust not a fox out on the heath)
*Und keinem Juden bei seinem Eid* (Nor a Jew giving his oath)

Seeds of hate were planted and grew, and anti-Semitic thinking was encouraged. Synagogues were demolished. We had one Jewish, and one half Jewish girl in the class at school, and I still remember their names, Ilse Levin and Ewa Lewantowski. Ilse's parents were the owners of a small haberdashery and cloth shop, and lived not far from our school. Ewa's father was Jewish, but her dead mother had been a Christian. She attended Bible classes with us, whilst a few of the catholic girls used to go and spend that hour in the common room.

Ewa always stressed her mother and her religion. She must have been told that this was important. One day she turned up, telling everybody that she and her father were going to emigrate to America, where her Uncle lived. A few weeks later she was gone, with all our best wishes.

Ilse was different. She was a quiet girl with a frightened look. We all liked her, nobody was unkind to her; she was always working hard, wanting to improve herself in the lessons, and generally very attentive to her classmates and teachers. There were several girls that came together to school because they lived in the same street, or passed one another's houses on their way to school, and she was one of a crowd. She didn't come to school one day, but nobody took much notice of this. After a few days, with Ilse still missing from school, whispers about her and her family started to go round the classroom. Suddenly she wasn't such a nice girl, and her parents had charged rather a lot for things in the shop, and they were really actually quite rich people, and did you know that she was Jewish?

'So what,' I said, 'I am Swiss.'

'Well, that is different, you are still an Aryan', was the reply.

The word Aryan was terribly important, but difficult to understand. Ewa, Ilse, my other classmates and I, we all looked the same, but Ilse was apparently different. My father tried to explain, pointing out that we were permitted to live in Germany as Swiss, but it didn't mean that we had to agree with the German thinking, or be convinced that Nazism was a good thing. But it was important for all of us not to upset people with expressions of different views, because we were not permitted to offend the host country. We had no Jewish friends, so we were not personally involved in anything that happened to them. We also lived away from the centre of Königsberg, where the Nazis, in the end, did strike out against the Jewish people and their possessions.

The next thing that happened was that the Levin's shop window had been smashed in with stones, and people had taken things out. The stones were still lying inside the shop, and nobody did anything about it. It happened at night, and the Levin family had disappeared.

Had they moved?

That couldn't be the case, because they didn't take any furniture with them. After all the rumours and whispers, and then this news, I decided to have a look for myself so, on the way back from school I made a detour, cycling through the road where Ilse lived, or had lived. I dared not stop outside her place, only cycled past slowly, because the road was empty, and I had the feeling that I was being watched from the houses opposite. Not only the shop windows, but also the windows of the two-storey flat above were broken by flying stones. Bricks were used for the two big store windows. Cloths and materials were unrolled and thrown about, some of them hanging out of the broken shop window, torn and dirty. Broken glass was scattered over the pavement and, by the wall under the broken shop window were some shapeless ladies and gent's hats, deliberately trampled.

Uneasily I cycled home. I was glad to be away from the destruction and signs of hate, which I did not understand and found disturbing. I didn't mention my trip to the Levin's shop but, when another bigger destruction took place in the centre of the town, I was so upset after seeing it that I told my mother about it.

We had a very big store in town called Stern. One could buy everything there. I had visited the store in the school holidays with my mother on one of her shopping trips to town, and was astonished by the size of it, and the amount of goods displayed on the three different floors. I never realized that the family who owned it was Jewish. Everybody knew Stern, because big advertisements were in the local paper every week, encouraging people to come and look and buy their goods.

News usually came through my classmates so, when they told me that the department store Stern had been broken into, I was determined to look at this also.

'The same happened to the Levins and now to Stern', the girls said. 'They are Jews.'

'Who does these things?' I asked.

I never really got a proper reply. Everybody avoided pointing a finger to a particular person, or to people, but somebody did once whisper:

'It is the SS' *Schutzstaffel* (protection formation).

I had known about the SA *Sozialistische Arbeiterpartei*, (socialistic workers party), who wore brown uniforms and boots, with the swastika band on their arm, but the SS were a new organisation, only lately visible in the town. They wore black uniforms, with the swastika band on their arm, and had black boots. I had not seen them locally, only the SA, because some of the fathers of my playmates at home had joined the SA organisation, and they wore the brown uniforms when they went to meetings.

We sometimes had an extra sports lesson in the afternoon, and I made this an excuse to leave home. I didn't take my bike, but caught the tram, as I wasn't allowed to cycle in the centre of the town yet; I was too young, only eleven years old, nearly twelve. It wasn't difficult to find the department store, because there were plenty of people crowded around, staring at it. The place looked awful. All the windows were broken, the large ones downstairs and the smaller ones upstairs, and the building stared at me with great big holes. Everything was broken inside too, the counters, the display units, all furniture. Paper, boxes, clothes, china, shoes, saucepans, cushions slit open, and feathers flying about. The police stood outside, preventing people from getting inside. The crowd kept a distance, but there was a lot of talking, and I overheard remarks like:

'They did it at night. Some of them left with armfuls of boxes, others with clothes, and even fur coats. It is not right to destroy things like that, but they are Jewish. Why don't they share the stuff out, there are plenty of poor people who would be glad of it. It is always the same people who take the most expensive things, and nobody punishes them because it is being done in the name of the SS and against the rich Jews.'

And then there were others who whispered:

'Be quiet, you don't know who is listening.'

When I got home, I told my parents about the visit. They were shocked, not having expected that I would go as far as the centre of the town. They had heard about it and my father had seen it, but he felt it was better for the rest of us not to know too much about it, or to see it for ourselves. I got severely reprimanded, and told never to do this sort of thing again. My father did explain that it was wrong and, if this was the type of party that had taken over the government of Germany, he hoped it wouldn't last long.

'The people won't back this type of crime,' he said, 'they will revolt, and stand up for decency and truth. I would do it if this was my country.'

He was wrong, but neither he nor I knew that at the time.


One of the things that Hitler altered was the way people greeted one another. Before 1933, we girls were taught to curtsy and shake hands when we were introduced to grown ups, and to say:

'*Guten Tag*' (good day).

The boys had to make a little bow. Ladies nodded their heads, and men lifted their hats and made a bow. Gentlemen sometimes kissed the lady's hand, accompanied by a small clicking of the heels, a custom particularly used by the officers in the army.

The new greeting was *"Heil Hitler"* ("Hail Hitler") and the lifting of the right arm to just above shoulder height. One was permitted to shorten the lifting of the arm, by bending it upwards from the elbow when greeting a friend or acquaintance. The distance between the two was often not long enough for a full-length movement of the right arm. It was also quite a tiring business to keep on moving the arm up and down and, even Hitler greeted his army or the people with a half movement of the right arm.

At school, we had to stand as soon as a teacher entered the class. The teacher would stand in front of the class, lift up the right arm (full length) and say:

'*Heil Hitler!*'

The whole class replied: '*Heil Hitler!*', with the right arm fully raised.

Now this was something my father didn't like. We were not allowed to do it at home, and had to avoid it whenever we could. He went to see our headmaster, and had a long talk with him about this new custom, and, I think, several other things, because he came back from this visit quite happy with the outcome of his meeting.

'It is all arranged,' he said to me, 'You don't have to say *Heil Hitler*. You are sitting at the back, so it won't be too obvious. You just get up with the other girls when the teacher enters, but don't say anything or lift your arm, and then you sit down when everybody else does. The teachers will know about it.'

At first, this arrangement worked out alright. The other girls in the class accepted it, after I explained again that I was Swiss, and the teachers had been informed by the headmaster. But things sometimes became difficult when teachers changed, which was the case between 1934 and 1937.

One day we had a new young teacher for history, who felt insulted that I didn't greet him with *Heil Hitler*. He went to see the headmaster about me, but could not alter the situation. He made up his mind to treat me differently from the rest of the class. I could never do anything right. I always got the most difficult questions to answer, and my homework never had a good mark. He was full of Hitler's new ideas of Great Germany.

He was a *Referendar*, a learner teacher, who, at the end of his practical time with us, had to give a lesson in front of an examining board, consisting of some of our teachers and our headmaster, and one or two professors from the education board. It might have been better for Mr S. not to pick on me, because he did not realise that, by then, I was quite a leader of the more unruly girls in the class. The class soon realised that Mr S. didn't like me, and I knew I had their cooperation when I said I wasn't going to do anything until the day of his examination.

Mr S. tried to prepare us for that day, by making us familiar with the subject he was going to ask us about. The subject was Napoleon, his conquest of Europe, and his defeat in Russia. We had to collect a big map and two large pictures from the library. The map showed Napoleon's progress through the different countries, and the pictures depicted his army. One the victorious army, and one the beaten one, which had underneath the sentence:

*Mit Mann und Ross und Wagen* (With man and horse and cart)
*So hat sie Gott geschlagen!* (So has God beaten them!)

Mr S. gave us two lessons, and after that he changed the subject for a few weeks. At the last lesson before the big day, he spent about ten minutes revising Napoleon, and asked one or two of us whether we remembered the words under the picture representing the beaten army.

We all knew the answers. At the end of the lesson, he asked the head girl to organise that somebody would get the map and the two pictures from the library for the next lesson, and also to see to it that we had chairs for the examiners. I told Anita, the head girl, that I would be responsible for chairs, map and pictures.

She looked at me:

'You won't get me into trouble, will you?' she said.

'No', I replied. 'Not you, maybe I will be in trouble, but I don't care.'

In the big break time, I got the chairs ready, making sure I got the oldest and hardest. The chairs were put along the side walls, and the examiners sat next to the pupils, one behind the other.

I discussed the lesson with the girls, and they all promised to be most unintelligent and unhelpful to Mr S. Nobody really liked him.

I got the wrong map and pictures, and struggled breathlessly into the classroom, just after the bell had gone. I apologised:

'I am so sorry Mr S., but the librarian wasn't there, and I couldn't find the map and pictures at first. The order papers had blown on to the floor, but I unrolled one picture and, when that was the right one, I knew this was the order.'

Although always so sure of himself, Mr S. had become nervous. First, he probably worried that there was no map, then the realisation that the chairs were hard and old, which would not get the examiners into a good mood, and then my bursting in like that with the map and the pictures.

He rubbed his hands, he smiled, he cleared his throat, he looked around. At last there was silence, and he could begin.

'A few weeks ago we talked a little about Napoleon, but today we will follow his travels and conquests across Europe in greater detail', he said, and, with that, the lesson began.

He started to ask a few questions, but nobody seemed to know the answers, or they were very unsure, and couldn't remember. So he decided to hang up the big map. It showed Europe, with each country in a different colour, and not the old map, with Napoleon's journey drawn in. Poor Mr S. even had difficulty in finding the places where the different battles had been.

'We had a different map the last time, but, never mind, the names of the places haven't altered', he said.

It was a struggle; the lesson just dragged on, and everybody seemed bored. The examiners made notes, nobody smiled. Our headmaster was most uncomfortable on his chair. I made crosses on the top of my desk with a rubber, showing the examiner next to me how bored I was.

'You ought to pay more attention to what your teacher is saying', whispered the examiner to me.

'Mr S. thinks I'm stupid, and all my answers are always wrong', I said, quite loudly, in reply, looking at the examiner.

For a few seconds there was dead silence in the room. The headmaster frowned and looked at me. I think this was the moment when he realised there was something going on in this class. Mr S. decided to ignore the outburst, and carry on with the picture of Napoleon's victorious army. He hung the picture up, and things went a little better. Mr S. smiled, he too started to feel better.

'And now we are coming to what happened to this army in the winter battles of Russia, and the return of the soldiers', he said, and, with that, he picked up the other picture, hung it up, undid the string and let it unroll. The last time, he had stood there like an actor, pointing to it and saying:

'Look at the defeated army!'

He had hoped to do the same but, when the picture unrolled, there was at first a gasp, then a few giggles, and then laughter.

The picture showed a cock, a hen, and the development of the egg into a chick. Mr S. realised then what had happened, and looked at me. I wasn't afraid of him, I had all my answers ready, but I wondered what our headmaster was thinking, and I looked at him. I could see that he had to hide a smile, and I also knew that he was now convinced that there was a pact in the class, to make Mr S. fail his final teaching practice. Before anybody could say anything, he got up and said:

'You will have to excuse me, but I have an appointment.'

Before leaving the class, he whispered to Mr S.:

'It is always advisable to check up on the equipment for the lesson, never trust pupils.'

The girls in the front heard it, and told me about it later.

Mr S. tried to make us remember what the picture looked like, and what the words were underneath, but somehow we had forgotten everything.

'I'm sure you know it', he said, and, helping us along, he repeated:

*'Mit Mann und Ross und Wagen. . .'*

Silence.

So he said the sentence on his own.

I am sure he was glad when the bell rang, and I am also sure he would have liked to wring my neck. Instead, he went to complain to the headmaster, who called me to his study the next day.

The interview went off better than I thought, as Mr Walsdorf seemed to accept my excuses for the mistakes. The mix-up with the picture and the map happened because I only checked one picture. He couldn't openly make me responsible for the lesson. I also told him about the *Heil Hitler* greeting, and what happened after that, and I had the feeling that he suddenly understood what was going on. He said that he was sorry that my father felt so strongly about the greeting procedure, and he also said that it might make it easier for me if the veto didn't exist. In the end, I decided it would probably be much easier to conform, and just say *Heil Hitler* like everybody else. In this way, I was no different to the other girls at school, and they soon forgot that I was Swiss. I did not tell my father about my decision.

There was no school in the afternoons, but we had obligatory visits to certain historic films, exhibitions, and some plays, usually with a Nazi theme. By not stressing this point at home, my parents did not see any reason why I couldn't attend. At school, I became one of the crowd, I blended in. It was different at home, where I had other friends and neighbours. Nobody from our district went to my school.

In 1935, it was announced that the Saturday was to be used by the Hitler Youth, and pupils, therefore, would not have to go to school on that day. Our school gave some of its rooms for the *Heimabende* (meetings) for the BDM *Bund Deutscher Mädchen,* (society of German girls). These were run by leaders, who were pupils in the school, and did not therefore interfere with the lessons. They were arranged in the afternoons or evenings, the free time for everybody.

It was decreed by Hitler that every German child, from the age of ten upwards, had to belong to the Hitler Youth and wear the appropriate uniform. The only excuse was bad health, and then a doctor's certificate had to be produced. There was one meeting during the week, and meetings on Saturday, often also on Sunday, making it a weekend. One joined a local group consisting of 15 - 20 girls or boys, not mixed, which was led by an older girl or boy. *Pfadfinders* (Scouts and Guides) had existed before, but now the new formation had become obligatory and nationwide.

I wasn't allowed to join, as my parents didn't agree with Hitler's government. Being Swiss, nobody could force me to do it. My friends at school assumed I had joined near my home as I lived so far away.

At school, it was terribly important to know what happened. We were encouraged to read the papers, listen to the radio, and anything to do with

Hitler was brought up at the HJ meetings. Although I did not attend these, my friends soon told me about them. Every history lesson started off with repeats of Hitler's achievements, and we had to learn the curriculum vitae of every important party member. Hitler's picture was hung up on the walls of several classrooms and suddenly pictures of Goering and Goebbels appeared also.

# CHAPTER THREE

## Hitler Youth - Traditional Christmas

At weekends I was often lonely because my friends were busy with HJ meetings. My father would not allow me to join. It was no fun to go cycling alone and, although I had Christel and Hans for company, I got bored playing with them all the time. We would play hopscotch, hitting the top with a string attached to a stick (called *Brummer*), roll a hoop, play with marbles, or play hide-and-seek in the garden. Sternchen would join us sometimes. I longed to be with my friends, boys and girls of the same age. Christa, Thea and Hilde, three of my local girl friends used to tell me about the BDM, and the things that they did there, and how much fun they had. One day I met the local BDM leader.

'Why don't you come along and have a look, to see what we are doing?' she said. 'You don't have to belong to the BDM straight away, you can come for a trial period.'

I asked my mother, but she would not permit it. I kept on asking and, at last, she said:

'Alright, you can go to one of their meetings.'

I told Christa, and she organised it. The afternoon meetings were held in the cellar of a big house. The room was whitewashed, and had an old carpet on the floor. There were trestle tables and folding chairs, and shelves along the wall, which contained books and boxes. Pictures of Hitler, Goering and Goebbels hung on the wall and, in one corner, stood the swastika flag. There were about 20 girls, all in brown uniforms, some of them familiar-looking as they were from my district. They were surprised to see me, particularly as I was not in uniform. Charlotte, the leader, explained that I had come along to see what it was all about, and that I might join one day.

At the beginning of the meeting, they all sang a marching song. After that, we sat down in a half circle, with Charlotte opposite us.

'As always, let's get on with the tests,' she said.

The tests were explained to me. Everybody had to pass them, and Charlotte recorded them in a book. After the passing of a certain number of tests, one received a bar, which was sewn on to the shirt sleeve, like sergeant's stripes. The tests consisted of knowing the curriculum vitae of Hitler, Goering, Goebbels, and a number of other top Nazis, including our *Gauleiter* (district leader), Erich Koch. Certain tasks had also to be performed before one could get a bar, like doing shopping for old people, bringing coal to them, or collecting old newspapers. I was surprised to discover how well things were organised, and how busy everybody had to be. The girls had brought a number of things along, like books, children's clothes, linen, toys, woollen clothes and even potatoes. Charlotte called out a name, then asked the questions. She said she usually tested five girls every week, and then told them what to prepare for the next week.

Just like at school, I thought.

The books were collected, and sent to German schools in foreign countries. The girls packed the books into boxes, then covered them with thick paper, put a string around the parcels, and labelled them. Clothes, linen, toys and the potatoes were allocated to certain addresses in the district and parcelled up. Charlotte then called out the names of the girls who had to deliver them. They had to do this after the meeting. The clothes went to poor people, and particularly those who had several children. We had some very poor parts not far from us, like the Kapornerstrasse, where my mother didn't permit us to go. Most of the parcels went there. I thought, I had better not tell my mother about this, otherwise she won't let me go to the meeting again.

After the packing of the parcels, the girls made toys. Some were stuffing dolls or teddy bears, others sewing on buttons as eyes. Two girls were making a doll's house from a wooden box. They covered it with bits of wallpaper. Another girl was making some of the furniture for it from match boxes. Some girls were cutting shapes with a fretsaw, some painting toys. Everybody was busy and happy, and I walked from one to the other, watching what they were doing.

'Would you like to do something?' Charlotte said to me.

'Oh yes, please, I would like to learn to use the fretsaw.'

'Alright, then. What about making a little doll's cradle and, when you have cut it out, you can glue it together and paint it and, if you like, you can also make the bedclothes for it, and knit a little doll, and stuff it.'

'That seems a lot to do.'

'Well, you will have to come again, then. Let's start with the wood.'

I hadn't done very much when the meeting came to an end. Everything had to be packed away, the floor swept, and then we all stood together to sing the National Anthem and the Nazi song, with right arm raised. At the end of the song, Charlotte called:

'*Sieg!*' (victory) and the girls shouted back '*Heil!*' (hail) and then again '*Sieg!*' and the reply '*Heil!*' and a third time.

Christa didn't have anything to deliver, so we could both go home straight away. The others collected their parcels; the potatoes were put on a little cart, which one of the girls pulled along.

'Don't forget to bring the cart to the next meeting,' called Charlotte, 'We will need it again.'

'How did you like the meeting?' asked Christa.

'I liked it very much, I only wish they wouldn't talk so much about Hitler and all those top people. That's the reason why my father won't let me join. I would like to finish the cradle,' I added.

'You will have to come again, then,' she said, 'but next week we meet earlier, because Charlotte has to go out in the evening. And talking about Hitler, we are the HJ, the Hitler Youth, we have to know all about the Nazi Party.'

'I am glad the meeting is earlier. I can then say at home that I am going to play handball.'

Charlotte let me come a few times without belonging to the HJ, but she said I would have to join officially if I kept on coming. This meant filling in a form, and taking the oath of allegiance to Hitler. I knew I would never get permission from my parents for that, so I never even asked.

Christa went away for several weekends with the HJ, and I was quite jealous. Charlotte said I could come with them if I paid for the journey. The girls were going to Nidden, a trip by train and boat. Nidden was a small fishing village on the Kuhrische Nehrung, a strip of land dividing the Baltic and the Kuhrische Haff. I kept on asking my mother whether I could go and eventually she had the courage to talk to my father. He wanted to meet Charlotte and talk to her. He liked Charlotte and I was allowed to go, but only this once. My father pressed the point that he was paying for all my expenses, and that he was not giving a donation to the HJ.

The Nehrung and the Haff geographically cannot be compared with anything. Both are unique. The Nehrung is a strip of land dividing two large seas, the Baltic and the Haff. The Baltic waters are not as salty as the North Sea, and one hardly notices the tide. The Haff is like a very big lake, with slightly salty water. It was formed by the Baltic Sea, which gradually covered the low-lying land, but left a thin strip of higher land called the Nehrung. The Haff has the shape of a triangle, with the town of Memel, which belongs to Lithuania, at the end of the Nehrung, where there is also an outlet to the sea, the Baltic. The River Memel, which for a great part is the border between Lithuania and East Prussia (it passes Tilsit), flows into the Kuhrische Haff.

Not many people live on the Nehrung. There are thick woods and marshes where the Nehrung is attached to the mainland. Gradually the trees become sparse, and so does the earth along the sides of the Haff and the Baltic, and the forest and firm land only carries on in the centre of the Nehrung, where there is also a good road. Along the coasts are the white and yellow sands of the bare dunes. A few small villages do exist, where fishermen and their families have settled. There is also Rossitten, with the well-known *Vogelwarte* (birds station and sanctuary).

After Rossitten comes Nidden, once a very small settlement, but now a thriving fishing village and holiday resort. It is built partly on the so-called *tote Düne* (dead dune), which once was a *Wanderdüne* (wander dune). The little fishing village of Nidden was covered several times by the *Wanderdüne*, until the esparto grass was discovered, which would grow on the white sand, and keep the dunes from moving.

We started for our camping weekend in Nidden on a Friday afternoon. Everybody had a rucksack, a sleeping bag and a rug. We all piled into the train, more than 100 girls and boys, all in HJ uniform. One or two were like me, just with a skirt and blouse. We were in the summer resort of Cranz in half an hour, and then moved off on to a sideline to Cranz-Beek, at the edge of the Haff. Here the steamship waited for the passengers.

We moved off, the mainland was left behind, and the boat went smoothly along the coast of the Nehrung. There were no waves; the Haff was as smooth as a pond, although we were told it could be pretty rough. At first, everything on land looked green, and one could see the thick woods where the elk lived. After an hour I could see in the distance that everything looked white and, when we got nearer to it, it turned more yellow, and then I realized that they were the empty dunes. Small, lost settlements broke up the emptiness, like little black dots and suddenly there was Nidden, with its small pier and lighthouse, and a harbour, shaped in a half circle.

The coastline of the Haff is very shallow, and a pier is needed for the bigger boats. When I got on land I was struck by the heat, and the strong sun late in the afternoon. The village, through which we had to march in twos, was quite big. Once through the village, we came to a thick wood, invisible from the pier, and a good road. We marched along the road, the leader with the swastika flag in front, singing and moving our legs rhythmically to the tunes. Suddenly we turned off the main road on to a smaller path which led to a clearing, and there was the camp. It consisted of two large huts, surrounded by wooden verandas. Now we had to put up our sleeping tents, which were kept in the huts.

Christa and I shared a tent, and it was fun putting it up. The cooking was done in one of the huts on an iron stove and the boys soon lit the fire. We all had to go into the forest to collect wood as there would be a big camp-fire in the evening. For supper, we set up big trestle tables and chairs outside, and we all had hot soup and big chunks of black bread and cheese. Charlotte gave me a tin plate, mug, and eating utensils. Everybody had to wash up their own plates, then we all changed into tracksuits, and sat around the big fire in the centre of the clearing, singing and chanting, clapping hands, and rocking to the music.

A whistle woke us the next morning. We had to line up for a run down to the sea and the sand. There we had our *Freiübungen* (exercises), then a run back, a wash, tent tidying, and inspection. Everybody had to stand next to their tent and the head leader came to look at us and our tents. Charlotte explained about me, because I was not in uniform.

'Helga is Swiss, and is thinking about joining us,' she said, 'but first of all she wanted to see what it was like.'

'I hope you will like it,' said the leader, 'and will be a member soon.'

We had breakfast, bread, jam, and *Ersatzkaffee*, (substitute coffee) and then we split up into groups. One group had to see to the dinner, another to clear up the camp-fire from the night before, another to get wood ready for the evening, while others went shopping or tidied the huts. There was one group, consisting of girls who hadn't been there before and didn't know Nidden, and I belonged to this group. We all climbed on to the *tote Wanderdüne*. It was hot, and the blinding white sand hurt my eyes, so that I had to close them a little. It was a hard climb and occasionally we saw the big foot marks of the elk, but we did not see the animal. The view from the top was beautiful, on one side the green sea, and on the other the blue Haff. The beach went on and on in small gentle curves, gradually becoming hazy, as far as one could see.

In the afternoon, we had the big *Schnitzeljacht*, (paper chase) a competition between the boys and the girls. This had been prepared by some of the leaders during the morning. The girls had to follow white pieces of paper hung on to the trees in the wood, look for certain objects, and bring them back. The boys followed blue pieces of paper, and had the same number of objects to collect. We were told what the objects were, but not where to find them. Amongst them was a spoon, a stone, a ribbon, a button, a horseshoe, a piece of string and a newspaper. The button was the most difficult to find, but somebody did find it. It was a big black button, stuck to a tree with a pin, and nearly invisible. To look for the objects, we divided into small groups and branched out into different directions. Sometimes we went wrong, and came upon the blue papers and met some of the boys; they, too, missed their guide papers from time to time. I kept with Christa; she knew about the game and was quite good, looking in branches, under leaves and moss or picking up wood. And then, suddenly, she grabbed my arm and put a finger to her lips. She stood quite still, and so did I, and then she pointed to the side. I heard a crackling in the wood and then, from behind some trees a great elk appeared, his head held high and his big antlers pointing proudly to the sky. There he stood, not looking at us, just listening, and wondering whether he, too, had heard something. And then he moved off slowly, away from us, and I caught my breath at seeing such a beautiful animal.

'We were lucky,' whispered Christa, 'they don't usually come so close to the camp. I have seen some on the dunes, but never in the wood'.

East Prussia was the last German province in which elk still lived free. The elk changes its *Schaufeln* (antlers) every autumn, and then they grow again, sometimes to a tremendous size. There were 1,200 elk on the Kuhrische Nehrung and in the marshes and woods around Memel before 1945, but after the Russian occupation all elk were completely wiped out.

I felt my day was fulfilled; the beautiful view from the dead dunes, a swim in the sea before lunch, and now I had seen the elk.

It was the boys who won the *Schnitzeljacht*. The button held us up, we found it too late. After supper, we again had our songs around the camp-fire, and hot cocoa, and everybody was really tired when it was time to crawl into our tents.

Towards morning it started to rain, which was a great disappointment. The tent kept dry inside, but it was no fun to crawl out of it and run into the hut to have a wash. Breakfast was in the hut, where everything was very crowded. It stopped raining, but the sky was still dark, and the leaders didn't know how long the rain would hold off. The decision was made to pack up and take an earlier boat back. We would have gone home after dinner in any case. It took quite a bit of time to break camp and, just when we were all ready, lined up to march down to the harbour with the flag leader at the front, it started to rain again. There was nothing for it but to march.

'Left, right, left, right,' shouted one of the boys, and another one started to sing:

*'Das Wandern ist des Müller's Lust . . .'* (to wander is the miller's happiness), and everybody started to move their legs to the call of left and right, and joined in the marching song.

By the time we came to the boat, the rain was running down our clothes. My hair was hanging like wet strings from my head, and my shoes squelched with the water in them. My rucksack, rug and sleeping bag had become quite heavy with the water from the rain, and I started to shiver. The boat was very full, as lots of people had the same idea of going home early. The Haff was not so smooth, and the journey back not so pretty or comfortable.

The train, too, was crammed, and so was the tram which I had to catch from the station. I looked a poor sight when I got home. As soon as I'd had a hot bath, I went to bed, assuring everybody that I'd had a smashing time, although nobody believed it at that moment. The next day, at school, I could compare my experiences of the weekend with the other girls, some of whom had also been away with the HJ, but to different places.

I was not allowed to join the HJ, and Charlotte would not let me attend any more meetings without being a member, so that was the end of my fraternising with Hitler's organisation.

There suddenly seemed to be uniforms everywhere, not only the young people, but also men and women. The men belonged to the SA or SS, and had meetings in the evenings or at the weekends, and the women had the so-called *Frauenschaft* (women's organisation). There was no school uniform, so I had no uniform at all.

One of the biggest meetings of all the Hitler groups was on May 1st, Labour Day. This was a holiday, and the day belonged to the brown shirts. People left their homes early in the morning, to meet in groups near their homes. Once assembled, they formed a column and then, with the swastika flag carried in front, they marched, singing, through the streets, their ultimate destination being the Erich Koch Platz. They came from all over the town, the BDM (girls), the HJ (boys), the SA, the SS, and the women, with their different *Standarten* (flags). Their uniforms were immaculate, the leather belts and high boots polished to perfection. The marching feet echoed from the walls, and the singing voices carried far. Some groups had bands, which joined one another when they met, and eventually formed a big band at the Erich Koch Platz. Eventually the whole Platz was filled with uniformed people and flags. Erich Koch stepped on to a platform and spoke to the crowd. His speech was relayed by a number of loudspeakers, which even extended into the road. But the highlight was Hitler's speech, heard by the whole country. One could visualise hundreds and hundreds of towns and villages, with places like the Erich Koch Platz, where people stood in uniform, and listened to the voice of Hitler. The final shout always was:

*"Ein Reich, ein Volk, ein Führer!"* (One state, one people, one leader), and then, with right arm held high, the German National Anthem and the Nazi song were sung.

After Hitler's speech, followed the May Day parade. The band played, and the different groups marched past the platform where the *Gauleiter* stood taking the salute. All this took hours, and some girls fainted, even boys and men felt poorly, and the Red Cross was kept busy. Finally, the marchers left the parade ground but a few roads away they broke up. Husbands looked for their wives and children, and walked together with them, often calling in for a beer on their way home.

I was one of the onlookers. Christel came with me sometimes, but my parents never came. It was probably just as well, because my father might have drawn attention to himself by not being in uniform. My parents didn't really like us to go, but there were plenty of people about, and not everybody had to attend in their Nazi unit on that day. Only the chosen ones marched as otherwise there would have been too many people. Apart from that, certain services of the town had to be seen to, like the running of the trams and trains, gas and electricity.

It was compulsory to join the HJ, but not the SA or SS, but if one joined, one could be sure of advancement in one's job, particularly as a civil servant. Hitler also wanted big families, and introduced the Mother's Cross for women with more than four children. This was like an Iron Cross, but silver plated, and attached to a chain. Hitler himself was godfather to every tenth child born to a family.

I remember my father being outraged when my mother had a letter asking her to attend a ceremony for the presentation of the *Mutterkreuz* (Mother's Cross) because she had four children. He wrote a furious letter in reply. Many women proudly wore their cross as a necklace for special occasions.

40

Christmas, although only once a year, started weeks before the 25th of December and, because of that, seemed to have been so much more of a family festival than today. At school, in art and needlework classes, little presents for the parents and Christmas decorations were made.

I was not very keen on needlework, but the teacher tried to encourage us all. One year I crocheted an oven cloth for my mother from thick string with a red border. I kept on dropping stitches, and it was most uneven when it was finished, but my mother liked it, and used it in the kitchen until it got scorched, having been left on the hotplate by mistake.

Another year I made my father a cigarette box. The teacher produced a box, and I had collected small pieces of amber from the beach, which were glued on to the box in a decorative way. The next year, my needlework teacher insisted that I ought to knit something for him, as we had now learnt how to knit. She suggested bedsocks, as my father travelled such a lot, and hotel rooms might not always be warm in the winter. I did not like the idea. I couldn't see my father in bedsocks, even in a cold hotel room, but when she showed me different colours of wool, I fell in love with some pink wool and started to knit. I was hopeless and my mother helped me, sometimes smiling a little at the thought of my father wearing pink bedsocks. My father was ever so pleased and surprised by my efforts when he unpacked his present from me at Christmas time. I am sure he had been forewarned!

'Pink bedsocks!' he called out and laughed. 'I think this is marvellous. At last I will have warm feet, especially as they are made of wool.'

I went to see him the next morning, but he hadn't got them on. He told me he would take them with him when he travelled, just as the teacher had said. I doubted whether he would, so I made a point, when nobody was there of searching the cupboards in my parents' bedrooms, and found them in the back of the drawer of his bedside table. In the end, they finished up in the cleaning box. They were probably good to put a shine on to the silver.

Christmas celebrations never changed in my childhood; every year they were held in the old tradition. I think it was my father's tradition rather than my mother's, because of the Christmas tree stand, which came from my father's father, and originally from Switzerland. It was a most unusual stand, and I have never seen one like it since. In the centre of a big square wooden board was a musical box, covered with a domed-shaped metal cover, which had a tube sticking out in the centre. The bottom of the trunk of the Christmas tree would be cut a little and forced into the tube, so that it was firm and steady. There were two levers

41

below the metal dome, which were used to wind up the musical box and the turning mechanism. Another lever was for stop and start. The musical box played four Christmas tunes and, whilst it was playing, the tree turned slowly round. My father would get the board from the attic one or two days before Christmas, but my mother would not start decorating the tree until after the midday meal on Christmas Eve. The tree had all the usual glitter and balls, but also some of the home-baked sweets and chocolates hanging from the branches, and real candles. On the top was a silver star.

During the Christmas holiday, we were sometimes allowed to have one or two sweet decorations from the tree, until they were all gone. My mother's birthday was on January 9th, and she would decorate the tree once more with sweets for all of us to share. It was great fun to go and choose something from the tree, much better than having been given a sweet.

The tree always stood in the alcove of the living room, and fitted so well into it that one could have thought that the room was designed with the tree in mind. The big dining room table was pulled out to its full length and stood against the wall and on it were all the presents or, if they were too big, they went underneath the table. Everybody had a *Bunte Teller*. This was a big decorated cardboard plate, full of apples, oranges, nuts, sweets and, on top marzipan. In front of the plate came the presents. Nobody was allowed to see the tree until it was time to go into the room and start the celebrations. My mother, with my father's help, would get everything ready. We, too, would collect our presents together. We laid these on the chair in my father's study, so that they were handy when we wanted them. At 5 o'clock on Christmas Eve - it was dark outside by then - we would line up outside the living-room door and wait. Sometimes my parents had forgotten something and would rush out again to fetch it. We could smell the tree, because my mother always burnt a few pine needles, to make it smell as if we were in the wood. We then tried to have a quick look, but were never successful. At last the time had come, and the door opened, and there was the tree, slowly turning, with the candles burning, and the musical box playing one of the Christmas songs. The rest of the room was in darkness, but one could just see the laden table, and my father sitting at the piano, with the little reading lamp bent over so that the light shone on to the music.

'Happy Christmas,' said my parents. 'Come in and let us sing some Christmas carols.'

I had to go and turn the music-box off under the tree. We all had to group ourselves behind and next to my father, our backs towards the Christmas tree and the table with the presents. I often craned my neck to see what presents I would get, but it was difficult, because we didn't always have the same place on the table, my mother mixed them up. The singing of the carols was sometimes a bit laborious. My father had learnt to play the piano when he was a child but, because he never played or practised during the year, he found it difficult to read the music quickly enough for us to sing in even time. He would start off with us all singing, and then, suddenly, he lost his place, or couldn't read the notes, and we would hold on to our last note, or stop altogether. He had ever so many excuses, it was never his fault!

'Helga, you sang the wrong note!' or

'Hans, you must stand still, otherwise I cannot play. Now let's start again.'

We had lots of beginnings, and sometimes we just sang on without the piano, and my father found a few notes later on. The last song was always *Stille Nacht* (Silent Night), and we knew that after that came the *Bescherung* (giving of Christmas presents). If the piano-playing didn't go too badly, we had lots of Christmas songs before *Stille Nacht* but, if the playing went badly, we had a short concert.

My mother would then take each of us to our place at the table, and wish us again a very happy Christmas. Once we had unpacked everything and enjoyed our presents, and said 'thank you', it was time for us to do our turn. We all had learnt our poem so, one after the other would say it, whilst my parents sat in front of us.

After the poems, we gave our presents to our parents, and then we all had something to eat. We always had potato salad and Frankfurter sausages with mustard. This was something which was prepared in the morning, and my mother and the maid would go quickly to warm up the sausages, whilst we cleared up the paper from the presents. We did not sit at the table as it was in use, but on the floor, whilst my parents had a card table, covered with a small table-cloth. We were allowed to stay up a little longer than usual and enjoy our presents, and the older we got, the longer we were allowed to stay up.

Christmas Day was the day for the big dinner. We always had a goose, stuffed with apples, and red cabbage and, as we were such a big family, there wasn't much meat left for the next day. My mother used to get up early to get the goose into the oven and by the time we came to have our breakfast we could smell apples, goose and red cabbage, and we knew this was the Christmas smell. My father would go for a brisk walk with us children before dinner, partly to occupy us, and partly for our health. We always had snow, and sometimes it was bitterly cold, but we never missed our walk. My mother, in the meantime, with the maid's help, would get the dinner ready. It was their turn to have a rest after dinner, because we three girls had to do the washing up. The afternoon was visiting time. We either went to see friends, or they came to us.

Christmas always went much too quickly, and then there were the few days before the New Year and another celebration. All the leftover food from Christmas was eaten up before the New Year. One of the items was called *Schwarzsauer* (black-sour). I don't think anybody liked it very much, but it was a tradition, and even my mother and father had this when they were children. It was made from the *Gekröse* (giblets) with *Backobst* (dried apples, pears and plums), lemon peel, sugar, spice and vinegar and, the worst of the lot, a little goose blood, to make it black. It was served hot, in a deep bowl, with dumplings made from flour and water, and there was always plenty of it!

The tradition for New Year was the *Bleigiessen*, (lead pouring), which was done after 12 o'clock midnight, and the bottle of champagne at the stroke of midnight. My father excelled in both, and he was always perfect in his timing with the champagne, so that the cork popped out at the first stroke of 12. He always had a bottle of Heidseck French champagne, even right through the war. We were only allowed a little sip, but had bubbly lemonade instead. For the lead-pouring, my mother usually bought a box with little lead figures, all different, and a spoon. She put the figures under identical cups, so that nobody could see what figure they would get, and we each chose one cup. We all marched into the kitchen with our figure, and my mother lit the gas on the cooker and put a bowl of cold water on to the kitchen table. One took the spoon, laid the figure into it, melted the lead over the gas flame, and then threw it quickly into the cold water. When taken out, it had a funny shape, and it was my father who was able to interpret the shape, and tell us what would happen in the next year. Small balls clustered together meant money; one year, I had a shape similar to a sailing boat and my father said I would travel. He could even read in the shape that one would get a bad school report, or win a trophy! I got both that year - how did he know? It was fun, and we loved it. We believed his prophesies at the time but, after the New Year had started, they were soon forgotten.

According to my parents, I did not work hard enough at school, I did not do my homework, I was naughty, and I often lied. All I wanted was to do my sport and read books, and I tried everything to fulfil this ambition. Today, one would say I was self-willed and high spirited. My father tried to change me with severe beatings, my mother by taking the books away, but nothing seemed to change me, so new punishments had to be found.

One year it was decided that I would not be allowed to spend Christmas with the family. I cannot remember what I did wrong, but it must have been something big. On Christmas Eve, as we were lining up at the living-room door waiting to be admitted to see the lovely turning musical tree and to get our presents, my mother took my hand, and my father opened his study door and said:

'This year you are not allowed to join us and you won't get any presents either, but your mother felt you should, at least, have a little tree. So we have put the Advent tree with the four candles into my study, and some fruit on the *Bunte Teller* (Christmas plate). There are some more candles, and you can replace the old ones when they are finished.'

I entered the study and on a little table stood the Advent tree with the spare candles and a box of matches. The plate next to the tree had oranges and apples on it, no *Pfefferkuchen*, (gingerbreads) no sweets and, of course, none of my beloved marzipan. The door behind me closed, and I could hear the others going in to the living-room.

Christel won't enjoy it, I thought. She always likes to be with me. Hans will feel funny, and Sternchen would probably think I deserve it.

Then I heard my father playing the piano, and everybody started to sing.

They will miss me, I thought, because I always sing the loudest, and often drown the wrong notes played by my father. I was right, they kept on starting the same tune, and then abandoned it and started another one. It was a short session of carols, and I couldn't hear anything much after that, even when I put my ear to the keyhole. I would have liked a book to read but, even if I had one, I would have had difficulty in seeing the print, with four little candles as the only light. If I turned the big light on, my parents might see it.

For years I had been making up stories, and telling them to Christel in the evenings. Often, when I went to bed and couldn't sleep, I would start imagining things, and then had the beginning of a story, and sometimes would continue this into my dreams. With nothing to do on this Christmas Eve, and the candles already being pretty low, I decided not to have any more light, but go to sleep on the floor, putting some cushions from the big chairs on to the carpet first. I blew out the candles, and made myself comfortable; at least I tried, it was rather hard on the floor. I dreamt about my very own Christmas, with plenty of books, and marzipan in lots of different shapes, hearts and big lumps, and small pink little piglets, with gold coins in their mouths. I kept on eating the marzipan, and there was still more to be eaten. I had to be careful with the piglets, because they had little pieces of wood in their legs, to prevent them breaking off and, if I didn't watch out, I could bite on to the wood.

Suddenly somebody was shaking my shoulder and everything was so bright.

I opened my eyes and realized where I was and that the big light was on in the study. My mother stood there, with a plate in her hand; my father stood by the door, frowning.

'I have made you a sandwich,' said my mother. 'You can take it with you into your bedroom. It is time to go to bed, we have finished our Christmas Eve celebrations.'

I got up stiffly, took the sandwich, and was going to leave the room, when my father said:

'Aren't you going to apologize?'

It was always very difficult for me to say sorry because often I was not sorry and I had been told not to lie! So I just looked at my father, and then left the room and ran upstairs. I heard my parents arguing, and I suppose my father would have liked to insist on an apology there and then, but my mother probably persuaded him to leave me alone, because I had already had my punishment by missing the celebrations and present-giving. Christel came after me and gave me some *Pfefferkuchen* and marzipan from her plate. She was always very kind to me and felt sorry that I had missed everything.

My father did not speak to me the next morning, and ignored me at the breakfast table, and during our morning walk. My mother begged me to apologize, so that we could have a peaceful dinner and, for her sake, I went to my father's study and knocked on the door. I did apologize to him, but I think even he felt that I didn't mean it and, although he was kind to me again, he looked at me thoughtfully during our meal, probably wondering what he could do to enforce his will over mine.

# CHAPTER FOUR

## Hitler in Königsberg - The Years 1938 and 1939

In 1938, Hitler visited Königsberg. Preparations were made well in advance. Old flags were cleaned and repaired, new ones were sewn, and the shops were full of little flags with the *Hakenkreuz* (Swastika), and pictures of Hitler, decorated with laurel and oak leaves. The Hitler Youth, the SA and the SS had practice marches and the bands practised every night in order to be perfect for the big day. Marches and *Wanderlieder* (Marching Songs) were played and sung on the radio all day, and the whole town was stirred up with great excitement. On the actual day, the centre of the town was full of flags and bunting, and the people filled up the pavements along the official route from the main station, the *Hauptbahnhof*, to the castle and the stadium. Hitler was arriving by train, driving for a short visit to the castle, and then attending the march-past at the stadium, from where he would also deliver one of his famous speeches, relayed through the town by loudspeakers and over the radio for those unable to attend.

All my school friends were very excited, because they were told that they had to be at the castle, in their HJ uniforms, early that morning. The children from our neighbourhood were allocated a section along the route of Hitler's journey to stand in their HJ uniforms along the road forming *Spalier* (guard of honour). We had no flags outside our windows and, being away from the centre of the town we thought it wouldn't matter much. We did, however, have the local *Sturmbandführer* (leader of storm troopers) from the SS calling on us to ask why our windows had no flags. He didn't know us and it took a bit of explaining on my mother's part, to convince him that our house could be without a flag. He wanted to bring some for us to hang outside. He went away grumbling under his breath, which worried my mother, so she phoned my father, who promised to be home by the evening of the big day.

47

Hitler arrived on a Tuesday, which was also the day for my piano lesson. Because of all the excitement and the crowds, Miss Wöhler, my teacher, would not come to us, but wanted us to have a double lesson the next week. I didn't like this, and said I would come to her.

I hadn't realized that Königsberg had so many people when I made my way to her in the town. I didn't have much of a lesson, because Miss Wöhler lived on the main road, which was absolutely packed with people, all shouting, whistling and singing, and her dog barked, not liking this unfamiliar noise. She was very upset about her dog, trying to pacify the fat animal, stroking him to make him keep quiet. In the end, she told me to go home, as I would have had difficulty getting through the crowds if I waited until after the motorcade had passed. I grabbed my music case and ran off. She was quite right; it was not easy to move along. Even close to the houses, there was hardly any space left. At the corner of a house, a woman was selling small bunches of violets for people to throw when Hitler passed. As I knew my father was coming home, I thought it might be rather nice to put a little bunch on his desk, so I bought one. I wasn't quite sure whether I had done anything wrong in his absence for my mother to complain about me, but I thought a little bunch of flowers would get him into a good mood.

I was hardly making any headway through the crowds, and thought it would probably be better to use the side streets. For this, I had to cross the road to carry on in the right direction to where we lived. The road was lined with SS and SA, also police and HJ keeping the crowds on the pavements and, when I tried to get through, an SS man stopped me from crossing the road. I realized I had to be crafty to get across, and found a section which was lined with the HJ, who were younger and therefore not so alert. A lot of shouting was going on around me, I thought I heard some motorbikes but, determined to push through, I took no notice of them. Suddenly I was through the crowd, ducked under the arms of the boys of the HJ holding hands, and ran into the road. I was in the middle of the road when I realized and saw the car with Hitler standing in it, coming towards me. I had been right when I thought I heard motorbikes, which always travelled in front of Hitler's car. They had passed, and now there he was.

*'Heil Hitler!'* shouted the people.

The noise was deafening, and I stood still, too frightened to know what to do. One of the SS men who always travelled on the running board of Hitler's car jumped off and approached me.

'Come, you can give the *Führer* your flowers,' he said, and put his hand on my shoulder.

He guided me towards the car, which had stopped. Hitler bent down towards me, stretching his hand out in expectation of the flowers. He smiled a little but there was no warmth, only a grimace, and his eyes were penetrating and seemed to hypnotize me, because my hand went up and he took the flowers.

'They are for my father,' I whispered, whilst a shiver ran down my back. His eyes were so strange, commanding, without any kindness. He never heard what I said, because the people were shouting and pushing, trying to get through the line of HJ, SA and SS.

'Why are you not in uniform?' said Hitler, having noticed that I must be over ten years old, being such a big girl. Anyway I was fourteen by then, and should have joined the party.

'I am Swiss,' I replied.

'Go back,' said the SS man, and gave me a little push, so I don't know whether Hitler heard me. I doubt whether he was really interested in me or the flowers, he was admired by so many, and wanted to wave to all of them.

The car started off again and I ran to the other side of the road, slipped under the cordon of SA men, and through the crowds to the back of the people. They were throwing flowers, streamers, bits of paper and rose petals from the windows, and everybody was shouting, cheering and whistling.

*'Ein Volk, ein Reich, ein Führer!'* That was the slogan called out by Hitler, and repeated in unison by the people at the stadium, when he had finished his speech that afternoon. I heard part of it on my way back home, as loud speakers had been erected everywhere and I had a long way to go because no trams were running until later in the day.

When I eventually reached home my father had arrived, and my mother was quite concerned because I was so late. I told them all about my adventure, and how I had lost my flowers. All my father said was:

'I hope this doesn't get into the papers. They love making a fuss of a girl presenting flowers to Hitler. This is good propaganda.'

It didn't get into the papers, but somebody who knew me must have seen me, because the girls at school knew all about it by the next day.

'Fancy you giving flowers to Hitler,' said Anneliese, 'you, who haven't even joined the HJ, and don't like to say *"Heil Hitler"*.'

I tried to explain, but nobody believed me. They were jealous, and envied me that I had been able to talk to "him", to be close to "him", to give "him" flowers.

I had thought that joining the HJ or BDM was harmless and full of fun, and resented the fact that my parents did not permit me to join but, seeing the adoration of my school comrades for the *Führer* and everything he did made me realize in what a subtle way the indoctrination of young people had taken place. I was too young to reason things out yet, I only knew that I did not have the same opinion as my school friends, because my parents would point out things which were never mentioned in the HJ. What happened to the Jewish people? Why was military conscription decreed in 1935, and a German Army and Air Force gradually built up again? I heard my father talking about it to his friends when they used to come to see him on his so-called *Herrenabenden* (gentlemen's evenings). He had these occasionally, and they would all meet in his study and smoke and drink beer and my mother would serve them little snacks. I sometimes was allowed to help to take in the plates and platters with the food, and later clear them away, and that's when I could catch snatches of conversation.

After Hitler annexed Austria in March of 1938, his popularity sky-rocketed. On March 14th, Hitler drove triumphantly through the streets of the country where he had once lived. The papers and newsreels were full of Hitler's journey into Austria. Everywhere people welcomed him with flowers and flags. If there was any opposition, that must have been quelled because, one month later, the Austrians voted 99.75% in favour of a union with Germany. Britain and France protested, but Mussolini of Italy sent his warmest congratulations to Hitler.

The next thing was the return of the Sudetenland to the "Homeland, Great Germany".

Hitler made another big speech from Nuremberg, to which we all had to listen at school. He declared that he would not tolerate the Czech oppression of the Sudetenland much longer.

'This definitely means war,' said my mother, and started to stock up food. We had to go to different shops and buy sugar, coffee, dried fruit, nuts and rice.

There was a conference on September 29th between Hitler, Daladier from France, Mussolini from Italy, and Chamberlain from England. The result was that Hitler got what he wanted. The Czech ministers were not consulted whilst the Western Powers talked. Poland and Hungary, too, had sent in their demands for territory, and got a certain amount of land and people in the next few weeks. Sudetenland was annexed. The German people had returned home!

Chamberlain returned to England, convinced that he had won a great diplomatic victory. The picture of him stepping off the plane with his umbrella in one hand, waving a piece of paper with the other, and telling the crowds that he had achieved "Peace in our time", was not only shown in England, but also in Germany and all over Europe.

In March 1939, the Czech President Hacha came to Berlin for a meeting with Hitler. It was announced that the fate of the Czech people was "trustingly" given over to Hitler and, on March 15th, German troops occupied Bohemia and Moravia, as the so-called protectors. The next day, Slovakia also came under German protection, and Czechoslovakia was no more.


Life was much too exciting and busy for me to worry about politics, as I had other things to think about. For one thing there was Helma, my local friend. I had grown lately, and was slightly taller than him, and he didn't like this. He also suddenly refused to have a race with me, or play football. All he wanted to do was to talk, or go for a walk. One day he told me he had discovered something, and wanted to show it to me.

Just past the tram station, in the Lawsker Allee, was a big hotel and restaurant called Reichsgarten which had stood empty for ages. First the hotel closed and then, after a time, the restaurant, because there was no demand for a big place like that, once houses were built around it. The front was fenced off with large gates which were securely locked since it was not occupied any more. Helma had discovered that the big lock had gone; one could open the gate by the handle and get in.

'Some people are working in the rooms inside,' he said. 'My father told me it is going to be a training school.'

'A training school for what?'

Helma's father was the chief constable at the local police station and, as a rule, full of good information.

'You must not tell anybody,' said Helma, 'but they are going to train people how to fight fires, and protect themselves against air attacks, in case of war.'

'Don't be silly, we are not going to have a war. It is only my mother who always thinks we are going to have one, because she went through the First World War.'

'I am only telling you what I heard. My father told my mother about it, and he is usually right. Anyway, what I want to show you is the big garden and park behind the house. We can get into it when the workmen have gone; they close the gate, but don't lock it.'

We agreed to meet at six o'clock, and he was right, the gate was open. First of all we climbed up to look through the windows. The rooms were empty, except for ladders, dust sheets and paint left by the workmen, so there was nothing of interest to be seen, but Helma was right about the decorating of the place. Behind the house was a wilderness of bushes, weeds and trees, but the further we went, the prettier it became, because we entered a park, with tall trees and overgrown paths. One path had been used before, probably by the workmen. It went down a small hill and, at the bottom, was a small stream.

'This is our Freigraben (stream),' said Helma.

It was the same little river which flowed along the Wahl, where we caught sticklebacks in the summer. The same river which froze in the winter. We had never realized this before, so now we tried to follow it to see where it went and how it got to the Wahl. We couldn't walk very far because the trees of the park gradually finished and in front of us was a huge field of nettles, behind which was a tall fence, announcing the end of the property.

'Ah well,' I said, 'that's it. I certainly won't go through those nettles and get my legs stung, and I shouldn't think you want to do it, seeing you have shorts on.'

'I might . . .'

'I don't believe you would do this.'

'I will do it if you give me something.'

'I have no money, no marbles and no sweets.' I said this quickly, because these were usually the things we passed on.

'It is nothing like that, it is something completely different, and you won't even miss it.'

'Alright.'

'You promise?'

'Yes, I promise! And I keep it, as you know.'

I didn't believe for a moment that he would go through the nettles, so it didn't matter giving a promise.

Helma looked at me, then at the nettle field, and suddenly he marched off, with the tall nettles covering his legs, and sometimes reaching up to his waist. He didn't stop until he got to the fence, climbed up a bit to have a better look, and then returned. I stood dumbfounded, I couldn't believe that I was seeing right.

Helma had red hair and pink skin but when he got back his legs were red, and so was his face, which was also covered in sweat. The pain must have been excruciating, but he didn't remark on it. He only said:

'It is the Freigraben alright. Let's get home, in case they decide to lock the gate tonight.'

I knew this was an excuse and that he wanted to get back to do something with his legs and, as I felt very sorry for him, I turned round and started to go back quickly. Suddenly I remembered his wish. He hadn't asked for anything yet.

'What am I suppose to give to you?'

'Not today, I will ask for it one evening.'

I shrugged my shoulders, I wasn't bothered. Whatever it was he could have, he had suffered enough for it, and maybe he would even forget it.

Helma didn't forget. I didn't see him for a few days, probably because he put something on his legs to take the burning away, and when we met again, he had long trousers on and looked very smart. He had arranged to meet me by sending a note along through my brother Hans, whom he had met in the afternoon. I had been out playing handball, and didn't get back until 6 o'clock. I'd never had a note from Helma before, and I was surprised when Hans produced it. All it said on the note was:

Meet me at eight o'clock, Reichsgarten.

That was the hotel where he had walked through the nettles, so I knew he wanted his present but, as he hadn't asked for anything, I couldn't take anything with me.

When I got to the gate, he was already there, and opened it for me. He walked on until we were behind the house, and then turned into the park, where it was already quite dark. Suddenly he stopped and looked at me, a little strange, and then said:

'You know what I want, don't you?'

I really didn't have the faintest idea, but I felt a bit funny because he made such a big secret about it all.

'I have no idea.'

He hesitated, and then he looked at his feet and his long trousers and said very abruptly:

'I want a kiss.'

'A kiss!' I called out, and put my hand over my mouth, because I thought I would burst out laughing, and I didn't want to do that after all the pain he had gone through. He wanted a kiss. What a silly thing to ask for! We were comrades, friends, pals. We didn't kiss.

'Oh, if that is all, you can have it.'

I put my arms around his neck, and kissed him on each cheek, then ran off, calling out:

'Good night, I must get home, it is late!'

I felt a bit embarrassed, and didn't want him to catch up with me, so I ran all the way home.

Christel knew I had gone out to see Helma and wanted to know what had happened, but I didn't tell her the truth. I just made up something, and went to bed.

I have had my first kiss, I thought, but it wasn't like it was described in books. Why did he ask me for it, instead of just kissing me?

In any case, I didn't want to be kissed by Helma. One only kissed when one was in love, and I was waiting for that dark, handsome and attractive stranger who would come and sweep me off my feet. I had read plenty of books, and hoped that the stories in them were not lies, or only made-up things. Helma was as old as I was; why did he suddenly think he wanted to kiss me? Now I knew why he wouldn't play with me any more, he felt he was grown up.

We didn't meet for a few days but, when we saw one another again, Helma didn't look at me, and we were both glad we were not alone, because some of the other neighbours' children were there too. We said silly things to one another, keeping up a conversation, in order to show that we had forgotten why and how we met the last time. When my brother came to tell me to come in because supper was going to be served, Helma came up to me and put his hand on my shoulder.

'So long', he said, and squeezed my shoulder a little, giving me a conspiratorial smile.

Suddenly our innocent friendship had gone, and I felt embarrassed and awkward. I avoided him after that, and missed him at the same time.


Helma was right about the Reichsgarten. The downstairs rooms were organised as lecture rooms, and people were encouraged to come and learn about protection against air attacks, and how to be an air-raid warden. My mother and I went to one of the courses because, although nobody thought there might be war, it was a good precaution, a chance to learn about First Aid. We did not only have lectures, but also practical classes. In the lectures, we were told how to strengthen one room in the cellar with posts in case of air attacks, and given a list of things one ought to have in this room, like a folding bed, blankets, emergency rations, water, a First Aid kit, toys and games for children. In the practical classes, we were shown how to use a gas mask and how to fight a fire. I thought it good fun, and quite enjoyed hitting the fire with a wet cloth attached to a stick, which we had to make ourselves. Looking back, it sounds all a bit primitive, but it made us realize what could happen, and got us used to not being afraid of gas or flames.

I had to take the course twice, because my mother was so impressed with the lectures and the practical side of them, that she thought it a good idea if Sternchen, too, would attend the classes. As these were only in the evening to give all working people the chance to come, and as it was then already dark, my mother didn't like Sternchen to go alone, but felt the two of us would be alright. I hit the flames with the wet cloth and stick much better the second time round!

At the beginning of 1939, the German government imposed a special tax on any food imports from Lithuania and, as this was pretty high, the imports stopped. Lithuania had a food surplus and, not being able to sell it, they had to destroy it. The milk which my father imported from Lithuania for his cheese and butter became very expensive. By the time he paid the farmer and the import duty, the milk cost him more than he could sell it for. Even by leaving the milk in Lithuania and producing the cheese and butter there in his two dairies he was losing money, because he had to pay import duty on the goods once he brought them over the border. My father carried on for a time in the hope that things would change, and so did a number of his dairy owner friends, but gradually one dairy after another closed. It was impossible to sell any businesses, because everybody had for years relied on the cheap import of milk, and the farmers in the Tilsit district had concentrated more on cattle for meat, and used the land for corn. With no more milk coming from Lithuania, the production of cheese and butter had to be curtailed as the local milk was needed for the daily use.

My father lost quite a bit of money. He sold one of the dairies in Lithuania to a concern of farmers, and was negotiating to sell the second dairy when, on March 22nd, Hitler annexed the town of Memel and the so-called Memelland at the eastern end of Prussia, calling it a return to the Homeland. The import tax for food and milk was reduced, and my father therefore did not sell the second dairy. Things had happened just in time for him, but not for some of his friends. Later, after the signing of the 1939 treaty which opened a corridor between Prussia and the Russian land, my father sold his other diary in Lithuania, and concentrated on the big one in Tilsit and another one which he rented in Ragnit.

Right through the summer of 1939, Hitler kept up his demand for the adjustment of the corridor, and the status of Danzig, but Poland would not give in. The Poles needed this corridor to reach the sea, the Baltic. On August 29th, Hitler delivered an ultimatum to the Polish government, giving them 24 hours to make a favourable decision about the corridor. On August 30th, the Polish government gave the Order to mobilize. Early in the morning on September 1st, the German attack against Poland began. A new type of war had started, the *Blitzkrieg* (lightening war), and it didn't last long. Poland was overrun with a speed that astonished everybody, even the German people.

At school, the war was made part of our lessons. We had a big map on the wall with part of Europe on it, and small flags were moved up when news came of how far the troops had advanced. There was the worry that France might march into Germany in the west, but we and the world were told, in propaganda speeches that the western fortifications were impregnable. In reality, that frontier had to be under-strength, because of the war in the east.

The flags on our war map at school moved pretty fast as the Polish army retreated everywhere, trying to get back to Warsaw in order to defend their capital. We had newsreels before the main picture in the cinema, and we could see there the *Luftwaffe* (Air Force) continually attacking the Polish headquarters. The roads in Poland were full of refugees, and the motorised Germans advanced faster than the Poles could retreat.

On the 17th of September, the Russians attacked Poland from the east. It was only later that we heard that Hitler had already asked Stalin, on September 3rd and 10th, to do this, which would have made it even easier for Germany to fight the Poles. The Russian armies didn't find a lot of resistance, as the Poles, who had not expected this attack, were occupied with the German army. The Russians took a lot of prisoners, as the soldiers had started to flee to the east. The Red Armies closed up to the German lines, with both sides being very careful to avoid a clash between them because of mistaken identity. After they met, each took a piece of Poland and, with that, the Polish state disappeared.

Hitler then announced that the central European situation was satisfactory, and he wanted negotiations with the Western Powers. The

Allies refused any peace talks, and it is doubtful whether Hitler was serious about a peace offer.

The surprising thing was that neither Britain nor France did anything whilst the Germans were occupied in the east. I am sure Poland expected it, and so did the people in Germany. Actually they feared it, because they knew it would be difficult to fight on two fronts. Russia didn't march into Poland until later, because they, too, waited for France and Britain to make a move. Only when it did not happen, did they enter Poland. It seemed as if no one in the west wanted to fight. The French sat in the Maginot Line, and the British dropped leaflets over Germany, which we were told not to read, but to hand in to the authorities. We didn't get any in Königsberg, but they had quite a number in the west. We were probably too far away.

Everybody seemed to be for the war. Amongst my school friends, a lot of fathers were called up, and some were fighting in Poland. In our neighbourhood, because of the police station, most fathers were in the police force, and they stayed at home at that time. Helma told me that he hoped that the war would last long enough so that he could join up; he was determined to go into the navy. He was only fifteen years old, and couldn't be a cadet for another year, until the age of sixteen. My mother, as usual, was concerned about the family, and how to feed us all. She had the experience of the First World War to look back on, and was now trying to find ways and means of stocking up food. Everybody realized that, with Britain having declared war, her navy would blockade Germany, and prevent any food coming in, so from now on we would have to rely on what the country could produce, or what it had stocked up. The shops still had their stored provisions, and rationing had not yet started. People went on a buying spree, particularly for things like coffee, tea, nuts, dried fruit, sugar, anything that would keep and came from foreign countries. Soon, the different grocers did their own rationing, allocating only small amounts to each customer. They also recognized people turning up again and again, and then refused to sell them certain items.

As the majority of men were called up into the army, there were vacancies everywhere and an announcement was made for volunteers to fill these, even if only on a part-time basis. My mother started to send us four children to the different grocers in the district to buy whatever we could, and she herself went too. We ignored one another in the different shops and in this way we were able to visit each shop five times. Often we only got a quarter of a pound of a particular item, and so we didn't collect a lot. Then my mother discovered a grocer not far from us who was terribly short of staff; his two sons, who worked full-time at the shop, had left to join the army. My mother convinced the owner that I would be a great help in the afternoons, after school. She told him that although I was only fifteen years old, I was strong, and could help to fill up shelves, and carry boxes and sacks into the shop from the store room. In other words, she got me a job at the grocers, so that I could help to fill our store cupboards!

There were no supermarkets in those days. The customers entered the shop and asked for the required items, which were then weighed and charged. Dried peas were kept in sacks, so were potatoes and unshelled nuts. Sugar and salt were in boxes or sacks, and coffee beans in tins. Everything had to be weighed, which took a long time. Mr and Mrs Meier served in the shop, and I had to carry in the stock from a back room. Some of the sacks were quite heavy, and I worked hard. I was the little girl who had to run about, tidy up, sweep and wash the floor and in the evening Mr Meier would give me some sugar, coffee or nuts as payment. My mother had arranged that I didn't get any money, but food which could become short later on.

The shop was sometimes very full of people and, when Mr Meier discovered that I knew quite a lot of the prices, and could even add up well, he allowed me to serve a little. Christel and Sternchen would come into the shop and when they saw me serving they would gently push through the people until they were at the counter where I would serve them, making out that I didn't know them. I was told to watch that people didn't come twice, but I never said anything about Sternchen and Christel. I only served when I had brought in enough stock, and when the shop was full of customers.

Mr and Mrs Meier liked me and, although I was on the go all afternoon and got very tired, they would not let me do things which were too heavy. The only trouble was that I couldn't do my homework, and I had to miss out sport. My mother gave me a note once or twice, saying that I had to go to the doctor or dentist, or that she was ill, and I had to look after my younger sister and brother, but she could not make excuses for ever. So, after a time, when my mother had quite a stock of food, I had to tell Mr and Mrs Meier that I couldn't come any more, because of my homework. They were very sorry to see me go but by then things had become difficult in the food line. There was talk of rationing and Mr Meier didn't get his full orders, sometimes even nothing at all.

Food rationing was introduced, and all items, even bread, were allocated. The worst thing was the milk; from now on, one could only get skimmed milk, except children under ten years of age, expectant mothers, or people with a doctor's certificate, who could apply for extra milk coupons.

We were all very interested in the war. At school, the war was the main subject. Nearly everybody had somebody in the war, a father, a brother, an uncle, a cousin, or a friend. I had no relatives in the war but some of our neighbours had joined. My friend Helma who was sixteen in 1940, left to enter the marine cadet school. People were advised to keep their radios on all day because extra messages were passed on at any time, interrupting the programmes.

In April, the German army occupied Denmark, and the navy landed troops in Norway which was strategically important for Germany. By occupying Norway, it had secured the transport of the iron ore from Sweden to Germany for the rest of the war. The German navy also had a safe place from where it could make raids into the Atlantic.

Chamberlain resigned on April 10th 1940 and Churchill took over as Prime Minister in England. On May 10th, an announcement on the radio told the German people that their tanks had crossed the Dutch and Belgian borders. Hitler was not waiting for France or Britain to attack. The war against France had begun.

At school the maps of Eastern Germany, Poland and Russia were put away, the Norwegian/Swedish map was hung on to the side wall, and the map with Holland, Belgium, Luxembourg and France was hung in a prominent place.

On June 10th, Mussolini declared war on Britain and France. When the German troops arrived east and west of Paris, the French government fled south. The capital was occupied, General de Gaulle fled to England and armistice talks were started. A cease-fire agreement was signed on June 25th 1940.

German troops paraded through Paris and visited the tourist attractions. We saw all of this on the newsreels. Some of my school friends had pictures of relatives in uniform standing next to the Eiffel Tower or under the Arc de Triomphe.

# CHAPTER FIVE

## Life at Home

At first, our lives did not change much because of the war. We still had to go to school, and carried on with the usual activities. In 1940, the summer holidays were made longer, and the beginning of the school year was transferred from the Spring to the Autumn. The school year 1940/41 had 17 months, from April 1940 until August 1941. From then on, one moved up a class after the Summer holidays, but the matriculation and the examinations after the sixth year were at Easter, so that pupils who had started at Easter, did not have to attend extra time at school. Pupils at our school could leave after the sixth year, called *Mittlere Reife*, (O-Level, first public examination) if they did not intend to go to university.

Lessons at school were sometimes cut because of shortage of teachers. The few male teachers left were transferred to the boys' schools, and sometimes it took a little time to replace them. The boys' grammar school was only a few minutes walk from our school, and the meeting place for all of us was the *Eisdiele* (ice parlour), at the corner of the Hindenburgstrasse, in which our school was situated.

In Autumn 1940, our whole class had to go into the *Erntedienst* (harvest duty). The summer holidays had been made longer for this reason. The excuse was, officially, that we wouldn't miss any school. Unofficially, of course, the Autumn term was very short, and the curriculum in the different subjects had to be condensed. Labour was needed on the farms, as most of the men were called up into the forces; it was decided to send the bigger school-girls for a few weeks, to help with any necessary jobs.

We were taken by lorry to the different villages where people had applied for help. I went to a very nice family with six children. The farmer was not in the army, but had been put in charge of several small farms where the owners were missing because of the war. Not everybody was called up, as it was also necessary to look after the farms and see to the grain and the animals. Mr Zimmermann, with whom I lodged, would organise the work on his farm early every morning, and then leave to see to the other farms which were allocated to him. I lived in the main house, sharing a room with the eldest daughter, who was 14 years old. I was treated as one of the family.

I did everything, from cleaning, bathing of the younger children, washing up, and I even learnt how to milk the cows, when one of the girls had cut her hand. The turning of the hay in the field was not too bad, but I hated it when we had to bind the corn. We had no combine harvesters in those days. The corn was cut by a man with a large scythe. It was fascinating to watch him. He had a certain rhythm, swinging the scythe through the corn with a swishing sound. At the end of the row, he stopped, took the stone out of his back trouser pocket, sharpened the scythe, and carried on. The women followed at a distance, picking up the corn to bind it. To make a sheaf, one took an armful of corn under the arm, and a few extra stalks in the other hand which were used to wind around the corn, finishing it off with a twist. There was a lot of bending to be done, and the inside of my arms soon got sore. Mrs Zimmermann gave me some old stockings with the feet cut off to put on to my arms but, even so, my arms still hurt.

After the cutting and binding of the corn, the sheaves were put into stooks to dry. Even that was painful after a time, because I had to lift the prickly sheaves. Mrs Zimmermann decided that it would be better if I carried on with the milking, and helping in the house, whilst the girls who were used to the reaping of the corn worked in the fields. But I had a go at loading up the waggon, drawn by two horses. The fork was pushed into the sheaves, and they were lifted up to the girls on the waggon, who stacked them. At first it was easy but the higher the waggon was stacked the more difficult it became to lift the sheaves. The best thing was the homeward journey, sitting high up on the sheaves of corn, with the horses slowly plodding along, the waggon slightly swinging in the rhythm, the girls singing and waving to the children in the village.

All in all, I enjoyed my time on the farm, and returned home brown, much tougher than before, and full of new experiences and an insight into another life, close to animals and the land.

Our *Gauleiter*, Erich Koch, decided that nothing must be wasted. Lots of things could be recirculated so we started the collection of paper, metal, including tins and aluminium. We had to go from house to house to advertise the collection, then give a date, and collect things and bring them to school, where everything was weighed and sorted. Our headmaster made it into a competition, writing down every week what everybody had collected. We also collected books, which were posted to German-speaking regions. This had already been done by the BDM (HJ), but was now also extended to the schools. At Christmas, in 1940, we all packed small parcels with little gifts and a letter to an unknown soldier at the front, again by orders of the *Gauleiter*. By now we were sixteen years old, and had started to be interested in boys, particularly men in uniform, and everybody hoped for a reply to their letter in the parcel. Some girls did get a reply, and carried on with their correspondence to their unknown soldier for a time, but I never got an answer. At first, I was a little disappointed, not because I wanted to write a letter again in reply, but the others were showing off their replies, even reading them to one another in whispers, and there was a lot of giggling, raising of eyebrows, and hiding of letters going on, in which I would have liked to join.

It was brought home to us that the war was not finished after conquering France when, even at school, we had to practice air-raid defence, fire-fighting, and had lessons in First Aid. The school also built out the cellars as air-raid shelters, where 120 and, in emergency, 212 people could easily be accommodated.

People were advised to build out one cellar room in their house as an air-raid shelter, and grants were given to those who wished to do this, but could not afford it. My father decided to have one cellar room strengthened with posts and beams, and a fireproof door. My mother put an old carpet down, some chairs, and a couple of camp beds, blankets, an axe, buckets of water, and some emergency rationing, First Aid equipment, gas masks, and a number of other small items she thought might be necessary.

My first boyfriend was called Gerhard Flach. Although I had Helma, I never really considered him as a boyfriend, more a comrade or playmate.

I was never in love with Gerhard, or even very excited about him. I was sixteen years old, everybody had a boyfriend or a soldier, and Gerhard Flach turned up at the right moment, when I was ready to accept anybody, so that I, too, could be in fashion.

We met at a sports competition in Insterburg, a small town 91 km from Königsberg. I was entered in the long jump, because I had jumped further than anybody else in our KTC club competition. I also had to play in the handball game.

We got to Insterburg by lunchtime, and had the first competitions by two o'clock. As expected my jumps were not much good and by three o'clock I had nothing to do except to wait until the others were finished, so that we could all return together to the school where we were staying. The handball game was not until the next morning, and I was really fed up, having now to hang around all the afternoon. There were lots of competitions going on, as it was quite a large sports arena, so I walked around to watch some of them. Boys, too, were performing and, whilst I watched the Hammer-throwing, somebody next to me suddenly said:

'Have you, too, finished for the day?'

I looked round and saw a boy, a little taller than myself, standing behind me. He had dark hair, and brown friendly eyes, and his nose was slightly flattened, as if somebody had given him a punch in his face.

'I have been watching you wandering around, as if you had nothing to do,' he continued.

I explained that I had finished, and found out that the same had happened to him. So there we were, both of us, with nothing to do all afternoon. He said his name was Gerhard Flach. I had to bite my tongue quickly, because I thought I was going to burst out laughing. Flach means flat and, looking at his nose, he had the correct name. Gerhard had been to Insterburg before; as a matter of fact, he knew it well as he had an aunt and uncle living there. So, when he suggested he could show me the town, I was only too pleased to go with him. But before going off, I went and found Ewa, one of my friends in the KTC, and told her what I intended to do. Ewa was still in the high jump competition, and had to wait for the next jump in her group, so she said she would cover for me. Gerhard and I had a lovely afternoon.

The next day I met Gerhard when he came to the sports field. We won our handball match. Gerhard watched the game and thought our team excellent, fast, and working well together. We met on and off during the day, but had to say farewell in the late afternoon because Gerhard lived in Allenstein, another small town. He promised to write and maybe visit me in Königsberg. He was joining the officers' cadet school in a month's time, and couldn't give me an address yet. I was not really bothered whether I heard from him or not. We'd had two nice days together and if that was all, I would not be heartbroken. Gerhard was already eighteen years old, and wanted to study architecture. Because of the war, he had to join the army. I was very surprised when I got a letter from him after two weeks, telling me that he had been called up earlier. He did not tell me where he was, as this was not permitted. His address was a number called *Feldpost Nummer* (field post number) or *Feldpost Nr. . . .* in abbreviation.

Everybody who was in the forces had a number, and sometimes also some letters added, and nobody knew where the addressee was situated. Postage was free to all *Feldpost Nummern*, whether they were letters or parcels. Gerhard was a good letter writer, and we kept up a correspondence. I liked to get letters from him, because I could tell my friends at school about him, and I think the same happened to him at the cadet school, because he could boast about a girl friend. Nobody, except Ewa, had met Gerhard, and I thought I must make quite sure that nobody sees him, because of his flat nose. I was very conscious of this small disfigurement in his face, which he had received through boxing.

For years my mother had a maid to live in but when the war broke out this had to finish. No German girl was allowed to go into domestic service as too many people had to replace the men who had left to fight in the war.

Our house was very big; we were a large family, and my mother could not manage on her own. She then found out that we could have foreign labour. Polish people were brought back to Germany to work in factories, or go into a household as domestic help. They were only allocated menial jobs, like sweeping the roads, working in the kitchens of hotels and restaurants or cleaning of buildings and toilets, like the railway stations, big banks and office blocks. They lived in camps under quite primitive conditions. Some girls were chosen to go into domestic service and were brought to the labour exchange, from where they were collected by a householder.

My mother had to go and sign a form that she would be responsible for the girl, feed and clothe her, and bring her back to the exchange when she was not needed any more, or when asked to do so. We had two hopeless girls, both of them not much good, until we had Olga. The real reason was that the girls came from very primitive backgrounds, and were frightened of all the new and modern equipment in German towns and houses. They had been forced to leave their homes and were often homesick. Some ran away, hoping to get back to Poland but if they got caught they were brought back and often punished by being put into labour camps.

None of the girls spoke German, and we didn't speak Polish. The first girl we had was quite frightened when she arrived. My mother had collected her from the labour exchange at the beginning of August in

1940. She was dirty, very poorly dressed, and had a small bundle of belongings. My mother brought her into the kitchen, and made her sit down at the table, because she thought she would give her something to eat first. She put a plate of hot soup in front of her, cut her a slice of bread from the end of a loaf and buttered it. The girl just sat there, looking at my mother then at me, and then she looked at the table with the soup, the buttered bread, and the end of the loaf still lying on the board. My mother smiled at her and told her to eat. Suddenly she grabbed the end of the loaf and, holding it in both hands, bit at it, chewed quickly, bit again two or three times, and then pushed the rest up her sleeve. My mother made a step forward and pointed to the soup, encouraging her to eat it, but the girl must have thought my mother would hit her, because she quickly put an arm over her head for protection. And then my mother saw that she was not only dirty, but also had nits in her thick long hair.

'On no!' said my mother, 'we cannot have this! The whole family will get the nits. We must give her a bath. I dare not let her go into the bathroom. We will have to do it in the cellar, in the washing kitchen in one of the big tubs.'

We heated some water in big saucepans. My mother told me to keep an eye on her whilst she went to find her some clean clothes. The girl's little bundle of belongings didn't look as if it contained any. The girl, in the meantime, drank the soup, just lifting up the soup plate and drinking from it without using the spoon and she also ate the buttered slice of bread. After that she looked at me, then put her folded arms on to the table, and her head on top of them, and pretended to go to sleep.

When my mother returned with some clean clothes, we poured the hot water into two buckets and tried to make her carry them. She would not let go of her bundle and could, therefore, only carry one bucket. My mother didn't want her to think that we intended to take her few belongings away, so she made me carry one bucket. It was not easy to explain things to her, even by showing her what to do in sign language, but she did pick a bucket up, and we were able to guide her downstairs.

Worse was to come, because she just wouldn't take her clothes off. She did understand what we wanted to do because every time my mother tried to pull her dress off, she held on to it.

'This is ridiculous,' said my mother, 'the water will get cold.'

We had poured the hot water into a small tub, and my mother had added cold water. She had shampoo and soap ready, also a soft brush and an old sponge, towels and a big comb.

'We will just have to pull her clothes off. If they tear, I have others here. We might have to burn them in any case if the smell doesn't come out after washing. You hold her, and watch that she doesn't scratch me when I get hold of her clothes.'

It was a proper fight, but we did get her clothes off. The smell was terrible, and the clothes were filthy. She was a big strong girl and, after a tremendous struggle, she gradually let us peel her clothes off. She had two dresses on, and several pieces of underwear. So, instead of having clothes in her bundle, she wore them all, probably thinking they were safer on her body than anywhere else.

The girl practically fell into the tub. My mother then washed her hair, finishing off with disinfectant to kill the nits. She did not use the brush to scrub the girl's body, as this was covered in weals from flea bites and she felt sorry for her. She used plenty of soap, and the sponge, but scrubbed her feet. The water was black when the girl got out, which she did quite willingly, and even tried to dry herself.

The next trouble came when my mother gave her some clean underwear. She didn't want the new clothes, but tried to get her old clothes back. Eventually my mother reluctantly made two piles of the girl's clothes, the underwear, and the two dresses. The underwear was pushed away, and my mother then laid the new, clean underwear on top of the two dresses. The girl seemed to understand, particularly when my mother soaked the underwear in buckets of water and made the signs of washing and rubbing them. I also thought that, maybe, she was only interested in her two dresses as she had hidden the bread in them, which she quickly grabbed from the pile of clothes.

It was difficult to comb her hair as it was so matted. I had to get some scissors in the end, and my mother cut some of it away. She then gave the girl the comb, which she quickly stuffed into her bundle. My mother told me to clear up the washing kitchen, whilst she took the girl upstairs to show her her bedroom.

I was just pouring out the water from the tub, when I heard my mother shouting:

'Come quickly, Helga, come, come, she has run away! Be quick and run after her! You must bring her back!'

I ran up the cellar stairs and out of the front door but could not find her. None of our neighbours had seen her. She had disappeared.

My mother and I were absolutely exhausted after this, and my mother was also quite upset. She was worried about the piece of paper she had signed, that she was responsible for the girl, and would look after her.

'I don't think that I can go through this again,' she said.

Nevertheless she phoned the labour exchange, and was told to come again on Monday morning. The office girl wasn't too concerned about a Polish girl running away.

On Monday morning I was at school but kept on thinking whether my mother would get another girl or not. She had said unless the girl was clean, she would not bring her back. I hurried home after school, and ran into the kitchen. Girl number two had arrived! She stood by the kitchen table, peeling potatoes with a knife, whilst the potato peeler lay next to the peels. My mother was cooking, and looked at me when I came in.

'Well, how did you get on at the labour exchange?' I said.

'I will tell you about it later,' she said. 'First you will have to give me a hand to wash her hair. She has got nits, but seems clean otherwise. So this time we will not go into the cellar, but wash her hair in the kitchen sink. She seems to be a little brighter than the last one.'

After locking the doors, my mother showed the girl what she wanted to do. The girl looked frightened. My mother filled up a bowl of water, and put the girl's hand into it to show her it was warm water. The girl's face showed surprise, but she would not put her head down over the sink for a hair wash. My mother kept on showing her, and explaining to her what she wanted to do, but the girl just wouldn't come near the sink. I could see my mother getting frustrated, when suddenly the girl took the bowl of water out of the sink, stood it on a chair, and positioned herself in front of it, looking at my mother.

'Maybe she is afraid of the sink, or the taps, or the hot running water', said my mother, 'but, never mind, she doesn't seem to object to a hair wash. So let's get on with it.'

We washed her hair, with the bowl resting on the chair, and I emptied the bowl, filling it with hot water several times. Hair wash, rinsing, disinfectant, rinsing again, drying, combing hair, the same routine as with girl number one, but this time no objection, as long as it was performed away from the sink. My mother gave her the comb in the end, which she quickly put into her pocket.

The girl had more belongings than girl number one. They were all stuffed into two string bags, and lying in the corner of the kitchen. From time to time she looked at them, making sure they were still there.

'You can go upstairs and show her her room,' my mother said to me, 'and unpack her string bags. If she has got another dress, there is a hanger in the wardrobe. I think she is more willing to understand things than the other one. After that, bring her down again. We had better not leave her alone for too long yet, she can help me in the kitchen again.'

The girl was quite willing to come upstairs with me but when I wanted to take her bags to empty them she wouldn't let me. The maid's room was small, with a bed standing under the sloping roof, a small wardrobe against the wall, with a washstand next to it, and a small chest of drawers. There was no carpet, only a little mat laid on to the wooden floor in front of the bed. I made signs that meant she should take her things out of the bag and put them into the chest of drawers and the wardrobe. She seemed to be very bewildered, and a little frightened. Eventually she laid the bags down and, together, we took the things out and put them away. Amongst her belongings was a crucifix, which I stood on the chest of drawers. She had two more dresses, all screwed up in the bags, which we hung in the wardrobe. She kept on looking under the bed, even crawling underneath, and I couldn't make out what she was looking for. She then pointed to her tummy, screwed up her face and crossed her legs, and I suddenly realized she wanted to go to the toilet. She had looked under the bed for the chamber pot. We had a toilet upstairs, but I thought I had better take her downstairs to the one next to the kitchen, as she would use that one more often during the day. I called out to my mother:

'I am showing the girl the toilet!' and then opened the door to let her in. She stared at the room, looked all around, even behind the toilet seat, and then she looked at me. It was obvious that she wasn't familiar with a toilet or, at least, not an indoor toilet. I called my mother as I didn't know how to cope with this situation.

'You will just have to show her what to do,' said my mother, 'you will have to demonstrate. Go on, get on to the toilet!'

I could see that this was probably the only way to explain it. I lifted the lid, showed the girl the inside of the toilet, pulled my knickers down, sat on it and performed. Her face was a picture of disbelieving awe. She stared at me with big eyes and an open mouth. When I got up, my mother showed her what I had done, and then pointed to her to do the same thing. Very slowly she lifted her skirt, watching us all the time, then her knickers came down, then she turned round and sat on the toilet and performed. When she saw we were pleased with what she did, she suddenly smiled a little. This was her first smile. She got up and dressed herself. After that, my mother showed her how to pull the chain to flush the toilet, or at least tried to show her. She took the girl's hand into her own hand, and then the two hands pulled the chain. The water rushed down into the toilet with a swishing noise and, with that, the girl screamed, pushed my mother and me away, and ran, screaming, to the locked front door. There she stopped, but carried on screaming and pulling at the door handle. My mother and I followed her and I put my arm around her to quieten her down. She gradually stopped and I brought her back, wanting to show her that the toilet was now clean. We had the greatest difficulty in getting her into the toilet but, eventually, she came to the open door, which my mother had wedged, and looked in. I held her tight, and my mother pulled the chain again, letting her watch what happened to the water.

The rest of the afternoon and evening passed uneventfully. The girl helped my mother, who taught her a few things like washing up and cleaning the saucepans. When it was time to go to bed, my mother took her upstairs and folded the bedspread back, showing her that she had to go to bed. She had no nightgown. I had told my mother this after I had helped her to unpack her things, so my mother had brought one along which she laid on her bed, telling her, in sign language, that she ought to put it on.

In the evening, I heard at last how my mother had got on at the labour exchange. She had decided to try and make a friend of the manageress, because she felt she would probably need the service of that office as long as the war lasted. To make a friend of somebody meant to do some black market business, in other words, to give them some food, or an article which was rationed, or in great demand, and difficult to get. Through my father's dairy, we had plenty of butter, cheese, and even cream, which my father brought home whenever he came. The butter was a little bulky to take along and, for the cream, one needed a jar, so another article had to be found. My father soon knew a number of people, and he exchanged butter for coffee beans. Coffee was very scarce, because only a few merchant vessels got through the cordon of British U-boats and battleships. My mother always carried a few coffee beans in envelopes in her handbag, just enough for two cups. They had to be beans rather than ground coffee, because of the strong smell. If my mother wanted something, and knew that the person had it, but wouldn't give it to her, or demanded coupons, she would suddenly whisper:

'I can let you have a few real coffee beans', and slide the envelope out of her handbag on to the table, covering it with her hand. It usually worked wonders!

My mother had insisted on seeing the manageress, Mrs S., at the labour exchange and, after waiting an hour, she was called into the office. Mrs S. was sitting behind her desk, and her secretary a little away, by a side table. This did not suit my mother at all, as she had hoped to be alone with the manageress. She started to tell Mrs S. about girl number one. At the same time, she took one of her envelopes out of her handbag, and laid it in front of her on to the table. She pressed her fingers over the envelope, as if playing with it, and the shape of one or two beans came through. She scratched the paper, and half a coffee bean poked out. There was a faint smell of coffee.

Mrs S. watched my mother's hand. The secretary was typing, and my mother carried on talking. Suddenly Mrs S. interrupted my mother apologetically and turned to the secretary, asking her to look something up in a file in the main office. As soon as the door closed, my mother handed the envelope to Mrs S. with a smile:

'My husband is Swiss, and we do occasionally get a little gift parcel from Switzerland. I thought you might like a few coffee beans. Next time I come, I will let you have some butter, if you are short, or some cheese.'

After that, Mrs S. was my mother's friend. By the time the secretary returned, the envelope had disappeared, and Mrs S. was explaining about the Polish girls she received for placement into domestic service. What she told my mother was not quite the truth. Either she did not know it, or she didn't want my mother to know it, because what happened was this:

Poland was now occupied by the Germans and, as labour was needed, people were forced to come to Germany. The SS went round villages collecting strong young men and women, herding them into railway cattle trucks and bringing them back to Germany. They hardly had time to take any belongings because the SS discovered that if it was known that they would come, all the young people would disappear into the woods. So they just arrived in a selected village with empty lorries, burst into the houses, and took the people. A lot of village people still lived very primitive lives, working for the local "count", and tending their rented land. There was no electricity, no running water or bathrooms, and the toilet was a little shed at the bottom of the garden with a wooden board with a hole, and a bucket underneath. When the bucket was full, it was emptied on the field as manure. The people were very poor and uneducated. They hardly had the necessities of life. There were only three important things: church, food, and paying the rent for the land, in that order of importance.

Mrs S. told my mother not to worry about girl number one.

'She probably had never had a bath in her life, and was frightened,' she said. 'Some girls do run away, but they don't get far. They cannot speak the language and, when they get hungry, they steal, and get caught.

Some sleep in doorways and get picked up. One or two come back here. I think it was awfully good of you to give her a bath and some clothes.'

She then looked at her file, and went outside into the main office where several girls were sitting on a bench. She came back with girl number two and, leaving the door open, told my mother that the girl looked pretty clean, and that she should try her.

'You might be able to teach her a few things,' said Mrs S. 'Our Polish interpreter said she comes from a bigger village, has been to school, and can write and read Polish. If she is not suitable, you can bring her back and, in the meantime, I will see whether I can find somebody else.' And then, speaking slightly louder, so that the secretary and the girls in the main office could hear her, she continued:

'I quite understand your situation, having such a large house, because of your husband's business, and four children still at school, you certainly need help in the home.'

And that's how girl number two arrived.

The girl certainly seemed more intelligent and willing. We had been able to wash her hair, and even calmed her down after the toilet incident, but the first morning turned out to be a bit of a surprise for my mother, when she went up to call her. She found her fast asleep on the floor, covered with the little carpet which my mother had laid in front of the bed. She had not touched the bed, nor the nightgown which my mother had given her. My poor mother was quite shocked. Nobody had ever slept on the floor in her house. The girl had also packed her two string bags again and was holding them in her hand. She hadn't even taken her clothes off.

It needed a lot of patience to teach the girl anything, because everything was new. She did not attempt to run away. She loved the garden. She never left any food. My mother tried to teach her a few words, but she would never repeat any. My mother was with her nearly all the time and, after a week, she felt there had been so little progress that there was no point in persevering. My mother never had any time for anything else, except looking after and teaching the girl. So she phoned Mrs S., and told her that she would bring the girl back. She packed some butter and put it into her big handbag, then she explained to the girl that she had to pack her things, gave her some money, and marched off with her to the labour exchange. Mrs S. was buttered up, but she had nobody suitable, and we were again without any help.

My mother was quite happy to carry on on her own; she was so much quicker, not always having to explain everything. It was as if a great weight had been lifted off her shoulders, and she was much more even-tempered.

On the last day of August, Mrs S. rang up. She was very excited and said she really had a good girl for my mother, but she must come and fetch her straight away. I don't think my mother was all that keen, she'd had such bad experiences with the last two girls, but she knew she could not last long without help. The fruit season would come, jam had to be made, plums bottled, apples and pears picked, and then the Sauerkraut had to be started, and the pickling of the gherkins. So off she went, and returned with Olga.

Olga, although again a village girl, had worked for the local priest in her native village and was quite domesticated. She was clean, small, but strong, with a plump face, and dark bright shiny eyes. She didn't look very friendly when she arrived. My mother introduced her to all of us, and said that Olga spoke a few German words, and understood quite a bit. She had already worked for another German family, where the man of the house had grown a little too fond of her, and his wife had brought her back to the labour exchange.

I took Olga upstairs and showed her her room. She was quite willing to unpack her little suitcase. I showed her the water tap, and made her fill up her jug; I showed her the toilet, and I even showed her the cellar. Nothing seemed to frighten her. She was a nice girl, I thought, and I gave her a sweet, which I had in my pocket. She smiled for the first time and said: *'Danke'* (thank you).

Olga was quite intelligent, and responded to kindness. She accepted new things gradually, even the vacuum cleaner. My mother had to show her several times what to do with it and, although she was frightened, she crossed herself quickly, then got hold of the handle, closed her eyes, murmuring all the time as if saying prayers over her rosary, and pushed the vacuum cleaner forwards and backwards. When she started, she had no idea why she had to do it, and just stood there, on the same spot, with eyes closed, pushing the cleaner forwards and backwards.

She was perfectly alright with most cleaning jobs, like windows, kitchen floor and dusting. She was in her element when she could peel vegetables, and enjoyed digging and weeding in the garden. My mother commented that she was better than any servant she had ever had, as they would never do any gardening. My mother went back to see Mrs S., to thank her, making sure there were a few things in her large handbag!

Sternchen didn't bother about Olga much, Christel was kind to her and tried to talk to her, Hans sometimes teased her by hiding behind the door and frightening her when she came into the room, and I made a friend of her. She was eighteen years old, and interested in the things which a young girl of that age would be. I gave her women's magazines, which she looked at for hours, and I took her for walks so that she started to know the district. Because she was Polish, there were a lot of restrictions for her.

The only amusements we had were the pictures, theatre or opera. There were no public dances; because of the war all dance halls had to close. One could organise small parties at home for dancing. Dancing classes were allowed, and all the best families in the town made a point of sending their sons and daughters to Albert and Erika Schmidt, who had a dancing school. They had won the German championships for several years in ballroom dancing and after that opened a school in Königsberg. Sternchen started at this school in January and went there twice a week in the late afternoon. She really enjoyed dancing and told us all about it, demonstrating the steps she had learnt.

The pictures were for everybody and, if the film was good, there would often be a long queue. Before the main film, we always had the *Wochenschau* (newsreel), in which we were informed about the victorious happenings of the German Army, *Luftwaffe*, and Navy. Olga, being Polish, was not allowed to go to the pictures. By Christmas 1940, having been nearly four months with us, Olga's German was quite good. So, as a Christmas treat, I decided to take her to the pictures. My mother was very worried, but I assured her that I wouldn't let Olga talk, and she would be with me all the time in any case.

I gave Olga an old coat of mine to wear, so that she didn't have her "P" on the outside, which would have been noticed. All Polish workers had to have a "P" on their clothes, Jewish people a Star of David, and later, the Russian workers had "Ost" (East) sewn to their clothes. We didn't go to the local cinema, but went to the middle of the town by tram, something Olga wasn't allowed to do either. To make sure none of our neighbours saw us going to the tram, or on to it, we left the house separately, and met at the second tram stop. All went well, even at the cinema. Olga never said a word, as instructed, and would only reply with yes or no to anything I asked her. After that, we often went together, and she was most grateful, as she knew what a risk I took.

# CHAPTER SIX

## War against Russia

In June 1941, there were arrangements made at our school for a fire watch. We had six girls and a teacher as lookouts every night. A rota was organised amongst the older girls and the teachers, and I also belonged to it. We had seven camp beds in the air-raid cellar to sleep on and took it in turns to walk around the school every hour. We thought it all great fun, and completely unnecessary, not realizing that it was an excellent foresight, because it was needed when the war with Russia broke out a few weeks later.

At the beginning of 1941, troops, tanks and equipment came through East Prussia, moving into occupied Poland, and everybody thought that they were getting ready for the Spring manoeuvres in April. Russia suddenly signed a neutrality treaty with Japan, which was a great surprise to everybody.

On June 22nd 1941, the German war machine attacked Russia without warning. At 6.30 in the morning, Goebbels read on the radio a proclamation from Hitler to the German people and, later on, Ribbentrop gave an explanation to the German and foreign Press.

I was on fire-watch at school in the night from the 22nd to the 23rd of June, and that's when we had the first bomb attack on Königsberg, in the early morning hours. After dropping a few bombs near the gas works, the planes turned towards the two high schools, the girls and the boys *Hufenschule*, and this was probably their main target. Between the two schools, along the Hufenallee, lived the Russian Consul, who doubtless had noticed that in the last few months the schools were partly occupied by high-ranking officers.

At school we had woken up from the noise of the planes and had run outside. This was, of course, wrong, but even our teacher came with us. We saw the big heavy Russian planes coming quite low over the school, when our teacher shouted:

'Get inside into the cellar!'

We all dived back into the school but, even before reaching the cellar, we heard the bombs, and the building shook. We all lay on the floor, terrified. We had forgotten everything about our air-raid training. I was holding my ears to keep out the noise and wondered whether this would be the end of my life, when I heard glass shattering and felt the building rocking again. After a time, the hum of the planes became less, and I took my hands away from my ears.

'We will wait a little bit longer before going outside and upstairs to see whether fire bombs have been dropped,' said the teacher.

Each of us had to take a bucket of water and the stick with the attached wet rag. A lot of windows were broken at the school, but the damage to the building was minimal. There were no fires and, after a couple of hours, the teacher decided that there probably wouldn't be any more planes and told us to go home.

The Russians dropped a few more bombs in the afternoon. One was a so-called *Blindgänger* (unexploded bomb), which fell near our Apollo cinema; one fell on a house in the Hornstrasse, where six people were killed, and one buried itself in the asphalt 20 m in front of the school. A few private houses were also destroyed, amongst them the home of one of my school classmates, Barbara. Her father was an officer in the army, but she, her brother, and mother, were at home. Barbara and her brother crawled out of the rubble with the help of some neighbours, but her mother got killed.

Nobody turned up at school in the next two days, because it was difficult to get there and then it was the summer holidays. When eventually we met Barbara at school again, she had changed. Her father had been allowed to come home for a few days to see to his children, and then Barbara with her brother moved to an aunt. She had been given her mother's jewellery, which had been in a safe in the bank, and she wore it every day, changing it to different pieces from time to time and showing it off. All the teachers were very nice to her, and so were all the grown ups, spoiling her, as they felt sorry for her. We, too, were all very kind to her at first, but gradually we got fed up with her, because of her showing off. I heard later that a few months after she left school her father got killed in Russia. She was then nineteen years old, and her brother sixteen, two young people without parents.

German soldiers were now all over Europe. We took the flags out of our map in our class where only the occupation forces were stationed, like in

Norway, France, the Balkan countries and Crete, and tried to carry on with the flags where the actual fighting was going on, like in the Mediterranean and Russia. Living in East Prussia, we were very interested in the Russian war as it was on our doorstep, and we all hoped that it would be finished before the winter. The German Army, particularly the tanks, were pushing forward at a tremendous speed.

The month of August was very hot, and we saw the tanks and infantry ploughing across the great Russian plains. Suddenly the German line on our map ran from Leningrad to the Crimea. Hitler announced that he would starve Leningrad to death and put up a blockade. Panzers were taken from the north and south, ready for a centre push to Moscow and, at the beginning of October, with autumn coming, the Germans attacked.

The rains came on October 7th, and it rained for three weeks. We saw terrible pictures on the newsreel and in the paper of guns, tanks, trucks, cars, and even soldiers sinking into the mud and having to be pulled out. This slowed down the campaign, but didn't stop it. Winter would come soon, and everybody knew that they had to reach Moscow before that. The last town before the capital of Moscow was Mozhaisk, and this fell on October 20th. We were now told that Moscow would be encircled, and that Bolshevism and the Red Army would be finished off.

By now the Germans were in possession of a great part of Russia's coal and iron reserve. They had destroyed or captured thousands of Russian tanks, guns, and aircraft, and the army was thoroughly beaten. But the Germans, too, had great losses and, because they were a long way from home, supplies became short.

Hitler decided to encircle Moscow, but this didn't succeed, because winter arrived earlier than expected, and it was the hardest in half a century. The temperature dropped overnight, and kept on dropping, and the cold wind from the North Pole had arrived. The German troops were still in summer uniforms, and there was only summer equipment everywhere. The lightweight oil in the guns and engines froze when the temperature reached 40 degrees below zero. The Russians were dressed for the cold. They fought with primitive but sensible equipment. They had horsedrawn sledges, ski troops, and mounted cavalry, which were better than the German tanks, with their engines frozen. They used vast numbers of soldiers, and their strength was the ruthless sacrifice of men. The German army was weak from the long trek across Russia. They were ill prepared and disappointed that they had not won the war before the cold winter hit them. Their Panzers came within 25 miles of Moscow on December 5th, but the next day, the Russians made a counter-offensive.

On December 7th, the Japanese bombed Pearl Harbour, and the USA was at war with Japan.

In the middle of December the troops fell back, shortened their lines, but had to leave a large amount of immovable equipment for the enemy. When Hitler discovered this, he fired the chief of the General Staff, von Brauchitsch, and took over the supreme command himself. He announced that the withdrawals had to stop, there was to be no more retreating, and the units had to fight where they were. Several other commanders were fired in the next month, and replaced by men who were prepared to listen to the *Führer*.

The firing of the generals did not stop the Russians, and did not help the retreating, ill equipped German troops. From time to time, there was heavy fighting, and our flags on the map in our classroom moved forwards and backwards.

Supplies did reach the troops, often brought in by the *Luftwaffe*. At home, everybody felt sorry for the soldiers in the frozen Russian territory and for Christmas we had to pack parcels again for the armed forces with little gifts and cheerful letters. In needlework we knitted balaclavas, mittens and scarves, which were posted as gifts. We collected illustrated papers, and posted them to the 18th army. We made thousands of envelopes for soldiers, folding and glueing them. We collected plants and dried them, like camellia and peppermint, to make tea. Grateful letters were received by a number of girls, and a *Staffelkapitän* (Group Captain) came in person to thank us whilst he was on leave in Königsberg.

Everybody was waiting for the spring and better weather. The newsreels showed the German soldiers on sentry duty, all wrapped up, so one could not even recognize their faces. They were only one hour on duty, sometimes even less, because of the extreme cold. The only interest they seemed to have was how to keep warm, how to organize wood or fuel to burn, and how to get hot food. There was not much fighting going on and by the end of February 1942 new lines had been formed. In March, the ice and snow melted, and everybody and everything was in deep mud. The weather through April and part of May stopped all fighting again, and the Germans, and probably the Russians, reinforced their supplies.

Albert Speer replaced Hermann Goering as economic dictator, and the homeland was now even more geared for war. Women without children had to work, either in ammunition factories, on the trams, post offices, or wherever necessary. More and more soldiers were needed, and Königsberg, as the capital of East Prussia, was used in the summer of 1942 as a collecting and assembling point for new armed forces. We had soldiers from the different satellite countries, Rumania, Hungary, Slovakia and Italy in the town, and there was also a volunteer Spanish division stationed in Königsberg for a time.

Everybody in Königsberg knew about the foreign soldiers and officers, because most of them didn't speak German, or had only a limited German vocabulary. On their days off they used to come to the centre of the town to have a look at the castle and the churches, to go into the parks, and to visit the cafés. We had no pubs in Königsberg, in any case, alcohol was scarce, but cafés served imitation coffee, made from roasted malted barley, and cakes with imitation cream.

My friend Ewa and I used to go into town in the afternoons, and have coffee at Schwermer's, a famous and elegant large café. Schwermer was well-known for their special marzipan and cakes, but now, with the scarcity of the ingredients, they only served cakes with imitation cream, and the marzipan was always sold out!

Schwermer was the café where the officers would come on their free afternoons. It was always full up with people, because the most important thing was not the food, but that one could meet somebody. Ewa and I were young girls, and we liked the look of the officers in their smart uniforms. We soon discovered that the soldiers from the different countries had different days off, and we called them the Hungarian afternoon, or the Italian afternoon, or the Spanish afternoon. We met a number of officers, but found it difficult to talk, as we had only been taught French and English at school.

And then, one day, we met two Spanish officers who spoke quite good German. This was really fun. They wanted to know about the town, and we made a date to show them the castle and the *Schlossteich*. We had a lovely day together, even hired a boat and rowed around the lake. Pedro and José had plenty of money and no idea what it was worth. They just kept on paying for everything. We met two or three times after that, always the four of us, although Pedro tried to persuade me to have a separate date. Somehow I didn't trust him. Once or twice he told me a different story about his background and, when he kissed me on our second meeting, I realized that he was quite an experienced man.

I talked to Ewa about it, and she, too, was worried. We were brought up very strictly, and even a kiss from a man, not a boy, was dangerous, we were told, as it could lead to something else which, of course, was completely forbidden. Ewa and I decided to stick together whenever we made a date with our Spanish friends.

Pedro and José had not volunteered as we thought but, as they were professional soldiers, they had to go where they were sent. They could have refused to come to Germany, but that would have meant no more promotion. By coming to join the German army in Russia, and doing a term of six months, they would move up from lieutenant to major in that time. Always assuming that they returned unharmed to Spain. Neither of them had been in any real fighting before. Somehow nobody ever thought of anybody being killed, only of victory, of promotion, and of the peace that would come afterwards.

Ewa and I enjoyed the company of our two friends and when, one day, they didn't turn up for a date, we realized that they must have left for Russia. I got a letter from Pedro two months later, in which he thanked me and Ewa for taking pity on two lonely soldiers. He confessed that he was a married man, but had been lonely in Königsberg. He promised to write again, and asked me to reply to his letter, apologizing for his bad German. He said José had been wounded, and he didn't know where he was. I felt his loneliness through his letter, and I also thought he was frightened. I did write, but I never had a reply. Ewa, too, never heard from anybody, and we wondered what had happened to them. There was no way for us as non relatives to find out anything, except by writing a letter. If Pedro got killed, the letter would be returned to me with the sentence, *Gefallen für Grossdeutschland* (Killed for Great Germany). So I wrote two more short letters, but I did not get a reply and the letters were never returned. It is possible that because he was Spanish only his Spanish relatives would be informed, and I had no Spanish address.

In May 1942, the Russians attacked, but were beaten, and the Germans pushed towards the Caucasus and the Russian oilfields. The 6th Army, under General Friedrich von Paulus, supported by a Panzer Army, was 40 miles from Stalingrad. The Russians fought hard, and held on to the Caucasus Mountains, and Paulus and his troops and tanks had to stop their push eastwards in the Steppes because of no supplies. The army used the petrol for the tanks and trucks faster than they could get replacement supplies. Hitler again rearranged his staff, as he was not satisfied with the progress.

By late November 1942 the German advance stopped, defeated by time and distance. General Friedrich von Paulus had already reached Stalingrad in September. The town stretches for miles along the western side of the great bend of the Volga, and was a major industrial centre. During the fighting, the Russian workmen carried on building their tanks and, when they were finished, they would drive out of the doors, with guns firing at the enemy. The battle of Stalingrad raged unceasingly. At night, the Russians would bring supplies over the river and, during the day their troops would fight behind broken walls and piles of brick and mortar. Neither the Russians nor the Germans would give up Stalingrad.

Casualties grew on both sides, and the Germans pulled in troops from their other fronts. Hitler was determined to have the city. Then, although early November, the temperatures dropped, and there was ice on the rivers Volga and Don. The Russians counter-attacked on three fronts along the river Don, encircling a number of German divisions. A Panzer division was pulled away from Stalingrad to help the German troops, which weakened General Paulus' position. The line was very thin, and consisted to a great extent of Rumanian, Italian, and Hungarian armies, and the Russians just scattered the troops. Field Marshal von Weichs urged Paulus and his 6th Army to move quickly, otherwise he would be trapped, but Paulus had to wait for Hitler's permission, which did not come.

So that was the position in the east by Christmas 1942, but there were also things happening in the homeland, where the civilian population was shown what it meant to be at war. In May 1942, thousands of British planes bombed Cologne. The fires raged for two days, and 20,000 homes were destroyed or damaged, apart from commercial properties, and 50 to 60 factories. Rail services, electricity, water and sewage were interrupted, and half a million people were homeless. Although raid after raid followed, German civilian morale was never destroyed. On the contrary, because of the ruin of their homes and the killing of their families, the Germans made even greater efforts to support the war. Children were evacuated from the bigger cities with their schools, and a number of them came to East Prussia. It was easier to bomb western Germany than eastern Germany, because of the limited range of the aircraft. Bombs rained on the cities every night. The British concentrated on Cologne, Düsseldorf, Essen, Dortmund, and the ports from which material was shipped eastwards to Russia, like Hamburg, Bremen, and Lübeck. Berlin was not forgotten either, as it was the capital. Hermann Goering, the head of the *Luftwaffe*, had boasted "No Allied planes will ever fly over the German *Reich*!", but he was wrong.

The Americans arrived in 1942, and soon joined in the bombing. The British concentrated on night attacks, hurting the civilian population and disrupting the war economy, and the Americans operated by day, concentrating their bombing at specific crucial targets, which were easier to find by daylight.

We did not have any bombing in Königsberg, but saw the destruction of the towns in the west in pictures in the paper, and on the newsreel in the cinema. Even so, the town got prepared and underground bunkers were built everywhere. The Vierbrüderplatz opposite us, where we used to play in the allotments, was now built up with houses, but the corner to the left of our house had not been touched. Here, a large underground bunker was being built to shelter 200 people.

Not everybody was allowed to go into this shelter when there was an air-raid, as there would not have been enough room. People who were entitled to go received a card, which they had to show at the entrance. It seemed rather silly to think that if the sirens went one would have to queue up to be admitted to this safe place, but everybody hoped that in an emergency one would be permitted to enter in any case. Our family did not get a card, because my parents had strengthened one cellar room and organised it with some equipment, so that it was quite a good air-raid shelter, and that was reason enough to make us stay in our own house.

In Russia, von Paulus was still stuck on the outskirts of Stalingrad, and forbidden by Hitler to retreat. Von Manstein, who was within 30 miles of Stalingrad, also urged von Paulus to attempt a break out, and link up with him. Hitler's orders were "No retreat, No surrender", and, by Christmas Eve, all hope for von Paulus' 6th Army was lost. In the brutal, snowy, windy, and cold weather, the Germans hung on. Hitler ordered Goering to supply von Paulus by air, and promised him five hundred tons a day. He made a speech, which we all heard on the radio, praising von Paulus, and the brave 6th Army. There were not enough planes and trained pilots to fulfil the promise of more supplies, even after the old planes from the training schools were brought in. Food rations for the troops were cut again and again, cartridges were handed out a few at a time, and there was no petrol. The 6th Army was gradually strangled. Hitler promoted von Paulus to Field Marshal, and he was ordered to hold on until death.

By late January, there were only 10 miles of German occupation left, and German soldiers wrote letters describing their hopelessness and suffering. One of the girls in my class had a brother fighting under von Paulus, and she brought a letter to school, where he described some of the terrible conditions. I think the most shocking part in the letter was the sentence that they had eaten their last horse. The girl was lucky that her family received this letter, because most of the letters were suppressed by the Berlin authorities, or partly blanked out with ink; bad news was not allowed to reach the homeland in those days. It was the last letter the family received; the next notification was *Gefallen für Grossdeutschland.*

On January 23rd 1943, the Russians took the last airstrip in Stalingrad and cut the German forces into two. The northern part was overrun and surrendered, and the rest stopped fighting on February 2nd. Field Marshal Friedrich von Paulus surrendered the rest of the 6th Army on January 30th, after five months of the greatest military blood bath in recorded history, with an estimated loss of 400,000 dead, and 500,000 prisoners. At the end, there were 280,000 men encircled, and only 42,000 were air-lifted out. Between 80,000 and 90,000 men were taken prisoner, including von Paulus, and most of these never returned to their homeland.

Hitler raged, and called them cowards. They should not have surrendered, they should have shot themselves. It was only later, when the truth was told about the terrible treatment of the German prisoners-of-war in Russia, that people thought that maybe Hitler was right after all about committing suicide rather than being taken prisoner. In reality, Hitler was not concerned about the individual soldier and his suffering. It was his pride that was hurt, that German troops had surrendered, and that his command to fight until death had been ignored.

Because of the Russian war, things at home changed too. I saw Zoppot, our family's holiday place by the Baltic, for the last time in 1940, when we had a very short stay there. My mother made arrangements to have it looked after, and the following year, with the Russian war in progress, my mother let the house for the summer to a family from Danzig. After that, it stood empty and, as Danzig is Polish now, I must assume that Poles live in our house, unless it was destroyed in the war.

Although we did not go away for the summer holiday in 1941, I still had a good time, going with my friend Ewa to the seaside, to Rauschen, 40 km from Königsberg. We caught the train early in the morning and in 40 minutes, we were on the beach.

Not far from Rauschen was Neukuhren, where a small airport had been extended lately to take bigger planes. Because of the expansion of the airport and the stationing of airmen, we met quite a number of them on the train. They travelled to Königsberg on their days off, and that's how I met Herbert. We just got talking in the train, and he asked me for my address. I had hardly got home that evening, when he rang up and asked for a date. Soldiers did not ask a girl 'when have you got time?' It was the other way round. 'I am off at such and such a time, may I see you then?'

In any case, you never knew how long they were stationed at the same place.

Herbert had some time off every day, and that's when we tried to meet.

I did not tell my mother about Herbert and, after the first phone call, he didn't ring again, but we made appointments from one date to the next. He did give me a phone number, but I was only allowed to ring in an emergency. We had a lovely week together, meeting every afternoon in Rauschen on the beach, and the weather was glorious.

Herbert was twenty-four years old, a N.C.O. in the *Luftwaffe*, good looking, and an absolute charmer. He was always laughing and didn't seem to have a care in the world. He loved flying, and told me when the war was finished he would stay in flying, making it his career. He put his arm around me and kissed me, then he looked into my eyes:

'I don't think I am passionately in love with you, you are much too young anyway, but I enjoy being with you, and I am very very fond of you.'

'I am seventeen years old, and quite grown up, and I sometimes wished you were more serious about things.'

His smile disappeared. 'Please don't fall in love with me, it is not worth it. I often laugh or joke, because I want to forget the war. I have already fought in France.'

After a week, the weather changed and when I got up one morning early to get ready to go to Rauschen, my mother stopped me from going, saying that it was silly to go to the beach on a dull day like this. She didn't know that I was meeting Herbert in the morning, as he had to be on duty at 12 o'clock. The real reason for not going to Rauschen was that Olga having left, my mother had no help and she wanted me to do jobs in the house. I promised my mother I would do it in the afternoon, and also said that Ewa would be waiting at the train.

'You can phone her up and arrange another time', said my mother.

I went into the cellar and started mangling the clothes. It was only 7.30 in the morning and the others were still asleep. I thought that if I finished the sheets and clothes quickly I could probably catch a later train and, even if Herbert and I didn't have much time together, at least he would know that I didn't let him down. When I had finished, I ran upstairs, but it was raining by now, and my mother thought me crazy for wanting to go to Rauschen.

I waited two days. When I didn't hear anything from Herbert, I went to see Ewa, and phoned the emergency number he had given me from Ewa's house. I asked whether I could speak to N.C.O. Herbert B. but was told that he had left. I could not write to him, because I did not have his *Feldpost Nr.* I kept on thinking about him, and hoped that he would write.

I received a letter after five weeks and, when my mother asked from whom it was, I said it was from one of the boys from the boys' school who had been called up into the army. Herbert wrote that he was at the front and did a lot of flying. I knew that the soldiers were not allowed to write where they were stationed, or where they were fighting, but the front meant Russia. It was a nice letter, thanking me for the lovely days he had had, and assuming that I didn't come the last time because it was raining. I was absolutely thrilled to have a letter and replied to it straight away, writing a really long one. The letter was returned to me after three weeks, and on it was written:

*Gefallen für Grossdeutschland*

I took the letter, ran upstairs and cried. He was only 24 years old, and so full of plans for the future. His laughing face haunted me for a long time.


Our meeting place in the *Eisdiele* got gradually depleted of boys, as some of them were already called up to the forces, before their eighteenth birthdays as officer's cadets. I was still in correspondence with Gerhard Flach, whom I had met in Insterburg at the sports competitions. He was quite a seasoned and experienced soldier by now, having fought in Yugoslavia and Greece. He had been on leave once, but didn't talk much about the fighting, only that he had seen the Acropolis in Athens, and several other temples and museums. Gerhard was my friend, nothing else, and he looked upon me as his girl pen-friend.

Another pen-friend was Ernst Heimke, one of the boys from the Grammar School. He had hardly left Königsberg when I received his first letter, but then he probably wanted me to have his *Feldpost Nr.* quickly so that I could write to him. He was a good letter writer, telling me quite a few funny incidents ánd happenings from the cadet school, and gradually I started looking forward to his letters. I took them with me to school and the *Eisdiele*, and anybody who knew him was only too pleased to listen to the funny parts of his letters.

My third boyfriend at the time was Helma, but I avoided him for a time. We had been happy children together, until the moment he wanted a kiss. After that, every time we met I made sure that it was only when somebody else was there. At the age of sixteen, in 1940, he joined the navy as a cadet and when he came on leave he looked very smart in his dark blue uniform. We were both a little shy when we met again, but now, being in the navy, I felt that I had to go for a walk with him when he asked me. We even went to the pictures and in the dark he put his hand on mine, quietly stroking it. He didn't attempt to kiss me until the last day, and then only on my cheek.

'I will never have another girl friend,' he said, 'I know you don't believe me, but you are the only one for me. You see, you will feel the same in a few years time.'

He didn't want me to write to him because, being in the navy, he would not get any post at sea and when the ship returned from an assignment the crew usually got leave. Although he insisted on being my boyfriend, I did not have to do any letter-writing, and I was glad of this, as I was busy enough with school, sport, and letter-writing to my other friends.

In September 1941, I had my first dancing lesson. There were about 25-30 young people, boys and girls, between sixteen and twenty years old. I recognized some of the girls from our school, even from our class, and also a few boys from our *Eisdiele* meeting place. We had to learn how to do the introductions. One did not dance with somebody without knowing his name. A young man was not allowed to dance with a girl to whom he had not been introduced. He had to find somebody first to introduce him to the girl. If he saw a girl he knew accompanied by her parents and wanted to dance with her, he had to ask the girl to introduce him to her parents and then, in turn, ask the parents for permission to dance with their daughter. A lady, too, was not allowed to address a man she didn't know. She had to find somebody who knew him and ask that person to introduce her to his friend.

Everything was very formal, but elegant, and once we knew how to behave, it was not difficult. The stiffness gradually disappeared too, and we became more confident and self assured. No casual dress was allowed either. The men wore suits and ties, and the ladies afternoon dresses, with a fuller skirt for dancing, and dancing shoes. We learnt the first two steps of the waltz in our first lesson, and then it was time to go home.

After my first dancing lesson, I received a little note from a Mr Wolfgang Hilmers, who invited me to the Operetta "Die Fledermaus" on the following Sunday, saying that, if I accepted, he would come and collect me. I was very surprised, and completely at a loss as to who he was. He did say that he had met me at the dancing class, but I could not remember him.

'This is marvellous,' said my mother, 'Now you will have a decent boy friend, somebody with a good background. It is most difficult to get tickets for the Opera House or the theatre. His family must have connections. You had better reply straight away that you accept, and then we will have to think about what you are going to wear. At last you are being treated like a lady, and not as a girl or a sports companion. It is time that you became more refined, and it looks as if this young man has appeared just at the right time.'

My mother had never talked to me like that. I never realized that she was concerned about me and my unladylike behaviour. I replied straight away, as I was only too keen to go to the "Fledermaus" in the Opera House. I had been to the theatre before to see several plays, some of them even with our school class, like "Goethe's Faust", and "Schiller's Räuber". We read these plays at school, and arrangements were made by our German teacher to go to the final rehearsal of the performances, which were free. But I had never been to the Opera House in the town, only to the *Waldoper* (Opera in the forest) in Zoppot.

My mother produced a beautiful dress for me, and I looked very grown up. She lent me her little evening bag and her opera glasses. I had a very nice winter coat, with a lovely collar, slightly too warm for the beginning of October, but my mother said I could leave it open, and give it up into the *Garderobe* (Cloakroom) in the Opera House.

'You don't have to worry about anything,' she said, 'you have got a gentleman to look after you.'

Mr Hilmers arrived, and rang the bell. I was told to open the door and to introduce him to my parents. I opened the door and in front of me stood a tall, very fair, blue eyed, elegant young man with a bunch of flowers in his hand.

'Good evening,' he said, and smiled, looking at me.

'Good evening. Please come in.'

He stepped inside, and then stood still, looking at me, not saying anything, but gradually getting red in his face.

Oh dear, I thought, he is shy.

I did remember him from the dancing class. I had dismissed him then as being much too shy, as I had had to do all the talking because he never said anything much. I would have never thought that he would have had the courage to ask me to come with him to the Opera House. Well, here he was and, if I didn't say or do something, we would probably stay here for ever, and my poor parents would never meet him. I looked at the flowers and, thinking they were for me, I said:

'What lovely flowers, how kind of you', and I stretched my hand out to take them.

'Oh no!' he said, 'they are for your mother.' And then he added quite firmly, 'I will bring you some next time.'

So there was to be a next time, I thought. He is not as shy as he looks.

I took Mr Hilmers to my parents, and introduced him.

'*Gnädige Frau, eine kleine Aufmerksamkeit*', (Madam, a small token) he said to my mother, and gave her the bunch of flowers, with his shy smile.

My mother was radiant; he had conquered her, she would never say a bad word about him, and he was assured of her affection until eternity! I could see all that in these few seconds. Even my father was impressed with this so well-behaved, clean and elegant young man. He thanked them for permitting me to go out with him, and promised to bring me back after the performance. After a little small talk, I got my coat, and we left to catch the tram.

At the Opera House, I soon realized that Mr Hilmers had been there before. He took my coat to the *Garderobe*, found our seats, paid for a programme, and was very attentive. The performance was excellent, at least we thought so. In the interval, he bought me an apple juice, and one for himself, and at the end he got my coat, and took me home by tram. We said goodbye outside our house, and he hoped to see me on Tuesday at our next dancing lesson.

Mr Hilmers went to the boy's *Hufenschule*, and lived not far from our school in a flat. His parents had a large farm but, because he and his sister had to go to school, they lived during term time in a flat in the town. His father was an officer in the army. He had been transferred to the Ministry of Agriculture in Königsberg, to be in charge of the food production of certain districts in East Prussia. He was responsible for supplying the army with requested amounts of food. For this he had to visit the different farms and was often away from home.

Life for me was sometimes hectic. Apart from my dancing classes and the new involvement with another boyfriend, I still had my sport, swimming, school, homework, going to the pictures, and the letter-writing to my other two friends, Gerhard and Ernst, to attend to. Then I heard from Gerhard that he was in a military hospital. He didn't say why he was there but, as he had been in some fighting before, I visualised him as being wounded. It could not be his right arm, as otherwise he wouldn't have been able to write. I felt very sorry for him, especially as his letter sounded rather forced, as if he didn't know what to say. I also thought he might be quite badly wounded, and didn't want to tell me or upset me. I wrote a cheerful long letter, and packed him a little parcel, with some homemade biscuits that my mother let me have. Actually, I had thought lately that I had too many boyfriends, and I had toyed with the idea of writing a farewell letter to Gerhard, but now, with him in hospital, my mother said I could not do this to him.

My mother had changed lately, or was it I that had changed? She suddenly became my friend, and treated me as a grown-up, discussing things with me, making suggestions, and not telling me off all the time and saying, do this, do that, help me with this. Because of this, I didn't mind telling her what I thought, and what I felt about the different young men in my life. We talked about Gerhard and Ernst and my new friend, Mr Hilmers. We both had a little laugh when we talked about his shyness.

'After Sunday, when he comes to us for coffee,' said my mother, 'you ought to try and change the formal address of Mr and Miss, to your Christian names. Usually a young man kisses the girl and, after that, the formality is dropped.'

I laughed out loud, imagining poor Mr Hilmers trying to kiss me.

'I don't think he has the courage to do that,' I said.

'Well, then you will have to do it first. Some boys do need encouragement. He is a very nice young man, and your father and I have complete trust in him.'

I wasn't quite sure what my mother meant with the last sentence, but I certainly started to think about how to get my Mr Hilmers to drop the formality and call me Helga. I also thought Wolfgang was a nice name and I practised saying it.

On Sunday, Mr Hilmers came, and the whole family met him at the coffee table. Everybody behaved well, even Hans, who sometimes dropped cake crumbs, looked extremely clean, with his hair combed flat with water. Usually he looked very untidy, with his hair sticking up at the back. He was not a great talker, but sometimes he would come out with some remarks which could be very embarrassing, even if it was the truth. He suddenly said to Mr Hilmers:

'You are the first boyfriend who has been invited for coffee. Sternchen never had anybody, and she is older.'

There was silence, whilst everybody looked at him, and then at Sternchen.

'Would you like another piece of cake, Hans?' said my mother sweetly, trying to draw attention away from Sternchen. Hans looked at my mother, surprised. We didn't usually get a second piece of cake because, with the shortage of food, my mother could not bake very often and we were always told before visitors came, that we were not allowed to ask for a second piece. My mother had made a mistake by asking my brother, because he replied:

'Yes, please', and she cut him a thin slice, although we all knew that she had hoped that he would refuse.

One Sunday, I was invited to have dinner with Wolfgang's family, so that at last I could meet them all. We were on christian name terms by that time. He had waited with the invitation until his father was able to be at home. I met his sister, who was three years younger, also fair, and not shy at all. His mother was a beautiful woman, very elegant, and I could see that Wolfgang resembled her. His father was much older than my father, and looked more like Wolfgang's grandfather. When one is young, forty seems old and fifty, well, that is really old.

I have no idea how old Wolfgang's parents were, but the two together looked like father and daughter, not like husband and wife.

Their flat was extremely elegant, with lovely old furniture, and beautifully polished floors. I felt a bit overawed, and taken by surprise. I had not expected Wolfgang to come from such an expensive home. He always said his parents had two big farms, and I thought of them as farmers. His mother looked as if she had never done any work in her life, with her beautiful fair and wavy hair, and her immaculate hands, with polished fingernails. His father was in a major's uniform, with his trousers and jacket pressed to perfection. They even had a German maid, an elderly woman, who had a white apron on, and served the meal. First she brought in the soup, after that the main meal, but Mrs Hilmers never helped her with anything. She only talked about the big house they had, and the riding stables, and all the things that were going on there, like the parties they had had before the war, and the sleigh rides in the winter. They said that I must come and see them in the country. They had plenty of space, and I would be company for Wolfgang. I looked at Wolfgang, who smiled at me, and I looked at his mother, and I thought:

She is not really a mother, she is like a doll, and her husband treats her like that. No wonder Wolfgang is shy, she overshadows him, and that's why he is so lonely.

I realized why he liked me, I was honest, I was down to earth, and my home was a home, not a showpiece.

My school report at Christmas was really bad. The reason was not the shortage of teachers at school and the cancelled lessons; I had too many interests, and never enough time for my homework. I used to get quite good marks in physics and chemistry, because I liked the experiments and enjoyed learning from them. Unfortunately, the practical work had to be omitted at school and, doing only theory, I soon fell behind, particularly with the chemical formulae. I was never any good at French and English and so, having dropped with the marks in chemistry and physics, I suddenly had four "no pass" marks. I got by with mathematics, because Wolfgang had helped me, and also with Latin.

By now I was too old to get a good hiding, so half my Christmas presents were taken away, and I had to sit down every day for two hours in the holiday, and do some revising. So the holidays were not exactly happy for me. The only interesting and good things were Wolfgang's letters. He and his family had left Königsberg to spend the holidays on their farm. Before leaving, Wolfgang and I exchanged Christmas presents, but promised one another we would not open them until Christmas Eve, at the traditional present opening time.

Wolfgang had hardly left when his first letter arrived. The writing covered eight pages, and he was sorry that I wasn't with him. He missed me, and hoped that I would come and stay with his family for a few days. After that, I received a letter every day. All his shyness disappeared in writing, and he poured everything out which he could not say to my face.

I still remember what he gave me for Christmas. He was most generous, and I think his mother helped him. I had a postcard size photograph of him, a powder compact with my initials HZ and the words Christmas 1941 engraved on it, and a small silver necklace, with a heart-shaped pendant encircling a four-leaf clover. I gave him a leather diary, and wrote on the last page:

*Ich schreibe mich auf's letzte Blatt,*
*Das seinen guten Grund wohl hat,*
*Denn wer Dich lieber hat als ich,*
*Der schreibe sich noch hinter mich.*

I write on the last page,
Which has a good reason,
Because who loves you more than I,
Can write after me.

His letters kept on coming and in each one he asked me to come and stay with him. After talking to my mother, we decided that I could go for a weekend. As soon as I had written, he phoned me up, and we arranged the visit for the following weekend. I was catching the train early Saturday morning, returning Sunday evening. I felt that was long enough. Actually, I quite enjoyed the two days I was there, particularly as we only met the grown-ups for mealtimes.

We had quite a bit of snow at Christmas so, when I took the train in January, I had to dress up warm, with boots and thick coat. Wolfgang was waiting at the small station, with a horsedrawn sleigh.

'I thought we could go for a ride straight away,' he said. 'The woods are beautiful, and some roads, still undisturbed from vehicles, have lots of snow.'

He was different, confident, taking over and telling me what to do. He knew his horse, and guided it well. We soon got into the woods, and everything was quiet and still, except for the dull sound of the horse's hooves, and the little jingling bells on the reins which Wolfgang held in his strong hands. We had a fur cover over our legs, hooked into the sides of the sleigh, and Wolfgang had wrapped a blanket over my shoulders. He had even given me a small muff to put my hands into as, apparently, his mother had produced it, and said that this would keep my hands warm. It was cold, but the air was clear and fresh, and the woods looked like fairyland, with the branches laden with snow, and the sun trying to filter through. Some of the paths into which he guided his horse still had undisturbed snow laying on them. He knew the woods, because we finished up at a clearing where he hoped that I could see some deer. He explained that if it was cold and snowy like this they usually fed the wild animals here, and he had often seen deer. We stopped and kept quiet, but no deer appeared, all I saw was their footmarks, and some leftover hay.

We reached the stables before dinner, where Wolfgang rubbed down the horse, and left it with some food. I helped him to put away the fur rug, blankets and cushions, so that they kept dry.

The house was old and beautiful, with large rooms, and one or two open fireplaces with wood burning in them, which gave out not only heat and comfort, but also a delicious wood burning smell. In the large entrance hall stood a beautiful tall Christmas tree, which should have been taken down before, but was left longer this time because Wolfgang wanted me to see it. My bedroom was quite large, but it was warm, as there was central heating all over the house. From the window, I could look over the garden, covered in snow, and then came fields and woods, all undisturbed and quiet and peaceful. Nobody would have thought that somewhere outside there was a war on, where people got killed, were starving and freezing, and crying in pain.

Wolfgang's parents and friends organised a sleigh ride after dinner, and we offered to strip the Christmas tree, after a walk around the stables and a general view of the so-called farm estate.

Everything took longer than planned, and we had not nearly finished with the Christmas tree when it was time for supper, so we finished it off in the evening, whilst the grown-ups played cards and talked. The next morning, we decided to build a snowman in the garden in front of the house. Although Wolfgang, his sister and I started off alone, rolling the snow into big balls, we soon had company, as nearly everybody decided to come and help. We finished up with quite a number of large snowmen, with red carrot noses, black coal eyes, sticks for a mouth and pipe, and hats and scarves for two of them. After that, somebody threw a snowball, then another one, and suddenly it developed into a snowball battle, without enemies. There was laughing, joking, calling out to one another, and snowballs flying everywhere, even some of the snowmen got hit.

In the end, we were all covered in snow and our gloves were wet. Before getting indoors, we had to brush ourselves down, and even take our boots off, as they were caked with ice and snow. Newspaper was put on to the floor in the hall for all the wet shoes and boots, and extra paper was pushed inside them to dry them out. There soon arrived hot Grog, a mixture of red wine with water, sugar, cloves and herbs, and we all felt happy and warm, with glowing faces and hands. Everybody ate well at lunchtime and, in the early afternoon, I had to get ready to be taken to the station for the journey home.

Wolfgang was sorry that I had to leave, and tried to persuade me to stay on as school hadn't started yet, but I knew that I wouldn't get permission from my parents, because I still had to do a lot of revising.

The big sleigh with the two horses took me and some of the other guests to the station. Wolfgang had volunteered to be the chauffeur, because he wanted to see me off. Again, I had to admire him for the way he handled the horses, this time two of them, and a big sleigh. This was his pleasure and his skill, not talking to people.

It had been a most enjoyable weekend, and I think I had fallen in love with Wolfgang, just a tiny little bit. We were both still so young.

# CHAPTER SEVEN

## Kriegseinsatz - SS visit - Wolfgang, Ulrich, Ernst.

In May 1942, we all had to finish school and go to the country for three months into the *Kriegseinsatz* (military employment), and I went again to the Zimmermanns. They welcomed me with open arms, and the one who was most excited was little Franzl, now six years old. I shared a room with Ulla, and little Franzl again followed me around the house and garden. There was a lot of soft fruit to be picked, like raspberries, strawberries, red and white currants, and Franzl helped. The fruit had to be bottled, or was used for dinner. I did my usual jobs, helping in the house, and also milking the cows. I enjoyed the hay-making, and my arms got sunburnt. I did not have to help with the reaping of the corn, as Mrs Zimmermann remembered my poor sore arms from the last time.

My birthday was in July and, as Franzl had never been to Königsberg, a big city, I asked Mrs Zimmermann whether I could have a few days off and go home, taking Franzl with me. She was delighted, and her husband took us to the station with the horse and cart. Franzl was very well behaved on the journey and at our house. Sometimes he was a little frightened, holding my hand all the time, particularly on the station in Königsberg, where there were a lot of people. The summer was beautiful that year and, because of the good weather, I could take Franzl to the Zoo, and to the big children's playgrounds in the park.

We were only at home for 3 days, and they passed quickly. I took my bicycle with me on the train this time, putting it into the luggage van. Whilst Franzl and I were sitting in the train, waiting for it to go, an air force sergeant entered our compartment. He put his bag on the rack, and sat opposite us. The train left, and Franzl jumped about at the window with excitement, shouting:

'It is moving, it is moving, sh-sh-sh- and now the whistle!'

And the whistle went as if by command, and I laughed, and so did the sergeant.

'That is not your little boy?' he said.

' Oh no! He belongs to a family where I am staying. I am in *Kriegseinsatz* from our school there. I have just been home for three days and taken with me; he had never been on a train before or to a big town.'

After that, we talked about what I was doing, and he seemed to enjoy listening to me, with Franzl adding a few sentences from time to time.

'But what about you, are you on leave? I must not talk about myself all the time.'

He looked at me, and then his hands started to tremble, and one side of his face twitched once or twice.

'I'd rather not talk about myself. I have not been very well lately. I have a pass to go home for a week, and then return to Königsberg to the military hospital after that.'

I felt sorry for him; he was obviously very shaken up, and I thought I'd better talk about harmless things, to make him forget the war. He appreciated what I was doing. He made a date with me for the following Sunday. We would meet in Rössel, where I could easily get to with my bike.

Theo and I enjoyed our day together. We explored the little town of Rössel, and had our lunch in a park by a small lake. I had told Mrs Zimmermann that I was meeting Theo, and how broken his nerves were. She knew the town, told me where to go, and packed us a picnic lunch. Theo had a little present for me when we met, a box with crystallized fruit and marzipan. I don't know where he got it from, because these things were impossible to get. He had to catch a train to get home, so I saw him off at the station, and then I returned to the farm on my bike. A few days later, I had a charming letter from Theo, thanking me for making the day so peaceful and successful. He told me he would write again when he got his new *Feldpost Nr.*, as he didn't know when he would return to the front. He wrote again from the hospital and, in his third letter, I got his *Feldpost Nr.* so, at last, I could write to him also. By then I was home in Königsberg, having finished my *Kriegsdienst* on the farm in August.

I never told Wolfgang about Theo. He still wrote to me, more often than I did, and then, in June, he was called up into the army. He was eighteen years old now, and knew that this would happen. As soon as the boys were eighteen, they were called up. They automatically got their matriculation without any examinations. Wolfgang joined as an officer cadet, and I was not even able to say goodbye to him, because I was not in

Königsberg. We were both sorry about this, but hoped to meet on his first leave. I had no idea where he was, because he was not allowed to write about places, at least not name them, but he described his training.

In September, I went back to school, having passed the end of term examinations, which did not exist! Everybody who went into the *Kriegsdienst* automatically went into the next class, as nobody could be at school for the examinations. So I was really lucky, because my school marks were still bad in a number of subjects. This time, I was determined to work hard, because we only had two terms before our matriculation, and the end of school at last!

At first, as I have said, we didn't really suffer much because of Germany being at war. We managed with food and clothes, and we children accepted the restrictions at school. Christel, being two years younger, had not been asked to do any *Kriegsdienst* yet, and Astra had finished school, and was then doing her practical year at Professor Peters from the children's hospital, who had five children. Our neighbours had accepted us, and also that my father was allowed to have a car. There were very few private cars on the road; most were confiscated, or hidden in a garage. Anybody driving had to have permission, and the petrol allowance was very small. Every time my father went to get his petrol coupons there were arguments and the rations were often reduced. If my father didn't have enough petrol, he couldn't come home so much. Even by train, he needed permission and, as trains were often requisitioned for the army, he could be stuck somewhere for hours, and it might take two days to come home. Often he could not inform us, because all telephone lines were taken over by the armed forces.

In 1942, Hitler's headquarters was transferred to East Prussia. The fortified compound called *Die Wolfsschanze* (Wolf's lair) was situated in the pine forests of Görlitz, a few miles from the town of Rastenburg. They often took over all telephone lines right across East Prussia and into Poland, and this could last for days.

The authorities, of course, knew that a foreign family lived at Metgetherstrasse No.1, but we were never bothered by them. Gradually even that changed. I don't know whether somebody, out of jealousy, had talked about us, or whether the authorities felt they ought to watch us, but one day the SS turned up, and asked questions. The first time, two SS men arrived, an officer and a sergeant, without an appointment, wanting to see my father. My mother asked them to come inside, and explained that my father only came home for the weekend, because of his business in Tilsit, and then only if he had enough petrol. The two men were quite polite. The officer asked the questions, and the sergeant wrote everything down in shorthand. He asked my mother whether we had any black market food, or guns and ammunition. My mother looked surprised why should she have guns and ammunition? The officer asked to see all the rooms in the house. Christel and I were upstairs doing our homework when my mother came into the room.

'The two gentlemen have come to see whether we have any black market food, or guns or ammunition,' said my mother, looking rather pale. 'I thought I'd start off showing them the rooms, from the top of the house to the bottom.' She looked at me whilst saying this. Was she trying to give me a message?

'Maybe you could tell Astra, in the study, that we have visitors,' she carried on.

This was really funny. The study belonged to my father, and Astra wasn't even at home! My mother kept on looking at me, and then guided the two men into the attic, where the washing was hanging because of the bad weather outside. Suddenly I thought, "black market food"; that was the brandy and the cigars in my father's study. I whispered to Christel to come and help me, and we sneaked downstairs into the study. We got two shopping bags, and filled them up with the bottles and all the cigars, leaving half a bottle of brandy, and one or two started bottles of some other spirit, and made our way into the cellar. I hid all the bottles under the stairs amongst the potatoes. We could hear the men and my mother coming down the stairs, and knew we couldn't pass them unnoticed.

'Let's get some Sauerkraut, and pretend we went into the cellar for this,' I said.

We had no dish, but we had some plates in the air-raid shelter, so we got two of them and filled them up with Sauerkraut. We met my mother and the two SS men in front of the kitchen in the hall.

'We've got the Sauerkraut for supper,' I said, 'Do you want us to get some potatoes, too?'

'You are good girls,' said my mother, smiling and realizing all was well. 'I don't know how long the two gentlemen will be, we might have to have supper a little later. Go and finish your homework first.'

With that, we went upstairs, and my mother carried on opening the doors to the different rooms. Eventually the two men left, and we ran downstairs to find out what had happened.

'Nothing has happened,' said my mother, 'not yet, anyway. Thank God you took the hint, Helga, and got the bottles away. From now on we will have to be prepared. They were quite polite, or at least not nasty, but they looked also into cupboards and wardrobes. I got quite frightened, and didn't like this at all.'

When my father came at the weekend, he didn't seem surprised about the visit, and told my mother to be very careful in what she said and how she replied to questions, so that she wouldn't upset anybody. He warned her that they would come again, different people, but always from the SS.

'Mention that we come from a neutral country, and that you have heard that a number of German officers are going to Switzerland to recuperate from their wounds,' said my father. 'It might remind them that we are not enemies.' And then he added: 'And not really friends either, but you must not say that.'

We now made sure that things were hidden, and my mother and I knew the places. We kept Christel out of it, as she couldn't lie, and we thought Hans, being four years younger, might talk about it to his best friend as a "secret", so he was not told about it either. The difficulty was how to hide the bottled food, because my father used to bring chickens, geese, and meat home, which my mother bottled and, as it was in glass jars, one could see through them. We stuck big labels all around the jars, so that the meat was not to be seen, and called them plums 2, or cherries 2, or blueberries 2, the number meaning it was meat, and plums was pork, cherries were chickens, and blueberries was beef. We also mixed the jars up with the fruit, and had big labels around the fruit jars also. The cupboard was pushed to the furthest end of the cellar, where the light was poor, and we pushed the smelly Sauerkraut barrel next to it. My mother also said that if I was at home and the SS came, I should get some Sauerkraut out when they went into the cellar, to make it smell really bad. This might make them leave the cellar quicker!

We had several visits after that; every time different people came, but they were always from the SS. Some were silent, but polite, others asked a lot of questions, and some were rude. My mother was frightened each time, and I was not always at home to help her. Somehow, she said she didn't feel so frightened if I was there, although I couldn't do anything. The SS always seemed to think we had guns, and they often looked through my father's papers, in and on his desk. They even opened post, which my mother had put on the desk for my father to attend to at the weekend. Usually my mother was silent and straight-faced, just opening cupboards and doors when asked to do so. I never heard my mother mentioning our Swiss neutrality, and I think she was afraid to talk in case her voice trembled and they realized that she was frightened, and then they would think she was hiding something.

I was at home when we had some extremely rude SS men coming to search the house. We could look through the window and see who was at the door and when the bell rang on that day I looked out and told my mother that three SS men were outside. She told me to open the door, whilst she was washing her hands, as she was preparing food in the kitchen.

'We would like to see your parents,' said the officer, when I opened the door.

My mother came along, still drying her hands on a towel, as she didn't want me to be alone with them for long. She was told, in a very abrupt manner, that they had come to search the house. I think the officer expected some opposition, because he looked a little surprised at my mother when she calmly said:

'Where would you like to start?'

'We might as well start here,' he said, and walked along the landing to my father's study and opened the door. My mother followed him, taking my hand. She wanted me to stay with her.

'There is no need for the two of you to come with us,' said the officer. 'You can get on with what you were doing. We will find our way around.'

My mother looked at him calmly and said: 'This is my house.'

The officer shrugged his shoulders, walked over to my father's desk which, this time, had no papers on the top, and pulled out a drawer. He took the drawer in both hands and turned it upside down, so that the contents spilled out on to the desk. He did this with the second and third drawer, and letters, files, and writing paper were mixed up.

'Look through these,' he said to one of the other men, 'and also through the rest of the drawers.'

With that, he walked over to the bookcase and took a pile of books out and laid them on to the table.

'Go over the bookcase also,' he said to the SS man, who had started to look through my father's papers.

'You can follow us when you have finished.' And, with that, he lifted the pictures off the wall, and knocked on the wall with his finger, hoping to find it hollow. He made a thorough search of the room, even had the carpet lifted up by one of his subordinates. He whistled when he saw my father's French brandy, even took the cork out and smelled it, but he did not help himself to a drink, although I think he would have liked to. My mother didn't offer him one. This could easily have been misconstrued and, in any case, my mother was furious because of what he had done with my father's desk. There was only half a bottle of brandy there. He never enquired where my father was, and I am sure the SS had my father watched and knew all about his movements.

All the rooms were searched more thoroughly than ever before. The carpets and pictures were lifted, and just left like that. I could see my mother getting more and more agitated. Her lovely home was ransacked. Nothing was taken, but drawers and cupboards were emptied, and the things scattered on the floor. The worst was my mother's linen cupboard. The officer opened the doors, and there were all the white sheets, duvet covers, pillowcases, and towels, folded neatly and in piles. He asked his subordinate to take them out. The man got hold of a pile and put them on to a chest of drawers. When he had the second pile in his arms, he looked around for a place to put them and hesitated, because there were some chairs in the room, and a bed, and he wasn't quite sure whether to put the pile on to the chairs, or the bed.

'Get on! Get on!' shouted the officer, giving him a little push, and then he went over to the cupboard and just pushed out the rest of the linen on to the floor. After that, he kicked it with his black boots, scattering everything, and said:

'Make sure no papers or guns are hidden in there.'

I kept on holding my mother's hand, as I didn't know what she was going to do. She had tears in her eyes, and was trembling, trying to control her emotions, but I also knew she wouldn't cry in front of these rude and cruel people.

In the cellar, I did my trick with the Sauerkraut and the officer soon left, telling one of his people to have a good look around. The two subordinates were a little embarrassed and when they were left to carry on with the search I noticed that they tried to tidy up a bit and did not empty any more drawers or cupboards out. My mother told me to get pen and paper. When I returned the search had finished; the men were just going to leave, when my mother said:

'I wonder whether you could write on this paper that you haven't found any forbidden goods or papers in my house.'

'We have not found anything,' said the officer, 'but that doesn't mean to say you haven't got anything hidden!'

'I am only asking you to write down that you haven't found anything,' repeated my mother. 'I will write it for you, if you will sign it,' and, with that, she wrote something on to the paper, dated it, and handed it to the officer with the pen.

'We will post you a note on an official form,' he said.

'I prefer your signature on this paper now. You are a very busy man, and it might take quite a time before I get it. I have dated it for today.'

He could see that my mother was determined so, suddenly, he signed the paper with his name.

'Please add your rank, and where you are stationed, as I am sure you are very proud of it,' said my mother.

He wrote this with a flourish underneath his name. My mother had hit the right note. My mother took the paper, folded it, and put it into her pocket. The officer suddenly looked at her:

'Why did you want that statement?'

'I want to send it to my friend, the Swiss Consul, to let him know that from now on the neutral Swiss must expect very thorough searching of their premises. He would never believe me if I didn't include a proof. I always thought the Swiss had a good understanding with the German people, particularly as they permit German officers and army personnel to come and recuperate in our peaceful country.'

This was quite a speech for my mother, and she must have thought about it whilst they were searching the house. Actually, the Swiss Consul was not really a friend of ours. My father had met him a few times when he called in at the embassy in Elbing. My mother probably thought it wise to stress that we were on very friendly terms with him.

'I am only doing my duty. I am not interested in your Consul,' said the officer. 'I have got two of my men as witnesses,' and he pointed to the two other SS men, who looked a bit embarrassed. I think the point had gone home. It wasn't so much that the house was searched, but the way it was done. My mother had pointed this out in an indirect way, and even the officer realized it. I am sure he would have liked to have the note back, but this was in my mother's pocket and if he had asked for it he would lose face in front of his subordinates.

'Lets go,' he said.

He clicked his heels, lifted up his arm, and said:

*'Heil Hitler,'* the usual greeting, turned round, and left the house, followed by the other two men, who also greeted us with *'Heil Hitler'*.

My mother never said a word. She closed and locked the door, went into my father's study, uncorked the brandy, and poured out one big and one small glass of the golden brown liquid and, sitting down, handed me the small glass.

'The small one is for you, you deserve it. It's a good job that you were there, it prevented me from losing my temper, and from crying.'

With that, the tears ran down her face, and she quickly gulped down a big sip of brandy, then another one, and another one, until the glass was empty. I sipped a little bit, it burnt in my throat and stomach. I'd never had brandy before, only beer and wine, but I, too, drank it up, copying my mother. She gradually cried more and more, until her body was shaking, and I felt terrible. I took her into my arms, or maybe she took me into hers, it didn't matter, we just had to hold one another. She cried and cried, and said:

'This horrible war, now it has reached us too, and I am always alone, having to cope with the house, the garden, the food, you four children and your education. Your father doesn't want any family responsibilities. He loves his freedom, and often still lives his bachelor life.'

She stopped as if she had said too much, but I knew what she meant. At eighteen years of age, I was not a child any more. I could see what was going on. I often wondered why my father didn't have a manager for the dairy in Tilsit, but then he would have to be at home all the time, and what would he do then? He liked being away and, every time he came home, it was as if he came on holiday and, when he got tired of domesticity, he left again.

When Christel came downstairs, she found us in the study. She had been doing her homework when the SS men came, and my mother had told her to stay in our room. Hans was not at home, but occupied with afternoon school sport. He had missed all the excitement, which was as well. Christel was shocked to see what a state the house was in.

I asked my mother whether she was really going to write to the Consul, but she said she would have a talk with Papa (father). At least she had the officer's name and rank, and where he came from. That was the main reason for the note, she said.

My father was furious when he heard what had happened.

'They have no right to behave in such a manner,' he said. 'We have done nothing to offend them, on the contrary, even now I am producing more butter and cheese. The demand has grown, because of the extra supplies for the armed forces. In any case, we belong to a neutral country.'

My father was quite proud of the way my mother had tackled the situation, but said there was no point in writing to the Swiss embassy, as the letter would never get there. The SS would intercept it. Petrol was very short, otherwise my father might have made the journey to Elbing, but this was situated in the opposite direction to Tilsit. Even so, my father did write a letter to the ambassador and took it with him, saying that he might be able to pass it on to somebody, so that it got delivered by hand. I don't know whether the letter ever got there, but we never had such a nasty search of our premises again. I am not even quite sure whether we had any searches at all after that.

I was looking forward to the end of my schooling; I felt I was grown-up now, and did not want to be treated as a school child any more. I imagined that once school was finished and I was at university life would be so much different. I didn't know in which way it would be different, but I knew it would be better. There were still many distractions preventing me from working too hard at my school work. Apart from my sport, and going to the pictures, I had too many boyfriends. I had hoped to finish with one, Gerhard, but then he wrote and said he was in hospital, so I wrote a nice letter back to cheer him up. In the end, I discovered that he had had tonsillitis, and I felt a bit let down, as I had imagined him severely wounded.

It was my mother who always insisted that I wrote to all my boy friends. As soon as I had a *Feldpost* letter, she would remind me to write an answer. She felt like a mother to all the young soldiers, being so far away from home, and often in danger of being wounded or killed.

'Letter writing and letter receiving is a lifeline for these boys,' she said. 'They wait for an answer, and worry when they don't get one. They want to know how things are at home.'

So I carried on, and wrote to Gerhard, to Wolfgang, to Theo, to Hans-Ulrich, to Ernst, and even to Heinz, who was Astra's partner at our last party in our home.

Wolfgang, who had been called up in June, wrote in November to say that he was in a military hospital in Königsberg, having had an operation for a *Leistenbruch* (rupture), and could I come and see him. By the time I visited him, he was already very well, and left the hospital a few days later. He was allowed to go home for two weeks, and we therefore had the chance to see one another quite often. He looked smart in his uniform and, as a soldier, he had certain privileges, like getting tickets for the cinema without queuing. We certainly made use of this.

Wolfgang had lost a little of his shyness and, in the dark in the cinema, he kept on holding my hand. He told me about his training at the cadet school, which was pretty rough at times. He was apprehensive about the future. He didn't like killing or wars, but felt that he had to fight for the future of his fatherland. Wolfgang was a peaceful young man, kind, soft and caring, not like some of the young men who couldn't wait to get into action.

'I don't like to be sent to the front,' he said. 'I like to stay at home and work on our farm, and for you to be with me for ever.'

'Is that a proposal?'

'More or less. You will wait for me, won't you? You are my girlfriend aren't you? There is nobody else?'

'I am not saying I will wait for you, Wolfgang. I am not waiting for anybody else either. I write to one or two boys, you know that, like Ernst from your school, who wanted a pen-friend, and Gerhard, whom I met in Insterburg, but I am not being tied down by anybody. I want to finish school in March and go to university. That is my next goal. We are both only eighteen years old, we are still very young, and one shouldn't make promises so early in life. They only get broken later on.'

'I never break a promise. I will write to you as often as I can, and you must promise to reply to my letters. Please, you will write, won't you?'

'Oh yes, I will write, but I don't know how often. I must get on with my school-work, you know that.'

Wolfgang was satisfied for the moment with the promise of letter writing, but not very happy to return to the army. He had joined the artillery regiment, because his father had fought in it in the First World War. He didn't like the tank division, nor the *Luftwaffe*, and didn't want to be in the infantry, but he liked horses, and some of the guns were still towed by horses. In this way, he hoped to be near his beloved animals. Unfortunately, he didn't see much of horses in his training, so he said, but had to know all about guns and *Ersatz* (substitute) equipment for them. Being an officer cadet, he also had training in how to handle and guide soldiers, make plans and decisions for attacks, retreats and self-defence. There was a lot of marching and practising on the assault course, which Wolfgang didn't like. This was very tough, as it was the preparation for the fighting, which everybody, later on, had to do. Wolfgang agreed that it was necessary, but he also felt that if the training was so tough, how much worse would the real fighting at the front be.

Wolfgang went back to his training after two weeks recuperation and, as promised, wrote a tremendous amount of letters to me. I think he spent all his spare time writing. I did not have the time to reply to all his letters, so I usually replied to two or three in one go. I posted a little parcel to him for Christmas, including some home-made biscuits, a little book, and a photograph of myself. He said that he liked the photograph best.

His next leave was in February 1943, just before my matriculation. He only had four days and knew that he would go to the Russian front after that. It was very cold, and the only place we could meet was a café in town, or the cinema. Wolfgang wanted to be alone with me, so he came to visit us. My mother said we could be in my father's study. We sat together and talked, and kissed and hugged one another. There were the silent questions:

Would we see one another again? Would Wolfgang get wounded? Would he get killed?

'Let's get married,' said Wolfgang suddenly. 'We are old enough to do what we want. We don't need permission from our parents. I want to know when I am out there in Russia that you are here when I come back. I want to make sure you don't go off with anybody else. I love you. I can look after you for the rest of your life. My parents' farm will come to me after their death. In the meantime I have my own money. My grandfather left me quite a nice sum, which I will get as soon as I am married. Please say yes, we have so little time, only four days. Let's make the best of these days, and be happy.'

I stared at him. What had happened to that shy young man who used to flush red just looking at me? And then I thought he was joking.

'I meant it,' said Wolfgang. 'I have told my parents how I feel about you. They like you, especially my grandmother.'

'The answer is "No". I want to go to university, and I do not want to be tied to anybody. Maybe one day I will feel different. Let's get this war over first, before we make any plans for the future.'

I felt that we were much too young to make serious promises to one another. Was Wolfgang selfish in his trying to bind me to him? There were already a number of young widows about who had hardly known their husbands. Or was I selfish, because I didn't want to be tied? I wasn't ready for marriage. There were so many other things to do first and when I married, I wanted to be a wife and mother, with a husband at home, and not one that was fighting in the war, and could be killed at any moment.

We had a lot of time together, even went sledging one afternoon, but when it came to the time to say farewell, this was not easy. We did not cry, and tried very hard to be brave.

'I don't want anybody to come and see me off,' said Wolfgang. 'I can make my way to the train by tram. We are to assemble in Tapiau, this is only an hour's trip by train. Some of my pals have their families coming to Tapiau to see them off, but I don't want that. I don't want to keep on saying goodbye.'

We hugged and kissed and held hands, and wondered whether this was the end. The fighting in Russia asked for a lot of bravery and sacrifice, particularly in the cold winter months.

The next soldier on leave was Ulrich, a neighbour's boy. His father, being a police officer, had never been called up, as he was needed in town. The family lived in one of the police flats next to the police station. Ulrich had always been a mummy's boy, very spoilt and protected. He was extremely fair and white skinned and as a young boy had never been allowed to play with us so-called rough children. He was an only child, and when the parents went for a walk with him on Sundays he usually held his mother's hand, or maybe vice versa. He glanced at us, with his head held high, pretending not to see us and the rough games we were playing, but I am quite sure he would have liked to join us. He was a little older than myself.

Sometimes he stood by the gate watching our games, and I tried to get him to join us, but he was quite honestly convinced that his mother was right, that our rough games were not good for him. He was called up to the army in 1940. Nobody really knew where he was stationed as he had never made friends with anybody. Ulrich's mother also was quite a snob, not talking to any of the neighbours. Her husband was one of the higher officers at the police station and they had one of the biggest flats in their block. My mother had tried once or twice to talk to her, particularly since Ulrich had left home, but she didn't get very far, Ulrich's mother was polite but uncommunicative. She would not say what Ulrich was doing, or where he was fighting, or where he was stationed. Every time Ulrich came on leave he was still an ordinary soldier, although one would have thought that with his excellent education he would have been officer material or, at least, have moved up a grade to sergeant. Goering always said:

*'Jeder Soldat hat den Marschalstab im Rucksack!'* (Every soldier has the marshal's baton in his rucksack!)

I went for a walk with Ulrich once and I liked him. He was very tall, intelligent, polite, and good looking in his uniform. Every man looks better in uniform. I had thought he would be shy, but he wasn't. He told me that he had been stationed in France and that he now would be transferred to another place, but didn't know where. We never knew when Ulrich came and when he left, because his mother didn't talk to anybody. With the other boys, we heard beforehand when they were coming on leave, and we all got a little excited then.

It was the end of November, just after Wolfgang had left for his final training, that Ulrich turned up. What a surprise, and what a change! The boy had become a man, and the soldier a lieutenant, with several decorations! Goering was right after all, bravery was rewarded. Ulrich and his parents proudly walked the streets and even stopped to talk to us rough lot! Ulrich had fought in Russia and got wounded. His arm was still bandaged, but one could not see this under the uniform. He had been very brave, saving the lives of two officers during a fierce battle, and had not only been promoted but had also been decorated by a general. It was unbelievable to see the development of this introvert young man. Even the way he walked with his parents was different. He had achieved something. People now looked up to him, and his parents couldn't stop talking about his bravery.

Ulrich was home about four or five days when Uwe, Helma's brother, came rushing to our front door and said to me:

'Come quickly, the SS are there, they have come to fetch Ulrich.'

I couldn't believe it, and ran outside to have a look. Sure enough, there stood a big car, with the SS chauffeur standing next to it, and this right outside the main entrance of the flats. The front door opened, and out stepped an SS officer, followed by two SS men, with Ulrich in the middle. Ulrich was handcuffed, the lieutenant's epaulettes on his uniform were torn off his shoulders, and the decorations were missing. He was deadly pale and trembling. The two SS men pushed him roughly towards the car.

'Ulrich,' I said, 'whatever have you done?'

He looked at me with frightened eyes. His lips moved, but no sound came. He lifted his hands to show me the handcuffs, or was it a wave?

One of the men gave him a push.

'Get in!' he said, and Ulrich fell into the car.

The two men sat either side of Ulrich. The officer got into the front seat, and the chauffeur settled himself behind the steering wheel and started the engine. The car roared off, leaving Uwe, some of the other neighbours and myself standing there in bewilderment.

'He could not have been an officer,' said Uwe.

'Nor have been decorated,' I added. 'They had torn it all off. Poor Ulrich, why ever did he do it?'

'He wanted to show off to his parents,' said one of the neighbours. 'He wanted them to be proud of him. He should have known it wouldn't last. It will kill his mother, and ruin his father's career.'

I went indoors, and told my mother about it. She was very upset, and felt sorry for Ulrich's mother.

'She will never have the courage to go outside again, because of what all the neighbours will think and whisper behind her back,' said my mother. 'I must go and see her.'

She put on her coat, took her handbag, and left the house. It was a long time before she returned,

'What happened to Ulrich?' I asked.

'It is all very sad,' said my mother, 'The parents blame one another now, and Ulrich's mother wants to move away. She cannot face her neighbours, or go shopping. Ulrich's father is going to apply for a few days leave. He is going to volunteer for the army. Firstly to get away from here, and secondly to make up for what Ulrich has done. He never was a lieutenant, or had any decorations. He wasn't even wounded; it was all a show, to impress people and, particularly, his parents. I am going shopping tomorrow with Ulrich's mother so that she is not alone when she meets some of the neighbours. Somebody has already put an anonymous note through her letter box, saying something about letting the *Führer* down. I found the paper and picked it up quickly when I left. I didn't show it to her, but there will be more notes.'

After a little while, my mother added:

'I wish her husband wouldn't volunteer for the army. It leaves her all alone here. He ought to stay with his wife and help her. I don't think she will ever see Ulrich again.'

My mother was right in her prophecy. She accompanied Ulrich's mother a few times when she went shopping. Some neighbours were nice, others pretended not to know Ulrich's mother. His father left to join the army.

Ulrich had a choice, either court-martial, or he could volunteer for the so-called *Kanonenfutter Regiment* (cannon fodder regiment). This was used in places in the front-line where it was known that there would be tremendous losses. It consisted of prisoners, soldiers who had absconded, deserted, or offended officers. In other words, men who should have been court-martialled for an offence. I don't know how long they had to stay in the regiment, but I do know that some of them survived. Unfortunately Ulrich did not. He got killed, but it was called an honourable death.

*Gefallen für Grossdeutschland*, and all was forgiven.

This was a very unhappy episode, and was talked about for quite a time in the neighbourhood. The attitudes of the people changed because of the war, particularly as things were not going so well, and there were fewer and fewer victories. People from the forces came home on leave, some of them telling good stories, and some of them describing the pain, the suffering and the hardship at the front. It depended where they were stationed or fighting.


Ernst posted a picture postcard from Paris and came home for Christmas 1942. He rang me up and wanted to go out with me, so we met in the town, in Café Schwermer. It was interesting to listen to his stories, as he enjoyed being in the army. He was in the occupation forces in France and had not been in any fighting. He said that all he had to do was to fill out forms, file papers, answer the phone, and run around the officers. He said he had needed a lot of courage to ask me to write to him that day in the *Eisdiele*, because he had no girlfriend. He still had nobody, as there was no opportunity, and he hoped I would carry on writing. He had one week of leave before being transferred to Sicily.

'I think we are going to North Africa,' said Ernst. 'There is talk that we might join Rommel and the *Afrika Korps*. I prefer Africa to Russia. I like the heat better than the cold.'

Ernst was not allowed to talk too much about where he was going to be transferred to, but promised to write and tell me what he was permitted to say.

My mother organised a little evening for us young people, so that we could dance and play games. Astra and Christel joined in, and also Klaus Katlus, a neighbour's boy, and Uwe, Helma's brother. Hans, my brother, had to turn the handle of the gramophone so that we had music. Astra felt we were all much too young for her, but she joined in because she liked dancing.

In some of the games we played we had forfeits. One of these was to empty out everything from our pockets. This was alright for us girls, we very often had no pockets, but the boys sometimes produced a lot of unnecessary things, which gave everybody the chance to pull their legs. Ernst was the one, this time, who had to empty his pockets. He was in uniform, and had to take everything out of his jacket, and then his trousers. He produced an awful lot, including his purse, his identity papers, string, handkerchief, a cork, French coins, and a little box, which he suddenly grabbed and kept in his hand. This was fatal, because we were now intrigued to find out what it was. Ernst stopped joking and smiling, and said very seriously:

'No, you are not going to look in the box. This is something we all have to carry in France, and if you don't know about it, I am not going to enlighten you.'

He looked at Christel and Hans and added:

'You are much too young in any case.'

He collected everything from the table, and put it back into his pockets. This was not a boy talking now, but a young soldier, and I think we all realized there was no point in trying to persuade him to change his mind.

'Let's get on with the game,' I said, shrugging my shoulders, but I was determined to find out the secret of the box.

Ernst was very reluctant to tell me what was in the box when I had a few minutes alone with him, but he also knew that I would not let up with my questions, so he told me it was a "Pariser". I had never heard of it, but was only too willing to learn. A "Pariser" is a French Letter or a Condom, and every soldier in France had to carry one, to avoid the spread of sexual diseases. Ernst didn't look at me when he gave his explanations, and felt most uncomfortable about telling them.

I was glad he had told me, because this was something which the girls at school had whispered about. He put his hand into his pocket, produced the box, and gave it to me.

'You can keep it if you like,' he said, ' but don't look at it now. We get them supplied in the army and can have as many as we like. Actually, you can buy them at the chemist, but most of the men don't like to ask for them there.'

Ernst left after Christmas, and the next letter I had came from Sicily. He didn't say that he was there, but wrote that his guess was right and that he would soon move on. In other words, he was going to join the *Afrika Korps*. The next two letters were not so cheerful any more. Life had become harder for him, there had been some fighting, and he had seen his first wounded soldiers. It was hot during the day, he said, but often cold at night. He hadn't heard from me, but then, post was not so important as ammunition and food. Everything had to be brought over to Africa by air from Sicily, and letters and parcels were often left behind.

Ernst never got any of my letters. They were returned to me in April, stamped: *Gefallen für Grossdeutschland*. I was absolutely shattered, and couldn't believe it. He had only joined the *Afrika Korps* a few months before. My mind was in a turmoil, and only one silly thought kept on coming up again and again.

'I do hope he has been able to use his little box'.

He was so young. A happy, honest, open, intelligent and sympathetic boy, who was hardly a man before his life was cut short. He was my friend, and had chosen me from amongst a number of girls to be his pen-friend, and had even come to see me on his short leave. I was sorry I had not always been kind to him, and often took too long to answer his letters, and even more sorry that he did not get my last two letters. I put a small ribbon around the letters from Ernst, including the two returned ones, and put them into a box where I already had Herbert's letters, and my returned one. A shiver ran down my back as I suddenly thought: How many more will I have to put into this box?

I did not cry, but I had a lump in my throat, and every time I thought of Ernst, I had to think of Herbert too, and the lump in my throat was sometimes difficult to swallow.

# CHAPTER EIGHT

## Matriculation - Kriegsdienst - University

At Christmas 1942, I received permission to take the examinations for my matriculation in the following Spring. We all worked hard at school, and homework piled up. It was now left to me whether I read books or learnt and revised because failing the matriculation would mean no university. My father was not at all in favour of girls going to university. He always felt it was a waste of time.

'Girls never finish their career when they study too long. They get married, and the money for their education is wasted.'

He wanted me to choose something different, maybe a teacher, where the training would not take so long. I stuck to my original decision, it was to be medicine, and my mother encouraged me. Just in case my father refused to pay for the university, my mother had already deposited some money for my studies in a special bank account, to which she added something whenever she could. My father knew what she was doing and sometimes jokingly threatened to cut my mother's housekeeping allowance. He promised to carry on paying for me if I passed the first big examination after two years, the *Physikum* (medical exam).

My mother always said that even if I did not finish my studies, at least it would give me the opportunity to meet some men from our social class and background. She was very conscious of this, and also that she had three girls, whom she had to bring *unter die Haube* (to marry them off), which would not be very easy, with so many young men getting killed through the war.

We called our school-leaving examination *Abitur* (A-level). It was also an examination to qualify for entrance to university. We had written and oral examinations, which were not set by the education authorities, but by the headmaster and teachers of the different schools.

We had to work for all the subjects in our *Abitur*, and have a pass in each one. The only choice we had was to take drawing and painting

113

instead of needlework. I was not much good at either, but drawing and painting did not ask for any homework, so I chose those. Everybody had to specialize in one subject. I chose German, because of my love of books and reading. This meant a lot of extra work, as I had to know a number of authors and their works. I also had to concentrate on one author in particular. I chose Walter Flex, who got killed very young in the First World War and therefore didn't write too much. He wrote short stories and a number of poems, most of them rather sad, because he spent hours in the trenches in France and saw the terrible waste of human lives. One could feel through his poems that he knew he would not return from the war, but wanted to leave something behind, even if it was only a picture of hurt, suffering, and sadness. A warning to the next generation to avoid another war.

I had to learn one of his poems, called *Die drei Lilien,* (The Three Lilies), which was quite long, and very sad. Our German teacher said she would ask me to recite it in class one day but when the time passed and we came near to our big oral examination days, I got worried that I might forget part of it, so I copied it out and asked one of the girls on the first desk in the class to keep it. If I had to stand in front of the class to do my recital and got stuck she would then be able to help me.

Right out of the blue, the teacher one day asked me to step in front of the class, and recite *Die Drei Lilien.* I had practised it many times at home, reciting it to my mother and to Christel, and once I had even made Christel cry with the sadness of it.

I didn't get stuck, I knew it all. I recited it slowly, leaving pauses where necessary to let the sadness sink through. When I had finished, there was silence in the classroom. The teacher disturbed it, she probably thought everybody was getting too emotional.

'That will do, Miss Zirkel. Quite well done, you may go and sit down. Now, let's get on with some different work,' she said.

I felt disappointed, having hoped for more praise. This came after the lesson from some of my friends, who felt that my recital was excellent.

We had a written examination in English, French, German, mathematics, geometry, history, geography, physics, chemistry, and history of art. All our written examinations were done weeks before the final oral one, and only the teacher would know whether one would be called for the final questioning. The final big day for the oral examinations was on March 15th, when we all turned up at eight o'clock in the morning with our sandwiches and thermos flasks, not knowing how long it would take. We had to wait in our classroom, and were called to the different examinations. As soon as the examined girl returned, she was asked what it was like, what subject she had been asked in for, and who were the examiners. The examination board consisted of all our teachers and the headmaster and this year we also had Mrs Förster, a *Regierungsdelegierte* (government delegate). This was not so good, as everybody knew that when Mrs Förster showed up somebody would fail the *Abitur*. Every year she went to a different school and this year it happened to be our turn. She would interrupt the questioning and ask some questions herself, often things the students would not know because they had not been covered in the curriculum.

I was only called in for two subjects, biology, which was *Pflichtfach* (compulsory subject), and German, which was my chosen main subject. Professor Dr Steinecke was as good as his word in biology, he only asked me questions about immunization, baby care, and hygiene, which I had learnt specially.

I knew that I would be asked questions for at least half an hour in my chosen subject of German, but I felt that as long as Mrs Förster didn't interfere in the questioning, I would be alright. Things went very well for the start. I had to make a comparison between my chosen author, Walter Flex's, sad outlook on the First World War and another author, and then I was asked by Mrs Förster whether I could recite a ballad by Walter Flex. He had written a number of them, also short poems, and Mrs Förster probably thought I would only have learnt the short poems. Well, I had learnt *Die Drei Lilien*, a long poem, and I would just insist that it was a ballad if she started questioning me about it.

*Die Drei Lilien* was the story of a young dead soldier, lying in his grave decorated only by a rough wooden cross and the three lilies, which also gradually died. I only remember one short line, which was repeated several times at the end of some of the verses:

*Keusch wie eine Lilie lag der Tote dort . .* (Chaste like a lily lay the dead there . . )

I was nearly crying myself when I had finished my recital, and I knew I had done well. There was a hush in the room, nobody moved, and nobody said anything, and they all looked at me. I had made a point of not looking at anybody whilst I was reciting, because I didn't want to see faces but concentrate on the words and the emotions I could put into them. I was astounded, therefore, when I looked at everybody, to see the different expressions. They were all moved by the sadness of the ballad, but there was also a look of disbelief on some faces that I, the one who was always so mischievous, and often in trouble, could recite something so delicate and full of feeling.

'Was that a ballad or a poem?' said Mrs Förster suddenly.

I looked at her, wondering what to say, because I did not really know the difference. I heard her adding grudgingly:

'That was a very good recital, and well learnt.'

Dear Mr Walsdorf, the headmaster, interrupted:

'Mrs Förster, may I point out that Miss Zirkel has already been questioned for over half an hour, exceeding the usual examination time for the chosen subject. There are still quite a number of pupils to be called in, and we are already running late.'

'Maybe you are right,' she said, and turning to my German teacher, she said: 'Before calling the next girl, I would like to have a word with you.'

'You may go Miss Zirkel,' said Mr Walsdorf, smiling.

By 9 pm, we were told that we could go home. The next day we were all assembled at 12 o'clock in our classroom, but we had to wait. The examination board had been in session all the morning discussing our results and did not finish until 12.45. (Miss) *Fräulein* Dr Stadie, our class teacher, came in, and called out two girls and, after a little while she came back and got their belongings and, nearly crying herself, she said quietly:

'They did not pass.'

Neither of the girls repeated the examination the next year. One of them got married a week later. We knew about this, and she didn't seem to care very much towards the end of her schooling whether she got her *Abitur* or not. She had a baby a year later, and was a widow 6 months after that, her husband being shot down over the Channel. The other girl went into the army as a radio operator, stationed in Königsberg.

At 1 o'clock we were called into the examination room. Mr Walsdorf informed us that we had all passed and would get our certificates in due course. He congratulated us, shaking hands with everybody, and then all the teachers did the same, and everybody said they were looking forward to the *Abiturfeier* (school leaver's party). There was no mention of the two girls who had failed. It had become true again; whenever Mrs Förster attended the final examinations, two people would fail.

Once outside the school building there were a lot of parents, friends, and relatives hanging about with questioning faces and I discovered that even my father had come to fetch me.

'Well,' he said, and tried to read my face.

At first I thought I could tease him, and pretend I had failed, but I was too full of happiness to hide my smiling face, and he could see that I had passed. He turned round and whistled and, from behind a tree came Hans with a large bunch of flowers, grinning sheepishly.

'Congratulations,' said my father. He gave me the flowers and hugged and kissed me.

'Congratulations,' said Hans, and gave me *eine Alberte*.

*Alberten* are pins or badges made from gold or silver in two sizes, 1.5 cm or 2.5 cm. It was in commemoration of *Herzog* (Count) Albert, who founded the *Albertina*, the Königsberger university. The shape of the badge was the top part of the body of *Herzog* Albert in his knight's uniform with his sword in his right hand and the inscription underneath: OVISACAD. ALB. On the back was a pin, which was stuck into the lapel. The tradition to give these badges to *Abiturienten* (young people who had passed their *Abitur*) was unique to Königsberg, because of the university. Parents, brothers, sisters, aunts, uncles, cousins, friends, anybody really could give an *Alberte* to the *Abiturient*, and often both lapels of a coat or jacket were full of this outward sign of school success.

Hans gave me a big *Alberte*, and my father produced a small one, explaining at the same time that, because they hadn't been sure whether I had passed or not, Hans had to hide behind the tree with the flowers. If my father hadn't whistled, Hans would have thought I had failed. I wonder whether they would then have given the flowers and the *Alberten* to one of the other girls from my class.

*Matriculation Hat and Alberten*

The second tradition was to wear a cap or hat made from red velvet and embroidered with gold thread. Each cap had to be individually made because on the flat top the initials of the owner were embroidered, in my case HZ. The rim was about 5cm high and had gold embroidered oak leaves on it. The cap was worn at an angle with an elastic under the hair to hold it in place.

We had a big celebration dinner at home. My father had organised a goose, my favourite meal in those days, and my mother cooked red sweet-and-sour cabbage with apples. I received several *Alberten* and got my little cap after a few days and wherever I went I wore them. It was the last year that the *Alberten* and the cap were worn, because already then it was difficult to get the gold thread for the embroidery, and the gold and silver for the pins.

If one wanted gold jewellery, one had to give up gold, even if a gold wedding ring was wanted. Gold plated jewellery, which wore off soon, could be bought. My mother had a beautiful amethyst ring made for me to commemorate this first big achievement of mine. For this, she had to give some gold, so she parted with a gold crown from her teeth, saying that she could replace it after the war.

All the girls in my class had now to go into the RAD *Reichsarbeitsdienst* (state labour service) for one year before they were allowed to go to university. It was all part of the Hitler Youth and was very organised. The work involved six months during the summer helping on the land, and six months in the winter, either working in war factories or helping as conductors on the trams in Königsberg.

Large manor houses were taken over by the RAD and the rooms made into dormitories for the girls, with a large dining room and reception room. My friend, Irmgard, told me about it. She had to wear a grey/brown uniform when off duty, and a blue dress with an apron when at work. The girls were sent out every day to different farms, but slept together in the house. They didn't work on Sundays, when they had political lectures, or singing or folk dancing. Irmgard said it was the same as when we worked on the farm before, when we did the *Kriegsdienst*, except that this time everybody had to return to the so-called headquarters and have the evening meal together in the dining hall. It was just like being in the BDM. She didn't like it.

'It is just like being in the army,' she said when I met her on a free weekend, which she got every two months. 'We have to get up early in the morning for outdoor exercises, then showers, dressing, bed making, and breakfast. After that, assembly in the hall, where we are told to which farm to report. Some girls get duties in the house, like cleaning, or helping with cooking the evening meal. The food is terrible! Every morning we have to march outside to raise the flag, and every evening we take it down again, never mind sun or rain. We hardly have any free time.'

Irmgard complained about the RAD, and I sympathised with her; I, too, was not happy. I had always assumed that, being Swiss, I would not have to join the RAD, but could go to university straight away after leaving school. Unfortunately this was not the case. When I went to register, I was told I would have to do some *Kriegsdienst*, as otherwise I would be too privileged, compared with my other school friends, gaining a whole year in my studies. There was also a kind of selection taking place as there were too many applications for the medicine course and a shortage of tutors and professors. I told the authorities that I had already done some *Kriegsdienst* through our school, but so had everybody else was the reply. The only thing I was allowed to do was to live at home and find myself a job in a needed place, like serving in a restaurant, working in one of the factories by the harbour, or as a conductress on the tram. I had to go to the labour exchange and get a list of the vacant jobs which were recognized as *Kriegsdienst.*

It was my father who came up with a good idea. He had a friend in town, a Mr Neff, who owned the restaurant and bar Hollatz. Mr Neff was always short of staff, and my father approached him, suggesting that he employ me. He applied to the labour exchange for a waitress and the job was given to me, together with a form that this was a recognized *Kriegsdienst.* I decided to work for him for three months (April, May and June), and then have three months duty on the tram (July, August, and September), after which I should be allowed to start at the university if I passed the selection examination.

Mr Neff put me on day duty, which meant serving the midday dinner, plus beer and non-alcoholic drinks during the day. My duties were from 10 am until 4 pm, often longer, because of the settling up of the money. The taking of the money didn't bother me, but it took some time to work out the food coupons. People who ate in restaurants had to give up food coupons. These were usually supplied in bigger amounts, like one pound of bread, one pound of sugar, half a pound of meat. Anybody eating out had to exchange their food cards at the Ministry of Food into smaller amounts first. Each menu had instructions as to how many coupons had to be given, and people often chose not what tasted best, but what needed the least coupons. Sometimes I could give smaller valued coupons in exchange for a large one, to help people out. All this took quite a bit of learning and time when one was busy serving hot lunches.

There was only one good thing about it. I got a free hot dinner every day, without coupons. I never had to serve in the evenings. I think this was an arrangement between Mr Neff and my father because, with the *Kneipe* (bar) attached to the restaurant, the evenings could become quite noisy. There were always a lot of soldiers and sailors in the town, and Hollatz was a favourite meeting place for them.

I found the three months quite hard and tiring, especially as I was not used to being on my feet all day. Like every other place, we were understaffed. Mr Neff was very kind to me and, in the beginning, helped me to sort out the coupons, and interfered if customers became too abusive or cross. Gradually he could see that I could manage and encouraged me with a smile, a few kind words, or a pat on the shoulder. Some days we were not too busy and then it was fun, particularly after I had been serving for a few weeks, and got to know the *Stammgäste* (regular customers). They were usually kind and patient, and they tipped well. I earned quite a bit of money, but couldn't do anything with it, as there was nothing to buy. Everything was rationed.

Wolfgang's letters did not come so often, but I tried to reply to them as soon as they did come because I could feel his unhappiness and his suffering, and he was my favourite boyfriend. He wrote very affectionate letters. He hung on to the thought that we would be together for the rest of our lives, once this terrible war was over. He embraced and hugged me in all his letters, getting in this way the warmth and comfort he needed. I realized that to him I was not only his girlfriend, but also his home, his security, his future and even his mother, who had never demonstrated a lot of affection for him. All his life he had missed the tenderness and caress of his mother and now, by showering it on to me, he felt that part of it came back to him. I got very worried at times because, although I was very fond of him, I was not yet ready to give myself fully to one person.

I was young, I was ambitious, I wanted to get on and do something with my life. I was afraid Wolfgang would ask me to marry him again, and I didn't want to hurt him by saying "no" once more. So, when writing to him I was very careful what I said, but he always thanked me for my loving letters which, in my opinion, were not so loving at all.

Theo, whom I had met with Franzl in the train, wrote to say that he would soon have leave and wanted to see me then. To my great surprise he arrived at the Hollatz restaurant one dinner time in lieutenant's uniform. Everybody turned their heads when they saw him coming in, because he was a very smart good-looking officer. Hollatz didn't usually have officers, it was not that type of elegant place. Theo smiled at me, pleased to have surprised me. I pointed to the bar, meaning I would meet him there, as I had a tray in my hand to serve some customers. When I met him at the bar, he kissed my hand, and said:

'I cannot kiss you on your mouth, so this is the next best thing.'

'You shouldn't do this,' I said, 'people are staring. They are not used to politeness here'.

He just laughed, and asked whether he could have some dinner without coupons. Mr Neff was very nice and let me serve him with some dinner. He also said I could have the next two days off. Theo was only three days in Königsberg. He didn't say what he was doing and why he was in the town, but he said he had two more days after that to go home to his parents. So we had two days together, actually only one and a half, because he had to stay on in the barracks one morning to do some paper-work. He had completely recovered from his nerve shock, at least that's what he said. He had taken another course and got promoted. He was much more relaxed and happy and liked to talk about the time when we first met, and how I helped him to forget the war on the day we went out in Rössel.

'I am not flying at the moment,' he said. 'I am teaching new recruits. As soon as they think I am alright again, I will go back to my old unit. They need me there, quite a number of them have got killed.'

When he said the last sentence his face did not move, but he had a faraway look in his eyes. He took a deep breath, and added:

'Most of us in the air force won't see the end of the war. It makes it easier to accept when one recognizes this.'

I didn't know what to say to him. I didn't think he was cured, and I was afraid to say or do anything to upset him. I couldn't bear to see his face trembling again, like it did that time in the train. I felt like shouting at him:

'Don't talk like that! Of course you will come back from the war! Look on the bright side! You must have hope!'

Instead, I changed the subject, and told him one or two amusing things that had happened at Hollatz in the restaurant.

On the evening of the second day he caught the train home and I saw him off at the station. He kissed me gently on my mouth, my cheeks, and my eyebrows.

'You are such a lovable person and can make a chap feel so much at ease. You are very understanding. You will make a good doctor, with your kind and helpful nature,' he said. 'Please keep on writing your cheerful letters, they do help.'

His dark eyes looked at me; they seemed full of tears, or did I imagine them? He didn't cry, and neither did I.

He got into the carriage, and opened the window so that we could see one another better. The guard blew the whistle, the train started moving. I stretched out my hand for one last touch of him. Theo took it and kissed my fingers.

'Farewell,' he whispered.

'Goodbye,' I called out as the train started to speed up.

I stood on the platform for a time, even after the train had disappeared. I had a foreboding that I would not see Theo again. He, too, had known it when he said "Farewell", I was sure of that.

He wrote to say he was back at the training school and in October of that year he was put into active service again, joining his old unit.

I never knew where he was stationed or what he did, but he was either accompanying bombing raids over England, or fighting English and American bombers over German towns. Once on active service, he didn't write much. The letters were short, sometimes only a few scribbled lines thanking me for writing, but always finishing with the sentence:

'I am looking forward to your next cheerful and entertaining letter.'

It was like a cry for help. My letters helped him with what he was doing and made him forget what he had seen and done.

Theo got killed just before Christmas. Two of my letters were returned to me with the usual sentence:

*Gefallen für Grossdeutschland.*

All his belongings were returned to his parents. His mother wrote to me asking me whether she could keep my letters, which had been included in his things.

'Your letters meant so much to him,' she said, 'I feel they are part of him now. Thank you for helping him.'

She sounded very much like Theo in her letter. I wrote to tell her that she could keep my letters.

I put Theo's letters in my box, to join the ones from Herbert and Ernst, and closed the lid with a sigh, and tears running down my face. Three young men, all different, kind, warm-hearted and sensitive, had gone. They had hardly lived when their lives were cut short.


At the end of June, I joined the tram personnel and became a conductress. We had some very intensive training first, as we had to learn all the stations where the tram stopped off by heart. Our instructress informed us that this was very important. At night, when it was dark, the black blinds in the tram were pulled down to avoid any light shining outside because of air-raids. As the passengers didn't know where they were, the conductor had to call out to inform the people of the name of the next station.

We were all supplied with a shoulder bag, a certain amount of tickets, and a float of money. At first I was a learner conductress, travelling with an experienced conductress for two days on an easy number route, and then three days on the busier routes.

Trams were always full in those days because there was no other transport in town. Cars were only for the army, SS or SA, and could only be driven by private people with a special permit, such as doctors, fire chiefs or important business people.

My five learner days were soon finished and I was left on my own. The first few days after that were a bit of a muddle, and I think a number of people got away without paying. The tram was sometimes so full that I had a job to squeeze through to take the money.

We had a number of soldiers in the town, some of them wounded. All of them were privileged to enter the tram first. Soldiers on crutches were entitled to sit down at the corner seats, which had to be vacated for them. There were no queues at the tram stops, everybody pushed, and tried to get in. It was often the elderly, the frail, and the shy ones who stayed behind. There was no time to hang around at the tram stops, so many times I just shouted *'Abfahrt'* (departure) to the next conductress, and then jumped on to the bottom step of the wagon whilst the tram was already moving.

Every driver and conductress had a free uniform. We had a black skirt, jacket and coat, a white blouse, and black walking shoes. We were allowed to wear our own stockings, which were always in short supply in the shops, but we were supplied with white ankle socks for the summer. We were glad of the shoes and the clothes, as everything was on coupons. Gloves and a cap were supplied for the winter. The cap could be worn in the summer, but was not compulsory, and I only used it when it rained. I wore the jacket, unless it was really hot, because it helped me with the carrying of my shoulder bag, which got quite heavy with all the coins after a few hours travelling. My shoulders used to get sore, even after moving the bag from one side to the other. Soon I got used to the routine of a conductress.

I hated the early morning shift. I didn't like to get up so early. I had my favourite tram numbers. No 4 and No 7 passed near our house. Actually it was the No 4's terminal, Ratshof, and I could tell my mother and Christel when I would be there, so that they could bring me a drink. We were allowed to eat our sandwiches, if we had brought any, at the terminals if there was time. If I finished at 1 o'clock, I would have my lunch at the canteen, where we did not have to give up coupons if we showed our identity cards. These cards were given to everybody who worked on the trams, and had a photo of the owner on them, to prevent them being used dishonestly. It also entitled me to free tram rides all over the town, when I was not in uniform.

I did not like tram No. 12, particularly in the evening and late at night. The terminal was near the harbour, and the part where civilians were not allowed. Ships used to come in there for refitting, and the whole area was full of sailors and navy personnel, as there was also the naval college. During the refitting of the ships, the sailors had time off and would catch the tram into the town, where they would drink and have fun. They often tried to make a date with me and tease me, preventing me from passing them to collect the fares from the other passengers, or they even refused to pay.

The worst time was always the last tram from the town to the harbour. By then, a number of sailors were pretty drunk, and wanted a kiss, and it was difficult to keep their hands off me. The other conductresses had the same difficulties. We all had a whistle, which we were told to use in emergency, so that the driver would stop.

My tram duty was for July, August, and September 1943 and, although very strenuous, I enjoyed it. I met a lot of people and could observe the behaviour of the different classes of society. The tram routes took me from the poorest to the richest parts of the

DER KRIEGSHILFSDIENST-
VERPFLICHTETEN

Helga Z i r k e l

SPRECHE ICH FÜR TREUE DIENSTE
IN SCHWERER KRIEGSZEIT
BEI
KÖNIGSBERGER WERKE UND
STRASSENBAHN G. M. B. H.
IN DER ZEIT

vom 1. Juli 1943 bis 30. September 1943

DANK UND ANERKENNUNG AUS.

BERLIN. DEN 30. September 1943

DER REICHSVERKEHRSMINISTER

*War Tram Service Completion Certificate*

124

town. In the evenings, I delivered people in beautiful clothes to the opera and the theatre and, in the morning I collected the workforce for the factories, and the business people for the town. During the day the general public travelled, including school children, and women going shopping into the centre of Königsberg and, of course, there were the soldiers and sailors and the civil servants. There were more women than men around, except for the ones in uniform. I learnt that there are kind and rude people in every class of society. When the tram was full, even a well-dressed and well-spoken lady would push and shout to get a place, and some addressed me like a servant.

Although the bombing of Königsberg had not started yet, accommodation was scarce because the bigger houses in the town were occupied by the army and war office department. People had to move out of commercial and private premises because of that, and the lucky ones who could remain in their houses were suddenly forced to give up some rooms.

The SS surveyed houses and flats, and people were told what they could occupy, and what they had to give up. We, too, had a visit from the SS. This time my father was at home and things went more peacefully. He was told that he couldn't be forced to give up a room in the house, but they would appreciate it if he co-operated. I don't know who suggested that the garage could be made into a workshop, but this is what happened. The garage was allocated to a shoemaker. He was a little man with crippled feet, walking with two sticks. He was very friendly and kind, sometimes a little shy, but we all got on very well together.

The other addition to our house was a new foreign girl, Sascha, this time from Russia. She spoke a little German, was quite well educated, and when she discovered we were Swiss she became our friend and couldn't do enough for us.

The six months of my *Kriegsdienst* came to an end, and I had to register at the university in September.

When I went to register as a medical student, I discovered more obstacles. Firstly, I was told that six months was not enough *Kriegsdienst* to give me permission to start my studies. Everybody had to work for twelve months, except if you had been in the army and returned wounded. I had quite an argument with the authorities, pointing out that as a neutral foreigner, I should not have thought that it was necessary for me to do any *Kriegsdienst* at all. The point was that I lived in Germany, was born there and went to school there. If I had come over from Switzerland to study in Königsberg, this would have been different. In the end, it was decided to let me start, but I would have to work during the Christmas holiday again, which I promised. I knew very well that if I didn't work in the holiday I wouldn't be able to start my second term.

Then I discovered the next obstacle. If I wanted to study medicine, I had to go through a selection process. Because of the war, there was only one professor of anatomy for first term students and, as there were too many students wanting to study medicine, a committee was formed, consisting of several professors and doctors who would interview the applicants and select the ones most suitable for this profession. If I had chosen another subject, I could have registered. I was given a list of people with whom I had to make an appointment to have an interview. After all prospective candidates were interviewed, the committee would meet, probably in two weeks time, and I would be informed whether I had passed their scrutiny or not.

I also had to produce a doctor's certificate that I was in good health, including the Wassermann test, used to diagnose syphilis and proof that I was an Aryan. These papers had also to be produced when applying for a job as a civil servant, and when getting married.

It was not difficult to get proof that I was an Aryan, because we had to research our *Ahnentafel* or *Stammbaum* (family tree) at school as part of a lesson. Being Swiss, my father had a *Familienbüchlein* (family book) where all dates of birth, marriages and deaths were entered and certified by our embassy and the home canton in Switzerland.

I went to our doctor who did the examination and the test, and then I made an appointment with the different members of the committee. When I showed the list with the names of the committee to my mother, she recognized the name of the professor of chemistry who was in charge of the laboratory in the *Stadtklinik* (town hospital).

'Mrs Jacoby is his secretary,' my mother said. 'I will give her a ring and talk to her, and also make the appointment for you.'

Mrs Jacoby was our dentist's wife, and a great friend of my mother's. Whenever my mother went shopping in town she would call and see her, and sometimes stay on for the evening. Mr and Mrs Jacoby would come for a Sunday coffee afternoon when my father was at home. Gradually, these Sunday afternoons stopped because Mr Jacoby was called up into the army, but my mother carried on visiting her friend.

The first person I went to see was a *Frau* Dr Grimonie, a lady doctor in the RAD. I have never forgotten her. She was a big bosomed, tough looking German Nazi, with short cut hair and cold eyes, dressed in the

RAD uniform. The moment I saw her, I knew I wouldn't like her and realized I had to be on my guard.

Things went wrong right from the start, because she greeted me with *"Heil Hitler"*, even standing up for it behind her desk with her arm raised. I just nodded and smiled and introduced myself, avoiding any kind of greeting and hoping she hadn't noticed it. I was wrong. Her cold smile vanished and she frowned. She motioned for me to sit down opposite her desk, and asked me straight away why I could apply to go to university in September, when the RAD usually lasted from March to March. I explained that, being Swiss, I could choose not to join the RAD, but that I had done six months *Kriegsdienst* and would do another turn on the trams in the Christmas holiday. She accused me of being workshy, not wanting to help on the farms because it was too hard. I replied that I had done two stints of farm work whilst still at school. She asked other questions about my life, and also about sport, something that was very important for every German, because it kept you healthy. I told her about my achievements in handball running and swimming. I could see she was astonished. She had hoped for something negative. She made a few notes, then smiled suddenly and became very friendly.

Her next sentences and questions were a shock to me. She suggested that I joined the RAD as a student of medicine, as they needed doctors. Although I was Swiss, she said, the Red Cross was formed in Switzerland, which was a neutral state, and very well thought of. She had been to Switzerland herself and the people around Zürich and Luzern were just like the German people. My parents would not have to pay for my studies, because I would be sponsored by the state and get a grant.

I would have to wear the RAD uniform during my studies, but could live at home. She had already got two students who started last year, and she would like two more to start this year. She was offering me the chance of a lifetime, free study for a very expensive course, and a job at the end of it. She pushed some papers around on the desk and produced some forms, which she said she could fill in for me to sign before I leave.

I was absolutely speechless. I just couldn't believe what she was saying. If I told my father that I had accepted this offer he would have had a stroke. The woman must be crazy to offer this to me. I just kept on looking at her, not saying anything, biting my bottom lip. I wondered how I could say 'no' without making her cross so that she would still recommend me. Suddenly I realized that there was no point in beating about the bush. I knew if I didn't accept her offer she would not recommend me and I would just have to make sure that the other committee members, whom I had not seen yet, would be impressed enough with me to overrule her veto.

'I am sorry, *Frau* Dr Grimonie,' I said, 'but I cannot accept this most generous offer. I do not want to be tied down to the RAD.'

She tried once more, saying that I only had to work for a few years as a RAD doctor, and could then choose to stay on or go into private practice. I am sure she was convinced that anybody reaching that stage would not change any more. She was very happy and satisfied as a RAD doctor and couldn't imagine or understand people with a different view.

I was quite firm in my refusal and when she realized that she could not persuade me, she changed back again into the cold unfriendly woman I had met first. She told me quite frankly that she could not recommend my application to the board because, being a foreigner, she could not permit me to take away the place from a German student. It would have been different if I had accepted her offer, because then I would have done something to help the German *Reich*.

I was dismissed again with *"Heil Hitler"*. This time Dr Grimonie did not get up, but carried on writing. She didn't even look at me when I got up and walked to the door. I said:

'Good day,' because I couldn't very well say *'Auf Wiedersehen'*, (goodbye) not wanting to see her again, and closed the door quietly.

My heart was beating loudly, I was furious, but also worried. This was the first interview. I would probably be alright with the professor of chemistry because Mrs Jacoby was working there, but what about the others? I needed strong support to overcome Dr Grimonie's opposition.

When I got home I told my mother how I had got on. She was very surprised about the offer of a grant, and couldn't understand this as I was not German.

'It is probably a new idea, and they are desperate to recruit students. It doesn't look as if it is a popular idea with the girls, if she even has to ask you. But you are right about being worried. Dr Grimonie will not have a good word to say about you. I will ring Mrs Jacoby and talk to her. She might have some suggestions.'

My mother was a long time on the phone. When she came back, she was smiling.

'I had quite a talk with my friend. These doctors and professors stick together and if we can get some to speak for you this will certainly help. This time it is not what you know, but who you know. We had an idea. You will have to go and see Dr Voss and tell him what happened.'

'But he is not on the committee.'

'That doesn't matter. Show him the list of the people who are on the board. He probably knows some. Dr Voss knows you and has always encouraged you in the idea of becoming a doctor. He might do something for you. Just go and see him. Don't make an appointment because that will take too long. You ought to talk to him before you see any of the other interviewers.'

My mother was probably right. Dr Voss had cured my back after an accident at school and after that I had visited his surgery several times with sprained ankles and wrists, even two broken fingers, and sometimes because of backache. All this happened through my sport. I usually finished up in his exercise room, working on the special apparatus, doing exercises on the floor and getting massage and heat treatment. I often helped the physiotherapists to pull the apparatus out and to push them back, demonstrating the exercises, and helping with plaster casts. The physiotherapists knew me well and, being understaffed, were glad when I helped. Dr Voss always said that he appreciated my staying on after my treatment. I had learnt how to do massage and sometimes was even allowed to do it on the patients if they permitted it.

I was still working on the tram, but my superiors knew that I had to go for interviews and, having done overtime before, to cover the extra free time needed, I rang up and apologized for not being able to attend the next day. I had to see Dr Voss in the morning, and some interviews in the afternoon.

Dr Voss was completely booked up, according to his secretary, after I told her that it was urgent that I saw him.

'Does it hurt?' she said, thinking I had had an accident.

'No', I replied, 'but I have to talk to him.'

'You will just have to wait and I will see what I can do,' was her reply. So I waited with the others in the waiting room. Patients went in and out, more patients came and went in and out, and I was still there.

Surely the secretary had told him I was waiting, I thought.

After three hours, Dr Voss came out and looked at me. He touched my shoulder and said:

'Come in, you have waited long enough. It must be important for you to sit still for so long,' and he laughed with a loud hearty sound.

Once in his room, I didn't know how to start. I wasn't shy and I could usually cope with even difficult situations, but this time it meant to ask for help and that was something I didn't really like to do.

'Come on, come on,' he said, still smiling, 'out with it, you must have had a good reason to come and see me. I won't bite you. I haven't much time either, I am a busy man.'

I blurted out: 'I need your help,' and then I took a deep breath.

He stopped smiling and looked at me kindly, searchingly.

'Are you in trouble? You can tell me if you are, we are friends, you and I, you know that, otherwise you wouldn't have come.'

I just told him everything, about the selection of the medical students, the committee, and the interview with *Frau* Dr Grimonie. When I had finished and looked at him, he roared with laughter. His big body was shaking and his big hands were smacking his knees.

'You know, I thought you had done something terrible, and had to go to prison, or run away from home because of a soldier friend. Come and sit here,' he pointed to a chair next to him, 'and give me the names of the people on the committee.'

He took the list and looked at it. I had also written next to the names the appointment times.

'You are not giving me much time,' he said. 'You have some appointments this afternoon.'

'I didn't see *Frau* Dr Grimonie until yesterday afternoon and I waited all the morning in your surgery.'

He didn't look up, but made some notes on his diary. After that, he copied the names from my list and the appointment times.

'Alright, that's that. You had better go for your interviews and don't worry. I think you would make an excellent doctor.'

He took my hand between his two big soft hands, holding it tight.

'I will tell you a secret. I am not very fond of *Frau* Dr Grimonie either. I met her at a conference.'

He opened the door, and pushed me into the waiting room.

'Thank you,' I said.

He was a kind man, and a good friend.

I can't remember how many interviews I had, and also not very much about them. Mrs Jacoby's professor was very kind. He asked me why I wanted to study medicine, where I lived, and whether I had brothers and sisters. The interview was quite short, and I felt that Mrs Jacoby had prepared him for my visit, and it was only a formality.

One of the other professors mentioned Dr Voss, saying what a brilliant man he was. I also guessed from the conversation with him that Dr Voss must have told him how keen I was, and that I had already helped for a time in the exercise room of the orthopaedic surgery.

When all the interviews were over, I returned to my tram duty and, after a week, I received a letter telling me that I had passed the scrutiny of the board and could register at the university.

My first day as a student will always stay in my memory. It was the beginning of October and my first lesson was in the Anatomy. By 12 o'clock I had to be back in the centre of the town for the next lecture, and some more lectures after that. It was a beautiful day and when I had finished I didn't want to go home straight away, but decided to sit amongst the flowers in the university garden. I was happy. I had a letter from Wolfgang, wishing me good luck with my studies and envying me that I had the freedom to do them. He was not happy in the army. He missed his animals, and he said he missed me. I promised myself to write to him the same evening. I sat for an hour in the garden, then cycled home, still full of happiness. I looked for Christel straight away, because I always told her everything, and found her doing her homework. I started to tell her, but she interrupted me:

'Have you seen Mama? She has got some post for you.'

'Post!' I said, 'how nice!'

I walked away from her, but she caught my arm and looked at me with loving eyes:

'I think it is bad news, so be prepared.'

I ran to find my mother. She looked at me sadly; with tears in her eyes, she handed me the two letters. One was addressed to Hans-Ulrich, whom Wolfgang had asked to accompany Astra to his party, and the other letter was addressed to Gerhard Flach. Both letters had stamped across them:

*Gefallen für Grossdeutschland.*

'No, no, no!' I screamed, 'not both of them!'

I ran upstairs and threw myself on my bed and cried.

Two more letters had to be put into my box. I had lost five friends now: Herbert, Ernst, Theo, Hans-Ulrich and Gerhard.

Was there a God? If so - Please, dear God, protect Wolfgang and Helma and all the other young boys from the Grammar School. They have only just left school, they are not men yet. -

I could not write to Wolfgang that evening, I was too upset. He needed a cheerful letter, so I left the reply for a few days.

Although we had to work hard at university, there was a lot of freedom. It was left to us to attend the lectures and nobody checked whether we were absent or not. There were also smaller study groups in natural science and zoology, where we studied plants and had to help with experiments on small animals, including a rota to look after them. For these studies we had a small book, and our lecturer had to mark in our attendance. At the end of the term it would be checked; 80% attendance was a must, otherwise one was not permitted to start the next term.

After each study year, consisting of three terms, there was an examination. One took the *Vor-Physikum* after one year, and the *Physikum* after two years. The first two years were devoted to theory. There was no hospital work; at least that should have been the rule but, because of the war, everybody was encouraged to do some time in hospitals or laboratories, because of the shortage of staff there.

I started in October. The weather was still warm. Christa, my new friend, had an uncle in Nidden who owned an hotel. She said it was completely empty because the season was finished and, in any case, people were much too busy to go on holiday. She had the offer of a free double room and suggested we have a weekend there; we would only have to pay for the food. We had two lovely weekends in Nidden, and each time it was still warm enough to lie in the sun and wander over the dunes from the Frische Haff to the Baltic.

# CHAPTER NINE

## War Progress in 1943/44 - At Home

After four years of war, by December 1943 we still had not seen or felt very much of it in Königsberg. Food was rationed, so was gas, electricity, and coal, but people had enough of everything and, if not, they tried to get some extras quietly on the black market. Trams and trains were still running, although not so frequently as before the war and train tickets were only allowed for short distances, unless one was in uniform or had a permit. There was a shortage of soap and toilet paper, so one had to use water only and cut up newspapers into small squares. Schools were put together to save heating two buildings. One school occupied the building in the morning, and the other in the afternoon. The town was full of people as we had a number of evacuees from the bombed cities in the west, a great many foreign workers, and officers and soldiers from the forces.

Christmas 1943 was very peaceful for us and we were all together in our home. We had a wonderful Christmas Eve, with plenty of presents and good food for everybody. Sascha joined us, as we all felt she could not really be left alone in the kitchen on this day. She had knitted a scarf for me, crocheted some oven cloths for my mother, and gave some other little presents for the rest of the family. She said I needed the scarf, because it was pretty cold in the winter, and I was working again on the trams. I had to work on Christmas Day, so we had an evening meal. My father had organised a goose, and my mother prepared my favourite red cabbage. We even had a Christmas tree and candles. The candles were not new. These were difficult to get, but my mother had always kept a number of candle pieces and so this Christmas we used them up. My father played the piano, with his usual mistakes, I even played a few carols, and Sascha tried to teach us a Russian carol, but we had to give up, because we were afraid somebody might hear us from outside.

As I had worked on Christmas Day, I had New Year off. We all stayed up to see in 1944. My father supervised the usual *Bleigiessen*, and we had his favourite champagne. My parents were concerned about the way the war was going. My mother felt it might be a good idea to get some money into Switzerland, but my father was too much of an optimist to believe that the Russians could ever get as far as Germany.

'All my business is here, I wouldn't want to go back to Switzerland,' he said. 'I would only have to start again there. The war will be finished soon, you wait and see. We are not suffering, we have enough to eat, enough coal to keep ourselves warm, the children have good schools and, really, it is not a good idea to uproot everybody. I have not got a lot of spare cash, having rebuilt part of the dairy just before the war.'

My mother was an organiser and a worrier, whilst my father could always see the bright side and, if possible, push worries away. Things would turn out alright in the end. I think my mother only wanted him to transfer a little money to Switzerland as a security, a nest egg in case it was needed. My father didn't listen. Later, when he realized that this would be a good idea, it was too late to do anything.

I had eight cold weeks on the trams and did not enjoy this time as much as in the summer. Several times I had to stay the night in the town when I couldn't get a tram back home. Accommodation was supplied in a school building in bunks; it was clean and not too uncomfortable. Sascha met me a few times in town in order to bring me something to eat and a hot drink. She became quite unafraid of travelling and walking around the town, with her "Ost" badge hidden under the fur collar of her coat.

My mother's birthday was on January 9th and Sascha presented her with a beautiful pot plant. She told us that she had found out that at the local nursery they were selling a few plants early in the morning every day. She had decided to go really early and wait until they opened the doors. She queued up from 6 o'clock in the morning, in the bitter cold weather, until they opened at 8 o'clock so that she could be the first customer. My mother was quite touched by her loyalty and kindness.

It was a very cold winter again and the newsreels showed the soldiers in Russia on duty outside their bunkers, all dressed up like mummies, with the ice hanging on their eyebrows, beards, and the openings in their balaclavas. Duty was only for one hour as nobody could stand the cold any longer. Everybody knitted scarves, gloves, socks and balaclavas and took them to the different collecting points, together with a letter to an unknown soldier. The temperature in Königsberg that winter was 25

134

degrees below zero for weeks, and they talked about 30 - 40 below zero in Russia. It seemed impossible that people could cope in such cold weather.

Back at university, I couldn't use my bike in the winter, because of the frost and snow. I had to go by tram, or walk. We were now asked to go and help in the military hospitals if we had any free time. More and more nursing staff were transferred to the front lines, and more wounded were brought back, a lot of them now with frostbite. I worked most Saturdays and Sundays in the hospital. Friday afternoon was my catching up day, when I got my lecture notes sorted out. In the evening, I wrote my letters.

Wolfgang still wrote regularly. He was in Russia, not quite at the front, and hoped to come back in April for a course at an artillery school, when he thought it would also be possible to come to Königsberg for a day or two to see me. He said it was very cold, but did not say where he was, what he was doing, or how he kept warm.

Heinz wrote occasionally and of course expected a reply. He was in a tank division in Russia, and wrote that everything was at a standstill because the fuel was frozen and the tanks had to be dug out every few days from the snow. He said it was bitterly cold; although they had a fire going in their bunker, he still had gloves on to write to me.

'I haven't taken off my clothes for weeks, and won't do it either until it gets warmer,' he wrote.

I sent both of them some cakes and sweets, and a cheerful letter.

Our work in the military hospital was more like that of cleaners and helpers. We were first year medical students and our medical knowledge was therefore almost non-existent. We were allowed to help with the making of beds, cleaning floors, washbasins, lockers, and bathrooms, carrying trays with food, and sterilizing the bottles and bed pans. There was strict discipline and we were taught how to obey. We learnt what the war was like in Russia, because soldiers talked and we saw their wounds. I saw that fingers and toes were not always shot off, but had fallen off in the frost. There was the soldier without ears, who had rubbed them off, not realizing that they were frozen. There were soldiers without toes, without some of their fingers, either broken off in the frost, or amputated because of gangrene.

The operating theatre was in use day and night and different professors performed their special operations. The military hospitals in Königsberg were transit hospitals. The doctors did amputations, removals of bullets or shrapnel if they were in dangerous positions, pinned bones and splinted arms or legs. Then after a short rest the wounded were transported to the

*Reich* for further treatment and recovery in hospitals and nursing homes. Nobody stayed long, because the beds were needed.

I was in my second term of medicine and therefore should not have progressed for another three months from the duties of floor and locker washing. Suddenly I was promoted. I was taught how to make beds with a proper corner at the foot of the bed, and it was my holy duty to tidy each bed before the big man, the *Herr* (Mr) Professor, made his daily visit.

My work in the hospital made me realize how naive I had been about the war up till now. I discovered more about fighting and enduring, and how people coped with them.


At the beginning of March 1944 I had a great surprise. Helma, my old playmate and friend, came home on leave. He never wrote or told me that he was coming, but just came to our house and asked for me.

I stared at him standing there in his smartly pressed sailor's uniform, with the square collar hanging down the back of his neck. He was pressing his sailor's cap with both hands against his chest. His red hair was cropped short and my familiar young friend seemed to have grown older. His face was flushed under chapped skin and his light blue eyes looked pleadingly at me, wondering what welcome he would get. He moved his lips, but no words came, and then he took a deep breath, got very pale, and the next moment the blood rushed back into his face.

I don't know how long we stood there staring at one another. I was so pleased to see him alive. He had changed, and I was not quite sure how to welcome him. Then I just threw my arms around his neck and kissed him, and pulled him indoors.

'Oh Helma, Helma, why didn't you tell me you were coming home. Come in, come in, I am so pleased to see you.'

He held on to me, not saying anything, just hugging me and pressing me to his chest with his strong arms, until I felt I couldn't breathe any more. I twisted myself away, and called my mother and my sister so that they, too, could welcome him.

Everybody was so pleased to see him. My mother soon produced cake and coffee and we all sat down, wanting to hear what had happened to him. He told us that he was on a destroyer and had just come back from the Norwegian and Barents Sea. It was the ship's duty to prevent British and American ships from reaching Murmansk, so that they could not bring supplies of armaments to the Russians. He didn't tell us where his ship was docked for repairs and refit, and didn't talk much about his experiences either. We had to get the map out to see where he had been. My brother looked at Helma with big eyes:

'You passed the Artic Circle! What was it like?'

Helma just stared at him. 'Freezing cold,' was his short reply.

There was silence in the room. Helma obviously didn't want to elaborate. He was glad to be home, sitting in a warm room, and interested in what we all had been up to since he left, a year ago.

He stayed at home for a week, and we met several times. I was never completely relaxed with him, remembering always what he had said before to me, that I was his girl and that he would never love anybody else. He had changed a great deal. He was quiet, not wanting to talk much. I always felt he was holding himself back, trying to keep himself under control. He was never very demonstrative, just gave me a quick kiss when we met or said goodbye, until the last evening.

We had been to the pictures in the afternoon and, although it was cold, with a little snow still on the roads, we decided to walk back home. We walked arm in arm, taking the longer way round through the park, the Luisenwahl. It was already dark, but the moon was shining and it would remain a clear night.

'Let's sit on the bench,' said Helma, pointing to one leading off the main path.

'But it is too cold,' I said.

'I am used to it,' he replied, 'and it is my last evening.'

We both had thick coats on. Maybe, it wouldn't be too bad, just for a little while. I could see Helma wanted to prolong our being together. He was not leaving until the following afternoon and, although I had skipped some lectures at the university because of him, I could not get time off the next day as I was on hospital duty.

'Alright, just for a little while.'

We sat close together, trying to keep warm. He took my hand between his two trembling ones, and said:

'I don't find it easy to talk any more because if I talk I remember things. Remembering makes me uneasy and sometimes I am frightened. But I have to talk to you, because I want you to know how I feel, and what you mean to me. If it wasn't for you, I wouldn't be alive today. It is hell out there in the Norwegian sea in the winter. I am not a rating any more, I have moved up, but I am not an officer yet, only a cadet, and the cadets have to do the rough work on the ship. Everything is frozen on deck, but we have to check the wires and ropes and that the lifeboats are in good condition. There is always deck duty, and I hate it. Look at my hands.'

Whilst saying this, he pulled off his gloves and showed me his hands. He could not straighten his fingers. The skin was rough, bumpy, and discoloured, and his hands trembled.

'My feet and legs are the same.'

I had wondered why he always put his hands into his pockets, or between his knees, when he was sitting.

'Put on your gloves, Helma, it is cold,' I whispered and after he had done that I held his hands between mine.

'You would die straight away if you fell overboard,' he continued. 'Nobody would even try and rescue you, because they would only fish out a body. I often thought I could finish my life quickly that way. It can look like an accident. We have lost several people like that. But every time I think about it, I see your smiling face, and you see that's why I say, if it wasn't for you, I wouldn't be alive today. I also know that I won't come back from this war. Once a ship is fatally hit, there are no survivors. I have seen it. It is terrible. There is no point in saving anybody; the water is too cold. You are not tied to me, but free to choose whom you love, and I hope you will be happy. I only ask you not to tell me if you have fallen in love with somebody else.'

His long speech quite shocked me. He was very serious about what he was saying. He was only nineteen years old, but had already resigned himself to the thought that his life would soon be finished.

I put my arm around his neck and cradled his head. Stroking his face, I tried to comfort him, because suddenly he cried - very quietly, with the tears just rolling down his face.

'I love you,' he whispered.

I felt shattered, not knowing what to do with him. Helma, my tough playmate, the boy who had been such a proud Nazi in the Hitler Youth, my young friend who had had the courage to walk through nettles to get a kiss from me, was a broken person at this moment.

'I am sorry,' he said suddenly, and wiped the tears away. 'Forget what I said, I don't have moments like this very often. It must be because of our last evening together. Farewells make me sentimental.'

He pulled me off the bench.

'Let's go, before we are frozen to the seat.'

We walked silently home, arm in arm, and I knew that Helma felt better for his outburst. In the back garden, we hugged one another for the last time, and kissed, and promised to think of one another often.

I did not cry until I got indoors and had walked quietly upstairs into my bedroom. I had a foreboding that Helma was right in what he had said.

Three months later, Helma's mother came to see me. She had received a letter from the War Ministry, telling her that Helma's destroyer had been sunk with no survivors. She was very calm and collected, and said:

'He knew he wouldn't come back, he told me so. He asked me to tell you the news when we received it. I am glad you were such happy children together.'

I never had a letter from Helma, only his picture. So I opened my box and added this to the letters and pictures of the others who had given their lives for "*Grossdeutschland*". Helma belonged to my childhood and although that had passed, I felt I had buried it forever at that moment.

Wolfgang wrote in April to say he would come back for a training course at an artillery school and hoped to have two days leave. Could I please make sure I got the time free for that, as he wanted to spend both days with me. As soon as I had definite dates, I organised my time. I was even able to have the Sunday off from the hospital and on Monday I would just skip the lectures.

I nearly missed Wolfgang at the station. I didn't recognize him in his new lieutenants' uniform. He arrived on Sunday morning and had to leave again on Monday, late afternoon.

He, too, had changed. He had been in Russia, but had not seen much fighting as he was not at the front. He did not tell me his duties. Soldiers and officers were not allowed to talk - the enemy might listen! Wolfgang had matured. He was surer of himself, having already been put in charge of people, although he was only just twenty years old.

'I want to forget the war,' he said, 'and have two lovely days with you. My mother is on the farm with my sister, so I have the flat all to myself and you can stay there too. Tomorrow I have to travel to the estate to see my family, and on Wednesday, I have to report for duty again. I will probably have to go back to Russia. Still, it is not so bad in the summer, I hope.'

He deliberately tried to be cheerful and quickly kissed me on my mouth.

'I don't think I will stay the night with you,' I said, 'I am not that type of girl.'

He looked at me searchingly. 'I didn't mean it like that. You can lock your bedroom door. I only thought that if you don't have to go home we can already be together for breakfast and there is no waste of time travelling to and from your home. You know it always takes over an hour to get to you and back, sometimes longer if the trams don't run properly.'

'I will have to phone my mother,' I said.

'She will say no, mothers always do.'

We went to the flat to deposit his suitcase and I phoned my mother. To my surprise, she didn't say no. On the contrary, she thought it a good idea as Wolfgang had so little time in Königsberg.

It was a beautiful Spring day and we decided to go to the Zoo, which was very close to the flat. We had lots of fun watching the animals, even going on to the children's playground and, as nobody was there, having a go on the swings.

Wolfgang's mother had left some food behind, so I made some supper. I was always very good at opening tins! When it was time to go to bed, Wolfgang produced a nightgown from his mother's wardrobe and a towel and said I could sleep in his sister's room.

'You don't have to lock your room,' he said. 'You and I are getting married when the war is finished and a girl is supposed to be a virgin until her wedding day.'

'You are very sure of yourself, and of me, aren't you? I have never said I will marry you. You know I want to finish my studies, and have a profession.'

'All girls say that, you just wait and see. I won't give up asking you to marry me, but I now realize that it is better to wait until after the war. We are still very young. If anything happens to me, I wouldn't want you to be such a young widow either.'

He kissed me good night and went into the bathroom.

Wolfgang was kind, considerate, loving, full of plans and ideas for the future, still a child and, then again, a man. He had no doubts, but knew what he wanted to do. He was convinced Germany would win the war. His roots were on his family estate, for which he was fighting at the moment. It was the place where he would live and work and start another generation. He had not seen the cruelties of the war yet, he had not suffered much, and Goebbels' and Hitler's propaganda had been successful with him, like with so many other young people of our generation.

Helma, in comparison to Wolfgang, was completely different. Here were two young men, nearly the same age (only six months difference), who had gone to similar schools, had been in the Hitler Youth, had been brought up under the same propaganda but, because of their experiences, finished up with different views. Wolfgang, probably through the help of his influential father, had not seen any fighting yet. He had been kept in the rearguard and been sent to different training schools and courses, whilst Helma was thrown in at the deep end straight away, experiencing and seeing the cruelty of war at sea. One had become a pessimist, a defeatist, and the other one an optimist, looking forward to a bright future.

Helma got killed, and Wolfgang had to experience what it was like to fight in the Russian war in the winter and, in the end, he too lost his home, his belongings, and his land.

Neither of us knew what the future would bring when we went to sleep in our different rooms that night. The next morning was dull and it soon started to rain. So we never went out, but found some records and wound up the gramophone and listened to *Schlager Musik* (pop music). Wolfgang also had some dance records. We rolled up the carpet and danced, and reminisced about our dancing classes and how we had met. We remembered the plays we had seen, the operas we had attended, even the pictures we had been to. After dinner, we just sat together quietly and talked; we both felt at peace, getting strength from one another.

Wolfgang didn't want me to come to the station because, being a gentleman, he wanted to see me safely home first, but I insisted.

'All girls take their soldier boyfriends to the train,' I said.

So, in the end, he agreed, and even liked and appreciated it.

The platform was packed with people, and we had to push through to the front, where the first class was. All officers went first class. Wolfgang got a window seat and we talked through the open window for a few minutes until the train went off. He smiled and waved and I waved back, feeling sad because of the parting.

He phoned me the next evening to say goodbye once more, and made me promise to write often.

It was a happy and peaceful parting for both of us. I did not know it then, that I would never see Wolfgang again.

A few days later another returned letter arrived. Wolfgang's school friend, Kurt Wöhler, who partnered my friend Irmgard at our last party, got killed in Normandy. It was another sad piece of news in my hand: *Gefallen für Grossdeutschland.* I had known Kurt more as a pen-friend but, at one time, I had been quite attracted to him, because of his dark good looks and charm. So it was with great sadness that I opened my box, and put in his last letter.

On June 4th 1944, the Allied troops entered Rome. The Germans were retreating, but their armies were not destroyed. In late July, the Allies invaded the South of France. A lot of propaganda was made about the rescue of Mussolini, who had been imprisoned by the Italian government. He was rescued in a daring coup by German airborne troops and brought back behind German lines. Mussolini set up a shadow Fascist government and managed to control a small portion of German held territory.

Living in Königsberg, we were, of course, much more interested in the war in the east. Hearing about the Allied landings in Normandy and seeing the newsreels didn't get us too worried; we were usually told that any retreat of German troops was only happening to consolidate the forces, ready for the next victorious push forward and, in those days, we still believed it. But what did worry us were the bomb attacks on the different towns, because there was always the thought, when would our town, our Königsberg, be the next target.

My mother's friend, *Frau* Jacoby, had a married sister living in Hamburg and, through her, we heard about the terrible destruction of the town. Her sister had lost everything, her house, her home, and her two children. Her husband was in the army and, being alone now, and having had such a shattering experience, she came to live with *Frau* Jacoby.

Total war had, by now come to Germany. First the killing of soldiers, secondly the killing of those who produced weapons for the soldiers, and thirdly the destruction of the efficiency of the German war machine, even if it was necessary to kill women and children.


In January 1944, the Baltic front exploded. Russian armies, backed by vast quantities of artillery, poured across the ice of the frozen Gulf of Finland in order to get back the city of Leningrad. At the same time, the Ukrainian and Russian armies attacked in the south and trapped the Germans there. In April, the Russians started their offensive in the Crimea and, by May, they were attacking the Germans along the Sevastopol fortifications, supported by 300 guns for every mile of front. The German defence crumbled against such artillery weight.

The Russians, with their different successions of attacks, made a decisive contribution to the western war. They destroyed the best of the German army, killing some 2 million men, before the first Allied soldier stepped ashore on the Normandy beaches on June 6th 1944.

The Russian summer offensive started at the end of June. Hitler did not permit retreat. He did not trust his Generals any more, and changed them, like figures on a chess board. The Russians succeeded in getting over the Njemen, and got as far as the Prussian border. Hitler gave a new order:

Every German soldier fights where he stands. He does not even step back 1m *freiwillig* (out of his own free will)!

In May and June, we had quite a number of reconnaissance flights, which meant that the sirens would go and we all had to run into the cellar or air-raid shelter. We had been prepared for air-raids for a long time. Because I had taken a course in air-raid drill, I had to join a student group as *Laienhelferin* (lay helper). If there was a bomb attack on the town, I had to report at the *Sammelplatz Schauspielhaus* (assembly point theatre) as soon as the siren gave the all clear. I had an identity card, which gave me permission to get through the streets, and ordered everybody to give me leave of absence, so that I could report at the assembly point. I still possess the *Ausweis* (identity card) for it.

My parents were also concerned about possible bombing and talked things over. They decided it was time to do something about the furniture and the more valuable items in our home. My father organized a room in a small town called Lötzen, and another room in Guttstadt. My mother and I started to pack up things in the home, like glasses and carpets. At

**Ausweis**

Der/Die    Helga    Z i r k e l  11. 2. 24  Melgathacke. 1
             (Vorname)    (Zuname)    (geb.)    (wohnh.)
ist Angehöriger der Studentenschaft Königsberg (Pr) und als
*Laienhelferin* eingestellt. Er/Sie hat
             (Aufgabe)
Anweisung, sich bei Vorentwarnung nach Bombenangriffen sofort am Sammelplatz der Studentenschaft (Schauspielhaus) zu melden. Alle Polizeidienststellen und Führer im Luftschutz werden aufgefordert, ihn/sie nach Luftangriffen, nach Beendigung der Schadensbekämpfung oder nach Entwarnung sofort zu beurlauben. Dieser Ausweis ist nur gültig in Verbindung mit einem amtlichen Personalausweis der Behörde oder Dienststelle.
(Nichtzutreffendes streichen)    11. April 1944
*Königsberg Pr.*        Gaustudentenführung Ostpreußen
             (Datum)
                                        (Unterschrift)
Bestätigt:                    Der Polizeipräsident
*Königsberg Pr.*        als örtlicher Luftschutzleiter
11. April 1944 (Datum)
                                        (Unterschrift)

*Air-raid Helper's Indentity Card*

first, my father took the things in the car in boxes, but eventually we were able to hire a lorry and bring the better furniture to these two places. We only kept the beds and some necessary items, like a cheap table and chairs.

People gradually left the town, and only the ones who were working stayed behind. My mother, too, moved eventually, and joined her brother, Erich, and mother in Tuchel, near Konitz, taking all the silver and other valuables with her. She became an evacuee.

Several things happened before my mother moved to Tuchel. Firstly, my brother, who was then sixteen years old, was evacuated with his school into the country, and Christel had to finish school because she was nearly eighteen years old. Our *Gauleiter*, Erich Koch, had declared Total War, which meant that all women under fifty years of age had to go to work, unless they had children below school age. All young people over seventeen years of age had to leave school, the boys going into the army and the girls doing war work. They had to replace the able bodied men who were still working in factories, so that they could fight in the forces.

Although Christel was Swiss, her school class being closed now, she was forced to do some war work, otherwise she would not get any food rations. All the girls were promised that they would get their matriculation without any examinations. Some of Christel's companions went into factories, some as helpers into the *Luftwaffe*, and some on to the trams.

My mother was very concerned about Christel. She was not strong enough to work in a factory and, in any case, my mother didn't like that idea at all. She knew from me what the work was like on the trams. She then had the idea that my sister ought to join the Red Cross but, if possible, not right at the bottom, or in a hospital, but in an office. She started to make enquiries, got names of important people, and tried desperately to find somebody who could help her, or have some connection. One day she said to my father:

'It is a pity you studied in Bamberg, otherwise you would have had some old *Studienfreunde* (student friends) in Königsberg and, maybe, could get help from them.'

'I met a friend once,' said my father, 'it must have been before the war. He had become a doctor, Dr Rudolf E. I don't know what he is doing now, but I could find out.'

It turned out that Dr E. was in charge of the Red Cross and all the nursing staff in Königsberg and district. He had a big office in town, where he occasionally turned up for meetings. Mostly he travelled

144

between the different military hospitals, according to his secretary. My father didn't like the idea of going to see him and asking him for a favour.

'You ought to go yourself,' he said to my mother and laughed. 'Rudolf was always very keen on the girls. You will probably have more luck than I. You are a very attractive woman. He is a married man with children and he will probably understand a mother's worry and concern.'

My mother phoned Dr E.'s secretary several times, pointing out that my father was an old *Studienfreund*. Eventually she got an appointment. At the last minute she had second thoughts and decided to take me along also. I was primed as to what to say and what to do.

'I am older now,' my mother said, 'but you are a young and pretty girl. He might take to you. It would be marvellous if we could get a connection with him. He is also a big Nazi, and seems to have influence in a number of places.'

'Don't you think you should take Christel with you?' I said. 'She is the one who is looking for a job, not me.'

'No,' said my mother. 'Christel is much too shy, she might spoil our chances. We are only going to enquire, in the first place.'

We both dressed up smartly and then went off for the appointment. My mother looked very elegant in her brown costume, with a cream coloured bow-tied blouse, and her gold chain around her neck, which was attached to her lorgnette. I, too, had a tailor-made costume on, the only one I possessed, because of the shortage of clothing coupons.

We didn't have to wait long in the office before we were called in. Dr E. was charming. He kissed my mother's hand, he clicked his heels (he was in brown Nazi uniform), and he shook my hand, smiling warmly. He was absolutely thrilled that a wife of his old *Studienfreund* had come to see him. Actually, I don't think he remembered my father at first, because he assumed that he was in the army, and was therefore surprised to hear that he was in Tilsit. When my mother mentioned that we were Swiss, he knew my father suddenly, because he only had one Swiss friend at university. Of course, he would be pleased to help us. Friends had to stick together in these difficult times. He kept on smiling at me, encouraging me to say a few words also. He was surprised to hear that I was studying medicine. Why did I suddenly want a position in the Red Cross?

'Helga doesn't want to join the Red Cross, I am talking about her younger sister, who now has to leave school,' said my mother.

For a moment I thought my mother had misled Dr E. on purpose, and I could see he thought the same when he looked at us. I was a tall, strong girl, very suitable for hospital work, but if little, shy, fair haired Christel had been here, Dr E. would not have promised help so quickly, I was sure of that.

'Helga and I have another appointment later on, and that's why she has accompanied me,' added my mother.

There was silence for a little while, whilst Dr E. seemed to sort something out in his mind. He promised my mother to look through the hospital vacancies, perhaps get an interview with one of the sisters in the hospital for Christel.

'Maybe Helga could phone you in a few days,' my mother said, 'because I will be going to Tilsit with my husband for a week.'

This was a very surprising statement. She never went to Tilsit with my father. But I had been told not to contradict her, so she must have had a reason for saying this.

Dr E. smiled again. Looking at me he said: 'Yes, that is alright. Just tell my secretary that you want to talk to me, and she will put you through if I am in the office, or tell you when I can be reached. I travel rather a lot.'

Dr E. kissed my mother's hand, murmured, *'Gnädige Frau'*, clicked his heels, shook my hand warmly, and we were ushered outside with the assurance:

'I will be in touch.'

'Well, that's it,' said my mother, once we got into the street. 'It is up to you now. He certainly has taken to you. Your father was right, he likes young girls. I am glad I didn't take Christel, she would never have passed his inspection. Now he only has to put in a word or two in the right direction, and you have to remind him. He won't forget you, but he wouldn't want to see me again. I told the little lie about Tilsit so that you will be the one who follows up this meeting. So let's wait and see.'

Nothing happened for a week and my mother got me to phone him. Sure enough, his secretary put me through to him. He was very apologetic, he had been rather busy, but he had started the ball rolling, and could I phone again the next day. Well of course I could, and did. This time he said he had made an appointment for Christel on the next day at the hospital, but would like her to have a letter of recommendation and, as time was short, maybe I could pick it up this evening from his home? He gave me his address, and stated the time to come.

My mother looked astonished when I told her and warned me to be careful in case he was alone. She reminded me of all the talks we had had. I always remember her warning:

'Kissing and cuddling is alright, but don't let him put his hand under your skirt. If he tries it, just say you don't think your father would like that.'

I was absolutely shocked by my mother; she had never been so outspoken before. Dr E. looked like a man who had always enjoyed all the pleasures of life, and never let an opportunity pass to seize what he wanted.

Dr E. was alone at home. His family was evacuated into the country. He asked me to come in and offered me a brandy, which I refused, saying that I didn't drink alcohol. He took me into his kitchen, and said that in that case we could have a cup of coffee. There was no shortage in this house. He had tea, coffee, sugar, biscuits and chocolates, all things short of supply everywhere. Even his cocktail cabinet was full of bottles. I saw this when he got himself a brandy after our coffee. He wanted to know about my studies, my schooling, my family, anything really to keep the conversation going, so that I wouldn't leave.

He said he was lonely without his family, and it was so nice to have me for company. He suddenly kissed me and stroked my hair, and his hand gradually worked its way down. I got frightened, and remembered what my mother had said.

'What time is it?' I said. 'I must not be late home, because my father is coming tonight.'

The spell was broken. Dr E. coughed, a little embarrassed, and looked at his watch. It wasn't all that late, but I felt that I ought to leave. He gave me the letter, and then fetched me a box of chocolates. He took me to the door, where we said goodbye. I kissed him as if he was my father, pretending the other kissing had never happened.

'You may call me Rudolf when we are alone,' he said softly, 'and, if you want any help in anything, just ring me. I have quite a number of connections and know a lot of people.'

As soon as I got home, my mother wanted to know how I got on. She was pleased to hear about the offer of help.

Christel went for the interview and was accepted as a Red Cross nurse, but had to live in the hospital. She got a uniform and when she came to see us on her day off she told us that Sister was very nice, but the work was hard. She had made friends, and thought that she would be alright. She had met Dr E. on one of his visits, but he had hardly taken any notice of her, which was as well, because she said Sister seemed rather sweet on him! Ah well, he was a charmer with women.


Erich Koch, the *Gauleiter*, called all people "to take up arms" (called *Volksaufgebot in Waffen*). Everybody had to work to save the homeland. The people who were really in command in East Prussia were the *Gauleiters* in Königsberg, Danzig, Posen, Stettin, and Breslau. They were promoted to *Reichsverteidigungskommissare* (defence commissioners). Hitler trusted them more than the generals and the army personnel after the attack on him on July 20th, and the *Gauleiters* used their power to the utmost. Erich Koch was the most powerful. He had moved up from *Gauleiter* of East Prussia, to *Reichskommissar* over the Ukraine, and had large territories under his command, from the Baltic to the Black Sea. He was an egoistical, ambitious man, domineering, with a lust for power, and without scruples. He had to leave the Ukraine when the Russians came, and now was only in command over East Prussia.

The East Prussians' defences were built according to his plans, and he refused to co-operate with the army. He also refused to make plans for a possible evacuation of the civilian population, because this would mean that it was possible that the Russians could overrun East Prussia. No German should even think that it was possible that East Prussia could fall into Bolshevic hands! East Prussia would stand like a man, and not even an inch would be given to the Russians.

Erich Koch did not trust the army. He relied on his *Volksaufgebot* (summoning of all the country's strength), and gave himself the title *Führer des Ostpreussischen Volkssturm* (leader of the Prussian people's home guard). He refused to put the *Volkssturm* under military command and, as *Reichsverteidigungskommissar*, he confiscated equipment and weapons which were supposed to go to the under-equipped army, fighting the Russians.


Astra was working and living in the Barmherzigkeit hospital, and seemed quite happy in her position in charge of the Diet Kitchen. Hans was in the country with his school, Christel lived in the military hospital, Sascha, the Russian girl, had left; my father came home only every so often, and my mother could now go to Tuchel, if it wasn't for me. I was still at home attending university and working at the hospital at the weekend. My mother was reluctant to leave me alone in the big house. It was my university friend Gitta who changed my mother's mind, and made her leave Königsberg.

Gitta and Krista studied medicine with me. We helped one another whenever we could. At one time, I had been quite friendly with Krista, when we had a few weekends in Nidden in her uncle's hotel but, after that, we only seemed to meet at lectures. All three of us were busy and involved in a number of other activities apart from university. Because I lived on the edge of the town, we didn't have a social life together. Krista then decided to do full time war work as she felt it was necessary and joined the *Luftwaffe* as a helper. She left Königsberg. She wrote one or two letters, to which I replied, and then I did not hear from her any more.

Gitta's life had gradually taken a very sad turn. Her father was an officer in the army, and was killed in the Polish war. She had twin brothers, who joined the *Luftwaffe*. Both were stationed in France, from where they flew to England on the different bombing missions. The news came that one of her brothers had been killed. She and her mother had hardly recovered from the shock, when they were told that the other twin was missing over the Channel. This was too much for Gitta's mother. She had a nervous breakdown, and Gitta had to take her into a sanatorium.

Gitta was now alone, so my mother and I suggested to her that she come to live with me, partly because we felt that she shouldn't be alone, and also because I would have company if my mother went to Tuchel. Gitta's aunt and uncle sorted things out with the sanatorium and helped to pack up things in the flat. I went along too, helping to pack all the small things into boxes, covering furniture, and generally preparing the flat for its future emptiness. Gitta moved to us and, from now on, we went together to our lectures.

The governors of the university decided that because of the war there should not be such long holidays between the terms and, by pushing the dates around, one could easily accommodate four terms of studies into one year, rather than three terms. Even so, we got three weeks holiday at the end of July - beginning of August. Gitta went to stay with her relatives. I closed the house up and decided to travel to Tuchel to stay with my mother. There was just one big difficulty. By now, nobody was allowed to travel by train, unless it was for a military or Party purpose, or very urgent, and one needed a pass to buy a ticket for the train.

Remembering what Dr E. had said, that he would always help me, I phoned him, and was lucky to get through to him. I didn't quite know how to put it to him, so I just said I needed help, but didn't know whether I could say it over the phone. What I really meant was that I wasn't quite sure whether he was alone, or whether somebody could overhear us. He gave me a different number to ring and when I did he answered the phone himself. He sounded quite jolly on the phone. I could hear voices in the background, as if he was having a party, but I don't know where he was. He knew straight away who was speaking and when I explained about needing a pass to travel, he said he would supply one. I could come and fetch it from his house. So we made a date and I went to see him.

I felt very uneasy, having to go to his home again, but I did need this pass. This time he even had some cakes and liqueur chocolates and, of course, I had to have my coffee. He put on some soft dance records, and, by dimmed light, asked me to dance with him. He was charming, and certainly knew how to make compliments. He held me close whilst we were dancing. His breath smelled of brandy and cigars, his eyes were closed, and all I could think of was:

He is a dirty old man who, even now, with the seriousness of war, grabs at all the enjoyment he can get!

It made me cross that I had to put up with this petting, just to get a pass for the train. I thought in a flash of all my friends who already had been killed, who had given their young lives for their fatherland, but surely not for a man like this, who still lived in luxury. I suddenly couldn't face any more and, when the record was finished, I just told him that I was on air-raid duty that evening, and had to return home, and asked him about the pass.

I think he realized that he would never get any further with me. Maybe he remembered that he, too, had a young daughter, because I had asked about his family earlier on. He would not have liked her to associate with an old man. He murmured something and left the room. When he came back, he had a number of papers in his hand. They were all blank train passes, stamped and countersigned by him. He told me that all I had to do was to put down the destination, the date and my name.

'You need one paper for each trip,' he said. 'One part of the pass is for your railway ticket, which you get free, and the other half, which you must keep, is your proof that you have to do this journey on behalf of the Red Cross. You probably want to go several times to Tuchel, so I will give you more than one pass. There are checks on the train, I think they will only glance at your paper but if anybody makes a note of it you had better give me a ring, so that I am prepared for any questions. I doubt whether this will happen, because I have signed them personally and I have never yet had a come-back. Before I got hold of the blank passes, I had already asked my secretary to type you a so-called *Marschbefehl* (marching order). You can use this for your first journey and, after that, you can fill in your own papers.'

With that, he handed me the blank passes and the *Marschbefehl*, and I said: 'I don't mind paying for the ticket.'

'You can't do that, not if you go with these passes. Don't worry, the railway will claim the amount of the fare from the government.'

Again he gave me a box of chocolates to take home, and hoped that I would have a good holiday.

'Get in touch with me if you need anything,' he said. 'It is such a pleasure to have an evening together with you.'

He kissed me goodbye. I was glad to leave, having accomplished what I came for. He had been most generous with the amount of papers he had given me, and also shown me how much he trusted me, so I forgave him for what he had done and, maybe, wanted to do to me. The passes later proved very useful.

Deutsches Rotes Kreuz
Landesstelle I

Königsberg (Pr) den 7.8.1944
Kastanienallee 39

M·a r s c h b e f e h l ·

-9.AUG. 1944

Die DRK-Helferin Helga Z i r k e l geb. am 11.7. 1924 in Ragnit hat den Befehl sich am 9.8.44 bei der DRK-Kreisstelle K o n i t z zwecks DRK-Einsatz zu melden.

Der Führer der DRK-Landesstelle I :

· DRK-Generalhauptführer

**Red Cross Travel Permit**

151

# CHAPTER TEN

## Hermann - Two Long Journeys

To have three weeks holiday was something which I had never expected. I had not made up my mind how long I would stay in Tuchel, as I also had to do some work for my studies and needed the university library for that. It took me all day to reach Konitz, where I had to change trains to the smaller line to Tuchel. We had delay after delay, were once diverted to a different line, and it was late in the evening when I arrived at my changing point, only to be told that the next train to Tuchel would not leave until 6 am.

I was terribly tired, and after eating a sandwich, I sat down against a wall and went to sleep. I regained consciousness gradually. My head was resting on something soft, which was odd, because I had started the night by sitting on my case, with my back resting against the wall.

I opened my eyes quickly and saw a smiling face looking down at me. I realized that my head was resting on the lap of a fellow traveller, and that I had slipped off the suitcase, leaning towards one side. I quickly straightened myself up, and apologized for having inconvenienced my neighbour. He only laughed, and said he had quite enjoyed having my head in his lap. He was an *Oberleutnant* (Captain) in the army, a very German-looking officer, fair, with bright blue eyes, glasses, a clever looking face, and at least thirty years old.

I looked at my watch and, realizing that I had another hour to spare before my train would leave, I decided to tidy myself up and have a little wash. I thanked my neighbour for his kindness, took my case, and went off to the washroom.

The train to Tuchel started from Konitz but, even so, I thought I had better go to my platform early. All the seats were already taken when I walked along the train, looking through every window. The first class compartments were in the front. I reached them, and was just going to turn back, when one of the windows opened, and the officer on whose lap I had slept the night before, looked out and called to me:

'There are plenty of seats free in here!'

'I have not got a first class ticket,' I replied.

'Never mind, leave this to me. I will straighten it out with the conductor. Come and keep me company.'

He helped me into the train, put my suitcase onto the luggage rack, and then introduced himself:

'Dr Hermann Fassbach'.

I told him my name and then sat down opposite him.

'Are you a doctor of medicine?'

'No, I am a doctor of physics and chemistry.'

I discovered that he was stationed in the Tucheler *Heide* (Heath-land), and would leave the train one station after me. The train left at 6 am, and the short journey to Tuchel went by very quickly. Being so busy talking I nearly missed the station, and had to say a quick farewell to my *Oberleutnant*, and jump out of the train.

'I will be in touch', he called out, and waved to me from the open window when the train pulled out of the station.

I told my mother about the trip and Dr Fassbach. She knew about the army being stationed in the *Heide*. She said that they had a number of officers and men coming into Tuchel to look for some amusements, but there were only two cafés there, and one poor restaurant, so they mostly went to Konitz. She thought there was a kind of secret training centre in the *Heide*, and none of the army personnel was giving much information to any of the civilians.

After an early lunch I went to bed to make up for the lost sleep of last night. I had hardly put my head on the pillow, when my mother woke me up and told me that *Oberleutnant* Dr Hermann Fassbach was on the phone, and would like to talk to me.

However did he find out my phone number? That was soon explained. I had said my uncle owned a mill in Tuchel, and there was only one mill. The reason for the phone call was an invitation to go out with him as it was such a lovely day!

To my great surprise, he turned up in an hour, driving an open staff car. Civilians were not allowed to go in military cars and if he wanted to take me out in a car, it would have been wiser to have a closed one, so that I could be hidden in the back seat.

Dr Fassbach assured me that it was perfectly alright to go out in his car, he had special permission. We drove into the heath-land, and enjoyed a walk on a sunny warm afternoon. When we got back my mother produced coffee and cake, which we had in the garden.

For two weeks Hermann "wooed" me, there is no other word for it. He had fallen in love with me when I slept on his lap and he did his utmost to make me fall in love with him also. He was thirteen years older than myself, divorced, and had already lectured in physics and chemistry at the University of Greifswald, where his father was a professor in the same faculties. He divorced his wife because she could not have children. Being sterile was a reason for finishing a marriage. Hermann was very German, and convinced that Nazism was good for the country. He wanted to be married and have plenty of children, as advocated by Hitler.

I liked Hermann. It was fun going out with him in his open car, with all the Tucheler people staring at us. Being older and more experienced, he was different compared to my other young friends. He was not shy like Wolfgang, very sure of himself, always in command of the situation, and made no secret of the fact that he was serious about me, although we had only just met. He brought flowers to my mother, and gave me little presents. When he heard that my father was coming for a few days, he said he wanted to speak with him.

My mother was already marrying me off again. Hermann was a very suitable husband, an academic who would have a job straight away after the war, and such a good-looking, honest and charming man. She could not understand why I hesitated. She was convinced that Hermann, being an intellectual, would permit me to finish my studies, on which I had set my heart, even after marriage.

I had to agree with everything she said, but . . . I was not in love with Hermann. To me he had cold eyes. There was no warmth in them when he looked at me. My mother thought that the reason for this was the glasses he wore. I disagreed with her. I always felt Hermann saw in me a good healthy mother for his future children, young, and strong enough to run a busy household, and the sooner he could get on with this dream of his the better. He had already lost a few years by having been married before.

His job was more important than anything else, which did not suit me, as I wanted to be number one. I soon knew he was working on a secret weapon, the V-2, because he searched the sky from time to time when we were together, and sometimes I, too, could see a silver ball disappear into the sky. Once he stopped in the middle of kissing me, looked at his watch, and timed the silver ball, which had come up in a curve from somewhere in the heather, and then disappeared. I knew that I couldn't live with a man who thought his science so much more important than the feelings of a loved one. My mother called me selfish but then, she didn't have to live with him for the rest of her life.

As soon as my father arrived, Hermann came to see him, and asked him officially for the hand of his daughter Helga. Hermann was a little old-fashioned, very correct, and extremely open with my father. He told him about his divorce, even brought all his papers along to show the reason for it. He said that he hoped my father would give his permission for me to get married as soon as possible.

'Helga is very self-assured,' my father said. 'I have not yet talked to her but, if it is her wish to get married, I will not stand in her way. She can have my blessing. There is no point in trying to influence her one way or another, she usually knows what she wants. I appreciate it that you have talked to me first but, in the end, it is my daughter's decision.'

After that, my father talked to me. I told him what I felt about Hermann, and also that it was my mother to a certain extent who was doing the pushing. My father laughed:

'Don't take any notice of your mother. She is like all mothers with daughters, afraid that you will remain on the shelf. I am more worried about Astra and Christel than about you. The few young men who will return from the war will have plenty of girls to choose from, that is true, but they will pick only the best, and you are one of them. So don't marry somebody now because you are afraid you will miss out later on. Just get on with life and if there is some enjoyment, like now with Hermann, take it. The war is serious enough. Only be careful; you are a girl, only the boys are safe when they are naughty.'

It was the first time ever that my father hinted that he was concerned about me. I also realized that he knew my mother's thoughts, and that my parents must have talked about us children. I suddenly liked my father. I was growing up, and understanding my elders better.

Hermann did not actually ask me to marry him. He only informed me that my father had no objections.

'No objections to what?' I asked him.

'To a possible marriage between us two,' he replied. 'We could get engaged, and then fix a date to suit us both.'

I felt Hermann ought to say it outright: 'Will you marry me?', but he did not say it.

Before I left Tuchel, Hermann suggested that I should meet his family, and I was all for it. There is a saying in German: *'Der Apfel fällt nicht weit vom Stamm!'* (The apple doesn't fall far from the trunk).

Hermann had told me a little about the rocket factory. He was very guarded in what he said, and gave no big secrets away concerning Peenemünde, where he had already been for years. The factory was built completely underground. It escaped serious bombardments until August 1943, when an unexpected raid surprised everybody.

The bombardment destroyed most of the V-2 construction blueprints, which delayed the first scheduled use of the V-2 from early 1944 until August/September 1944. The Peenemünde rocket project was so secret that when an experimental V-2 crashed and almost destroyed a nearby *Luftwaffe* base, news of the catastrophe was covered up. It was then decided to test the rockets elsewhere. Some were tried out in the Tucheler *Heide*, others from a range at Blizna, near Warsaw, in Poland.

After my holiday in Tuchel, I went back to the university again and Gitta joined me in our home. We now seemed to have the sirens going nearly every night and, in the end went to bed in a track suit, so that we didn't have to dress again when we had to get up suddenly. We each had a small suitcase packed, which we stuck into the garden hedge when running to the air-raid shelter.

Although we had a reinforced cellar as an air-raid shelter, we often used the main big one at the corner of Lawsker Allee, which was specially built. The warden there had given us permission because he didn't like the idea of us two girls being alone in the house and cellar.

People who had no cellars came running along the roads towards this centre point as soon as the siren went off, amongst them neighbouring family Lange, with all their children. Dora had put her four children into a big washing basket, the size of a child's bed, and Hilde, my friend, stuck little Fritz into it also. The basket contained a mattress covered with a sheet, a pillow for each child, and a small featherbed as cover. The children were often fast asleep whilst Dora and Hilde carried the basket, one on each side, running along the road. Sister Margot and grandmother followed with the nappies, bottles with milk, a few biscuits, and some cuddly toys.

Eventually we had two terror bombardments by English planes on August 28th and 31st. These destroyed the Königsstrasse, Rossgarten and the centre of the town, including the old castle. All that was left were the suburbs to the north of the river Pregel, Hufen, Ratshof, where we lived, Amalienau, Juditten and, south of the river, the workers suburb of Ponarth. We were extremely lucky that we escaped, the only reason being that we lived so far away from the centre of the town.

Both times Gitta and I went to the big air-raid shelter. Through our student group we were ordered to report at the Theatre after a bombing raid, so that we could be organised into helping groups. The second bombardment was the worst. Gitta and I had the greatest difficulty getting to our appointed collecting post. Everything was burning, and the yellow light of fire lay over the town when we started to walk towards it. We hadn't got very far when the sirens went again, and another wave of bombers arrived. These planes only had to drop their bombs into the darker part of the town to complete the disaster.

We quickly dived into the next house, but there was no cellar, so we both stood trembling against the wall just past the entrance door. The house shook and vibrated, and we wished that we had not left our air-raid shelter so quickly. Luckily we were still quite far away from the centre and, although some windows broke in the house, the rest was undamaged.

We made another effort to get to the Theatre after the all clear. It was hot, there were fires everywhere, houses had collapsed and blocked the road and, after a time, we were lost, not recognizing anything any more because of the destruction. We met people stumbling about, having come from the city, and telling us not to go any further until the flames had died down. So we turned back, and reached our own house in the early morning hours; it was still safe and sound, except for the shoemaker's big shop window, which was broken.

The town burnt all day and the next night but the following day we made another effort to get into the centre. There were no trams running because of the bomb craters, which had destroyed some tramlines. The town was unrecognizable, and it was impossible to get into some parts of it. Gitta and I were frightened when we met the first people who were coming towards us away from the city. Some were badly burnt, carrying children with scorched clothes, looking for nurses, doctors, or a hospital, even if it was a makeshift one. They told us about people being burnt or suffocated in their houses or their cellars, about the fire storm that was so tremendous that it sucked people into the flames. Some finished up naked and dead, the fire storm having pulled off their clothes.

The Theatre was bombed also, but we got there eventually, and were allocated to help with a soup kitchen. The centre of the town was closed to everybody, and the home guard and soldiers had taken over collecting the bodies and searching through the debris.

Gitta and I served soup all day. There was a never-ending queue of people. They were all shocked, shattered, some crying, others silent and in a stupor, in dirty and sometimes scorched clothes. Some took the soup and the bread, and then sat down, never touching the food, just holding it in their hands. I had no time to talk to them.

Gradually we heard more about the disaster, particularly from the soldiers who came back from the centre of the town for a break. They told us about the Kneiphof, the island in the town centre, with the Dom (Cathedral) on it which was completely destroyed. All five bridges spanning the River Pregel which connect the Kneiphof with the town were destroyed and people could not get off the island. Some jumped into the river with burning clothes and drowned, others just died in the flames. The beautiful old Dom was a ruin, and not one house or *Speicher* (warehouse) was left intact. Hundreds of people were burnt or suffocated in the town, because they could not get out. Some of the dead in the cellars were unrecognisable, or could not be brought out. They were destroyed with flamethrowers. The main railway station was full of bodies, and so were the trains which had stopped there. The station cellar, too, was full of dead. The people had suffocated. The bodies floated in water which poured out of burst water pipes into the cellar.

Large diggers made mass graves in the *Stadtfriedhof* (town cemetery) so that people could be buried. It was difficult counting the number of dead, as often only parts of the body were found. In the end, the dead were only counted if a head was found, as often nothing could be recognized. Hundreds of other dead, often only parts of the body, or bodies which, from the heat, had shrunk to children's size, were burnt in the cordoned-off city centre.

Gitta and I helped in the soup kitchen for four days, and were then allowed to go as by now we really needed a wash and a change of clothes. Gitta decided to see what had happened to her mother's flat, and I made my way to the Barmherzigkeit where Astra was working to find out what had happened to her. The hospital was partly destroyed, and I was told that Astra had been allowed to go home for the day to see how things were going there. So, whilst I was looking for her, she was looking for me.

After that, I made my way to Maraunenhof, where Christel was working as a nurse, and found her hospital undamaged but bursting with injured people needing attention. All beds were full, and even the corridors were occupied with makeshift beds. Christel was alright, very tired, like myself, but not able to have time off to come home. I could at least talk to her and reassure her that Astra and I were alright.

I stayed the night with Christel, having a good wash and borrowing some clothes from one of the nurses, as it was much too late for me to walk home. There was still no public transport. Christel and I had to sleep in the same bed. We comforted one another and promised, whatever happened, to keep in touch.

On the way home next morning, I passed the bombed Theatre, our meeting station, and found a notice there to all students. It said that because the university and most of the institutes, including the anatomy, were destroyed, studies would finish for the moment. All students had to report to their local labour exchange, and the medical students to the nearest hospital for allocation of war work.

I decided to go home, have a good sleep first and see Astra, who would, by now, be very concerned about me, as I had not left a note at home where I was to be found.

Astra was in the house, listening to the radio.

'There has been one short announcement about the bombing of Königsberg whilst I was in the Barmherzigkeit,' said Astra, 'but nothing about how bad it was, and they have never mentioned it since.'

She was glad to hear that Christel was alright, and pleased to see me. She had been concerned because Gitta was missing, too. She said the shoemaker had put a board over the broken shop window, but had not come again to work after that.

Astra told me about the bombing, and when the Barmherzigkeit was hit. They were lucky as they had had no fire bombs and the only parts destroyed were the buildings where no wards were situated. The Barmherzigkeit, being a civilian hospital, would now probably be closed but at the moment all the staff had to help with the patients.

'The kitchens are destroyed,' said Astra, 'and, as there is even talk of closing the hospital for civilians, I can see there won't be a job for me now. In any case, I haven't been feeling well lately. I have lots of headaches and feel giddy when I stand for a long time. I have already written to Mama. She wants me to see the doctor. I am not going back, and have brought my suitcase with me with all my things.'

After a little pause, she added: 'They want me to help in the wards, as they are bringing food in from a communal kitchen. I can't do that, I am not strong enough.'

So that was it, I thought, she wasn't strong enough to work in the wards, but she was strong enough to carry a suitcase home from the Barmherzigkeit, quite a long way.

I never believed much in her illnesses, and now realized that she didn't want to go back because of the different type of work she had to do, which she didn't like. I also knew that my mother would support her if she was here. The trouble was that we could not use the phone for long distance calls, these were only allowed for party members and army personnel. The phone was working, we had tried it, and we could make some calls, but it was not possible to contact my mother.

Suddenly I had an idea. When I was in Tuchel, Hermann had given me a number to ring if I wanted to contact him and I had done this once when I was at my uncle's mill. I told Astra about Hermann and the phone number, and then decided to ring him.

The girl at the telephone exchange asked me with whom I wanted to speak and I told her I wanted to talk with *Oberleutnant* Dr Fassbach. I think the Dr did the trick; she probably thought it was a doctor of medicine.

'We only have very few lines from Königsberg at the moment because of the latest bombing,' she said, 'but I will try and contact the number and ring you back. It might take hours.'

The call came through late in the evening. Hermann was pleased to hear my voice, but also surprised that I had contacted him, until I told him about the bombing of Königsberg. He hadn't heard anything, and doubted whether my mother would know about it. He promised to contact her, and would even try and get her to phone me.

He must have an important position if he can achieve that, I thought.

Sure enough, my mother phoned the next day, very worried about everything, the bombing, Astra's bad health, the closing of the university, and poor Christel and her work in the hospital.

My mother decided that it would be best for Astra to come to Tuchel, to recuperate from the strenuous hospital work!

'Let her go and see our doctor. She knows all about Astra's health,' said my mother. 'She will give her a note so that she can get a railway ticket, having to travel to Tuchel for health reasons. Once she is here, I can look after her.' She added: 'Hermann has been most kind and helpful.'

This meant that he had organised the telephone call for her, but she couldn't say that openly on the phone.

Astra went to see our lady doctor, but I didn't go with her. She came back with the news that the doctor thought she had some trouble with her lungs, as she often had difficulties in breathing.

'The doctor thinks I ought to have a *Röntgen Aufnahme* (X-ray), but this is difficult to get for civilians, particularly as at the moment a number of hospitals are bombed out. Still, I have got a note to travel to Tuchel, so

I will go tomorrow to Mama. I have got a letter for her, explaining everything.'

She smiled all over her face:

'I haven't had a holiday with Mama like you. Now I am going to catch up with it, and have a lovely long rest.'

Trains were not going yet from the main station, but our own little station, Ratshof, had a train going out of the town, where Astra could then change for Konitz. I took her to the station, helping her to carry her case. She had no difficulty in getting a ticket once she showed the doctor's certificate and for once the train left on time. When I got back home, I found Gitta packing her things.

'Oh Gitta!' I said, 'you are not leaving!'

'Yes,' she said, 'I am going. I have joined up as *Luftwaffen Helferin* (Air Force helper). I want to get away from everybody and everything here. I hate the war and what it is doing to people.'

Suddenly she cried, and I put my arms around her. She had suffered such a lot, and had been so brave all along.

'I don't care about anything any more. I would like somebody to tell me what to do until the time comes when we are all dead. Believe me, none of us will survive this war. The world hates us. Do you remember what Goebbels said in his speeches? He said the enemy wants to destroy Germany and, with it, all the people that live in it. He is right, you can see that. The bombing of our town was to destroy people and homes, it was not aimed at the army or at factories who supply ammunition. This was systematic killing. By joining the *Luftwaffe*, I will not have to make decisions. I will get a bed to sleep in, have my food given to me, get up when told, do the work when told, go to bed when told, I like the thought of being regimented.'

She looked at me, to see my reaction to this long outburst, but I kept quiet. What was I supposed to say? She had lost her father, and her two brothers, and her mother had lost her mind, all because of the war, and now her only relatives, her aunt and uncle, had lost their home. Maybe she was right; in the *Luftwaffe* things would be organised and she would be looked after.

Gitta didn't want me to come to the station, and I didn't insist, but I made her keep the key to the house and told her that she could come here at any time, even if I was not there. We both had tears in our eyes when she left and after she had gone I kept myself very busy in order to avoid too many thoughts going through my head.

The next day, I reported to the military hospital where I had worked before at weekends, and everybody was pleased to see me. I had brought a small case with some clothes and night things, knowing that I would have to stay some nights.

As soon as the trams were running again, I was able to go home occasionally. At first I was upset every time the tram took me through some of the destroyed parts of the town. People still lived there in the ruins and got on with their jobs, life having gradually returned to near normal.

One day I went right into the centre to see what the Kneiphof looked like. The island could now only be reached by boat. All that was left on it were charred buildings, and the ruin of our beautiful 14th century Dom. I kept on staring at it, remembering the school visits, and what we had learnt about it. It had stood there for 600 years and, in one night, it was destroyed. Nobody returned to live on the Kneiphof; it remained a dead place, with rats and mice the only inhabitants.

The view of the destroyed buildings was, in the end, a familiar sight. One's mind got dulled, and one accepted it, because it was there, and would remain until the end of the war. Some small roads were closed for ever, but the big ones were cleared, leaving the rubble at the side, often covering all the pavements. We had water and electricity, shops were open, trams and trains were running, with the main station open again, although without a roof, and the ticket office a little wooden hut. We even had post, with the post-women delivering letters every day.

My mother wrote from Tuchel, saying that she was very concerned about Astra's health, particularly her lungs. She had started to make enquiries in the south of Germany for a possible place for Astra in a sanatorium in the mountains. She wrote:

'If I can get a place for Astra, I will have to take her there, and I would like you to come with us, to help with the luggage and to keep me company on the return journey. You have still got your papers from Dr E., I hope?'

This was a hint for my railway passes. I still had several left. I was very surprised by my mother's letter. I never believed in Astra's poor health. I felt a little guilty for having doubted her, but looked forward to the possible trip to the south of Germany.

At the end of September my mother wrote, asking me to come to Tuchel so that we could start our journey to Oberstdorf, im Allgäu, as she had found a place for Astra in a clinic. The hospital staff were sorry to hear that I had to leave, but they could not stop me as I was working voluntarily. I promised to come back, because I liked the staff, had got used to the routine, and had gradually also been allowed to help the nurses, rather than only being ordered to do the cleaning jobs.

I went to see Christel to say goodbye. She was quite upset because, although we did not see much of one another, she always felt I was not far away and she could contact me in an emergency.

'Don't worry,' I said to her, 'I will be back soon. Mama and I are not staying in Oberstdorf. We are only taking Astra and, after a day or two, we will come back. I will get in touch with you as soon as I am back.'

My trip to Tuchel over Konitz was, this time, uneventful. A surprise was waiting for me in my uncle's mill. My brother, Hans, had come for a few days and my father came the following day to say goodbye to Astra. I had written to Hermann that I was coming to Tuchel again and he phoned up so that we could make a date.

Hermann and I had a few days together. The autumn that year was beautiful, leaves changing early from green to yellow to brown, and I loved the smell of the heather. Hermann was charming, but did not press me again with his marriage proposal. He said that he would like me to meet his family. As soon as he was ordered to Peenemünde he would send me a telegram, so that I could come to Greifswald.


Our trip to Oberstdorf took three days. We caught the train from Tuchel to Konitz first, and then got the express to Berlin. Astra had two large suitcases. She had packed in nearly all her clothes, not knowing what the weather would be like in the mountains, and winter was coming soon. My mother and I shared a small case, as we never intended to stay more than a day or two.

When we got to Berlin, we were late and had missed our connection. The next train wasn't going until the morning, and we had to stay the night in the station. My mother had found a corner seat on a bench, and Astra and I sat on the big cases. None of us slept much that night. The train we caught the next morning started from Berlin, so it was empty when it arrived. We had arranged that my mother and Astra would get into the train straight away when it pulled in, and occupy three seats, whilst I would struggle with the cases. This worked out alright. Astra and my mother had a window seat, and reserved one seat for me. We realised only later how lucky we were when the journey dragged on all day, through the night and the next day. The seats were upholstered, because my mother had second class tickets. Only the third class compartments had hard wooden seats. First class were reserved for party members and officers. The train again was very full, and stopped not only at the advertised stations but also in-between, often somewhere in the country. A few times we were pushed on to a siding and had to wait there.

Trains with ammunition and fuel had priority, and civilian trains were cleared from the main lines if these important trains needed the track. The longest wait was at night. We were pushed on to a siding and stayed there for hours in the half dark train. The black blinds were pulled down, and the shades over the lamp bulbs had only little slits. Everybody tried to sleep a little. At least we in the compartment could rest our heads on the backrest, and the seats were soft. Some people in the gangway lay down on the hard floor. There was nothing to eat or drink and the toilets were dirty and without water. As soon as it got light outside, my mother suggested that we have the window open for a little while because, by now, the air in the compartment was really bad.

The stopping and starting carried on. We slept, we dozed, we walked a little along the corridor to get the circulation back into our legs, and felt increasingly hungry, thirsty and dirty. We reached Oberstdorf in the evening, and enquired where our hotel was, which my mother had booked beforehand. Our hotel was a small guest house, run by an elderly couple, who were very pleased to see us, having expected us a day or two earlier. They were shocked to hear about our long journey and showed us our rooms straight away, so that we could have a wash, promising us a meal after that, and also that somebody would collect the cases from the station.

My mother and I shared a bedroom, and Astra had her own room. I remember that the meal was very good, but I was so tired that I only wanted to sleep. I had a lovely soft bed, with a big featherbed to cover myself, and it didn't take long before I was asleep.

When I woke the next morning and looked out of the window, I thought this was the most wonderful view I had ever seen. It took my breath away. The sun was just coming up behind the snow covered mountains. There were green meadows, with wild flowers and cows and, dotted up the hills, were chalets, with flower boxes full of red and white trailing flowers.

I was allowed to go and explore things after breakfast, whilst my mother went with Astra to the sanatorium. The owners of the guest house, Mr and Mrs Sulzer, told me about a *Wanderweg* (footpath) through woods and meadows up the mountains. They packed some food and drink into a small rucksack and helped me to put it on to my back. Mr Sulzer even produced a map and a stick, and I was off. I walked and climbed, and stopped and looked back, and enjoyed the view, the air and the sunshine. I got hot and sticky and found a bench under a tree, where I sat down for my lunch. Everything was quiet and peaceful here. Nobody had mentioned the war and there did not seem to be any shortage of food. Nothing was bombed out, everything looked clean and well looked after. Killing, fighting, destruction, and suffering, had by-passed this place.

When I got back I asked Astra what she had been doing all day. She said she had seen the doctor and had had some examinations. She was not all that communicative, which made me realize that things had not quite gone the way Astra had wanted them. She was always like that when she didn't get her own way, or when somebody found out that she was in the wrong.

When my mother and I were alone in the bedroom, I asked her how she had got on. She told me that Astra had seen the doctor in the sanatorium, who had examined her, taken *Röntgen Aufnahmen* of her chest and in the afternoon they had gone back to hear the results. Astra was not as bad as my mother had thought. She said:

'Our own lady doctor had frightened me a little. Astra had brought a letter from her to Tuchel. I wished she had taken some *Röntgen Aufnahmen* of Astra's chest. She was so poorly in Tuchel that I felt she must come into the mountains. Now the doctor here thinks she has grown too quickly as a young girl and is rather thin, but there is only a slight weakness in her lungs. The sanatorium is quite full and, as Astra is not really ill, they cannot give her a room there, only the treatment. The doctor said that if I can find her some accommodation, she can then come every day after breakfast and join the other patients in the sanatorium, remaining until the evening meal. She will be under medical supervision during the day. The patients rest in the open air, go for walks, have breathing exercises, and are generally occupied. They are also on a special diet, worked out for each one. Astra must put on some weight. She will then be able to do more, without feeling tired all the time. I have asked Mrs Sulzer whether Astra can live here, and whether she will keep an eye on her. She is quite willing to do this, but I am worried about this arrangement. It would have been so much better if she was all the time in the sanatorium and under supervision. Your father wasn't very keen on the idea of mountain air for Astra so, if he hears that it was not such an emergency after all, he might say we should have brought her back. I feel we had such a terrible journey to get here, and the doctor does think Astra will benefit, so I have decided to leave her here. She is twenty one years old, and was already quite independent when she worked in the hospital in Königsberg; she ought to be alright.'

This was quite a long speech for my mother to make, and it showed me how worried she was. I thought again:

Why is it only me who can see when Astra is exaggerating or pretending an illness. This time, even my father had doubted it.

My mother had a talk with Mrs Sulzer and paid all the bills, so that we could make an early start the next day. We had been advised to travel to Lindau am Bodensee and catch the express to Berlin from there, so that we had a better chance of getting a seat.

Astra was quite happy with all the arrangements, and looked forward to her stay with Mrs Sulzer and the sanatorium. My mother had told her to open a bank account, and she would transfer some money to it as soon as we got back. There were no tears when we parted and my mother said she would come and visit Astra, if possible, in two months, or arrange for her to come home for Christmas.

We both got a window seat in the train in Lindau. It was easier this time, because we only had one small case and a bag with sandwiches and drinks. This time we were prepared for a long trip. The journey to Berlin took a day and a night, in a very full and rather noisy train, with us being shunted into sidings when necessary. My mother developed a migraine; by the time we got to Berlin, she was quite ill, and she had to spend a day in an hotel.

As soon as we arrived in Tuchel at the mill, my aunt gave me a letter from Hermann.

'Hermann brought the letter two days ago,' she said, 'but I couldn't tell him when you would be back, or whether you would come here or carry on straight away to Königsberg. He left the letter and said he would forward a telegram to Königsberg, because he had to leave. He would like you to come to Greifswald.'

Oh dear, I thought, I have done enough long distance travelling.

I opened the letter and it was just as my aunt had said. Hermann was transferred to Peenemünde; he would get a few days off to come to Greifswald as soon as I could come to stay with his parents.

'As soon as you get back, take the next train and come to Greifswald,' wrote Hermann. 'There is no need to write, as you probably will be here before your letter. I don't know how long I will be in Peenemünde. There is talk of me being transferred somewhere else.'

I was sure Hermann knew where he had to go. He was always very careful what he said and would not put anything in writing either. I wondered whether his transfer was to France or Russia.

My mother said that I had to go, and should start off the next day. There was no point in going to Königsberg first, and then back again.

I could have gone from Berlin if I had known about this. It was a good job that I still had some of Dr E.'s rail passes left. I had used two of them to go to Oberstdorf and back, and I had to keep one to get myself back to Königsberg. Using two to go to Greifswald, I still would be alright and have one spare when I finished all my travelling.

I started off the next morning. The journey was long and tiring, with several delays. When I arrived, late in the evening I had to find my own way to Hermann's parents' place. They lived in a flat, in a big old house which belonged to the university. I climbed the two flights of stairs and rang the bell, feeling a little uneasy about meeting people that I had not known before.

To my great surprise, Hermann opened the door. I had not expected him to be at home. I was really pleased to see him and probably overdid the welcome, because he just wouldn't let go of me, hugging me. In the end, he pulled me indoors and introduced me to his mother, who had come to see who was at the door.

*Frau* Professor Fassbach looked old to me, with long grey hair pinned at the back of her head into an untidy bun. Everything about her was plain, colourless, and old-fashioned. She had a friendly face and kept on talking, hardly giving me time to say anything. I was ushered into a large living-room, full of heavy dark old furniture. Thick curtains were drawn over the windows, and the light from a small table lamp was shining on to an open book on a small table next to a large soft armchair. Somebody had just been sitting there reading, probably Mrs Fassbach.

I was asked to sit down. Hermann took my suitcase and stood it by the door, whilst his mother kept on talking. Both then sat down. They kept on asking questions, but did not wait for any replies. At the same time, they were telling me things which did not sink in because I was so tired. Gradually I started to understand what they were telling me. The reason why Hermann was at home was the sudden illness of his father, who had had a serious operation. Hermann had been given compassionate leave, because his father had had to have his leg amputated. Hermann's father had got over the operation very well, and was coming home the next day. There had been no time to tell me all this before. Hermann had heard about it just after I left Tuchel. His transfer to Peenemünde was put forward, so that he could combine it with a visit to Greifswald. Even so, they all wanted me to come, because it meant Hermann could see me again, and his parents could meet me.

The room was very dimly lit, but my eyes gradually got used to the semi-darkness. I noticed a grand piano with dust on top, a large bookcase, and several worn but comfortable looking chairs standing on a threadbare carpet. I had not imagined that Hermann would live in a place like this. There was nothing really wrong with the room. Everybody in those days had thick curtains because of the black-out, but the whole impression was of untidiness, and a non-interest in making things look attractive.

All I could hear was the talk about the poor man, who now had to get used to walking with crutches because it would take a long time before he would get an artificial leg. In the meantime, I sat there, tired and hungry, making the proper sympathetic remarks, and thinking:

I don't like this place. I wonder when they are going to ask me whether I want something to eat, or how my journey was?

It was Hermann who eventually got round to it:

'I think Helga is tired, I had better show her where she sleeps. It is already quite late.'

With that, he took my suitcase, and brought me to a little bedroom, which had belonged to his sister.

'We thought that you might like this room, as it is nearer to the bathroom. Lotti, my sister, still uses it when she comes home occasionally, but she has taken most of her things with her.'

I knew that his sister was in charge of a laboratory in the south of Germany. She was younger than Hermann. He also had an elder brother, Ludwig, who had studied agriculture, but was now in the army. Nobody had mentioned any food. I said good night to Hermann and, as everything was so dark everywhere, I didn't go and find his mother again to say good night, but went to bed.

The next morning I woke early, went to the bathroom, got dressed, and found the living room again. I opened the curtains. There was a view of a wide street with old houses opposite. A few people were about, and it looked a sunny, warm day. I did not like to explore any of the other rooms, in case I walked into a bedroom, so I had a glance at the books in the bookcase. There was quite a selection, from science books to novels to poetry, and a set of red bound small books. I took one out, and discovered that they were Mrs Fassbach's diaries. She had been writing in them for years. I quickly put them back, as I didn't want anybody to think that I was prying, but I made up my mind there and then to have a look at them again, if I got the chance. It might tell me something about the family, and Hermann.

I could hear somebody moving about, so I followed the sound and found Hermann in the kitchen, trying to make some breakfast.

'I thought I would start the breakfast,' he said. 'My mother is not very domesticated, and we often make our own food.'

'Let me help,' I said. 'I have brought some food. I had better get it from my suitcase.'

Anybody visiting during the war always brought some food, because of the rationing. I had brought quite a bit of butter, cheese and coffee, which my mother had packed in, and this was as well. We only found a tiny piece of margarine and bread in the pantry and, after some search, Hermann produced a jar with a little dried-up jam. We made toast and coffee and carried it into the dining room. Mrs Fassbach appeared, saying that she could smell real coffee, which she had not had for ages. Hermann fetched another cup.

Afterwards, it was decided that I would stay in the flat, whilst Hermann and his mother fetched Mr Fassbach from the hospital. He was coming by ambulance, and they were going to carry him upstairs. He had been taught how to walk with his crutches; they could not supply him with a wheelchair, because they were needed for the wounded soldiers.

'You can look at some of the books,' said Mrs Fassbach.

'There is plenty of choice. I am sure you will find something you like. I don't think we will be away long. The ambulance is organised, and the hospital is within walking distance.'

I watched them walking along the road from the window and, when they went around the corner, I got myself some of the diaries, and sat down by the window. I could see the arrival of the ambulance from there.

I also got myself a small book of poems, which I could have read if I was asked.

Some of Mrs Fassbach's diaries were quite old, so I put them back, and then I read about Hermanns's wedding. This was interesting. I hadn't realized that he had left the church, and could therefore only be married in a registry office. His fiancée would have liked a church wedding, but had to give in because of that.

That was not a good start to the marriage, I thought.

Mrs Fassbach complained that she didn't see much of her daughter-in-law, although the couple lived in a small flat on the campus, not far away. It was the next item that surprised me. Apparently her daughter-in-law had a miscarriage, and she hadn't even been told that

Hermann's wife was expecting a baby. She seemed more upset about not being told than about the loss of the baby. Hermann had never told me about this, and I felt sorry for the young woman. She was probably not able to have any more children after that, and that was the reason for the divorce.

This certainly was a slightly different picture to the one I had imagined, and I felt that what had happened to her was cruel. On the other hand, she might have been quite glad to get away from Hermann and his family.

Mrs Fassbach seemed to entertain quite a bit, because the diary was full of names, and descriptions of people. She was very musical, played the piano, and gave concerts in her drawing room. All these things were not very interesting to me. I didn't feel guilty at all for prying, having found out something about Hermann's wife, and also discovered that there was no love lost between mother and daughter-in-law. It certainly gave me something to think about.

They were soon back. I saw the ambulance coming round the corner, and quickly put the diaries back, leaving the book of poems on the little table.

The ambulance men carried Mr Fassbach upstairs on a stretcher and sat him into an armchair. His wife fussed around him, pushing a cushion into his back and laying a blanket over his legs, covering the empty trouser leg. I had noticed the amputation was just above the knee.

I looked at Mr Fassbach. He was a very thin, pale man, and looked a bit like Hermann, only much much older. His wrinkled face had the same cold blue eyes, and he wore the same glasses as his son. His skin looked transparent and he was so frail that I thought he would fall off his chair. The little bit of hair he had was long and swept back and, because he was so thin, his ears and nose seemed rather big. He reminded me of the wizard who came out of the bottle in one of the fairy stories.

Hermann introduced me. He smiled at me, and nodded his head, but didn't say anything. He put his head against the backrest of the chair, and shut his eyes, whilst his hands pulled the rug a little higher, as if he was cold. He looked absolutely exhausted.

'I think we had better let him have a little rest whilst we go into the kitchen and see about some food,' said Mrs Fassbach.

She had no idea what to cook for dinner. She found some macaroni and even a tin of tomatoes. As I had brought the cheese, I suggested having macaroni cheese. She thought that was a good idea, but admitted that she was no good at making a white sauce.

'I always get lumps in it. I usually cook the macaroni and just pour the tomatoes over it and grate some cheese on top.'

I offered to do the sauce. Mrs Fassbach got the macaroni on to the boil, then went to lay the table. She didn't come back into the kitchen, so I carried on making the meal. By now I had discovered that she wasn't a cook, and didn't seem to bother about dirt either. Before I could cook, I had to clean the stove, as there was still food stuck on from the last few meals. The whole kitchen needed a springclean, but I wasn't going to do that!

Everybody complimented me on my cooking, not realizing that my knowledge, too, was very limited. Hermann and I washed up, whilst Mrs Fassbach played the piano. She was a marvellous pianist.

After that, Hermann and I went for a walk, and he showed me the little flat where he had lived with his first wife. It was unoccupied, very nicely furnished, and Hermann said we could move in, as soon as we were married.

I reminded him that I had not said "yes" yet, but he only laughed:

'You were very pleased to see me yesterday when you arrived. You didn't hide your feelings then!'

He wouldn't understand if I explained to him that it was only the relief at not being confronted by strangers after the long tiring journey. He was always right in whatever he said!

When we got back, Mr and Mrs Fassbach had visitors, another professor and his wife. He told everybody about his operation. Suddenly he stopped talking, pressed his hands on to the arms of the chair, and then lifted himself slightly up. At the same moment Mrs Fassbach started to talk, as if by command. Her voice was louder than usual, her speech fast, mixed with loud laughter recording a funny thing that had happened to her. Mr Fassbach dropped back into the chair, and carried on talking to his friend the professor. I was not sitting very far from Mr Fassbach and I noticed that somebody had made a bad smell. I looked at him but he just talked. I looked at everybody else, but nobody seemed to take any notice. A little later, the same thing happened. Mr Fassbach raised his bottom, Mrs Fassbach started talking loud and laughed. This time I was watching Mr Fassbach, and I could hear and smell what he was doing.

You dirty old man, I thought, and his wife knows all about it and tries to cover up for him.

I got up and went outside. I was not going to sit in that stinking room all the afternoon. After that I made quite sure I never sat near him again.

That evening Mrs Fassbach found a tin of soup and, with another bouillon cube and some water added to it, we made enough for the four of us. There was some bread and sausage, and my butter and cheese. During supper, and washing up with Hermann afterwards, I decided that I had had enough of Greifswald. I could see that I would be left with the cooking and maybe even finish up having to clean the flat. I informed Hermann that I would take the night train the next day back to Stettin, and then to Königsberg.

Hermann was surprised but understood when I explained that I had to report back to the hospital, where I was needed.

'All medical students have to work now in the hospital,' I said. 'It is going to be part of our practical time, and will be recognized as such.'

Hermann took me to the train. We promised to write to one another, and I promised to think seriously about his proposal. We kissed goodbye and I waved to him from the train until I couldn't see him any more.

I thought of Wolfgang, who also wanted to marry me, and I knew that I preferred his youth, warmth, and inexperience to Hermann's clever and cold personality.

# CHAPTER ELEVEN

## Bombs on Ratshof - Hospital Work

As soon as I got back to Königsberg from Greifswald, I reported to the hospital. From now on I had to work like everybody else, or I wouldn't get my ration cards. I phoned Christel and we arranged that our free days would coincide, so that we could meet at home. Christel told me about her work in the hospital. She had passed the stage of cleaning and bed making and was mostly helping sister, who seemed to be quite fond of her.

We talked about the war, but did not think we were in any danger yet. There had been some foreign planes over Königsberg at night, because the sirens went several times, but there had been no bombing any more. We promised one another that, whatever happened, we would keep in touch.

There were several things that frightened me in November. One was another night bombing attack of Königsberg, and then there were the stories that two wounded soldiers told us, who had fought to get back Nimmersdorf. This was the first town in East Prussia to be overrun by the Russians. Five days after the town was lost, it was taken again by the Germans after heavy fighting. The soldiers were shocked to discover that scarcely a single inhabitant was alive. Women had been raped and then nailed to barn doors and farm carts, children had been shot, along with forty French prisoners-of-war who had worked on the farms, and old people had been tortured until they died. The cruelties which the Russians had endured at the hands of the SS had produced a backlash, in which the innocent suffered with the guilty.

We were told on the radio in propaganda speeches that the East Front was strong from Tilsit in the north to Kattowitz in the south, and parts of East Prussia were only vacated to consolidate the armies. From now on, the Russians would be stopped. In any case, the new *Wunderwaffe* (wonderful weapon) would soon be used, and final victory was on the horizon. We listened to the reassuring speeches, and believed them.

The bomb attack on Königsberg happened when Gitta was on leave. She was given three days off before being transferred to the *Reich*, and decided to spend these days with me. She looked very smart in her uniform, and said that she was quite happy living in army quarters with women and men soldiers. It was strict, there was marching, inspections, and there was training. She had been trained to manipulate the big searchlights, used in night attacks, but was now transferred to the Flak the *Flugzeugabwehrkanone* (anti-aircraft or ack-ack unit) and had to report in two days time to Wolfenbüttel, near Braunschweig.

'They have 8.8 guns there, which protect the H.G.W. (Hermann Goering *Werke* (works)) and we will be trained to use them' she said.

'You are just like a soldier, Gitta. Not like a woman. Do you mind that?'

'I don't care, it doesn't matter,' she replied. 'You just do what you are told, and the comradeship amongst us girls is great. If there is not enough food, we share, if we are cold, we organise a party to go and find, or steal, wood. We had an iron stove in our barracks. I hope it is going to be the same in Wolfenbüttel. It should be, because we are all transferred together.'

After a little while, she added:

'I have given your name as next of kin, I hope you don't mind. I couldn't very well give my mother's address. I haven't told anybody about her and I didn't want to give my aunt's name. It is only a formality; everybody had to fill in a form.'

She talked quite matter of fact, as if this was an everyday occurrence, but I was shocked to realize that she had been transferred to a dangerous location and that she might even get hurt or killed.

It was pretty late when we went to sleep and, when the siren sounded, I didn't feel like getting up. Gitta jumped up straight away and grabbed her clothes. Her training had been excellent! She looked behind the curtains.

'You had better get up quickly,' she said. 'There are searchlights in the sky, I think this is going to be a big one.'

I jumped up, pulled on my track suit, grabbed my emergency bag, and we ran out into the garden. I quickly pushed the suitcase into the hedge and we crossed the road, then crept along the walls of the houses. We could hear the low humming of the heavy planes, and then the Flak started. The sky was alight with searchlights, which occasionally caught a plane in their cross-beams. The first bombs were dropped; we could hear them, and saw the flash when they hit the ground. It wasn't far away from us, at least it didn't seem far, and I thought it was coming nearer.

'We can't cross the road to the bunker,' said Gitta, 'we might be hit.'

Trembling, we stood in the shadow of a house, leaning against the wall and feeling the building shake. Suddenly there was silence.

'Come on!' I shouted, and pulled Gitta, running across the road. The door of the air-raid shelter was already closed, and it took a few minutes to find the handle and open the heavy door. The warden looked surprised, but quickly pulled us in and closed the door again. He had hardly closed it when there were some heavy dull thuds, the bunker shook, the lights went out, some people screamed, children started to cry, and then the bunker shook again.

The warden put the emergency lights on and started to walk around to look at everything. People calmed down once there was light. The air-raid shelter, being purpose built, would withstand some bombing, we knew that, but what about the houses outside? Somebody said, after a while:

'It is quiet now, let's open a door and look outside.'

The warden walked towards a door and tried to open it, but it wouldn't move. He tried another and another; the same thing happened, none of them would move. Even the door where we had come in wouldn't open. Still, there was no panic. We knew somebody would eventually come and get us out.

The warden came back to our door. He looked at me and Gitta, who was in uniform. Thinking that she must be more knowledgeable than anybody else and might be able to give advice, he whispered:

'The fans are not working either, and I think that even the air holes are blocked. If we don't get out soon, we will suffocate.'

We both stared at him, then I said:

'You had better keep this quiet as long as possible,' and Gitta added: 'Tell the people it might take quite a time before we are rescued, and that they ought to try and have a sleep, lie down on the benches, and the floor. They won't use so much oxygen then.'

The warden was quite an old man. He looked frightened and for a moment I thought that he might be the first to panic. Gitta could see that too; she said:

'You are responsible for a lot of people, you are doing very well, and everybody accepts you as the authority here.'

With that, he straightened up, turned round and, walking further into the bunker, told some people to stop talking so that others could sleep, and suggested to everybody that they should have a rest whilst waiting for the rescuers. Some people tried to sleep, others just couldn't keep quiet, and carried on talking but in whispers.

We could not hear anything from outside. It became hot in the bunker. People started to sweat and got short of breath. Somebody wondered loudly what was the matter with the fans, and where were the air holes? Eventually people guessed what had happened, and a woman near us screamed hysterically:

'We are all going to die. That's how it was last time, when they bombed the centre of the town, and then they found all the bodies in the cellars. They had all suffocated.'

I could see that there would soon be a panic after this outburst. The warden had gone to the other end of the bunker, and I decided that I had to do something. I walked towards the woman, put my hands on her shoulders and, shaking her to stop her screaming, I said:

'Now be quiet. Screaming and shouting will not help. I am a nurse, so listen to me.'

It was the mentioning of nurse which made her stop. All the others around her looked at me and I had to say something.

'I am sure there is some air coming in somewhere, otherwise we would have suffocated by now,' I said. 'We have been here over three hours. Let's try and preserve the little bit of air we have by keeping calm. Screaming, shouting, talking, all need more air, so does movement, like walking. If everybody keeps quiet, we will last much longer. I am sure they have started to get help to us.'

As I said this, we could hear banging, and I took my shoe off and banged on to the wall in reply. I did this several times, and each time there was a reply. This seemed to satisfy people for the moment. I walked slowly back to Gitta, and sat down beside her on the ground with my back to the door. As we were the last ones to enter, we did not get a seat, and I did not want to go away from the door, because I wanted to be near one when it opened.

I was not the only one who thought so. People gradually moved to the different doors and sat down. The air was very thin by now and the first few people started to faint. I, too, had difficulties in breathing, and Gitta suddenly collapsed on to my lap. People did not have the strength to panic any more, but were fighting for breath. I could hear noises by our door; they were coming to get us out!

Let's hope they are in time, I thought, feeling quite dizzy and light-headed. At last somebody was trying to push the door - there was a crack, and fresh air was coming in. I breathed deeply, feeling giddy, and then stood up, pulling Gitta up also.

'You must help me,' I whispered to her. 'I cannot lift you, or carry you. I haven't got that strength.'

Gitta stumbled to her feet. The door opened slowly, and new air rushed in.

As soon as it was realized that it was our door that was opened first, everybody pushed towards us and an absolutely frantic mass of people tried to get out. The weak ones and the ones who had already fainted were trampled on as the hysterical crowd tried to reach freedom and fresh air.

I dragged Gitta outside and away from the door, and we both fell onto some earth, gasping for air. We had no idea where we were, because the road which we had crossed four hours ago to get to the bunker had gone. We were in a kind of crater, a hole, and had to climb out of it. Once on top, we looked around. It was still dark, but there were fires further away, probably houses burning. Everything smelled of earth, brick dust, fire, and there was a lot of smoke, which made it difficult to recognize things.

I shivered. The night was cold, and I was frightened, wondering where our house was and what it looked like. Gitta just sat on the earth, with her head bent down, taking deep breaths of air. More and more people stumbled through the opened door, some carrying children, or helping others who hadn't got the strength to reach the door on their own. The Lange family tried to push the basket with the children along as they hadn't got the strength to lift it, so I got up and helped them to push, until they got to the top of the crater.

The children were awake, but quiet, and the three sisters and their mother just stood there staring, wondering where their road was with the house they lived in.

At first people had spilled out through the door, stopped a little, then climbed up the crater and sat down. Eventually there was only a trickle of people, and then nobody came out any more.

'What about the others?' somebody said, and mentioned a few names.

The helpers who had dug out the door went inside the bunker and I followed them. I was confronted by a sad and frightening picture. People who had been at the other end of the bunker had fainted because of lack of oxygen, and some had suffocated. The old and the weak even children, had dropped to the ground and been trampled on. I picked up the children first and carried them out, one after the other, and tried to revive them. More and more people helped and we were able to save a few. Some had terrible wounds where they had been trodden on. These, if still alive, were laid to one side to have first aid treatment, but there were only a few. Most of those brought out from the bunker were dead and when we counted them it came to sixty-three, women, children, and a few old men, all from our neighbourhood. A number of faces were familiar, even if I didn't know them personally; they had lived in our district, and I had seen them.

I looked around. There were a lot of people just sitting, not moving, afraid to go home because of the uncertainty of what they would find. There were rows and rows of dead bodies, and there were the wounded, already attended to by friends and relatives. All were scattered in a wide area, on top of rubble, bricks, and earth.

Gitta was coming towards me; she, too, had helped. She looked shocked and grey, and tired, and dirty.

I must look the same, I thought. But why aren't we crying?

'Let's go and see what is left of our house,' I said. 'Look, the sun is coming up, it is getting light.'

The smoke and dust in the air had cleared away and it was a beautiful morning with a lovely red and pink sky. We both stared at it but, when we turned round, we could see in the distance smoke and burning houses.

'It looks as if we have had no fire bombs here,' said Gitta. 'It is the other side of the town that is burning.'

'We were lucky that they opened our door in the bunker first,' I replied, 'otherwise . . .', I didn't finish the sentence, I just couldn't say it, but looked meaningfully at the dead bodies.

We both made our way over the ripped up earth and rubble in the direction of our house.

Bombs had been dropped at the corner of Lawsker Allee and Wiebestrasse. They had hit the big Police station, the Reichsgarten, the big old hotel and restaurant where we had our aircraft defence training, and the park with the Freigraben. The police station had disappeared, and the debris from the building covered our bunker, blocking all air holes and doors. The houses next to the police station were on the whole alright, except that the blast had broken windows and doors and brought tiles off the roofs. The road was cracked, and we had difficulties getting across. We made our way to the corner of Metgetherstrasse and, with a sigh of relief, I said to Gitta:

'Thank God, our house is still there.'

Hilde Lange came to see me and asked me whether I would come the following morning to the funeral service for all the dead from the bunker.

'The vicar has given permission to have a mass grave dug by the church. The funerals will be tomorrow morning at 10 o'clock, with a service in the church first. I said I would go round to everybody, and tell them.'

'Yes, Hilde,' I said, 'I will come. Tell me, how are you all?'

'We are alright.' She stopped, took a deep breath, and then said:

'Mrs Faust and her daughter Thea, who lived above us, are dead.'

When Hilde said this, the tears started rolling down her face, and suddenly I, too, felt like crying.

'Oh Hilde,' I said, 'I am sorry.'

'My Mum told the authorities to inform Mr Faust', continued Hilde, 'he is in the army, but he won't be there by tomorrow morning for the funeral.'

Before she left, Hilde said:

'By the way, nobody will be able to get any flowers, so we thought, if everybody could bring a few bits of greenery from the garden, that would help.'

'Of course, I will cut everything that is green, the winter is practically here, in any case.'

We had no electricity, but we had water, and my mother had a small bottled gas cooker in our cellar air-raid shelter which I brought upstairs. We tried the telephone, but that was not working either. Later in the afternoon, a woman from down the road knocked on to the door and asked whether I had some spare sheets or blankets.

'They have laid out all the dead in the church, but we feel they ought to be covered, or wrapped up. There are no coffins,' she said. 'It would help us if you could give us some sheets or blankets.'

I promised to let her have some and she asked me to take them to the church. As soon as she had left, I took some of my mother's sheets, and got two blankets out of the *Bettkasten* (large ottoman) in the attic. I told Gitta where I was going, and then went off to the church.

After passing the collapsed tower, I came to the big area of grass next to the church where the small flower beds and benches used to be. A huge noisy digger was pulling the grass up, then the earth, and gradually making a big hole for the mass grave. The grass was covered with the debris from the tower. There were no flowers in the beds as it was the beginning of the winter, and the benches had already been put away to preserve them during the cold months. Nothing looked pretty any more. The big church doors were wide open and when I stepped inside I could feel the draught and the wind, coming through the broken windows. The church was full of dead bodies. Candles were flickering everywhere; some had been blown out by the wind. A few women were busy wrapping up some of the bodies. I gave them my sheets and blankets.

When I got back, Gitta had cooked a small dinner, and we ate it by candlelight, because we still had no electricity. It was very cold at night. In the early morning hours, Gitta and I slept together in one bed to keep ourselves warm. When we got up, we realized why we had been so cold. The temperature had dropped to 5 degrees below zero. The winter had come. It was November.

I took Gitta to Ratshof station and we said a tearful goodbye. Gitta was travelling to the centre of Germany. This was a long way, and she would not get leave again to come to Königsberg because of the shortage of the rail passes. We promised to write and not to lose contact. I said that if I did get time, and the trains were going, I would go and see her mother.

Afterwards I just had time to cut some greenery and the bottom branches of a Christmas tree which we had planted years ago. They were stiff and hard from the frost.

I went to the church, and was surprised to find it packed with people. They even stood outside. I couldn't get in, and didn't hear what the vicar was saying, until he came outside and walked to the place where the day before a large rectangular hole was dug. The people stepped to the side, forming a guard of honour, and leaving a passage for the bodies to be carried through. Old men from the home guard carried them on stretchers and laid them down gently next to the hole, going back for more bodies. In the meantime, other men lowered them into the hole, where two men laid them side by side. The children came last, and that's when some of the women started to cry.

The two men climbed out of the shallow grave and pulled up the ladder which they had used. The bodies looked like mummies, wrapped up in blankets or white sheets. The vicar was murmuring a blessing and throwing some earth on to the bodies; others followed suit, gently throwing the earth in. Some dropped greenery, and one woman had some flowers, which she scattered on to the small children's bodies. Three men got hold of some spades and started to cover the bodies with more earth. It was not easy for them, as they had to chop away at the frozen earth heap. Gradually they covered the bodies. The vicar started to sing the old Lutheran hymn:

'*Ein feste Burg ist unser Gott* . . ' (A strong fortress is our God) and everybody joined in.

When the hymn was finished, he walked to some of the bereaved relatives, and talked to them. I walked to the edge of the grave, and said a little prayer, thinking all the time of Thea, and I cried like the others. I laid my Christmas tree branches by the side, hoping that when the grave was completely covered and finished, somebody would put them on top of the grave. I had seen the digger behind the church and realized that when everybody had gone, the grave would be finished off with this mechanical device.

Hilde was at the graveside with her sister Margot, and her mother.

'We left Dora at home to look after the children,' she said. 'I had better say goodbye now, because we are leaving tomorrow morning, all of us. The authorities have got us a place in the country. It will be safer for the children.'

There are sixty three people dead here, I thought. Others are leaving the town. What about me?

I said farewell to the Lange family, and then went home. After all the crying and the sadness of the occasion and the cold outside, I was glad to get indoors. I felt exhausted, and made myself a hot drink when, suddenly, the telephone rang. I couldn't believe it, the phone was ringing! I ran to it straight away, and heard Christel's voice. She was relieved to hear me answering. Her hospital was alright, but she had heard rumours that the one where I was working had been destroyed.

'It wasn't a big bomb attack,' she said. 'They only dropped a few bombs, but this time they wanted to destroy the barracks along the Kasernenstrasse. Unfortunately they dropped them on the wrong side of the road and hit all the hospitals. You had better go and find out whether you can help.' With that, we were cut off.

I wrote a letter to my mother, then I packed a little shoulder bag, in case I had to stay in the hospital, and put on my Red Cross uniform. There was a shortage of nurses' coats and capes, and I had not been given one, so I put on my winter coat and my boots and started off. It was already well after dinner time by now. I decided to walk around the Vierbrüderplatz, so that I could pass the church once more, as I wanted to see what had happened to the big grave.

It didn't look like a grave when I saw it. The digger had filled it up and piled the rest of the earth on top, so that it looked like a big earth hill, covered with green branches and fir, and little notes stuck in-between the leaves with heartfelt messages to a loved one. Some people had made a little cross from branches, and stuck it into the earth.

I was able to use the tram for part of my journey to the Kasernenstrasse but even so it took me two hours. All the buildings, the hospital ones on one side of the road had been hit. The other side was intact, except that all the doors and windows were missing. Men with red arm bands, the *Volkssturm*, were covering up the windows with wood. I asked one of them what had happened to all the wounded and the staff.

'There were not many alive after the bombing,' he said 'They took them to different places, like school halls. Some of the doctors and staff have gone to the *Stadtkrankenhaus* (town hospital). The operating theatre there is in the cellar, and they can use it day and night.' He looked at me and my Red Cross uniform under my coat. 'That's where you could report. It's no good looking for anything in those bombed buildings; there is nobody alive there any more. They stopped looking for people. You might as well leave the bodies buried, it saves a funeral, and the earth is too hard to dig a grave.'

He turned round, and slowly walked back to his job of covering the windows with wood. He didn't sound bitter or sad, just giving me some facts, and then getting on with what he had been told.

Just like Gitta, I thought. Not caring any more. Glad to have a job, and being told what to do, and therefore not having to think.

By the time I found the *Stadtkrankenhaus,* it was evening and dark. The hospital was completely full. There was hardly any space between the beds in the wards and even in the corridors, patients were lying on mattresses on the floor, leaving only a narrow space to walk through. I could not see any staff and made my way along the corridor to Sister's room, only to discover that this, too, was given over to accommodate wounded.

I found a Sister in the laundry room, where she had one corner for her desk and records. I didn't know her, so I introduced myself, apologizing that I had not reported any earlier because of the bombing of our bunker and the tragedy that followed. She said that there were a few people from the Kasernenstrasse hospital here and that she would be only too pleased if I would work here, as they were very short of staff.

'You will have to learn things quickly,' she said. 'None of my staff does any cleaning, they are too valuable to do that. Cleaning, tidying and sometimes even taking food to the patients can be done by the walking wounded, the ones who are on the mend. My staff do the nursing. You can start with me tonight and, tomorrow, I will get you into a rota. There is not much free time for anybody. Accommodation for nurses is scarce so, if you can sleep at home, that is fine. In an emergency, you can shake down here in this room on a palliasse, but it won't be quiet here.'

My work started. Sister Helena was on night duty, and responsible for over 100 patients in two large and four small rooms, and along the corridor. We had a very busy night, with hardly any time to stop for a drink. There were two more nurses on the wards who got the patients ready for the operations and also attended to them afterwards. There was only one operating theatre, but it was in use day and night, with different shifts of doctors, nurses and helpers. I was working with an auxiliary nurse who knew the routine. It was our job to change the sheets on the beds for patients who had left for the operating theatre, to turn patients who were too ill to do it by themselves and thereby prevent bed sores, fetch and empty bedpans and bottles, give drinks to thirsty soldiers and generally do what we were told by the two experienced nurses and Sister Helena.

The night just flew by and by 4 o'clock we had to start with the morning wash. Quite a number of wounded soldiers were able to have their own wash, some could even get up and visit the bathroom, but there were others who were hardly conscious, or could not move, or had no hands or no arms. I was told not to spend too much time with each patient, otherwise I wouldn't get round. This was true, but the ones who were conscious asked questions and wanted answers, and I could ask about their experiences, and how and where they were wounded, and all this took time. Sister Helena soon stopped this:

'No more talking, Sister Helga, just get on with the washing of the patients. And, by the way, next time you take a bowl of water to somebody who can attend to his own toilet, fill the bowl up with water to the top and then stand it in an empty bowl. In this way you can carry two bowls. You share the water when you reach the bedside. We have to economize with our time, and half a bowl of water is plenty for each patient.'

She then smiled, and said in a low voice:

'You are doing well for your first night here.'

By the time I came off duty, I was tired. Sister Helena decided to keep me on night duty for a week as I had already started. I would then have half a day off and move on to the day duty timetable. In this way a rota was established for me. I went home to have my sleep, and a break away from the hospital and the smell of blood, disinfectant, soap and water, and the steam from the autoclave. The trams were running quite frequently, and I was therefore able to do the journey in half an hour, with a bit of luck.

185

I was lonely at home, because most of our neighbours had moved into the country. I missed Gitta and the Lange family. I had letters to which I had to reply. Wolfgang was at the eastern front, but I had no idea where. He said that it was bitterly cold, and he had frostbite. Hermann wrote, but didn't say where he was. He didn't mention any fighting, or the cold, so I assumed that he was working as a scientist again. He said that his father was better and quite mobile on his crutches. Gitta wrote:

'We are up most nights to attend to our duties.'

Which meant that they were on the Flak each night, shooting.

My mother wrote a long letter, telling me to give up the hospital work and come to Tuchel. She was working in the office of the Rösler*mühle* (mill) which belonged to her brother and I, too, could have a job there, or maybe apply for a nursing position in Konitz. Christel also ought to ask for a transfer to the Konitzer hospital. She said that she hadn't heard from Papa lately and wondered whether he was in Königsberg. I had hardly received the letter when my mother turned up. She had been able to persuade the authorities to let her have a rail pass, because she had to go and see her bombed out house and save what she could from it. She was shocked when she saw what had happened to the neighbourhood. Our own house didn't look bad, as I had been able to put in the windows from the double glazing but, of course, she saw the bombed police station, and the houses without windows.

Christel came home for the day, and my mother again tried to persuade us to come to Tuchel.

'I am worried,' she said. 'The Russians are in East Prussia and, although everybody is convinced that they will be driven out again, I feel Tuchel and Konitz are so much further to the west, that we will all be much safer there. We also have no bombing in Tuchel.'

Christel liked her job, and the staff. She didn't want to change, and I, too, had settled down in the *Stadtkrankenhaus*. I had been told that this hospital service would, later on, be recognized as practical time in my medical studies. I would probably not get this recognition if I worked in the Konitzer hospital as it was a much smaller one.

My mother was disappointed. She was also very worried about my father, not having heard from him. He never really wrote to anybody, just turned up, or was able to phone either Tuchel or Königsberg but this time it seemed ages since we had heard from him. My mother asked me to try and get hold of Dr E., to beg him to arrange for a trunk call to Tilsit, but I was not able to do this. He was not in Königsberg.

Before leaving for Tuchel again, my mother went to see her friend, Mrs Jacoby. When she came back, she looked very serious. From time to time she started to say something to me and then stopped. I could see that she was debating with herself whether she should tell me whatever it was or not. Eventually she made up her mind.

'Come and sit down, I want to talk to you quite seriously.' Her face looked troubled and worried. 'As you know, I went to see Mrs Jacoby this morning and we had quite a talk. She is leaving Königsberg with her sister and going to stay with relatives, who live near Stettin. She doesn't know where her husband is, except that he is on the eastern front. He was called away from Königsberg's military hospital about a week ago. Mrs Jacoby is very worried about the Russians. She said that they have pushed much further into East Prussia than we are told on the radio. She is convinced that the Germans will lose the war. She said that you and Christel ought to leave and come to Konitz but, if you don't want that, you could go to Greifswald. At least you have your future in-laws there and it is far enough away from the Russians.'

'They are not my future in-laws, I wish you wouldn't talk like that. We agreed to leave things as they are for the moment, so please don't mention it again. Anyway, I have explained to you that I must stay here. They rely on me at the hospital; I cannot let them down.'

'Forgive me, but I had to have another try, before I come to the next thing which I want to talk to you about.'

She stopped, hesitated, and looked at me.

'We have already heard terrible stories about the animal behaviour of the Russians and, particularly, the way they treat women, raping and violating them. If the Russians should come to Königsberg, God forbid that this happens, you might think that it would be better to be dead than to be desecrated by them. Mrs Jacoby has given me some poison. It is cyanide, a very quick killer. I have two little phials. Her professor got them for her, as he is also very concerned about the situation. He got one for his wife. Mrs Jacoby and her sister don't need them now as they are going away, so she passed them on to me. She said that I ought to give one each to you and Christel. I have been thinking and worrying about it, and decided not to mention this to Christel. It would frighten her and I don't think she would ever have the courage to use it. Or she might panic, and use it at the wrong time.'

My mother was watching me, trying to read my reaction in my face. I just looked at her and thought that she was over-reacting like Mrs Jacoby, because, only this morning, we had been reassured again that the Russian front was strong. On the other hand, working in the military hospital, I also had first hand news from the soldiers about the terrible atrocities performed by the Russians, and I would rather be dead quickly than raped, and then, maybe, nailed on to a door.

'What does it look like?' I asked. 'I mean the poison.'

My mother opened her handbag, and took out two small glass phials, about one and a half inches (4 cm) long, with a little screw top.

'I suggest that you have a linen thread on it and carry it around your neck.'

After a little pause she added:

'You haven't said what you think about it.'

'I am twenty years old. I neither want to be raped, nor do I want to die. I just do not know whom to believe - the news on the radio, or you or what Mrs Jacoby has said. I will take it, and think about it.'

'The reason why I am so scared is because I have not heard anything from Papa,' said my mother. 'He should have come to Königsberg by now. What if the Russians are already in Tilsit?'

I looked at the clock, and said:

'I have to go now, or I will be late. Don't worry about Christel. I will be with her. We promised one another we will stick together. If we really think the Russians are coming too near to Königsberg, we will take the train and come to Konitz. Don't worry about Papa, he usually knows what to do, and will just turn up.'

I got my things together, and left for the hospital.

I was back the next morning to see my mother off at the station. We hugged and kissed and we were both crying when the train left.


Two days after my mother left, I had a letter from the military command, informing me that Gitta had been killed. She had given my name as next of kin, and they informed me that *Flughelferin* (woman air force helper) Gisela K. had given her life for *Grossdeutschland*. It was a printed form and in the last paragraph I was asked to which address her belongings should go. There was also a letter from the commanding officer, informing me that Gitta had been killed whilst on duty at the gun, together with a number of other girls, and that they all had a combined funeral.

I could not believe what I read. Fate could not be so cruel as to finish off a whole family. Her mother would never know what had happened to her because, even now, she was still expecting visits from her husband, who got killed five years ago, and from her two sons, one of them killed, and the other one missing over the Channel. Her daughter, too, would now never visit her again, and she would wait in vain.

I had lost so many friends and dear ones by now that I felt quite numb. There was the big lump in my throat again. There was also a lump in my stomach so that I couldn't eat, but I did not cry. I just sat and thought of Gitta, and the time we had together at the university, and the last night in our house, when we slept together to keep warm, and I whispered:

'Dear, dear Gitta, you are not really dead, you are asleep somewhere. Rest in peace. You will not be forgotten.'

I replied to the letter, saying that her personal things could be posted to my address. They arrived in a small parcel. There were letters and photographs, and a few knick-knacks, amongst them a little coloured box. I opened the lid, and on the inside of it was a drawing of the God Eros, with bow and arrow shooting into a heart. Underneath it said:

*Stube 103* (room 103).

Gitta mentioned in one of her letters that she was in room 103, so I thought that the girls from this room must have given her this box. She had my letters in it. I took them out and burnt them with other letters, but I kept the box. This box is still in my possession and when I look at it I think of Gitta, not with sadness, but with affection, and I remember my youth, and the war, and the hardness of the time which was so long ago, and I am grateful for today, and appreciate the good times and the peace even more.

My mother wrote at the beginning of December that she still hadn't heard from my father and feared that he was not alive any more. She also said that she had heard from Astra, but didn't like the news she had from her.

'Astra has met a man,' she wrote, 'and although she hardly knows him, she wants to get married. She is very vague in her description of him. He is Austrian by birth, and a forest warden. Why isn't he in the army? Is there something wrong with him? And why is there such a hurry to get married? I don't trust Astra, she is not a good judge of men, she always wanted them too much. I have applied for a rail pass and, if I get it, I will go to Oberstdorf and fetch her back here to Tuchel for Christmas. I will only be away a few days, but I will let you know when I leave.'

This news was a great surprise to me, but what astonished me most was the sentence:

'I don't trust Astra, she is not a good judge of men, she always wanted them too much.'

So my mother knew what Astra was like and, maybe, she also knew that she had often tried to take my boyfriends away.

I wrote to my mother and told her to leave Astra alone and let her make her own decisions, whether it was a mistake or not, but she never got my letter because two days later I had a quickly scribbled note, telling me that she had left Tuchel.

In December, the work in the hospital increased. It was bitterly cold and, because of the coal shortage, the wards were hardly heated. More and more wounded soldiers arrived and we didn't know where to put them. We heard from them that the Russians were coming nearer. In the town, the first pathetic-looking refugee columns arrived. We were short of medical supplies and received parcels with paper bandages, which were hard and often painful on the wounds. I hardly went home, because my work day was twelve hours and, by the time I had finished I was much too tired to travel home. We nurses shared beds, so they were occupied day and night. I had my own sheets, which I put on the bed of a night nurse on duty if I wanted to sleep on it, or a day nurse on duty, if I slept during the day. The other nurses did the same.

From time to time, I was on *Bahnhofsdienst* (station duty). Trains arrived with wounded, who had to be sorted out. The station, having been bombed, was draughty, cold, and full of trodden-down snow and ice, and the stretcher bearers walking along from the trains slipped and slithered. We handled hundreds of wounded men, only picking out the more seriously hurt, who needed attention straight away. The others were transported further, to the main part of Germany. Many lightly wounded men were deeply relieved to escape the battlefield with honour. We were glad of the aid of the new miracle of medicine, penicillin, which was used in great quantity and which, therefore, often ran out.

The doctors walked along the train looking at the wounded, deciding on quick emergency treatment, and allocating the patients to different hospitals, or ordering them to remain on the train. I had to cut away mud-stained battle dress and bloody boots, which revealed the terrible tragedies beneath. Soldiers were often just dumped into the train because there was no field hospital, and Königsberg's main station was the first place where they could get medical attention. Many only lay on straw and a thin blanket in goods trucks. Some were already dead from their wounds and the frost and cold in the carriages. We often had 20 degrees below zero.

190

The only way to cope with this was to keep one's mind blank, not to think, but to pick out the ones who needed the most attention and ignore the others, even if everybody thought you were hard and without feeling. Like the time when I stepped over splinted limbs and stretcher handles, ignoring the plea for more blankets and pain killers, and moved to the man where a penetrating wound of the chest needed a large firm dressing to contain those ominous sucking noises.

'Keep him upright,' said the doctor, 'get another pillow.'

'You see to him,' said sister to me, and followed the doctor, who was already two stretchers ahead. Sister always had three or four nurses around her to pass on some of the jobs.

The doctor, in the meantime, kept on with his running commentary:

'Stomach here - get this one to our hospital as number one - quarter of morphia, Sister, straight away - another one for the hospital with a note for two pints of blood, one of plasma - gun shot, mortar blasts, mines, incendiaries -'

The doctor stopped, chewed his pencil, looked around. Who had priority? Of all these desperately wounded men, whose need was the most urgent? And the frightening thing was that none had travelled very far. So where was the Russian army, and how many German soldiers were there to fight them? Were we told the truth, or was there a cover-up?

In the hospital I was known as being hard, but that was not true. There was always so much to do that there was often no time to take off a bandage slowly to avoid pain, or to stop and sympathize with somebody who had lost a limb. But the ones who really needed an encouraging word or a little kindness because they had suffered too much did get it from me. Like the small sixteen year old who had lost both legs, and whose body was riddled with shots from the *Stalinorgel* (multiple rocket launcher). We all knew he wouldn't live long. He was often delirious, calling for his mother, and complaining about the pain in his legs, although they had been shot away. From time to time he was conscious, and I would go and hold his hand, and he would smile. He knew that he had no legs, but he never talked much about his wounds. It was as if he knew his time was limited, that he would die soon. When he was conscious, he would watch me going around the ward and wait until I came to him, and then he would smile. When he was asleep, or when his mind had gone, he would call his mother again and if I held his hand then he used to think I was his mother, and tell her that he was in pain. We were short of painkillers, too, and had to economize. I had no access to them and could not help him, but I could wash the sweat off his face and give him a drink, and say

191

a few kind words. I never knew whether I would see him again when I went off duty, so I always made a point of seeing him before I went.

One day he wasn't there any more, and I went into the laundry room and cried. Sister Helena found me and told me off but, just before I left the room to get on with my work, she suddenly put her arms around me and gave me a hug, without saying a word.

She, too, had been fond of the little soldier boy, I thought.

Everybody was in awe of the big man, Professor Strauss, who performed the more complicated operations. He visited the wards occasionally, only stopping to look at patients that he had operated on. He was always accompanied by a number of doctors and, of course, Sister Helena who by now was in charge of all the wards, and was called *Oberschwester* (Higher Sister). Professor Strauss was a brilliant surgeon, but also, according to the gossip, a little queer. He sometimes behaved irrationally, particularly since the big bomb attack against Königsberg, when he lost his wife and daughter, who was also a medical student. He had even walked out in the middle of an operation, I was told. He had suddenly stopped, looked at his assistant, and said:

'You can finish off the operation.'

Then he walked out into the so-called scrubbing up room, pulled his gloves off and his gowns and cap, changed his shoes, got his coat, and walked out of the hospital. Nobody knew where he had gone to, and nobody tried to find him either. He returned the next morning as if nothing had happened. The staff were now wondering whether this would happen again, and anybody assisting him during the operations was very alert in case he suddenly had to take over.

I had nothing much to do with Professor Strauss except if he was coming I had to take off the bandages before he arrived, so that he wouldn't lose any time waiting before the wound was exposed.

One day I was very busy doing just that, and I got behind because some of the bandages had stuck on. This always took longer, as they had to be eased off. On this particular day, there were more stuck-on bandages than usual, and I was attending to the last patient when Professor Strauss walked in. He marched through the whole ward, straight to my patient, having decided to start at this particular end of the ward.

'Sister Helga,' hissed Sister Helena, 'you haven't finished the preparations of the patients for the *Visite* (doctor's rounds).'

As a rule, one didn't reply to Sister Helena if she was in company and under no circumstances if surrounded by Professor Strauss and his staff, but I had been very busy, even hurting people in trying to be quick and being told off by the patients for it, that I forgot about the unwritten rule of silence. I said:

'It is the last patient, and a lot of bandages were stuck. The *Visite* also started from the wrong end . . .'

I stopped. Oh dear, I thought, now I have done it! I replied in front of Professor Strauss, his staff and, worst of all, Sister Helena.

Her face was a furious mask. She dare not reply, but I knew that she would send me away in a minute, and carpet me later on.

And then we heard Professor Strauss laugh loudly.

'Somebody did have the courage to reply to you, Sister,' he said, looking at her with twinkling eyes. 'There is going to be trouble later on,' he carried on, and looked at me.

'Is your name Helga?'

'Yes, *Herr* Professor.'

'Just like my daughter; the same name, and she, too, was a medical student.'

He could see that I was one because we students wore badges, indicating that we were medical and not nursing students.

'How old are you, and how long have you been at university?'

'I am twenty years old, and I have had three Semesters (terms) at university.'

'Helga,' he said, 'everything just like my daughter.'

He looked around the ward, then at his staff and Sister Helena, and then back at me .

'I am sure you have learnt all about bed-making, bedpans and bandaging. It is time to have a look-in at the operations. You will learn more there.'

With that, he turned towards Sister Helena:

'Make the arrangements, Sister. She can report at the Theatre in the afternoon. - Right, now let's get on, and look at this patient here.'

The *Visite* had started, and Professor Strauss walked through the ward, stopping at the patients that he had operated on, and taking no more notice of me.

Sister Helena didn't tell me off and I heard her talking on the phone to the Theatre Sister:

' . . he had one of his crazy ideas again. He wants one of my nurses, a medical student, to have a look-in, as he calls it. Her name is Helga, like his daughter. Something must have clicked, so that he suddenly wants her there. I hope it doesn't last long, I need her here badly . .'

In the afternoon I reported at the Theatre, and Sister there was just as autocratic as Sister Helena. She warned me not to faint, and then she said:

'Professor Strauss might have forgotten all about you. If that is the case, you can quietly slip away and get back to your ward where you are desperately needed. He does get funny notions occasionally. If he remembers you, you just have to watch what he is doing, but don't faint. Look at the floor if seeing blood puts you off, and watch the way he is cutting away on the patient. Always remember, they don't feel anything.'

Professor Strauss had not forgotten about me.

'Where is Nurse Helga?' he asked and, when he saw me, said:

'Good, I am glad you are here. Today you can just watch, and get used to seeing how things go. Tomorrow you might get a little job, if you haven't fainted today. A lot of them do the first time.'

He was quite an understanding man, I thought. Nobody ever mentioned that.

I, too, had to have a gown on and cover my hair before I was allowed into the Theatre. I was quite apprehensive. I would have preferred a job, because then I could have concentrated on it, but just to stand about, and watch that I was not in the way made me feel uneasy.

The soldier to be operated on had shrapnel in his thigh and, according to Professor Strauss, this was quite a straight forward operation. He had performed hundreds of them, Sister said. Professor Strauss was also a lecturer and he had a number of young doctors around him, apart from his assistant. He kept up a running commentary about what he was doing.

It was the first incision that shocked me, because he cut deep and sure. Although there was a lot of blood, busy hands around him seemed to know what to do to stop it. I felt queasy and quickly looked at my feet. I heard a voice behind me whisper, 'breathe deeply', and a hand in my back grabbed my gown and held me. I was determined not to faint and just stood where I was, taking deep breaths. I heard Professor Strauss' voice, but what he was saying didn't sink in, until he suddenly addressed one of the doctors and said:

'You may finish the operation and do the stitching up.'

I looked up and saw a startled young man gazing at the Professor.

'You have to learn,' continued the Professor, 'so get on with it. I will advise you if you get stuck.'

He stepped to the side and let the young doctor take his place. I was so fascinated with this switch over that I forgot all about my feeling queasy and watched the closing up of the wound and the stitching. The young doctor hesitated from time to time, but carried on, with an encouraging word and a little advice from the Professor.

There were four shrapnel operations that afternoon and, after a break, there was going to be quite a big chest operation. Each time, Professor Strauss asked another doctor to finish off the patient. I felt quite exhausted after the fourth operation, although I had done nothing except watch and stand about.

'I am glad you didn't faint,' said the Professor to me. 'You had better not watch the chest operation, you have seen enough for the first day. Come back tomorrow afternoon.'

I was dismissed. One of the nurses showed me where I could hang my gown and she said it would be there for me for the following day. The nurses were talking about the operations, and one of them said:

'He was nearly his old self again this afternoon. Not only a confident surgeon, but also an excellent teacher. He hasn't allowed the others to do anything lately.'

She turned to me and said:

'He hasn't permitted medical students into the Theatre either. Maybe Sister is right, it must have been your name that triggered it off, being the same as his daughter's.'

The next day, I worked on the ward in the morning and was in the Theatre in the afternoon. This time I got a job, cleaning and sterilizing the instruments, and I watched how they were laid out. I did not see all that much of the different operations because these jobs had to be done at the same time. Some operations followed one another very quickly and the instruments had to be ready.

Gradually I got into a routine; the mornings were spent on the wards, the afternoons in the Theatre. Professor Strauss addressed me from time to time when he saw me, but sometimes didn't even recognize me, because we all looked the same, or very similar, in our gowns, with our caps on.

After three weeks, he was suddenly transferred, and Sister Helena asked Theatre Sister to transfer me back to the wards. I had been an extra pair of hands in the Theatre, but I had never been fully occupied and could have been of more use on the wards.

Christmas was nearly upon us and the war news was bad. We all felt very uneasy because of the advancing Russian troops and, particularly, tanks, especially as nobody knew exactly where they were. I had been home once or twice for a few hours to look for post, but there was only a letter from

Hermann, who wrote regularly. Once I met Christel at home. We both felt we were the only ones left from our family except, of course, Astra in Oberstdorf. We had to assume that my father was dead, but we didn't know what had happened to my mother or to Hans.

My mother only wanted to be away a few days, but had left Tuchel over two weeks ago. My brother, although not a prolific writer, had usually posted us little notes informing us how he was doing with his schooling. He, too, hadn't written lately. All this was very worrying, and Christel and I wondered whether the Russians were maybe making a big circle around Königsberg, and we would be closed in without realizing it.

'The express train to Berlin is still going every other day,' said Christel. 'They only take wounded, mothers with children, if they have a rail pass, and I have heard that nearly all the party members have gone.'

I was sorry I had no more rail passes. I had even tried to contact Dr E., but he was not in Königsberg; even his secretary had gone.

They are *auf einer Dienstreise* (a business trip), was the reply I got.

Christel and I decided to wait until the New Year. If we hadn't heard from anybody by then, we would both find a way to leave the town, but together.

'Mama and Papa would never leave us alone for Christmas if they could come to us. They would at least send a message,' said I to Christel. 'Even if Mama decided to stay with Astra, she would write, unless there is no post any more.'

And then I remembered:

'I do get letters from Hermann.'

I didn't say that this must mean something had happened to our mother, I didn't want Christel to get frightened.

Christmas passed, and so did New Year, and there was no news from our parents. Neither of us had time off, but there were little Christmas celebrations in the hospital.

After New Year I rang Christel at the hospital to remind her of our arrangement and to ask her to come to our house. We had arranged that when I phoned her she would just leave without telling anybody and come home. We would then pack a few things and try and get on to a train and make our way to Konitz, then Tuchel. We both felt this was further west, away from the Russians, and my uncle would surely know what had happened to my mother.

Nobody seemed to know where Christel was at the hospital. I eventually got put through to a Sister, who informed me that Christel had left with a transport of wounded on the train to Pillau harbour.

'We are getting as many wounded away as possible, a number of them by boat from Pillau.'

I couldn't believe this. Christel had promised not to go without me. And then it struck me. They are evacuating the hospitals. At least they seem to have started with Christel's; ours was still working and nobody had said anything. There had been a lot of whispers, a lot of talk. Soldiers had warned us, but Sister was strict and would not allow any talk about the war situation.

Time must be getting short before the Russians are expected, I thought.

There was, of course, the possibility that Christel had made her way to our house, rather than accompany the transport of wounded. I never said anything at the hospital, but just walked out, taking my few belongings with me, and made my way home.

The tram was still going to Ratshof, but when I got home, I suddenly felt lost and lonely. The house was cold and dark. There was no electricity, no phone, no letters and no Christel. She hadn't been home to leave me a note, and she hadn't collected any of her things either.

What was I going to do? Was it better to return to our hospital and hope that the wounded would be transported with accompanying nurses to the *Reich*, and then I could go with them, or should I make my own way out of Königsberg? Where should I go, and how should I travel? There had not been any mention of evacuation of people from the town, and only Christel's hospital seemed to have started with some of the wounded. Our hospital might have been chosen to remain in service until the Russians arrived and that was the reason why nobody was allowed to talk about the advancing Russians. Well, if that's what was going to happen, I was not going to stay. I would make my own way to Tuchel or, failing that, go to Greifswald. These were the two places my mother had suggested, and I might find some news of her there.

I looked through my things. It was difficult to decide what to take. I found a big old rucksack, which we children used to have for picnics. I could carry that on my back. I also decided on a suitcase, and thought I could put this on a sleigh. Warm clothes were important, and a thick blanket. I had never heard about sleeping bags in those days. Money was another important thing. I had organised this already. For the last few weeks I had gone to the bank, and gradually drawn out nearly all the money from my account. I did have quite a bit, because my mother had started this account years ago when my father announced that he wasn't in agreement with me studying medicine. Although my father had promised to pay after my *Physikum,* my mother had never reduced the amount in that account.

I wondered how to carry the money. Some I would have to have on me, but the rest I put in the box which I had from Gitta, and this is the reason why it is still in my possession. The box went into the rucksack and I wrapped some clothes around it.

I also packed a few bottles of brandy, cigarettes and matches. We always had these things in the house for the purpose of bribing. I found two large, thick, hard smoked sausages, which I knew would keep, and took all the black bread I had organised for this purpose. I did not forget my first aid kit and some painkilling tablets, and I also hung the little phial which my mother had given me around my neck.

I cannot remember what else I took, except a small satchel with a few personal things, instead of a handbag, in which I also put some photographs. I was able to carry this across my shoulder.

I decided to have one more night at home, just in case Christel should turn up, then try the station in the morning, and get the latest news about any trains.

I did not sleep very well. It wasn't the cold, because I had a thick featherbed and blankets, but it was the worry about the next few days.

I wrote a note in the morning, describing my plan of travel, and left it on the kitchen table. I even tidied everything in the house. I was convinced that I would come back. Surely the German army would be able to push the Russians back. Hundreds and thousands of people were frightened of them, and soon the new *Wunderwaffe* would be in use. Even Hermann had hinted this.

I locked the front door in the morning and hid the key in our usual place at the back stairs in the garden. I had my rucksack on my back, my satchel over my shoulder, and the suitcase on the sleigh. I marched off, and I did not look back, because I was afraid I might cry.

This was the journey into the unknown, away from the familiarity of my youth, my childhood and my friends.

I did not know it then, that I had lost them all at that moment, and that I would never return.

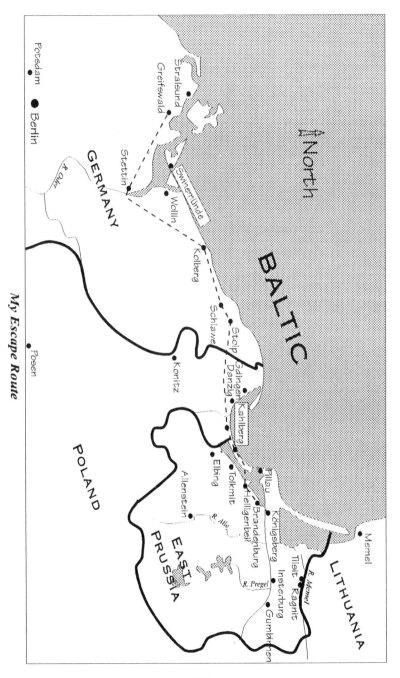

My Escape Route

Potsdam

Berlin

Stralsund
Greifswald

Stettin

GERMANY

Wollin

R. Oder

Swinemünde

Kolberg

BALTIC

North

Schlawe

Stolp

Gdingen
Danzig

Kahlberg

Konitz

POLAND

Posen

Elbing

Tolkmit

Allenstein

Heiligenbeil

Brandenburg

Pillau

Königsberg

R. Alle

EAST
PRUSSIA

R. Pregel

Insterburg

Tilsit
Ragnit

R. Memel

Gumbinnen

Memel

LITHUANIA

199

# PART TWO

## THE GREAT ESCAPE

# CHAPTER ONE

## The Russian Advance - Joining the Refugee Treks

At this point, it is necessary to describe what really happened in Germany and, particularly what happened in East Prussia.

Not being allowed to listen to any foreign news, we only received the information which we were supposed to hear. Goebbles' propaganda machine was very efficient. To doubt Germany's victory was treason, and to voice it could mean death to the unbeliever. In the first days of January 1945 we in Königsberg did not know the true state of the war. It was not until after the war that I found out how lucky I had been to start off from Königsberg when I did, and how cruel it was to leave us all in such ignorance. People could have been evacuated much earlier, in a proper fashion, when the trains were still going.

In January, most of the preparations by the people to hold back the Russian forces were useless, because there were no soldiers to occupy the fortifications. Many of the anti-tank ditches had fallen in. Hitler had sent more and more divisions to fight the Allies in the west in the Ardennes, as he thought this more important than East Prussia. He did not believe in a Russian offensive and we in East Prussia had no idea that there were hardly any forces at the border.

In the west, and in Italy, German troops were pushed back. Gradually the soldiers got disheartened and lost confidence in a possible victory. Some German units started to surrender to the Allies, others moved eastwards, pounded by Allied shells from north and south, and suffering under fighter bomber attacks from first light to dusk. Long columns of men, horse drawn carts, and a few surviving tanks and vehicles struggled eastwards. The dead were left behind, unburied, in the roads and fields, and everywhere were the stinking carcasses of horses and cattle, the ruins of field cars and trucks. Tanks, damaged and overheated, crawled along. Petrol was drained into canvas buckets from abandoned vehicles, until there was no more fuel to be found and they had to be blown up. After that, the crews started walking, just like the rest of the German army. Anybody speaking openly about the hopelessness of the military situation was posted to the Eastern Front, where now, as the winter had come, nobody wanted to fight.

The Russian offensive started on January 12th 1945, and this was the beginning of the catastrophe that broke out over East Prussia. The Red Army was a tremendous fighting machine when they entered East Prussia, determined to repay the Germans in their own kind for their Russian policies. The long harvest of bitterness which the Germans had sown was ripe for reaping, and the Russians showed this by the slogans on their tanks:

"For the Motherland" and "Death to the Germans".

They were successful with their offensive because of their mass of people and equipment, containing long-barrelled giant guns, Stubley Howitzers, and Katushas which fired rockets. The Soviet artillery men boasted:

'Where Katusha strikes, nothing lives.'

The result of the Russian offensive was the great flight of the civilian population to the west. It began in the worst German winter on record. The snow storms blowing over East Prussia came with even more force after the middle of January. They built snow mountains on the road, the like of which had never been seen before. All roads and paths were covered with refugees. Snakes of carts, people, and animals, pushed slowly forward. As soon as the snow clouds cleared a little, Soviet fighter planes appeared, dropping their bombs on to the helpless columns.

In the north, everybody was on the march to Pillau, the Baltic harbour. People, soldiers and wounded who reached that part, did have some hope of getting away from the oncoming wall of the Russian might by boat.

In the south, the Russians made their way to the 6,000 square kilometre industrial complex of Schlesien (Silesia), which they hoped to envelope to the north and south, but otherwise bypass. The area had a great many industrial installations, which the Russians later bodily removed to Russia. They now avoided any combat in that zone. They left an escape route to the south-west for the Germans. Machinery and equipment was therefore saved, but not human life.

Hitler left Ziegenburg, and moved to the Reichskanzlei in Berlin on January 16th 1945, directing the war from a bunker there.

Everybody believed the messages from Berlin and Posen (Poznan), and the propaganda given out day after day that the Russians had been stopped. There was great surprise when they suddenly heard the noise of guns firing. The misled inhabitants often didn't leave their villages until the last moment, and then got between the German and Russian fronts. If they got away, they only moved to the next village, believing that they would return soon.

Hitler refused again and again to divert any troops or tank divisions to East Prussia as he needed them in the west, and in Hungary, where the big oil wells were. The lost army in East Prussia had no fuel, and very little ammunition.

In the meantime, the Russians surprised unprepared villages, estates and farms, and ransacked them, raped women and young girls, and shot or hanged the men. They burnt down farmhouses and barns. There was plunder, devastation, violation, and abduction. Anybody alive after violation and rape was herded together and had to march to the north-east, in the direction of the Weichsel. They never saw their families again. If they were still alive, they had to make their way into the unknown, a way which for most of them meant the way to their death. Even the Poles suffered. They were treated the same as the Germans, as they often worked on the farms which were given to the *Auslandsdeutschen* (German expatriates) in the once Polish districts. All this was hell, living hell.

The Russians had a saying:
"The first wave gets the wrist watches,
The second wave gets the girls and women,
The third wave gets what is left!"

In February, it got even colder. The temperature dropped to 25 degrees below zero, and the wind got stronger and icier. German divisions and tank groups were scattered, often moving backwards without a leader. The roads were covered with ice, like glass. Anybody wounded just dropped and was left; the cold finished them off. The refugees started to move with the soldiers and the tanks.

As soon as the Soviets entered German land, they confiscated everything. In every village and every town, camps were organised where the *Beute* (loot) was collected. Everything was moved out of the houses, even floors, doors, windows, washbasins, toilets, lamps, wires and switches. Electrical installations and telephones were often put on to Russian lorries with shovels, showing the primitive organisation and mind of the Russian soldier.

The Germans were not allowed to stay in their houses. Men were collected, women, children, invalids and old people were pushed together into one building. The only exceptions were large estates with animals, where people were needed to look after them. The animals, if not killed for meat, were collected into big herds, and driven through Poland into Russia. Most of them died on the way from neglect and cold.

Nobody knew how many people had started to flee from the Russian armies since the beginning of January. They moved along the roads and by trains, or walked along the railway lines, through villages and towns, in the bitter cold and frost, through snow, ice, and thaw, and new frost again. And into the midst of these lost people, who thought they had found somewhere to stay for a while, fell an Anglo-American *Bombangriff* (bomb raid) in the town of Dresden, on 13/14th of February 1945.

The bombing of Dresden took place in three stages. Large areas were erased, and whole parts of the town wiped out. The fire fighters were helpless, they could not save anything. It was impossible to get into some parts of the town, and the actual number of deaths could not be established. Parts of the town, and their dead, lay empty for years, particularly the small streets. Stations, streets and meadows had been bombed, which were full of people and refugees. The estimated number of dead was 135,000 people.

The whole of East Prussia was suddenly on the move. Nobody wanted to stay behind and wait for the Russian tanks and their soldiers. People started to flee, with hastily packed wagons, carts, and sledges, in big columns. There were no able men left, and French prisoners-of-war, women, young boys, and a few old men had to lead the carts with the horses. They had often only just been reassured by propaganda speeches or a party member that the Russians would not enter their town or village, and had stayed until they heard the shooting, then grabbed a few belongings, and tried to leave by train, or on foot. Trains soon did not run any more, so it was that everybody had to walk. On the roads were a mixture of panic-stricken people, and retreating soldiers. It was bitterly cold and, in normal times, no creature would have been outside.

Russian planes shot at anything moving along the roads. The old, invalids, children, and sufferers from the attack were left behind on the road, or in the provisional and simple night quarters vacated by the refugees.

It was impossible for the weak German army to push the mighty Russian force back. Hitler changed his generals too often, replacing them with people he felt he could trust, often party members, who were not capable of commanding an army.

The refugees had hoped to get a free road to the Weichsel but, when this did not happen because of the advancing Russian tanks they moved north and north/west. Then came the news that the only free way now was the frozen Frische Haff and, by going over the ice to the Nehrung, one could get to Danzig and Pommern. Russian tanks, followed by motorised Infantry, had reached Allenstein, and were pushing further over the railway line towards Elbing. Being provided with more and more masses of Russian manpower, they were able to reach the Frische Haff, and the encircling of East Prussia was accomplished.

Headquarters was not concerned with how many refugees suffered, froze to death, or perished. Erich Koch, the *Gauleiter* of East Prussia, had secretly left Königsberg at the beginning of January, leaving a number of party bosses behind. He insisted that he was not only the Gauleiter of Königsberg but of the whole of East Prussia, and had to position himself where he was needed. He occupied the best hotel in Pillau, at the harbour, together with his *Stab* (staff). When this was bombed, he moved into a house in Neutief, but let the people, particularly Hitler's headquarters, believe that he was still in Königsberg. He was prepared to flee if necessary and for this purpose he had a *Fieseler Storch* (small German aeroplane), and an ice breaker standing ready at all times. He gave everybody the impression that he, personally, would defend Königsberg, and was even prepared to perish in the town. Hitler trusted him, not realizing what a coward he was. Erich Koch had been the master of the east, and he was unwilling to lose this post, which would happen if East Prussia was lost to the Russians. Anybody in the army preparing or suggesting retreat had to be replaced. Koch saw to this, by informing Hitler at headquarters.

When I left home, the big Russian offensive had just started. The first refugees had already reached Königsberg. They and the wounded soldiers had told us about the Russian tanks and their armies, pointing out how much nearer they were than we were told.

I decided to go first to the main station because, even if I couldn't get a train there, I would meet people with the latest news of the Russian advance, and what other ways there were to get away from the town. I discovered that trains were still going, but only one or two a day because of coal shortage, and then only for people with permits. The SS stood at the barriers with guns, preventing the mass of people from pushing through and getting on to the trains.

'They shot two people yesterday who ran for the train,' said a woman next to me.

She had been at the station for two days and hoped to get a place on an extra train, which was promised for this morning. I waited with her, because she said the train was going to the west, probably Berlin.

It was bitterly cold. The station had been bombed, and the roof replaced only with a few boards, preventing the snow from coming in. There were no windows, only large gaping holes, but the walls still existed, and one could shelter behind them from the wind. There were crowds of people, all waiting for this special train, but there was no food or drink, and no toilets. By late afternoon, I was desperate to go to the toilet and also to have something to eat. I was afraid to open my case where I had my food lest people could see what was in it and ask me to share it, and then I would not have anything for later on.

I moved away from the people and tried to find a place where I could be alone. I left the station and made my way to the *Güterbahnhof* (goods depot), hoping to find it empty. There were a few wagons, occupied by refugees, and some people had huddled behind a little house where they were sheltered from the wind. I discovered that it was the railwaymen's toilet and still working, so I used it! Nobody took any notice of me, so I explored the place, and found the signal box. Most windows were broken and boarded up, some were cracked, and the door, which one reached by going up some steps, was a big board without a handle. I could see a figure moving about and there was smoke coming out of an iron pipe.

I pushed my sleigh and suitcase under the stairs and climbed up the steps. I lifted the board to the side and entered the room.

'Close it!' shouted a voice. 'Don't you know that it is cold outside?'

This must be a joke, I thought. Of course I knew it was cold, not only cold, but freezing, and at least 15 degrees below zero.

I put the board back and could feel the warmth in the room. I looked at the old man sitting next to an iron stove watching me.

'What do you want?' he said. 'Nobody is allowed in here, I am on duty, moving the points.'

'I am very cold,' I said. 'I have waited all day at the station for the extra train to Berlin, but it hasn't come yet.'

'There is no train,' he said.

I looked at him in disbelief, because I couldn't imagine that all the people in the station, including myself, had just waited there for nothing.

'Come and warm yourself,' he said suddenly and, when I got a little nearer, he added: 'You can have a little hot soup.'

I noticed that he had an old pot on top of the stove and, when he lifted the lid I could smell the soup. He poured some into a mug and gave it to me.

'Thank you,' I said. My hands were trembling when I took the mug. It was a very thin soup and tasted more like salty water, but it was hot, and it warmed my inside.

'Sit down,' said the old man, pulling a box forward. I think he was glad to have some company, because he didn't seem to have anything to do. When I had finished my drink, I gave him the mug back, but he told me to keep it and hang it on to my rucksack as I would need it.

He knew a lot about trains, at least about the railway lines, because trains were hardly running. He advised me not to wait for the Berlin train because if I didn't have a permit I would not be able to get on to it. Only party members and their families could travel and if there was a space they would take a few wounded. He told me that my best plan would be to make my way to the harbour and try and get on to a boat travelling along the *Seekanal* (deep shipping lane) to Pillau. There I could get a boat to Danzig, or Gotenhafen (Gdingen), and then further to Stettin. He had heard that one didn't need a permit for the boat, and that refugees were transported from there. He warned me that it was no good relying on trains. I would never get on to one, particularly with a sleigh and the suitcase. He turned out to be a very nice old man, who wanted to help me.

By now it had got very dark and he suggested that I slept in his signal box on some sacks and started on my journey in the morning. Until his suggestion, I hadn't realized that he lived in this building, but I didn't mind; at least it was warm here. He had odd bits of wood, which he collected from the goods yard, and he organised coal from some of his engine driver friends. I brought my suitcase and sleigh into the signal box and gave him a piece of sausage, because he had shared his bread and soup with me.

The next morning I made my way to the Pregel harbour, together with hundreds of other people, hoping to get a place on a boat. Torpedo boats and even a mine-sweeper went from there, and there were also the big coalboats, which usually went along the canal. The coalboats pushed in front as icebreakers, and the others followed in the opened channel.

I had assumed that when I got to the harbour there would be some kind of organisation or guidance to get the refugees on to the boats; that one either bought a ticket for the boat, or even got the travelling free, with the government footing the bill. I soon learnt how mistaken I was when I saw the crowds of people with their different belongings piled up at the harbour. I couldn't even get near a boat, and there certainly was nobody selling tickets.

The captains of the coalboats used the need of the people to make themselves rich - necessity knows no law. They asked for high prices. They took jewellery, money, or other valuable items, and some desperate families gave all the money they had. When people argued about the high prices, the captains pointed out the risk they were running, as Soviet planes bombed a number of boats.

I listened and talked to people. Most of them were in groups, or families were together, whilst I was alone. In this way, I could get around from one group to another. I thought that even if I paid a high price and got to Pillau, I would have to pay an even higher price to get away from there because the next crossing of the water, the Baltic, was much longer. I could not spend all my money now, with the uncertainty of the future.

I discovered that some people had already waited days and nights, although they were prepared to pay, because the few boats going along the *Seekanal* through the Haff to Pillau had to come back again to pick other people up. Everybody was frightened, cold and hungry. Some people decided to walk back to the town in the morning, others resigned themselves to stay there, while some started to walk along the icy road to Pillau, hoping to get a ship from there.

There were also those who decided to walk westwards, along the coast of the Haff, because they had been told that they could cross the frozen Haff further along, and get to the Frische Nehrung, the small land strip dividing the Baltic and the Frische Haff. Walking along the Nehrung, one could reach Danzig, and a ship to the west.

It was bitterly cold and even with my blanket wrapped around me I could not get warm that night. I thought of the kind old man in the signal box and the thin hot soup. I chewed a little of my black bread, and a bit of sausage, taking a long time over it. I debated what to do, and which way to walk.

It was much too cold to stay for days in the harbour and wait for a kind captain who would take me on his boat for a reasonable price. I was not going to pay the exorbitant sums asked for. In any case, the longer I waited, the nearer the Russians would come. If I walked with the others to Pillau, I would again be confronted with having to fork out a large sum of money to get on to a boat, not even being sure whether there were boats. In any case, I didn't like sea journeys. I always had to fight sea sickness and, at this time of the year, it would be very cold indeed to sit on deck, where I usually went, for the fresh air. If we were bombed or torpedoed, we would never survive in the cold water, with the temperature between 10 to 15 degrees below zero. I also never intended to go to Danzig. I still had the idea of going to Tuchel, and that was the way to the west. I decided to go with the people who wanted to go along the edge of the Haff towards the west, and then make my way to Elbing. I also thought I could call at the Swiss Embassy in Elbing, which was neutral; surely I would be protected there. Walking would be much better than standing around or sitting in this freezing cold weather.

Once I had worked out what I was going to do, I soon went to sleep. When I woke, I couldn't move anything.

I am frozen stiff, I thought, and got frightened.

Gradually I was able to move my arms, my hands, and my fingers, then my legs, but my feet were like lead and I could not feel them. I mentioned it to a woman next to me.

'Take your boots off, and rub them with snow,' she said.

I did what she suggested, but it took a long time before the feeling in my feet came back. I never forgot her advice and, whenever after that I couldn't feel my hands or feet, I would rub them with snow.

The harbour was full of wagons and carts. There were prams, bicycles, sledges, motorbikes and people, people, people. As soon as it was light, there was movement everywhere, and the columns started off in different directions, spurred on by the stories they had heard about the terrible revenge of the Russians, leaving behind the people who were frightened to start the march into the unknown.

I joined the column that went to the west. It started to snow and an icy wind was blowing. I wrapped my blanket over my head also, and walked behind a cart, so that I was a little sheltered from the wind. I tied the rope from the sledge around my waist, keeping my gloved hands under the blanket. When the cart stopped to let the horses rest, I, too, stopped. The woman who had guided the horses took a box and sat down by the side of the cart. I pulled my sleigh up and sat on top of my case next to her, using the cart as a back rest. I took a piece of bread and sausage out of my pocket, and ate them. The woman did the same. Neither of us spoke, or offered the other food. She got up and pulled some hay down from the back of the cart and gave it to the horses. I noticed that there was an old woman in the cart, and two small children, huddled in featherbeds.

I followed the cart again when she started off. I had no idea where we were going. There were no sign posts, but it was a big icy road, and other people had gone along it before us, because there were dead bodies in the ditches. The road was jammed with the column of refugees, driving their herds of cattle and horses, and moving along like a grey-brown snake.

Everything stopped in the evening and some people tried to make a fire to warm themselves. I was just thinking of joining them, when others shouted. We could hear the noise of planes. Russian night fighters were soon there, and a whole column of refugees was shot at with machine guns. There were many dead. The snow was too high, and the earth too hard, to dig a big grave. I helped to attend to the wounded but in the morning they were left behind unless they could walk. From now on there were no more fires allowed at night.

The cart which I had accompanied the day before was not moving when I decided to start in the morning, so I just joined the ones who had started. I had rubbed my hands and feet again with snow, but I could not get warm. I thought of running a bit, but felt that I had to preserve my energy, not knowing how long this wandering would last.

In the afternoon I had a great surprise. I suddenly met some neighbours from our street, Mr and Mrs Katlus. At first, I was really pleased to see them. I had been very lonely, and I also felt that as they were more my parents' age, actually a little older, it would probably be quite a good idea to stay with them. I am afraid that I soon changed my mind, and even regretted that I had met them.

Mr Katlus had lost a leg in the First World War and walked with a stick. He jokingly said that he would not get frostbite in his wooden leg. He and his wife were carrying far too much stuff with them. He had a large homemade rucksack, which was hanging down his back up to the hollows of his knees. His wife was the same, burdened with a big heavy rucksack. They were marching very slowly along and I felt that I could get on much faster without them. Mr Katlus then suggested putting his rucksack on top of my suitcase saying, of course, that he would help me to pull the sleigh. Before I could reply or make an excuse, he stopped, pulled the rucksack off and tied it to my sleigh. He did help with the pulling, but we gradually moved to the back of the column because of his slowness.

Before, whenever the road sloped down, I would sit on top of my case on the sleigh and toboggan down hill. Going up was not too bad, because I only had one case. Now we had to hold the sledge back when going down and when going up it was hard to pull. Mr Katlus had the greatest difficulty, as he kept on sliding backwards. His wife would help him, and I had to struggle on my own to get sledge, cases, and large rucksack up the hill. Having my own rucksack on my back, I felt like a packhorse. I needed a plan of how to get away from them. They were very grateful for my help, and said so, but they never realized that they had forced themselves on to me, or did they do it on purpose?

Late in the afternoon we saw a village, with a small road leading to it. The column carried on along the main road, but Mr Katlus suggested that we ought to go to the village. We could maybe get some food there. He said they had nothing to eat. Mr Katlus was the sort of man who suggested things, but didn't wait for a reply. A suggestion to him was a command, one had to do it. He had hardly finished speaking, when he had already turned off towards the village. When we got there, we found the place empty. The people had already left, but at least we could spend the night in a barn. There was no food anywhere and Mr Katlus didn't ask me whether I had any. He said that we would just have to go to sleep hungry and look for some food in the morning. We crawled into the hay, but after a little while, Mr Katlus said it was draughty where they were and he and his wife moved with their rucksacks to the other end of the barn.

'You will help us again in the morning, won't you?' said Mrs Katlus anxiously.

'Of course she will,' said Mr Katlus, 'she is our neighbour, and we will look after her as she has no parents.'

'Good night,' I said.

After a little while, I could hear movements, then silence, then movements again. I kept very still.

'Are you asleep?' asked Mrs Katlus.

I kept quiet. She repeated the question, but I didn't stir.

The moon was shining and some light came through a little window. I lifted my head up gently and saw Mr Katlus sitting up, leaning against the wall and eating something. His wife was taking things out of the rucksack.

Up till now I had felt sorry for them, but that settled it. I made up my mind to leave them early in the morning. As neighbours they had never done anything for us; we were only on speaking terms, that was all. Having made me help them all day and then to tell me they had nothing to eat was most unfair. I had nearly offered them some of my bread and sausage!

I now took a little out of my pocket and ate it quietly. Every morning I had put some in my pocket, so that I didn't have to open my case during the day. I was very thirsty, but I dare not get up to go and eat a little snow, which I had done before to quench my thirst, in case Mr Katlus realized I was not asleep.

It was still dark when I got up and left the barn silently with my belongings. There was no movement from the Katlus couple and, although I had made up my mind to leave them behind, I felt a little guilty.

I made my way back to the main road and when it was light I met the column again, some of them already marching along. People didn't talk much; most of them just walked along, trying to keep themselves warm. There were only a few old men, the rest were women and children. Everybody who could walk did so. Only the old, the invalids, and the very young were allowed to remain on the carts and wagons. This was to save the horses.

In the ice and snow we pushed forward slowly, step by step. Peoples' faces were hardly visible. Many had put sacks over their heads with little slits. Some carts were without covers because they were hastily packed. The people walked in silence; the only noise was the horses' steps on the snow and, from time to time, the high pitched noise of a badly-greased wheel axle.

The first bigger place we reached was Brandenburg, on the Frische Haff, where every house, every yard, and all roads were full of people with carts and wagons. Somebody said there were barracks where one could stay the night and, having had already some nights in the open, I decided to find a covered sleeping place. I moved through the wagons, carts and people, and eventually found the so-called refugee camp. They were old wooden buildings, full of dirty, foul-smelling straw, filled with hundreds of people. They were so crowded that many sat back to back. There were one or two fires outside, and people brought more wood to keep the fires going. I tried to get near one to get a little warmth, but this was impossible. In the end, I just sat in the street, like everybody else, resting my back against a house wall, and having to be content that I was at least sheltered from the wind.

There was a lot of talk about crossing the frozen Haff to the Nehrung, and then walking along this narrow land strip to get to Danzig, but some people said it would be better to go further, towards Heiligenbeil, because the Haff was not so wide there. I looked at my map and could see that this was true, so I decided to carry on walking. Heiligenbeil was also a bigger town where I maybe could get some food, because my bread and sausage were nearly finished.

I quietly took a sip of brandy from a small bottle in my satchel. The liquid burnt down into my empty stomach. I realized the bottle was nearly empty so, in the morning, I would have to find a quiet place where I could fill up my small bottle. I had several bottles of brandy in my rucksack and case, but carried a small one in my satchel.

It had snowed again during the night, but I had been lucky. Where I was sitting the roof was overhanging a little, and the snow hardly touched me. The storm and wind had blown the snow into metre-high dunes, and the carts and wagons looked like lumps, with the snow on top of them. I wondered what the people looked like who were underneath.

I started to walk again, joining a trek to Heiligenbeil. I had been able to fill up my brandy bottle. I ate my last bit of bread and sausage and took a sip of brandy.

I do not know how long I was walking before I reached Heiligenbeil because, not having any more food, only a little brandy, things were a bit hazy at times. I slept in barns or sheds, and was able to crawl under some straw in a barn one night, and sort out my case and rucksack in a little privacy.

The road where our trek went along was marked with abandoned goods; prams, suitcases, bundles, bags, sacks, children's toys, boxes, bedding, even sewing machines. Nobody really knew where the Russians were, and we were all afraid that they would turn up at the next village or town.

In Heiligenbeil, the town was again full of people; more and more arrived and there was no space for them. This time we also met soldiers, a number of them wounded, who had come from the battle front. Everybody moved about in hopeless heaps through the snow-covered streets, trying to find a place to stay, in schools, barracks or barns.

At least there were a few soup kitchens, which had been started by the army, and people stood in long lines, waiting patiently for a piece of bread, and a mug of soup. I joined a queue and, when I had finished my soup and bread, I very quietly joined a second line for another helping.

Women, covered like mummies to keep out the cold, walked from house to house, begging for a bed, or some warm milk for their babies. There were children, who pulled along their ill mothers on sledges, or even sitting on suitcases, asking for a doctor, a bed or, at least, a warm corner. I, too, walked along to find a place to stay, and also to get some food, as I had eaten my last piece of bread and sausage. There were no shops open, and the remaining inhabitants of the town were afraid of the thousands of people occupying their streets and buildings. Many were afraid that they might have to take in the refugees, so they bolted their doors and windows. But I also saw a few who gave warm milk to the children.

In Heiligenbeil, I was able to get some bread in exchange for some cigarettes. The same people allowed me to stay in their garden shed, if I could dig it out of the snow. I went to look for somebody to help me, and found two wounded soldiers, who were willing to give me a hand. One had his arm amputated, but was very strong and dexterous, and the other had a stiff leg after a bullet had hit his knee. We worked hard, and soon had the entrance of the shed clear of snow, and also a small window. We pushed the contents to one side, and made enough space to stretch ourselves out on the wooden floor. There were rags and papers in the shed, which we used as mattresses; at least they covered the floor a little. There was no heating, and no comfort, but it was a place away from the crowds, sheltered from the wind and, with three of us close together, warmer than outside, where the temperature had dropped to minus 20 degrees Celsius at night.

My two new friends told me their stories. Max was married, with three children, and lived in Berlin. He had to have his left arm amputated because after being wounded it took a long time before he had proper hospital attention and by then gangrene had set in. He was quite philosophical about it and, in a way, glad to be able to make his way back home, having finished now with fighting in the army. Friedrich, on the other hand, being younger and keen on sport, was unhappy about his stiff leg. It would stop him from a number of things, not only sport, but also dancing, and climbing steps and stairs, etc. Still, at the moment, there were more urgent things to be considered, like where to go from here.

Max and Friedrich had been on a motorised transport for wounded, going the same way as I had come, when the Russians had shot at them from the air. Their lorry was hit and burnt out, and they were told to get to Heiligenbeil where they would get some transport. They soon realized that this was an empty promise when they arrived in the town. They had even further bad news for me. I had intended to make my way to Elbing, but they said that by the time I got there, the Russians would have arrived there also. They had already reached Güldenboden, just before Elbing. Max said:

'There are no more trains going to Berlin. This morning at the station I met wounded soldiers whose train had returned to Heiligenbeil because the Russians were shooting and bombing Elbing. They will take the town soon. The door to the west is then closed.'

216

I could not understand this. We had always been told that the German divisions would hold the Russians when they entered East Prussia, and now the Russians had even come from the south. Max and Friedrich, with the help of my little map, informed me of the reality of the situation.

The only way out now was across the frozen Haff to the Nehrung; then, walking along this strip of land, one could reach Danzig or Gotenhafen and hope to get a boat to the west. I told Max and Friedrich that I had hoped to reach Konitz and then Tuchel, where I had relatives, and could, maybe, get some news about my mother.

'This is impossible,' said Max. 'The Russians are already crossing the frozen Weichsel between Thorn and Graudenz, and it won't be long before they are in the Tucheler *Heide*. You will have to cross the Haff with us and get to Danzig, and then plan the next step.'

I liked the two words "with us", meaning that we would now stick together. And to show that I accepted my two new friends, I produced my bread and asked them to share it. They were even better off than I, having quite a bit of food, amongst it a few tins of corned beef. The army had supplied them with some iron rations, too, and extra food and blankets and warm clothes.

At night, we slept close together and, for the first time, I felt a little warmth creeping into me. In the morning, I suggested taking some of their things onto my sledge, but they preferred their rucksacks and satchels. Max, although he had only one arm, was excellent, the way he managed. Friedrich's leg was very stiff in the morning, and the wound on his knee looked angry and red. I made him a new bandage and applied a thick layer of antiseptic cream, hoping that it was only the cold that had discoloured his wound.

We marched off in the direction of the Haff. The columns of carts, wagons, animals, and people were crawling along the road, and the fields and meadows towards the ice of the Haff and, once we all got there, we just stood, and waited, and stared. There were at least 3,000 carts pushed together in endless rows. The wheels of the vehicles stood in brown/white earth, which had thawed, and then frozen again.

It had started to snow, and a cold wind came from the Frische Haff, which made not only us, but also the animals, shudder. We found a spot amongst the carts, a little sheltered from the wind, and we waited, like everybody else. Further back, I could hear the wheels of other carts creaking. They pushed along until they reached the queue of the refugees, making the snake of people, animals and vehicles even longer. Much further back, we could suddenly hear the sound of guns and fighting and, when it got dark, we saw the fires from burning villages. Everybody started to get restless and frightened, but the army was there and assured us that there would be a road staked out in the morning, to provide a kind of bridge across the Haff.

This was the first time that I really got scared. Now I could see for myself how near the Russians were, this was serious. Max and Friedrich had told me about it, but now I saw it with my own eyes. We whispered together, and decided to move as near as possible to the ice, so as to be some of the first ones ready for the crossing. In a way, it was reassuring to have soldiers here.

In the night I heard the hungry cattle bellowing, and I shivered. I was jealous of the people in their carts and wagons, who pushed together in the straw under the tarpaulin. Muffled up women stood guard by the horses and wagons, so did a few old men, French and Polish prisoners-of-war. The flight of millions through East Prussia, which was like a witches cauldron, had made everybody hard. Despair had killed the natural honesty of people. Some who had lost their horses on the way, tried to take the horses from other wagons. So the guards were there to protect the horses, and also to be prepared to move when the word came, so that they would not be left behind on this terrible coast. Most of the people were women and children, some were babies, and there were the wounded who were capable of walking.

As soon as it started to get light, there was movement everywhere. The animals had to be fed if the people had food for them. Children cried because they were cold and hungry. A woman had died in the night, and some of the old men had started to dig a grave in the hard earth. When they laid her into it, people arrived with other bodies, children and newborn babies who had died of hunger because the mother had no milk.

'Please bury the baby with the others,' a mother said, giving the bundle to one of the men. 'I don't want to leave it behind on the roadside.'

Her voice was monotonous and weak, without feeling.

It was so terribly cold that most of the time I was shivering. Max tried to warm me. Friedrich was quiet and never said much, waiting for Max to make the decisions. I decided not to look at his knee in the morning, but hoped the cream had worked.

Somebody had made a fire, and there was hot water. Friedrich had some bouillon cubes, so we all had hot soup for breakfast, dipping in the hard bread. We sat near the fire, and I got a little warmer; at least, I could feel my feet again.

The army had made a bridge over the Haff with the help of fishermen and pioneers, who had staked out a route where the ice was safe. There were wooden boards at the coast, so that the thin ice there would not break, and also to cover the unfrozen edge. We were told that we had to cover about 8-10 km of ice, and must keep 15 m distance between the wagons, otherwise the ice might break. Two officers rode along the trek, enquiring whether there was room on any of the wagons as hundreds of refugees were incapable of walking any further because of frozen feet. Even if there was space, people would not take anybody. They had become very selfish. The horses had to be considered; they still had a long way to go, and it was better to have a lighter load.

The ice bridge across the Haff had been bombed by the Russians two days ago and when the men, who had staked out a new route came along the coast, everybody tried to get near them to ask whether it was still possible to get over the Haff. The question was whether the 4th army division would be able to hold back the Russians long enough for all the refugees to cross.

'Yes, the ice will hold,' said one officer. 'Thousands of people have already crossed the Haff. Only make sure you keep your distance, and watch for cracks and splits in the ice.'

The trek started, and gradually the wagons and the people moved. Some horses refused to go onto the ice, but the soldiers pulled them across the boards, and onto the hard, white slippery surface. Max, Friedrich and I, stepped over the boards on to the ice and started to walk. Friedrich needed a little help at first, but soon found a way of balancing himself with his stick. Max insisted on helping me to pull my sledge, so I didn't tie the rope around my waist. We made sure we kept a distance of approximately 15m from the cart in front of us. This was as well, because the wheels of the cart threw up melted ice water, forming a spray behind.

It creaked under the wheels and the horses hooves, and we were worried that the ice might break. Right and left from our staked-out path lay the sacrifices from the last few days; sunken carts, horses which had either frozen to death or been shot to save them the last suffering death. But the worse things were the human bodies, frozen stiff and lying in grotesque positions on the ice. I avoided looking to the side, because I started to feel sick with fright.

'Keep going,' said Max, and Friedrich added:

'Look straight ahead.'

Soft ice was covered by boards but even that was not always safe; we passed a wagon which had only recently broken in and was left behind.

Sometimes a wagon that had broken in could be pulled out again. Before this was undertaken, it had to be unloaded. There was a stoppage when this happened. Max and I helped one such wagon and the people were most grateful.

Suddenly the ice cracked, and a big ice floe like a triangle broke away, carrying a wagon along. I stopped and caught my breath, but it was alright, because the ice moved towards a bigger piece and the horses jerked the wagon across and back into the old column.

A woman fell through the split ice and people screamed. They tried to get her out with a pole. Was it worth it? She would only freeze to death with her wet clothes. We did not look to see what happened because it was snowing now, and walking against the wind became more and more difficult.

My father always used to say that one can talk oneself into things until one believes them and I kept on repeating to myself:

'I am not cold, I am not cold, I am not cold.'

Slowly I pushed along with my blanket over my head, nearly covering my face, and repeated these words. Gradually I came to the conclusion that my father was wrong.

It stopped snowing and, suddenly, there were the Russian planes. I could hear the shots of the machine guns and the pom-pom of the little bombs. The horses got frightened, reared up and galloped away. The distances were forgotten and whole groups of horses and wagons broke through the overloaded ice. The horses sank, pulling the wagons with them. Women and children screamed for help. People ran around in helpless despair, where mothers and children had disappeared into the ice-opening formed by the bombs. They ran to the other wagons and begged for help. A woman knelt on the ice and shouted with folded uplifted hands:

'Please don't leave us - help us!'

But who could help? Everybody had difficulties with their own wagons and horses.

Even so, I stopped and looked and wondered what I could do. I heard Max shout something - a warning - but it was too late.

The ice split behind me and I could feel a tremendous pull on the sledge rope, which made me fall over.

'Let go! Let go!' shouted Max and at the same time he threw himself over my body.

I let the rope go. The sleigh disappeared into the crack in the ice, pulling me along towards it. If it hadn't been for Max's weight on my body, I would have fallen into the hole. In this way, only one side of my body dipped into the water, and Friedrich was already pulling at both of us, having thrown himself flat on to the ice. He got us away from the edge of the hole.

'Get up,' he said. 'It is much too cold to lie on the ice.'

He pulled the wet blanket and my rucksack off me, then took his rucksack off, unrolled his blanket and wrapped me in it.

'Have you got some brandy left?'

'In my rucksack,' I said. I was shivering all over, and my teeth were chattering.

Max had already opened the rucksack and found the bottle. He held it to my mouth.

'Drink!' he commanded. 'And don't spill any, it is too precious!'

He, too, had a sip. Both men then started to rub my wet side. They told me to keep on moving, and not to stand still. We moved away from the split ice, and I put on my rucksack again. They wrapped Friedrich's blanket over my head and made me walk, pulling me and pushing me. I was a little drunk from the brandy, and so tired, and so cold, I didn't really want to walk any more. I stumbled along, shivering all the time.

Suddenly we could see a strip of land, covered in a faint mist.

'The Nehrung!' somebody shouted. 'Look, there it is!'

But there was still a long way to go, and the land didn't seem to come any nearer. At one spot there were so many dead people and animals that one could see that people had not taken enough care to keep their distance once they saw the land again. It started to snow once more, and the sky changed colour and looked yellow. The coast of the Nehrung with its pine trees became invisible. I felt disheartened and sick and full of despair. I thought we had walked for hours and hours and seeing all the dead and frozen animals and people made me aware of the danger all around me. Every time the ice creaked I shuddered, and now we had seen land, and then it disappeared again.

People started to throw things from their wagons to make them lighter. Other wagons rolled over sticky soft flour sacks, pieces of cloth, and even smoked pork sides and bags of potatoes. Max stopped and picked up some potatoes. We pushed them into our pockets, and I squeezed two into my satchel. The pork was frozen, but Max broke a few pieces off, holding one end with his foot and bending the other end until it cracked and broke. We had to watch where we were going because it was now snowing hard, and I nearly fell over two thin long pieces of wood pointing upwards.

They turned out to be the shafts of a wagon of which nothing else was to be seen.

Suddenly the horses seemed to pull harder; they could smell the land. With a last effort, and encouraging words from the women drivers, the horses pulled the wagons over the edge of the Haff on to a small embankment then stopped amongst low bushes. The three of us followed the wagon in front of us. We watched the woman who had guided it throw her arms around the neck of one of the horses and rub her face in its wet mane, as if she wanted to say thank you.

Once on land, Max and Friedrich collected wood, cutting branches off the fir trees, and made a fire. My clothes had become very stiff from falling into the Haff; the water on them had frozen to ice. I had to sit close to the fire to try and dry my clothes. Of course, they never did get dry, but they got soft again. Friedrich also tried to dry my blanket. We put some potatoes into the fire and melted some of the pork. At least we had food, even if the potatoes tasted rather funny, as they had been frozen. It got dark and we had to put out the fire so as not to attract the Russian planes. We picked more branches from the fir trees as a foundation for a bed, and all three of us huddled close together, wrapped in all our blankets, to try and keep warm in the night.

Max and Friedrich made a fire again the next morning. We melted some snow for warm water to rub our feet with and clean our teeth. I hadn't done this for a long time. We had a hot drink of tea and ate the bread which I had exchanged for cigarettes in Heiligenbeil. We talked about the day before, and I said that I was sorry for having lost my case and sleigh. I now had no more cigarettes and only one bottle of brandy left, but I still had all my money, and I was still alive.

# CHAPTER TWO

## Village of Hell - Flight to Stettin

The exodus of people reached from Königsberg and the Samland, and from the ferries between Pillau and Neutief over the Frische Nehrung, through the Weichselniederung and Westpreussen (West Prussia), and Pommern to the River Oder. It was a singular train, with cart behind cart, often three rows next to one another, and, by the side all those who dragged themselves along on foot, with bicycles, prams, sleighs and even wheelbarrows. Max, Friedrich and I were in the middle of them. We walked along the rough and sandy Nehrungsroad, originally built to take small fishing wagons, and which now had to accommodate military transports, travelling from Danzig to the east, and from Pillau to the west. The refugees had to make room for these transports, because they were the only hope of holding the Russians back.

The snow kept on falling. The Russian artillery shot from the Ermland on to the road, so that we escaped to the Baltic side, where we threw ourselves into the snow. Big lorries came from Neutief with trailers, pushing the people with their wagons and carts to the side. Some lorries were open. All were full of wounded, covered only with a blanket and, bumping and banging, they passed us. As soon as there was a stoppage, people made a fire, so that they could have a hot drink, and everybody looked for wood and twigs, so that they could share the warmth. When the column started again, the fires were extinguished, and the kettles were carried along to be put on to the next fire when the column stopped again. Whole families sat under trees and bushes on their wet bundles, resting before marching along again. They, too, had little fires as long as the matches lasted. This carried on all day but as soon as darkness came there were no more fires.

To prevent the Russians from moving along the narrow land strip of the Nehrung, people had built barriers from wood and rubbish and because of that the wagons and carts often had to move along the frozen

223

sand beaches of the Baltic, and we had to do the same. The road was covered in high snow, and the wind was blowing, and the sand beaches, although mostly frozen, had wet parts where the going was even harder.

It took us three days to get to Kahlberg, one of the bigger fishing villages on the Nehrung. Just before we entered the village we were shocked to see some of the open trailers from the hospital lorries that had passed us before by the side of the road. They were full of wounded soldiers covered with thin blankets. The snow lay on top of them, but nobody moved; some of them were probably already dead.

Kahlberg was full of people, animals, carts and wagons. There was no bread, or food for the animals. People queued already in the night in front of the shops, hoping for some bread to be sold in the morning. The horses were fed on fir twigs and beach grass, a poor substitute after the hard work they had done. There was no water, because the Nehrung had no wells. One could only melt the snow, but this was dangerous water, as one could see the sick people by the side of the road, twisted in pain with intestinal trouble.

There were a number of officers and soldiers in the village, and the talk was that a new front was going to be formed near Kahlberg, if the Russians had reached the western part of the Weichselniederung. It would be a front made up of lost people, without hope - the enemy in the west, the enemy in the east and, to the north, the sea. There didn't seem to be any sense in fighting any more, but a resistance had to be maintained, to help the fleeing crowds to get away from the Russians, their revenge and their atrocities.

Max said that he would try and get some bread from the soldiers and disappeared. We made a fire, melted some snow, and let the water boil. It took a long time, but so did Max, before he returned. He did bring some bread, and also quite a bit of news, having talked to a number of soldiers.

'All those lorries we saw with wounded,' said Max, 'are going to Gotenhafen, because it is the headquarters for the wounded from the east. They are going to transport them from there by ship to one of the ports along the Baltic, going as far as Lübeck, if possible. They only transport the badly wounded in ambulances and lorries; the slightly wounded have to find their own way. They were just sorting the people out when I got there. They are short of fuel for the lorries and have to economise, taking only half of the vehicles along. Even the wounded with crutches have to walk. They look a pitiful sight. Some of them haven't even got a coat. They were given some food rations, and I queued up also, showing my empty sleeve. I was told to make my way to Danzig, and then to Gotenhafen, where I can have a place on a ship. Friedrich, with his bad leg, could also go.'

He looked at us both and produced the food, bread, corned beef, some other tins, and packets of hard dried biscuits, the iron ration.

'I will have to go on my own then,' I said, 'because I do not want to go to Danzig and Gotenhafen. I want to make my way either to Tuchel or to Greifswald.'

'I want to go to Berlin,' said Max.

'I want to get to the west, as far as possible,' added Friedrich, 'so a ship to Lübeck would suit me, but I don't know whether I can make it to Gotenhafen. My leg is giving me a lot of pain. Also, I do not want to hold you back, because I know you could walk faster than me.'

I had inspected Friedrich's leg in the morning, and didn't like the look of it. He definitely had frostbite; it had started to get black.

'If there are so many wounded here,' I said, 'they must also have doctors and medicine. Friedrich, why don't you try and see a doctor now, at least your leg would get professional attention.'

'Good idea,' said Max. 'I know where the transport is. In any case, we can stick together until we get off the Nehrung, and come to Steegen, where the autobahn to Marienburg starts. We can then decide which way to take.'

We made our way to the camp, where we found a number of abandoned lorries and ambulances. They were draining the petrol out of the open vehicles to fill up the covered ones. Two doctors and a few nurses were there, and one doctor eventually looked at Friedrich's leg. He told him bluntly that he had to have it amputated, the quicker the better.

'Get with the transport to Gotenhafen,' he said. 'Come and see me there and if they have some facilities, as they have promised us, I will do the operation.'

He looked around, and then walked to an ambulance, which was just going to start off. The driver had already got two wounded soldiers sitting next to him, but the doctor said:

'Push together,' and, pointing at Friedrich. 'Get in there.'

Friedrich hadn't even recovered from the shock of being told that he would lose his leg, and now he was told to leave us. He hesitated, not knowing what to do. The doctor walked off, the driver started the engine, then looked at Friedrich and shouted:

'Come on, man, you are the lucky one, not having to walk. I have no time to waste.'

Max pulled off Friedrich's rucksack, winked at me, and we both helped Friedrich into the ambulance lorry, giving him his rucksack to hold on his lap. It was a tight fit, with all the people in the front, and we had a job to close the door.

'Good luck!' I shouted. 'Thank you for saving my life.'

'Goodbye', said Max. We both waved, as the ambulance roared off.

Friedrich shouted something, but the window was closed, and we couldn't hear; it probably was only a goodbye.

I never saw Friedrich again, but I like to think that he got back to his home town and his family.

It was again very cold but it didn't snow, so Max and I decided to carry on walking until nightfall. It was always warmer to move about than to stand or wait, and the snake of people and wagons was on the move until dark.

It was another day before we reached Steegen and the autobahn to Marienburg towards the south. Here we had to decide whether to go towards Danzig, and hope for a ship, or carry on over land towards the west. Again we saw a lot of soldiers. There seemed to be no organisation, because refugees and soldiers were all in the same columns, moving along the roads. We soon found out that the Russians had started to push towards West Prussia, Pommern and Neumark, and we had met part of the divided and lost retreating army. There were also men from the *Volkssturmeinheiten* (civilian home guard), who mingled with the refugees moving over the frozen and snowstormed country, occupying every road towards the north and north-west.

'The Russians are in Elbing,' said some soldiers, 'and the first tanks have reached Tolkmit, on the Haff.'

This was the town on the other side of the Haff from Kahlberg, where we had met the hospital transport. We never realized that the Russians were so close. Nobody seemed to control anything, and everybody only had one thought, to get towards the west and away from the Russians.

'The Soviets will soon be in the Tucheler *Heide*,' said Max. 'You had better give up the idea of going there and make your way to Greifswald.'

I had to agree with him and, as he didn't want to go to Danzig either, we both decided to try and make for Wollin and Stettin.

When Max and I arrived in Steegen we believed, like everybody else, that the Russians would be stopped, and that they were further away than they really were. None of the villages had names; these were taken off to confuse the enemy, but it also confused us at times, and we had to make sure that we travelled west or north/west. Max always tried to get information from soldiers and officers. They were more reliable and knew the facts better than the civilians.

In Steegen was a large camp site with a big fire which some of the soldiers had organised, and we were able to get a hot drink. Max said he was going to get information about the latest happenings and would return. I got as near as possible to the fire, to get warm. A number of women were just sitting near the fire, some of them rubbing their hands or feet. One woman, she was still young but looked fifty, shivered from time to time, and seemed very frightened. Suddenly she started to talk in a monotonous voice, as if forced to pass on the information:

'We were always between the Russians. They came into our village. They shot my mother and father. They took our rings and watches and, if they couldn't get them off quickly enough, they chopped our hands or fingers off. After that, they did with all the women what they do everywhere, rape them.'

She stopped, looked at the ground, then continued:

'The first Russians left again. A number of them spoke a little German and they said that we ought to get away, because the Russians who would come after them were worse. And so we left, and followed these Russians. I thought, these have passed, and the next ones won't come until later. I only wanted to stay between the two waves of them. I ran and walked and ran. But then other tanks came, and the soldiers were Mongolians, and it started again.'

She stopped and looked into the fire.

'When it was all over, I stumbled on and in the evening I saw some big lorries coming along the road. I wanted to hide in the snow by the side of the road, when I realized they were German soldiers. I ran on to the road and begged them to take me along. I told the soldiers about the tanks and the Mongolians and what they had done, and they swore. They took me along. There were other women and children on the lorries also. When we got into a wood we heard shots. The lorries stopped. We hid in the wood but, when the shooting had stopped, we returned to the soldiers and the lorries. The soldiers didn't want to fight any more. They had no ammunition and thought it would be better to become prisoners. One of them said that if they didn't fight the Russians the SS would hang them. Everybody had seen the bodies of soldiers hanging by the roadside, who had been found hiding amongst the refugees. One sergeant argued with them, and told them that they had to protect us women, because the

Russians would not have any mercy with us. And that is how I eventually got here.'

There was silence when she had finished, and I thought that she felt relieved that she had told her story. Some people stared at her, others moved away a little, and I felt that she needed some sympathy, some sign that we would not ostracise her, but would understand what she had gone through. I got up and sat next to her, and put my hand on her trembling knee, pressing it gently. Others, too, came and sat next to her. She looked at us and said:

'I won't go through it again; the next time they can kill me.'

I touched my little phial around my neck and thought the same.

Max came back. He made a movement with his head that he wanted me. I moved over to him and he whispered:

'Come on, we are getting a lift!'

I couldn't believe it, but it was true. He had met a driver of a lorry from Berlin who was going to try and get through to Stolp. He had a load of fuel and sacks of food for an army division staying there.

'They are taking provisions to a column of SS,' said Max. 'Three lorries altogether. They are really full up but if we can squeeze in my new friend will take us. They are leaving at 1 am. We will have to try and get into the back of his lorry between 11 pm and 1 am, when he is on guard duty. He will look the other way.'

Cautiously, we moved away from the camp fire and went to see where the lorry stood, so that we would be able to find it in the dark. A lot of refugees mingled around the three vehicles, trying to find out where they were going and whether there was room on any of them. Two soldiers with guns were guarding them. It was already getting dark, but at least we could plan how to get into the lorry.

'My friend said that there is a small space on one side, where he climbs in to get some fuel. Otherwise the lorry is packed full to the top. We will gradually have more space, when he uses the next lot of fuel. He doesn't keep the empty canisters. At first we both might have to stand in the lorry.'

'At least it is a transport,' I said. 'I am sure I will be sick. I had better be on the outside, so that I can lean out.'

'You will be alright, you'll see. Anyway, if we really can get to Stolp, that is a good bit of the journey. We can then get along the coast to Kolberg, Wollin, and eventually Stettin. If we are lucky, and get there before the Russians, we might even get a train from there, you to Greifswald, and me to Berlin. In any case, I think they are going to hold the Russians back. Surely they are not going to let them get as far as Berlin.'

It started to snow again. There were no more fires going, because of the Russian planes. Max and I dared not go to sleep, in case we didn't wake up at the right time. I still had my watch, and I think it was keeping good time, but we often didn't know what day it was, or what date. By now it definitely was February, and so it was three weeks since I had had a wash, or sat in a comfortable chair, or had a sleep in a bed, or even taken off my clothes. When would all this end?

Max and I moved over to the lorry when it was time. We couldn't see a guard, but then it was dark, so maybe the guard was on the other side. We then noticed that each driver was sitting behind the steering wheel, waiting for the accompanying sergeant, or officer. Because it was snowing, they were probably told to sit in their vehicles.

'Which is the right lorry?' I said to Max. 'Do you recognize your friend?'

Max sneaked around to find out which one was the right lorry. He came back and we made our way to the back of one which Max pointed out. We knew it was the right one, because the strap from the hood was undone on one side. It was high up, and quite difficult to climb in. Max, with my help, went in first and took the rucksacks, and then I climbed in. There was hardly any space. We could stand, or sit on our rucksacks, but we could not do anything else. They certainly were on time because at five minutes to one o'clock, we heard voices, clicking of heels, meaning an officer was saluted, and then a voice said:

'I will check the back straps, sir,' then the sound of footsteps. The corner of the hood was lifted, I saw a grinning face of a soldier, and then the strap was fastened. A few minutes later the lorry started off slowly. They had to drive with very little light, or none at all, and seemed to crawl along the road. We were rocked and shaken about, and it wasn't long before I was sick. This was a pity, because we were always short of food and to bring it back was unforgivable, but I couldn't help it. I undid the strap, and just spat it out of the back. It was lucky that we were the third lorry, so that the other two couldn't see us. After that, we both sat down on our rucksacks with our knees hunched up because there was so little space. Gradually, the swaying of the lorry made me go to sleep and, when I woke up, it was daylight. Max, too, had gone to sleep, but was awake soon after I opened my eyes.

We realized that we had woken up because the lorry had stopped. We kept quiet, wondering what would happen next. I was terribly stiff, and couldn't sit any more in the hunched position, so I tried to get up and stretch my legs.

Max did the same. We heard voices, but couldn't hear what they were saying, and we dared not look out. It was very difficult to stand in the little space, and my arms and legs were aching.

'I need a good stretch,' I whispered to Max.

He nodded his head, but didn't reply. Then we heard a voice outside:

'I will get some more fuel, sir,' and, with that, the hood was unfastened, and our soldier friend looked in.

'Sir,' he called out, 'we have got some stowaways!'

Max and I looked shocked, but the soldier put his finger on his lips, and smiled a little. An officer, a lieutenant, came to the back of the lorry, and stared at us.

'Get down!' he shouted, 'How did you get in there?'

'We climbed in when nobody was looking. It is pretty cramped, but driving is better than walking,' I said defiantly, and started to climb down. Max handed me the rucksacks, and then he, too, climbed down, quite nimbly with one arm.

Even if we don't get any further, I thought, we have had a good ride.

The soldier got told off by the lieutenant for not having watched the lorry better, but he seemed to know his superior, because he looked sheepishly at him and said:

'He is from Berlin, Sir, that makes three of us.'

The officer looked at him. He must have realized that the soldier had met us before, because how else could he have known that Max came from Berlin? Suddenly the lieutenant said:

'Fill up the tank and also the other vehicles, that will give the two a bit more space in the back of the lorry.'

With that he walked off. Our new friend grinned, and said:

'He is also from Berlin. He is not a bad officer. I have been with him now for six months, and we get on alright. He has accepted you, so now you don't need to hide.'

He filled up the lorries which made a little more space in the back. We loaded up our rucksacks again, then climbed in and were off. Max produced some bread and sausage, but I only ate the dry bread because I was still feeling sick.

We hadn't travelled very far when Max sat up straight and listened:

'I think I can hear planes,' he said.

He got up, opened the back, and looked out.

'I am right, there are Russian planes. I am sure they are going to attack us. On the white landscape we are a good target. The drivers won't hear the planes because of the noise of the motors.'

He pushed and rattled the canisters to make some noise, shouting to attract the driver's attention, but the lorry crept along slowly on the icy road.

Max looked out again in the back, and then he shouted:

'They are coming for us, get out, jump into the snow,' and he threw our rucksacks out.

I jumped into the high snow by the side of the road, and saw Max doing the same further along. Our two rucksacks lay in the lorry tracks, whilst the vehicle moved away from us. I looked up and could see three planes diving down to the road, and then I heard the tack-tack-tack of the machine guns. Suddenly there was a terrible bang. The lorry we had travelled in exploded, with the fuel canisters being thrown up into the air.

I buried my head in the snow and held my ears. When I looked up, all three lorries were burning, and the planes had left, being only visible as spots in the sky. Max came walking towards me. I got up and collected the rucksacks.

'Do you think they have all got killed?' I asked.

'Let's go and see,' he said. 'They might have got out before the vehicle was hit.'

A sergeant and two men from the first lorry had jumped out, and were alright, but the occupants from the other two vehicles never had a chance. Being loaded with fuel, it only needed a spark to blow the whole lot into the air. We all stood silently around the hot debris and warmed ourselves. Tears were running down my face. I thought of the driver from Berlin with his cute grinning face, and the young lieutenant, of whom he had said, 'he is not a bad officer', giving him a compliment in his way of thinking. We had not met the other occupants, but there were three of them, I was told. So the attack took three lorries with supplies, and five lives.

Looking around, we could only see snow and the icy white road that we had come along, gradually disappearing into the distance. I was surprised that there were no refugee columns, but there were signs that carts and horses and people had travelled along the road because by the side there were the frozen carcasses of animals, and the bodies of frozen people. We were on a large plain, and it looked to me like a shroud, all silent, and bright in the sunlight, blinding us.

Dear God, I thought, why can't you just fold this shroud around us, and drop us back into a normal life, with peace.

'We shouldn't have been on the road,' said the sergeant. 'We had been told that Russian planes come along here. That's why everybody travels at night and hides in the woods and villages during the day. We had orders from the SS to arrive in Stolp this evening, otherwise we would be shot. We were late, so the lieutenant decided to take a chance. Now he is dead, and the SS won't get their supplies either.'

The sergeant showed me on my map where he thought we were, and we decided to carry on along the main road, until we came to the next village. It was still a long way to Stolp, particularly on foot. The sergeant and the two men were not very keen to turn up in Stolp without the supplies. They said that nobody would really know what had happened to them and if the lorries were found, they could have perished with them, like the others. The sergeant said that if the planes came again we should bury ourselves into the snow next to a corpse, because the Russians only shot at anything that moved.

We walked and we walked and, although I didn't like to look at the dead bodies by the side of the road, I found this easier for my eyes than the white snow. It really was a most beautiful day and the sun was quite warm, melting the snow and frost on the stiff bodies by the roadside. We could see some carts and wagons in the distance. They didn't seem to move, and the nearer we got, the more frightened I became. They looked like ghosts, and I wondered whether I was imagining them, like a mirage in the desert. I asked Max:

'Are those real wagons in the distance? Maybe it is a refugee column we could join?'

'Let's wait and see,' said Max.

The sun disappeared behind thick clouds before we reached the wagons and it started to snow again, so that we could not see into the distance any more. We came on to the carts very suddenly; they were like ghosts, an unbelievable picture which I have never forgotten. The carts and wagons just stood there, in the same way as they had travelled, but the horses were dead, lying between the shafts of the carts, shot through by machine guns from the air. Here and there, a man or a woman or a child were still sitting on the vehicle, just sunk together, after a bullet or grenade splinter had hit them. They were frozen stiff.

There were about half a dozen wagons and a number of bodies by the road side. I looked at it all without crying, just as if it was an everyday happening. I was cold and numb, and it didn't seem to matter that they were all dead. I wondered how long they had stood there. Maybe it only happened a few hours ago, when our lorries got attacked.

One of the soldiers climbed on to the back of a cart and came back with a blanket. He had no coat as he had jumped out of the lorry so quickly when we got attacked. At least this would keep him a little warmer. We decided it would be a good idea to have a rest, and we all climbed into a cart with palliasses. We had something to eat and, as it was still snowing, we crawled under the straw and went to sleep. It was at least sheltered here and the palliasses kept us warm.

When I awoke it was dark and had stopped snowing. It was very quiet and I thought for a moment that I was all alone; I couldn't even hear anybody breathing. I felt towards the side where I knew Max had laid down, and he caught my hand and said:

'It is alright, I am here. The others have gone. I woke up, and heard them whispering, but I kept quiet. They just climbed out of the cart and walked off. I think they don't want to fight any more and will try and make their way towards the west, the same as us. I don't blame them, but they will be called deserters and, if caught, will probably be shot. Under the circumstances, it is better if they keep to themselves and not stay with us.'

There was really nothing I could say to that. Max asked me after a little while:

'Shall we get on? It is probably better to walk in the dark, because of the Russian planes. We should find a trek soon; they can't all have made their way to Danzig and Gotenhafen.'

I agreed with him and we climbed off the cart. The night was dark, but not too dark. We could still see where the road was. I wrapped my blanket over my head because it was very cold, and we walked and walked.

Just before daylight, we met another column of refugees and, together with them we entered a village, which was still occupied. The people stared at us. They didn't want to believe us when we told them that the Russians were not far away. They had been told by their *Bürgermeister* (mayor) only the day before that there was no need to be concerned about the Russian planes. There were only some reconnaissance flights undertaken by the enemy. The German tanks had already pushed the Russian forces back, and no evacuation was necessary.

We tried to get a hot drink, but people had become very selfish. Nobody would let us indoors because we were dirty and we smelled. This was the first time in my life that I had become a beggar. I begged for a cup of hot soup or tea, I begged for shelter, even if it was only in the hallway of a house, but the doors were locked to us and the food refused.

Max and I just accepted the refusals. We had seen such a lot of misery, we had experienced such frightful moments, we were so cold and hungry and weak, that we didn't have the strength even to get upset any more. We just kept on walking and I thought that maybe we would just walk until we dropped, like all the other people by the road side. At the end of the village we found a barn. This time Max didn't go to find the owner, but just opened the door a little, and we slipped inside. There was some straw in the back behind some farm machinery. We crawled inside it and I was soon asleep.

The people in the village were so sure that the Russians would not advance as far as Pommern, because they were blinded by German propaganda. I had seen burning villages and attacks by Russian planes and knew that things were different. I did not know the facts, or the Russian plans of how and where they would attack and push forward, and it was only luck that I eventually reached Stettin, on the Baltic. It was a hair-raising journey at times, and I was often only just in front of the Russians, and sometimes even behind them. I had a map, but that was only occasionally useful. The villages had no signs, and we only got information from the bigger places, where people were left behind, or from the few still organised troops, who were also marching to the west.

We never made it to Stolp, but then, there was no need to travel so far north, as it was our intention to reach Wollin or Stettin.

The lorry had probably taken us just over half way, and well past Danzig. The three drivers had avoided the big towns, because their fuel and their supplies could be confiscated by higher authorities; that was also the reason for them keeping to smaller roads. Because of the continuous snowing, roads often disappeared unless they were used by troops or refugees, and Max suggested that we ought to find a railway line. Going along the line, we would at least go in the right direction.

We joined any trek going west. These were usually the refugees with carts and wagons and animals, because they knew that they could not get on to a ship with them. Others walked east, making their way to Danzig and Gotenhafen, having their belongings on prams, sledges, handcarts, and wheelbarrows, or just in big rucksacks on their backs. We often travelled at night, and tried to find a place to stay during the day. Food became very short. Nobody would share, and sometimes there were fights when somebody tried to steal some potatoes from the ones who still had food. The people with the wagons usually had some food hidden away but if they shared they might not have enough for themselves later on.

At first we found the villages still occupied, but the Russians pushed towards the coast and people left, taking with them as much as they could carry, or load on to carts and wagons, as long as they had horses to pull them. At night we could see fires on the skyline. These were burning villages, and a warning that the Russians were coming nearer.

Gradually our food ran out. It became more and more difficult to walk on an empty stomach. One day, we discovered some *Mieten* (clamps) on a farm, and dug up some potatoes. Max made a fire and we half cooked the potatoes. I filled up my pockets and satchel, and put some in my rucksack. We quickly put snow on to the fire and, still munching the potatoes, we were off, in case the smoke had attracted any planes. We also found some corn scattered on to a barn floor. We soon picked it up, cut it and broke it into small granules, and ate it going along.

Once I was so weak that I didn't want to go any further. My stomach had got used to being without food. I didn't get the hunger pangs any more, but I just did not have any strength. Max peeled off the dark bark from a tree and cut some of the white wood from underneath.

'Chew it,' he said. 'When it is soft enough, swallow it, so that you have something in your stomach.'

I did what he said, but all I remember is that it hurt my teeth.

We met a column of soldiers and went with them. They still had an officer in command. They were told to make their way to Schlawe, where they should be able to get a train to Kolberg, which was declared a *Festung* (fortress) by Hitler, and had to be held and fought for until the last man.

At night we were surprised to see a number of soldiers without guns joining the column. They came out of the darkness of empty farms, sad figures with heavy rucksacks and sticks. They marched with the troops, but disappeared in the morning. We heard that they were the ones who had thrown away their guns, and would hide during the day. They were really deserters, but they didn't think so. They were the pitiful remnants of a once big and well equipped army, who felt that it was hopeless to fight without ammunition, and hoped to get as far as the Oder, and cross it to the west.

Max and I were much too weak to keep up with the marching pace of the soldiers and had to slow down. At least they had given us some food, a tin of corned beef, and some iron rations, together with a piece of hard bread. We were very careful what we ate, as we had starved for a long time. Even so, I couldn't eat the corned beef; it was too rich for me, and gave me stomach cramps, so I only ate the bread, chewing it for a long time. Max was alright, but he only ate a little; we didn't know how long it would have to last.

We reached Schlawe and tried the railway station, but there were no trains. The town was full of refugees. There were two soup kitchens, organised by the army. We queued up at both of them and got a bowl of soup and a piece of bread. The *Bürgermeister* had opened all schools, halls, and any big buildings for the refugees, and we found a place in a dance hall for the night. There were two iron stoves, with pipes sticking out of the windows, which gave out quite a bit of heat. Everybody collected bits of wood to keep them burning. For the first time for ages I got warm and had a good night's sleep. We had some soup and bread again in the morning, and then carried on walking along the railway line in the direction of Kolberg, towards the west.

Just outside the town, they were digging a mass grave, and I stopped. I looked at it, remembering the one that we had had in our district in Königsberg, just after the air-raid attack. It seemed years ago, and yet it was only just over two months.

People were bringing bodies from everywhere. Carts passing suddenly stopped, and somebody would carry a wrapped up figure to the grave. The small ones were children; none of them looked heavy. All were people once loved by somebody, and now starved or frozen to death. I stood there and saw the grave gradually being filled up; there were so many, and I could feel that heavy lump in my stomach again.

'Come on,' said Max, and he pulled me away. I looked at him. Suddenly I realized that he didn't look well. His face was swollen, and I was convinced that he had a black eye. It wasn't frostbite; his face looked as if somebody had hit him. He turned his back towards me.

'What is the matter with your face?' I said.

'Nothing, come on, we have to get on,' he said.

This convinced me that there was something wrong, but I left it for the moment.

Max had always wanted to go along the railway line and now we did it. We could see that trains had been running quite recently, and Max thought it might even be possible for us to get on to one. I doubted this, as one could see that a number of people had had the same idea. They just sat there under the trees waiting for a train, whilst we passed them.

For the first time, we knew which way we were going. For days we had wandered along, joining different groups, sometimes being alone, then finding trodden paths in the snow, or empty farms, but we were never sure whether we hadn't lost our direction. Max said we would stick to the railway line now until we got to Kolberg.

On the second day, towards the evening, we saw a village, quite a bit away from the railway line. Even so, we decided to find a barn or house there where we could sleep, as we had been so very cold the night before. The place looked empty when we got near to it and was ghostly silent. I suddenly felt very apprehensive. Farms were often completely empty, but villages usually had some life left, a dog, a cat, the odd chicken, and even one or two old people and invalids incapable of being taken away. I could see that even Max seemed to hesitate. We were quite a few people who had veered away from the railway line to look for night shelter, wrapped up women and children with their sledges and rucksacks.

The first women in our group entered the village. We were somewhere in the middle, because Max and I had started to slow down. Then we heard a scream. A terrible scream, which kept on and on, and was joined by another scream.

Suddenly there was silence again - ghostly silence. Everybody stopped walking and stood still, frozen to the spot, not from the cold but from fright. Only the people in the back of our column still moved, closing up the gaps in the trek as they had not heard the screaming.

'The Russians!' shouted a woman near us and, with that, panic broke out.

People tried to turn round and get back on to the small path which we had trodden in the snow; others just stumbled to the side, sinking into the deep snow, but trying to get away, and some just stood petrified, not being able to move for shock.

'If the Russians are in the village, it is no good running, they will get us in any case,' said Max. 'The place is too quiet for Russian soldiers to be there. Let's just wait a little while.'

Some of us stood and waited, but the ones who had started to flee carried on back up the trodden path to the railway line, or across the white field with the high snow.

Two women came back from the village, stumbling and swaying, an expression of horror on their faces. When they reached us we tried to find out what had happened, but they couldn't talk. One of them kept on shaking her head, and saying all the time:

'No, no, no.'

I thought that she was probably the one who had screamed, because she looked as if she was going to scream again.

'Let's go and see,' said Max. 'It must be safe, otherwise the two women would not have come back.'

What we saw in this village was so inhuman, so cruel and shocking that for months afterwards I would wake up at night in a sweat, when the picture of it had intruded into my dreams. All my life, I have pushed it into the background, just said to myself:

'It was terrible, don't think about it, don't bring back the detailed pictures. It is finished. What happened there was not done by civilized people, but by savages, by animals. In any case, people wouldn't believe that this had happened, if I told them.' Even today, I feel sick to think about it but maybe the time has come to describe some of it.

The Russians were not in the village when we entered it, but they had been there with their tanks, as the marks showed in the snow. The big vehicles had even rolled over people, flattening them into the ice and snow. The houses had broken windows and doors and in the streets were broken china, household appliances, chairs, tables and furniture. The buildings had been completely ransacked, everything just thrown into the streets, or smashed up inside, like washbasins and toilets. Even the floor boards were ripped up in some of the houses, and the featherbeds slit open. Linen and clothes were pushed into the cesspit.

A few houses and barns were half burnt out; some of them were only a heap of rubble and ash.

That was the extent of the material damage. It was what had happened to the people that made the women scream, and made even the hardened ones amongst us retch, and be sick and be absolutely petrified.

Women had had their clothes slit open. Some were naked. They had been raped and lay on bare floors, or in the street, frozen stiff and dead. There were young girls, no more than fifteen or sixteen years old. There were old women, age didn't seem to matter. Some must have tried to run away, because they were shot in the back, or stabbed, and were lying in grotesque, twisted, stiff shapes by the side of the houses, as if they had been kicked into that spot.

An old man was nailed upside down on to the door of a shed. This must have been a special punishment; maybe he tried to protect his wife. Along the wall of a house were a row of bodies, all old men and young boys, shot in the back. They probably had to line up there to be shot. But the worst thing was the well, which was in the centre of the village. This was completely filled up with bodies, the last ones only half submerged, with their legs hanging over the edge, or sticking stiffly into the air.

There was no life left anywhere. We all stared, were sick, trembled, turned, and walked silently away to stop the rest of the trek, so that the children would not look at this hell on earth.

I touched the little phial which I wore around my neck, and I knew that if a Russian came near me, I would not hesitate to take what was in it. It gave me some comfort, but did not stop me from trembling and being sick.

I had forgotten all about Max. The horror I was seeing blotted everything else out. I had to hang on to the belief that this was not real, otherwise I would have screamed, or cried, or raved. I kept on clutching my little phial, and I suddenly remembered my mother when she gave it to me. Even she could not have known then what the reality was like. It is one thing hearing about horrors, but a completely different thing when one experiences them, and sees them with ones own eyes.

I must get out of here, I thought.

Max was suddenly next to me and took my arm. I looked into his swollen face; it looked sickly yellow/green. His eyes were very big and one of them had a black mark.

He has been in a fight, I thought. Probably last night. I must ask him about it.

'Let's get out of here,' he said. 'They are all dead, even the animals. We will have to be quick, and get away.'

I must ask him about his face, I thought again, and kept on saying the same sentence to myself again and again, only so that I could push the other horrible pictures out of my mind. Even so, we had to go along the village street again, making our way through the broken possessions, and passing the twisted frozen bodies. I tried to look only at my feet, and noticed they were floppy.

I am not walking properly, I thought. I am stumbling, as if I am drunk. Max pushed and pulled me.

'Come on, come on,' he said impatiently, 'or I will leave you behind.'

He had never said this before. I was afraid to be alone now after what I had seen, so I stumbled a little faster, and we got out of the village. It was dark by now, but we made our way back to the railway line and then, a little further, we stopped in a wood.

To our surprise, we found a small detachment of German soldiers there under the guidance of two officers, and quite a number of refugees with their carts, wagons and horses. The soldiers had moved along the railway line as they, too, had been ordered to march to Kolberg, to defend the so-called *Festung*. Somebody told them about the village. They were shocked, but said that it must have happened a day or two ago, and probably by an advanced group of Russian tanks, because they had not seen or heard anything, on their march along the railway line.

'We could not have helped them,' said the officer. 'You cannot fight Russian tanks with bare hands and an empty stomach. We have no vehicles, hardly any ammunition, and have nearly finished our iron rations.'

Max and I sat on our rucksacks, leaning against a tree. I was absolutely exhausted, but couldn't sleep, because every time I closed my eyes the pictures from the village came back. Suddenly I remembered Max's face.

'What happened to your face, Max? You have been in a fight, haven't you?'

At first he didn't answer. He was sitting crouched up on his rucksack, with his arm folded over his tummy, pulling his blanket tightly around him. I could not see his face because it was dark, but I had the feeling that he was in pain. He had been very quiet all day, not only after we had been to the village. I was convinced that he was ill.

'Max, please, no secrets. We are friends, I have to know if you are not well.'

'I got hurt two nights ago in Schlawe. I could smell bread, and followed my nose. I found a baker busy baking bread and asked him to give me some. He wanted a black market price for it, said that's what people pay now. I refused, took two loaves, and wanted to get out quickly. Having only one arm, I couldn't open the door. The loaves under my arm hindered me and the baker caught me. He hit me in my face with his fist. I dropped the loaves and hit him back. I was a good boxer once and knocked him out straight away. I picked up the loaves, but when I got through the door, his assistant stood there with a thick piece of wood in his hand. He hit me in my stomach. It really hurt, but I stumbled away with my two loaves, not wanting to drop them again. They are in my rucksack. We could have something to eat if you like.'

'That would be nice, Max.'

He had spoken very quietly, and I answered in the same way, just as if it was an everyday conversation, but I knew he was hurt and in pain. I felt guilty for not having taken any notice of it before. He got up awkwardly and I got one thick black loaf out of his rucksack. I broke off a few pieces and put the rest back. We sat close together, munching our bread. It tasted delicious and I said so, also that I was grateful that he had taken such risks. He never replied, just pressed my arm.

At midnight, the soldiers got ready to move off, and Max said that we had better go with them. Some of the refugees joined in, too, a few carts and wagons, and people on foot. Max seemed very stiff. I could see that he was in pain. We had eaten some bread again, and I only hoped that we would not get a tummy ache from the fresh bread. Max had difficulties in keeping up with the marching soldiers, and I pretended not to be able to walk fast either. He knew what I was doing, because he suddenly said:

'I don't think I can keep this up for long. You will have to leave me behind because I want you to get to Kolberg as quickly as possible to have some protection. It won't be long before the Russians catch us up.'

'Don't be silly. After all that we have been through, we do not part, but stick together. You help me, and I help you.'

Max did not have the strength to argue. Gradually, we fell behind the marching soldiers, together with other walking refugees. Only the carts and wagons seemed to be able to keep up with the soldiers' pace.

We met other small military units, everybody making their way to Kolberg. They were a pathetic group of soldiers, sometimes having been collected from leftover divisions.

By the afternoon, Max couldn't walk any more. I touched his forehead and realized that he had a temperature and, when I made him sit down on his rucksack, he suddenly turned to the side and spat out blood.

By now we had left the railway line because there was a good road to Kolberg, which was busy with refugees and small army units. Sometimes even a car or a lorry passed. I knew that I had to get Max on to a vehicle, because now he was incapable of going any further. One could see that cars and lorries were very full; they just blew their horns for the refugees to step to the side because, if they stopped, they would have too many people begging for a lift.

Towards the evening the treks thinned out; only a few people were still on the road, as most of them had stopped somewhere for a rest. Suddenly a single lorry came along and I made up my mind to stop this one, even at the risk of my life. I stepped into the middle of the road and waved my arms. The driver blew his horn without slowing down. He was not going very fast because of the icy road, but he would skid if he put on his brakes suddenly. He came nearer, and I thought:

He will just have to run me over, and, with that, I collapsed and lay in the road, pulling my blanket up over my head.

The driver must have braked and skidded, because I could feel the spray from snow and ice on my back. A strong hand pulled me up, my blanket fell down, and so did my cap, and I felt the icy air on my face and ears.

'You silly, silly creature, I could have run you over, I could have killed you!' said a voice. I looked into the face of an elderly soldier, probably the driver.

'That would only mean another frozen body in the ditch, then,' I replied. 'What does it matter? Please, I do need help for a soldier over there.' I pointed to Max, sitting on his rucksack. 'He has already given an arm for his fatherland and now he is hurt internally. He is spitting blood and he has got a temperature. Please take him with you to Kolberg. Maybe he can get medical attention there. In any case, he cannot walk any more.'

I said all this very quickly, because I was afraid that he might not listen to me, just push me into the ditch and drive off.

'We have no room on the lorry,' he said.

'Surely you can get one more person on. I am only asking for a place for him, not for me. He is a soldier, he has done his duty. He wants to get back to Berlin now, to his wife and children.'

I hoped that by saying this the old soldier might remember his own family and take pity on Max.

'Come on, man,' shouted a voice from the lorry, 'what is the hold up? It will be completely dark soon, and we have a long way to go yet.'

'Sir, it is a girl, begging for transport for a wounded soldier,' called the driver.

'Alright, try and push him into the back of the lorry,' came the reply.

I ran over to Max and tried to pull him up. He was very heavy, or maybe it was that I was weak. If it hadn't been for the driver, I would not have been able to help him to the back of the lorry. It was true, there didn't seem to be any room, but somehow we lifted Max in, and willing hands helped. I ran back for his rucksack, dragging it along the road. The driver lifted it into the back, and then turned round to me:

'See whether you can squeeze in also,' he said, and started to take off my rucksack. He handed it to the other soldiers, and then helped me up into the outstretched arms of several of them.

'It's a girl, it's a girl, come on, let's have a cuddle,' some of them shouted in good fun. I was embraced by arms in rough uniforms, and kissed by unshaven and bearded men. I didn't care, I felt safe, and Max didn't have to walk any more. Sitting on a soldier's lap, I fell asleep.

It had started to get light when I woke and I felt refreshed. Somebody gave me some dried biscuits, but I refused the tinned meat, knowing that that would make me sick. I asked about Max. They said that he was very ill, and had been delirious during the night. He wanted nothing to eat, only a drink, and somebody gave him some water. Soon after that we reached Kolberg.

The small town of Kolberg was full of refugees, and it was impossible to move in the streets. Our lorry stopped at the station. The accompanying officer got his small unit lined up and marched them off, leaving a guard for the lorry behind. I was told that I would have to find a place for Max, as the lorry might be needed again. Some of the soldiers kissed me goodbye, and I thanked everybody for keeping me warm and giving me food, because a few had passed on their iron rations to me, saying that they would surely get some more in Kolberg. Max was very weak. He could hardly sit up, and he was looking at me all the time, probably wondering what I would do now.

'I will go and see whether I can find some medical help for you,' I said to him. 'I will be back.'

'You don't need to come back,' he replied. 'Try and get to Wollin or Stettin.'

I didn't reply, but just climbed out of the lorry. I took my rucksack with me, not because I didn't want to come back, but because I was afraid the lorry might be moved, and I wouldn't find it again.

In the streets I met people who had seen the Russian tanks, and said that they were encircling Kolberg. There were quite a number of soldiers in the town. Guns, ammunition and food, although in short supply, were still there, and one could queue up for bread. The best news that I got was that there were still hospital trains going to Stettin.

I queued up for some soup, and then for bread and after that made my way back to the station, where I found the lorry still parked, with Max in the back.

The guard said that he had given Max a drink, but he had brought it back, with some blood, so he had just covered him with another blanket and left him asleep. I told Max that I was going to look for a hospital train, but I didn't know whether he was conscious enough to hear me.

The station was full of people, but there were no trains. I went to the goods depot, where I saw some cattle trucks with little smoking pipes sticking out of the roof. The trucks were guarded by soldiers and when I got near them I was stopped.

243

'No civilians are allowed near the train,' said the guard.

'What is in the trucks?' I asked.

'This is a hospital train,' he said.

I could not believe that wounded were transported in cattle trucks but if the guard said it, it must be true. This was just what I was looking for. I tried to find a doctor or a nurse, but was unsuccessful.

I explained to one of the guards about Max, and he said that if I could find some stretcher bearers and brought him to the train, he would see that he got in.

'But you must hurry, because the train is going soon.'

I could not find any stretcher bearers, and I thought that, if I could find two soldiers who were willing to carry Max, they could do so by using my blanket. I did find two soldiers, but I had to see to Max's rucksack. Max wasn't heavy, we both must have lost weight on our journey. His rucksack was quite a weight, at least I thought so, and I pulled it behind me like a sleigh. We got to the train, and the guard opened one of the cattle truck's sliding doors. I was shocked when I looked inside, but had to be quick to get Max into the truck, because the soldiers wanted to go, and the guard wanted to shut the door. I had told the guard that I was a nurse and he said that, in that case, I had better look after Max, because he could see that Max needed attention.

On the floor of the truck was straw, and on it lay the wounded. There were a few buckets as toilets, and a can of water, and an iron stove with the pipe sticking out of the roof, with bits of wood next to it to keep the fire burning. The smell was shocking, not only from the toilet buckets, but also from the wounded, some of them bandaged with toilet paper. It reminded me of the days in the hospital in Königsberg, when we had paper bandages. Some wounded were moaning with pain, others lay very still; one or two were sitting up, leaning against the wall of the truck.

A soldier on crutches hobbled over to me and said:

'I try and look after them, I can at least get up and move my arms. I keep the stove going for some warmth. A doctor looks in sometimes, but he has no medicine or bandages.'

I smiled at him and tried to make Max comfortable, rolling him gently into his blanket and resting his back against his rucksack.

'They are guarding the train,' continued the soldier, 'because the refugees try and get in otherwise and there is no room. That's what they say. I would have thought they could take a few.'

Suddenly we heard shouted commands outside, clicking of heels, feet marching, and the opening and shutting of the truck doors, and then our door was also opened. Icy cold, but fresh air came inside. I saw some SS men, with an officer, standing next to the truck. They all looked inside and when the officer saw me he shouted:

'Get out! No civilians are allowed in the hospital trains! How did you get inside?'

He turned round to one of the men, and commanded:

'Get her outside!'

The man jumped into the truck, pulled me roughly on my shoulder and pushed me outside.

'I am a nurse,' I said. 'I have just brought a severely wounded soldier along.' I pointed to Max.

'Let's see your papers,' he said.

I had no papers, only my student card, which showed that I was studying medicine, and I didn't think he would accept that. Even so, I looked for it in my satchel and produced it to the impatiently waiting SS officer. He only glanced at it.

'Students are not nurses,' he said. 'Shut the door!'

'My rucksack is still in there and my blanket,' I called out.

He took no notice of this, but called to one of the soldiers guarding the train to get rid of me, and marched on with his small group, opening and shutting the next truck door, and the next, and the next.

I clenched my fists in my pockets. Looking at the guard, I said pleadingly:

'I must have my rucksack and my blanket, it is all I have got.'

The soldier looked frightened. He glanced at the departing SS party and said:

'You had better go quickly, otherwise there might be trouble.'

'Please,' I said again, 'I will be cold, and I have no food.'

Suddenly I saw the truck door being slightly opened, and a hand pushed my rucksack outside, followed by my blanket. I recognized the wounded soldier with the crutches. The guard quickly turned his back towards the other side, and I heard him say under his breath:

'Take it and run, for God's sake disappear. You will get us both shot.'

I grabbed the rucksack and the blanket and, pulling both behind me, because I had no time to put them on to my back, I stumbled off in the opposite direction to the SS men.

Max, I thought, oh Max, now I will never see you again. I only hope they give you some medical attention soon.

I asked one of the guards at the back of the train when the trucks were leaving, but he didn't know, so I made my way into the town again. This time, there was something different going on. People were standing more in groups and they looked frightened. There were no soldiers about, like in the morning. Everybody was whispering the news that the SS had taken over command, and that every soldier had to fight, to hold the town against the Russians.

'They are going to hang the deserters,' said one woman. 'I heard the new commandant giving the order to look through the refugee wagons and carts, through the empty trains, and through all houses and cellars.'

That's why they opened all the trucks in the hospital train, I thought.

I also remembered the soldiers who used to join the marching troops and refugee treks at night only, and then disappear during the day, but I doubted whether they would come to the town.

I got some soup and bread again, and found some shelter in a school building. A number of refugees were waiting for boats to take them to Lübeck, but there were still trains going to Wollin and Stettin, and I decided to try the station in the morning. I didn't sleep very well. I dreamt about the village where the Russians had been, and I woke up because somebody was shaking me, telling me to be quiet. Apparently I had been calling out in my dream. I missed Max. There was no point in trying to go to sleep again, so I got up, and made my way to the station.

I was surprised to see a number of people about already, again in groups, and whispering, and I heard them say:

'They have done it, we had better not talk loud, otherwise it will happen to us. Go and look in the market square.'

These were frightened whispers, and I thought that I must go and have a look, because nothing could be more frightening than what I had seen before in that silent village; or could there be anything worse?

What I saw in the market square in Kolberg was horrible. The SS had hanged some deserters from lamp posts and trees, and attached labels around their necks:

*"Ich hänge hier weil ich zu feige bin weiter zu kämpfen."* (I hang here because I am a coward to carry on fighting).

*"Ich hänge hier weil ich ein Defätist bin."* (I hang here because I am a defeatist).

*"Ich bin ein Deserteur".* (I am a deserter).

*"Wer zu feige ist, für das Vaterland zu kämpfen, stirbt den Tod der Schande."* (Anybody being too cowardly to fight for the fatherland, dies the death of shame).

*"Ich hänge hier weil ich nicht an den Führer glaubte."* (I hang here because I did not believe in the *Führer*).

It was a sickening spectacle, German people were killing German people, life was not sacred any more. I felt like shouting, but I only shivered, and stared, and felt lost, alone and disheartened.

Kolberg was full of people. More and more treks of refugees arrived with their wagons and carts, or just walking. Although there was some provision for refugees in school halls and larger buildings, there were no hospitals or any official medical aid. Some of the refugees had met the Russians, and pale and frightened girls looked for a doctor, to confide their terrible experiences. Women gave birth in barracks or halls, even doorways, with the help of a kind neighbour, or no help at all.

There were also the old people, who could not go any further, or had lived all their lives in the town and had resigned themselves to the fact that they would not get much help from anybody.

There were the *Wahnsinnigen* (insane), with their frightened eyes, who went from house to house, and from cart to cart, asking about their mothers and children.

There were the wounded soldiers and the invalids, who were afraid that they would be left behind. They often had a weapon under their blanket in order to force the *Sanitäter* (medical orderly) to take them on to a ship or train, or to kill themselves before they fell into the hands of the Russians.

The town also had Russian prisoners-of-war, who were supposed to be transported to the west. They were in a very poor state with their wooden shoes, balaclavas pulled down nearly covering their faces, and paper cords holding their coats together.

There were a number of small steam ships, some of them hardly seaworthy, which took people, wagons, carts and animals. Long queues were forming in the hope of getting on to this transport.

There was corruption, and there were fights, as high prices were asked for the tickets on some of the better ships. Women tried to hide their men in boxes, or dressed them as women to get them on board, whilst the SS searched for them to make them join the *Volkssturm*. If any soldier was discovered by the SS having tried to get on board ship disguised, he would hang next day from a lamp post in the harbour as punishment, and also to frighten others.

The news that a ship had arrived travelled like wildfire. People moved along the roads to the harbour, crawling out of ruins, and the mass would reach the ship and fight for a place. The ships were overfull, but even the people in authority didn't care. They pushed the people back when there was no space left.

There was no comfort on board, only iron decks and empty hulls, hardly cleaned from the last load of refugees. Often there were still signs of dysentery, which most people had by now from the cold ship floors. The fright made people sit on the iron floors, or stand so close together that even if one person fainted, they would not fall.

Ships with refugees went to Swinemünde, Lübecker and Kieler *Bucht* (bay). Some of them did not return for more refugees; some of them sank from being overloaded, torpedoed, or bombed. Very few made a second journey.

As planned, I made my way to the station again and straight away had a look at the goods depot. To my great surprise, I discovered that the hospital train had left. Although I was glad about this, I was also sad, because I missed Max. At the same time, I saw another train standing there with a mixture of goods trucks and passenger coaches. Smoke was already coming out of the chimney of the engine so this train was ready to leave. There were people getting in, SS and SA men in uniform, but also women in fur coats, some warmly dressed children, and luggage. A number of boxes were put into the goods trucks.

The whole train was guarded by the *Waffen SS* (special force SS), who I knew would not hesitate to shoot at anybody trying to get near it. I realized that the party members were secretly leaving the town with their wives and children and their belongings. There would be no train at the station platform; this one was going to leave, unannounced, from the goods depot. I knew in a flash that this was the last train. People came rushing along, waving papers, probably their permits, which were checked before they were allowed to enter the train.

I was standing next to a small railway hut observing all this, unnoticed by the guards. I kept on racking my brain on how to get on to this train, because it would be my last chance to get out of Kolberg without having to walk. I wondered whether there were the same number of guards on the other side of the train. Thinking that I might stand a better chance from there, I made my way to the other side, having to go rather a long way round.

There was only one guard on the other side, marching along the train, from the back to the engine, then stamping his feet, and a quick turn, and back again from the engine to the end of the train. He was just in the middle of the train, marching towards the engine, when the siren went off, announcing Russian planes. The guard broke into a run towards the engine, shouting something. There was more smoke coming out of the chimney, and the train started to move.

I was not very far from the end of the train, so I ran and jumped on to the buffer. The last truck was not very high, an open one, covered by a tarpaulin. I tried to climb on to it, when suddenly the tarpaulin was lifted a little and two hands pulled me over the edge of the truck wall and underneath the tarpaulin, whilst another hand covered my mouth in case I screamed.

It was dark underneath the cover. Somebody pushed me down into a sitting position, because the walls of the truck were not high enough for anybody to stand. A little light was coming through a 2" (5 cm) hole in the back and the edges where the tarpaulin was fastened to the goods wagon. I could feel people next to me, and hands were still on my shoulders, but the hand over my mouth was gradually taken away. I couldn't see anything, but I knew my eyes would acclimatize themselves to the semi-darkness. Everybody else probably thought the same, because nobody spoke. I could feel the train moving, and bumping over points, and I also could hear the dull crash of some bombs.

They are bombing Kolberg, I thought. Or are the Russians already so close that they are shooting at it? Let's hope the train gets through.

Gradually I got used to the near darkness and noticed some figures, and a number of boxes, bulging sacks, and crates. There was not a lot of space, and one or two figures were lying on some boxes.

'Who are you?' I whispered loudly.

'Who are you?' came the reply from a deep man's voice, and then:

'Are you armed? A pistol? A knife?'

'No,' I replied. 'I am a refugee from Königsberg.'

There was silence for a minute. I had spoken loudly this time, because the deep voice hadn't whispered.

'Are you a woman?' asked the deep voice suddenly.

Up until now I had not been afraid, but this question made me feel uneasy. There was no point in lying, so I said: 'Yes'.

This reply stirred the other passengers in the truck into some action, and I felt some hands touching me, trying to find out whether this was true. I knew that they couldn't feel much through my thick clothes but, even so, I didn't like the idea of being pawed about, so I said loudly:

'Leave me alone.'

The reply was loud laughter from one or two, some whispering, and a loud voice saying roughly:

249

'We haven't had a woman for a long time. Come on, make us happy, we might all be dead by tomorrow.'

I thought that I had fallen into the hands of some soldiers, probably deserters, with no discipline or morals, determined to get away from the fighting, and I started to get afraid. My heart was beating like mad and, as hands were still pulling me, I hit out in all directions. I knew that I had hit one or two, but I didn't care. At the same time, I called out:

'You are a dirty lot. Keep your hands off me. I thought only the Russians behaved like that. I haven't run so far in front of them to be seduced by you. Who are you anyway, probably deserters, and that is nothing to be proud of.'

There suddenly was silence in the truck, and the deep voice said commandingly:

'Go and sit down. She is right, we are not like them.'

The train was by now going pretty fast, and we were rocked about quite a bit. I could still hear shooting in the distance.

'How old are you?' said the deep voice.

I didn't reply. Firstly, I didn't know whether it was better to pretend to be older, or to tell the truth, and secondly, I was too upset to reply calmly. I was afraid my voice would tremble.

'Nobody is going to touch you against your will,' said the deep voice, 'but you might as well tell us the truth. How old you are and where you come from. There are not many single girls moving in the refugee treks, usually families are together.'

He had realized that I was young, and I had the feeling that I would be alright with him. He seemed to have some authority, because the others had obeyed him. I told them that I was 20 years old, and a medical student from Königsberg. How I had left the town, made my way to the harbour, then went with the refugee treks along the Frische Haff, crossed it with my two wounded friends, broke through the ice, walked along the Frische Nehrung, got Friedrich on to a wounded transport, had a lift in a lorry that got hit and blown up, came to the village that had been ransacked by the Russians, how Max got ill and how I got him to Kolberg and then on to the hospital train. How I was then left alone, and discovered this train in the goods yard.

There was a long silence when I had finished. All we could hear were the wheels on the railway lines, running in their plonking rhythm.

'I am sorry,' said a voice. It sounded like the rough one from before. By now I had got used to the little light in the truck, and noticed quite a number of soldiers with rucksacks and guns.

'We are not deserters,' said the deep voice, and I saw it belonged to a sergeant.

'We are ordered to hide under the tarpaulin here as extra guards in case the people on the station discovered this train and stormed it.

I am sure that we were supposed to stay behind in Kolberg, but the train moved off fast because of the siren, and we decided that we might as well stay with it. The Russians must be pretty close, otherwise all those party members in the front of the train would not have left. They usually know more than we do.'

I thought of all the people still waiting in the station for a possible train, and of all the trucks on this train with luggage and belongings from the party members which could have been left behind to make space for them.

I didn't say anything, because I didn't know how the others felt, but I had that hard lump in my stomach again, which I always got when I was upset or frightened.

I don't know how long we had travelled, when the train suddenly braked, slowed down, and then stopped.

'Do you want me to go and have a look, sergeant,' said one of them.

'No,' was the reply. 'They might think that we jumped off before the train left Kolberg, so let's just keep quiet, and do what we were told, only to come out if the refugees storm the train. The further we get to the west, the better.'

He looked through the hole in the back. He also lifted the tarpaulin gently, to have a look around. He whistled and said:

'Be prepared, lads, we might have to get out fast. We have met Russian tanks, I can see marks in the snow. They are probably at the front of the train, that's why it has stopped.'

I started to tremble, and my hand went to the phial around my neck.

'We will jump out on the left side, because there are some bushes and trees which will slow the tanks down and give us a chance to get cover. Don't shoot. Keep the few shots you have for an emergency.'

He looked at me and then said:

'You can either run with us, or stay behind rolled up in the tarpaulin where they might not find you. Either way, we cannot protect you, not against tanks.'

We waited. It seemed an eternity and the sergeant whispered that nothing was to be seen except snow, and tank marks on one side of the railway line. I decided to run with the soldiers, and leave my rucksack behind, only taking my blanket. I could run better without a pack on my back.

Suddenly we heard shots. The train started to move again. The shots were further away and the train soon got up speed.

'There they are!' called out the sergeant, looking through under the lifted tarpaulin. We all had a look, and saw three large Russian tanks racing towards the train.

'It's a good job that they are such bad shots,' he said.

We could see the Russian tanks shooting at us, but the shots dropped short of the train. The engine went faster and faster and if the driver could keep up the speed we might outrun the tanks, as long as there were only the three which we could see. Nobody said anything; we were all holding our breath.

'Maybe they have blown up the rails,' said one of them, but the sergeant said:

'This is probably only a small advance group, some scouts, finding out whether there is any resistance. The railway line goes south/west from Kolberg to Stettin; there was always the danger that we might meet some tanks. They talked about it last night, but the report was that the Russians had only broken through at one point, and were being pushed back. Let's hope that we have passed that point, and let's also hope the reports are true.'

So we were going to Stettin, I hadn't known this until now. Maybe we would even get there. I wrapped myself again into my blanket.

'We are leaving the tanks behind', said the sergeant after a while.

Everybody sat down again, close together. It was bitterly cold; the tarpaulin cover was not like a roof. My teeth were chattering, and I started to shake from the cold and the fright of seeing the huge tanks, with their smoking gun barrels. Somebody put another blanket over my knees and an arm came around me and a kind voice said:

'It's alright, they have gone, don't worry. I will keep you warm.'

The soldier on the other side of me moved closer, too, and gradually I calmed down and relaxed. The train was going at top speed, and we were moving from side to side. A few times I thought the wheels might jump off the rails.

When the train eventually slowed down again, the sergeant had a look, and said:

'I think we have made it. I can see a number of houses, it must be Stettin. We will probably be guided into the goods yard again, everything has to be hush, hush.'

He looked at me.

'We cannot take you with us, you shouldn't be here. Let's see whether you can jump off somewhere. You are alright now, but keep going west; you have seen how close the Russians are to the River Oder.'

I put my rucksack on and stood at the back of the truck, all ready to climb out when told.

'Get ready,' he said suddenly. 'We are entering the goods yard, and there are plenty of trucks about where you can disappear.'

I could feel the train going very slowly, and also the bumping over points, and the excitement was building up inside me. I had the same feeling as I used to have before a race, or when our team ran on to the playing field when we had a handball match. The memory of this was like a flash, and seemed years ago, when I was a happy child.

'Now!' said the sergeant, 'come on, the train has practically stopped.'

He folded the tarpaulin back and helped me over the top, holding my arms until my feet touched the buffers.

'Thank you,' I said.

'Good luck,' replied the sergeant, and some voices repeated it.

I jumped off the buffer, and zigzagged my way through a number of trucks which were standing in the yard, soon losing sight of the slowly moving train.

I seemed to be in the centre of a maze of trucks. So that I would not make my way in a circle, I decided to walk just in one direction. I climbed through the connections of the trucks hoping all the time that the trains would not move. It was a large shunting yard, and I got very tired when, eventually, I reached the side. I was on an embankment and, although I could see a road at the bottom, I could not get on to it, because there was a fence or, at least, there could be a fence. The snow was so high, that only the tops of the fence posts were visible, and I did not like to chance the slide down in the snow, and then find that I could not get through, and have a laborious climb back to the top again.

There was nobody about. The trucks looked as if they had been standing there for days, because there was a lot of snow on their roofs and between the railway lines. I listened for a time. Then I thought I could hear the noise of an engine, the puff, puff of the smoke escaping from the chimney, and decided to walk towards it along the railway line. At least they kept the lines free of snow, so it was not such a hard walk.

I was in luck; it was the right direction, and soon I saw houses by the side. The embankment levelled out, and I found a gate, where feet had trodden a path. The gate was open, and I assumed the railwaymen were using it. I followed the path on the other side of the fence, which eventually led to a road where, to my great surprise, another trek of refugees was slowly moving along. I quickly joined them. They were all making their way to the town to cross the bridge over the Oder. Everybody felt that if they could get to the west bank of the river they would be alright.

'In any case,' said one woman, 'Stettin is such a big place, surely they won't let the Russians take this town, too.'

It is impossible to describe the confusion, fright and hope, doubt and belief, sorrow, and wishful confidence which we all felt in those days. We had all come such a long way in our flight, we couldn't imagine that the war would roll over the whole country.

# CHAPTER THREE

## The End of my Flight - The End of the War

Stettin was a big town, the biggest I had so far encountered since I left Königsberg. Life there still ran pretty normally. There were trams, there was electricity, and there was some food in the shops. Because of the unending stream of refugees, there were several refugee camps. Cinemas, theatres, school halls, any large building, had been provided with bunk beds for the homeless. There were toilets and washing facilities, but no showers or baths, and only cold water. I got a bottom bunk allocated in a school hall, and was even given half a piece of soap.

I had left Königsberg in the middle of January, and it was now the end of February. In all that time I had only changed my socks occasionally, not to wash them, but to let them dry in my rucksack. I never had the opportunity to have a wash, or change or wash my clothes. I had lost my suitcase whilst crossing the Frische Haff, and discovered only one set of underwear in my rucksack, but no trousers or pullovers. I wore three pullovers because of the cold. Still, I felt that I had to take off my rags and have a wash.

I was shocked to see how thin I was, and I never stopped shivering all the time I was trying to wash myself. I put on my clean underwear and the dirty trousers, pullovers, coat and blanket, and hoped that people could now see that I was cleaner than before. I tried to wash my underwear, but some of it fell to pieces. I hung it up, like everybody else, on a string over my bunk underneath the bunk above me.

The big room was quite warm, as it had several iron stoves going. We were also supplied with hot soup and bread. This was luxury indeed, warmth and food. It wouldn't matter if I stayed here for a day or two.

There were plenty of people who could tell me what was going on. I found out that trains were still going to places, but one had to apply for a permit.

So it should be possible for me to get a train to Greifswald, I thought. But it was too late to apply for a permit the same day; I stretched out on the bunk, and was soon asleep.

Two things woke me up: a pain in my chest, together with a cough, and the itching of my arms, legs, even my body. I jumped up and peeled off my pullover, thinking that maybe the soap which I had used was irritating my skin. I saw that I had marks on my body from bites. The hall was dimly lit. I couldn't see very well, but I could make out little things crawling up the wall, over my blanket and on to my palliasse, tiny red creatures. I started hitting them, and shaking my blanket, when the woman occupying the bunk above me said:

'They are *Wanzen* (bugs). I am used to them. I rub myself all over with the soap they gave me, it helps a little. They come out in the dark, or the semi-dark. It is alright during the day when it is light.'

She looked at my bites on my arms.

'Go and sit under the light; you will be alright there.'

I put on my pullover again, and took my things and moved towards the single bulb burning near the entrance. There I sat on my rucksack, leaning against the wall, coughing and scratching myself. All the weeks that I had travelled, I had never caught any bugs, or had a cough and now, when I finally found this warm place, I got both. I suppose that in the cold and frosty atmosphere germs did not spread, and bugs could not live. I did not return to my bunk that night, but slept like I always had slept, fretfully, sitting hunched up against the wall.

The next morning, I got my pathetic washing and, after a bowl of soup and some bread, made my way to the town hall to get my permit. The cold air outside hurt my chest, my cough was worse, my arms, legs and body were sore from scratching, and my skin was covered with red lumps and weals.

There was a tremendous queue for train permits, and there were fights when somebody wanted to push in. Some people had waited days, others had reached the desk, and were then refused a permit. There was, as always, the SS to keep order.

I did not think that I would ever get a permit. Besides that, I realized that I was not at all well and it would be very dangerous to queue there, outside, through the night. Instead, I made my way to the station, where I found out that trains were going to Berlin, Hamburg and Stralsund, the last going through Greifswald. The Stralsund train had already gone for that day. I stayed at the station, and watched what would happen if one of the other trains arrived.

Before the Berlin train came, people were already allowed on to the platform. At the barrier there was a railway woman looking at the tickets, and two SS men with guns. The platform was absolutely packed with people; more were queuing up to get through the barrier. When the train came in, there was pandemonium, with people pushing to get through the barrier, waving their tickets, and the people on the platform trying to get into the train through doors and windows. There was not much more control at the barrier. The two SS men and the conductress didn't seem to mind, because they probably knew that these people didn't stand much chance of getting on to the train, because even all the people on the platform could not get in.

Watching all this, I learnt one thing - I could get into the train without a permit. The permit was only needed to get the ticket. If I could slip through the barrier in a crowd without a ticket, just waving my hand, pretending I had got one, I would get on to the platform and have a chance to get on to the train.

I stayed the night at the station. I didn't want to go back to the hall with the bugs. I had had some soup and bread in the evening, but the next morning I had difficulties in swallowing, so I gave the bread to a child, with the surprised mother thanking me profusely.

This time, people were not allowed to get on to the platform for the train to Stralsund too early. I had stationed myself not too far away from the gate to the platform and, although people were pushing and shoving to get through after showing their tickets, I did not move until I saw the train arriving. I then waved my hand with a piece of paper in it as a sign that I had a ticket and pushed forward. Others did the same, but there were also some without tickets who thought they could have a try. The two SS men shouted out that only ticket holders could get through, and pushed the people who did not wave their hands with papers away, helping the arm waving crowd on to the platform. I slipped through and disappeared into the crowd of people on the platform. The train stopped, an open door was nearly in front of me and, as I had only a rucksack on my back and my hands free, I was able to push everybody away and get into the train.

I did not get a seat, but that didn't matter. I was used to sitting on my rucksack and once I was inside the compartment I sank, exhausted, on to it. I was feeling very hot and thought the train must have been heated. It wasn't long before the whistle went. Somebody tried to shut the carriage door. There were so many people in the train that this was difficult to do.

We all got pushed together, squashed, but eventually the door clicked in, and the train started off.

I don't know how long the journey to Greifswald took, and I don't remember much about it either. I was hot, and I was cold, I dozed, I slept, I woke up, because we had stopped somewhere, but it was not Greifswald, and the train went off again. Somebody asked me whether I was alright. I wanted to say that there was nothing wrong with me, but it was such an effort to speak that I just smiled or, at least, I tried to smile, and went to sleep again.

They did tell me when the train stopped in Greifswald. It was dark, so it must have been evening, or even night. I got out of the train and, pulling my rucksack behind me, I staggered along the platform, together with a number of other passengers.

I don't think I have got the strength to walk to Hermann's parents' flat, I thought, and then a funny thing happened. The floor of the station platform came up and hit me. I shut my eyes and thought: I have made it. I don't have to fight any more. I can sleep now for ever. With that, I relaxed and went to sleep.


It was not a relaxed sleep. I felt hands touching me, I felt that I was being carried. Somebody was washing me with warm water and a soft sponge. I was given something to drink, but then I was sick. At times I couldn't breathe, and then I heard a kind reassuring voice encouraging me, and telling me to have another drink. I was sure I was in a bed, but I couldn't open my eyes, because my eyelids were too heavy. Something seemed to press on my chest, and it hurt. The Russians were shooting again. The ice broke, and I sank into the water, and I screamed. Somebody pulled me out and brought me into the village which the Russians had ransacked, and I started to run. I ran, and ran, until I was so short of breath that I could not breath any more. I was fighting for air, and the kind reassuring voice was there again, and called my name. It was a woman's voice, and she called me Helga. This made me feel better, but not for long, because the pain in my chest started again, and the water in the Frische Haff was so cold. Max and Friedrich pulled me out. All the dead bodies were suddenly not stiff any more. They walked like ghosts over the ice and came towards me with outstretched arms. I knew they wanted me to come with them, they came to fetch me. I didn't want to be stiff and frozen, so I screamed, and told them to go away, and then they did, gradually disappearing in a snow storm.

My eyelids got better, and I could open my eyes. The pain in my chest had gone too. I looked around.

Where was I? I had never seen this place.

I was lying in a comfortable bed, with white sheets, in a small clean room. There was a door, and a window with curtains, and the usual blackout. There were two chairs and a locker. It was daytime, and the sun was shining, and I felt warm and comfortable.

Of course I am dreaming, I thought, so if I don't move, and just lie here quietly, and carry on dreaming, I will be warm and comfortable for a little while longer.

I heard footsteps, and I got frightened. The door opened, and in stepped a nurse with a friendly and kind face. She was not young, and she was not old, she seemed ageless. She moved quietly, gently, and silently. She came to my bed. She picked up my hand and stroked it, saying softly:

'I am so glad that you are better and awake at last. We were all very worried about you.'

'Where am I?'

'You are in hospital in Greifswald, you have nothing to worry about any more.'

I did remember going on the train to Greifswald, I even remembered arriving, but not what had happened after that. Gradually, I found out what had happened.

I was already quite ill whilst travelling in the train. People had been concerned so, when I left the train some passengers watched me and, when I collapsed on the platform, they got the nurse from the First Aid station to come and have a look at me. Nurse said that I had a high temperature and was very ill, and must get into hospital straight away.

I was unconscious when I arrived at the hospital, so somebody looked through my things and discovered my name, and that I was a medical student from Königsberg. Nurse Wanda told me:

'You were in a terrible state. We had to burn all your clothes. You even had bugs. We thought you were about 35 years old, or even older, and we were surprised to see from your papers that you were only twenty. You suffered from malnutrition, some frostbite, and your skin had a lot of sores. On top of that, you had a touch of pneumonia and pleurisy. You were very weak, and we sometimes thought you would die, because your stomach refused to accept food. I made you drink chicken broth. We had to cut your hair quite short. We could not comb it, because it was so matted. You talked during your illness, and we know quite a bit about your terrible journey. The only thing we were all wondering was, why you chose to come to Greifswald. Have you got relatives here? Maybe we could let them know, so that you can have some visitors.'

I had already been over a week in hospital. I looked at my thin white arms and hands and asked for a mirror. The face looking back at me from it was only vaguely familiar. It was very white and thin, with two big eyes, and funny, short cut hair. Surely I could not look like that. I was too tired to tell Sister Wanda about Hermann, so I went to sleep again.

I had the greatest difficulty in keeping any food down, but everybody was patient with me. The doctor I saw was an old man, who was very kind and who seemed to know a lot about me. I must have told everybody my story in my delirious state. He said that as soon as I was a little better, he would transfer me to the bigger ward, so that I had company.

Sister Wanda asked me again about my journey from Königsberg, but I didn't want to talk about it. Every time I thought about it, I felt uneasy, and started to shiver, and get cold, and she quickly dropped the subject. I did tell her about Hermann and his parents. She said that she had heard about Professor Fassbach, who was quite well known in the town. She promised to go and see him on her day off, and find out whether he had some news of my family.

It was only a day or two after I told Sister about Professor Fassbach that she came into my room, smiling broadly. She walked up to my bed, took my hand and said:

'I have some good news for you, but you must promise not to get too excited, because you are still very weak. I have a visitor for you outside, and the doctor said that you can see her for a little while. It is only a short visit.'

Thoughts were racing through my head who the visitor could be. At first, I thought it might be Hermann, but Sister Wanda had said "she".

Oh dear, I thought, I hope it is not Mrs Fassbach. I never did like her, and I didn't want to see her yet, not until I was feeling better.

I had said this to Sister Wanda before and she had promised to respect my wishes.

Sister Wanda opened the door and an elegant, tall lady dressed in a fur coat walked in. She looked just like my mother. I stared at that loving, familiar, face, and saw the tears which were running down from her wide open eyes.

'*Mein Kind, mein liebes Kind, was hast Du alles durchgemacht um hierher zu kommen,*' she said softly.

(My child, my child, what have you been through to get here.)

I could feel my heart beating loudly in my ears, like a drum. I could not think straight. How could a woman walk into my room, and look, and behave like my mother. And then I realized that this was my mother.

'Mamuschka,' I whispered. 'Mamuschka, oh Mamuschka,' I tried to lift up my arms to embrace her, but I didn't have the strength. My arms jerked, and my hands trembled, and then my mother was next to me. She embraced me, and my head sank into the soft collar of her fur coat.

I felt like a little child that had run away and had now come home, and I started to cry. I had not cried for a long time, and now that I had started, I couldn't stop.

'Sh, sh,' whispered my mother. 'You must stop, otherwise they won't let me stay. It is alright, don't worry. I am staying in Greifswald in Hermann's flat and I will come every day now.'

I just could not stop crying. My whole body was shaking and, although I tried to say something, no words came.

Sister Wanda came in again and, when she saw me crying in such a hysterical way, she left quickly to fetch the doctor. Both of them returned and tried to calm me down, so did my mother, but reassuring words and their kindness did not help. Eventually they gave me an injection and, before drifting off to sleep, I heard my mother's reassuring voice: 'Don't worry, I will be here again tomorrow.'

The next morning I felt much better. I kept on asking Sister Wanda whether it was true that my mother had visited me the day before, because I thought that I had dreamt it.

'Your mother is coming to see you again today,' she said, 'but the doctor will only allow the visit if you promise not to cry.'

'I am sorry I cried,' I said, 'I don't cry often. I haven't cried for years. I don't know what came over me yesterday. I will try not to cry today.'

'We all understand,' said Sister Wanda. 'You have got a good excuse, you have been ill.'

She really was a very kind and understanding person.

When my mother arrived, Sister Wanda came in to warn me again. It was not really a warning, but a preparation. She tidied my bed, combed my short hair and fussed around to give me time to get used to the thought that my mother would come in. I was still not strong enough to sit up on my own, but she had pushed a number of pillows into my back, and I was now lying in a raised position.

When my mother came in, I again felt that hard lump in my stomach. My heart was beating loudly, but I didn't cry. This time Sister Wanda watched me for a little while but, when she saw I would be alright, she quietly left the room.

My mother took her coat off, and we embraced and hugged one another without saying a word. I felt again like crying but, remembering Sister Wanda's warning, I suppressed it. I knew that once I started to cry I wouldn't be able to stop.

Neither of us was in a hurry to find out what had happened since we met last. For the moment, it was enough to hold hands, and to look at one another. Eventually I did ask:

'Have you heard from anybody else? Papa, Christel, Hans? Did you see Astra?'

'I have not heard from anybody else, and I never went to see Astra either,' said my mother.

She did not have a long story to tell. I knew that she had left Tuchel to travel to Oberstdorf to see Astra, because she had informed us that she was getting married. My mother never got to Oberstdorf. On the way to the south of Germany, she suddenly heard that the Russians had broken through in East Prussia. She decided that she must return to be with us, and got a train back to Berlin, only to discover that all trains to the east were for troops and military equipment. She tried for several days to get a train east, but this was impossible. Neither could she get any accommodation in an hotel, and had to sleep on a bench in the waiting room at the station. She then thought that she had better travel to Greifswald, and discovered that, by now, it was even more difficult for civilians to get a rail pass. She was not sure whether to travel south to Astra, or Greifswald. We had discussed things before, and we all had Hermann's address. Everybody had felt that if anything happened, it would be better to make our way to Greifswald, as this was in the north of Germany nearer to Königsberg. We had all agreed that the Fassbach family was our anchor point. We would either travel there, or get into contact with the family, and so my mother made her way to Greifswald and turned up at family Fassbach.

The few days sleeping rough in Berlin, the queuing for a rail permit, and the journey in a train packed full of people and luggage had been an exhausting experience for my mother. She arrived at the Fassbach's very tired and hungry, and with one of her terrible migraines. The welcome was not very enthusiastic. Still, they made her up a bed, but forgot to give her something to eat. Hermann, of course, was not there, and Mr and Mrs Fassbach were strangers to my mother. After my mother had had a good sleep, the two women talked things over, and it was decided that my mother would move into Hermann's flat for the time being. My mother had hoped to have a letter from us, and was very worried that there was no news for her from anybody.

Whilst my mother was in Berlin, she had taken out a lot of cash from her bank account, and she took nearly everything out whilst in Greifswald. She reckoned that the money was safer in her hands than in the bank, in case the German economy collapsed. She was, therefore, alright for money. She registered at the labour exchange, and even got a job there. She was then entitled to get her ration book. She only worked half days, mostly typing. As she said to me, if it wasn't for the worry about her husband and children, she could be quite happy in the little flat. It was comfortable, warm, and well situated, close to her work, shops, and even Mrs Fassbach, although the last would not have mattered.

Sister Wanda had gone to see the Fassbach family, who told her about my mother. As it was not very far, Sister Wanda went to Hermann's flat. My mother wanted to come straight away to see me, but the Sister prevented her, telling her that she had to calm down first, and said it would be better to wait another day. And that's how my mother had turned up at the hospital.

After that my mother came to see me every day, sometimes in the morning, and sometimes in the afternoon, depending on her work. At first she did all the talking as I was too weak to talk much; often I drifted off to sleep, and felt guilty afterwards. For the first time in my life, I really loved my mother deeply. She had nobody in those days, only me, and she told me things which she would probably never have told me in normal times. I had never thought much about my mother when I was young. She always protected Astra and Christel, spoilt Hans, and I went my own way. Now things were suddenly different. I was weak, I was ill, I needed care and protection, and I was all the family that my mother had at that moment. She showered me with love and affection. She brought me little things like food and fruit. I don't know where she got them from, because she had nothing to exchange it with, as in the days when she had butter or coffee beans. I didn't ask; I felt relaxed and happy. She asked me questions about my flight and my journey, but I didn't like to talk about it. Every time I thought of it, I remembered Friedrich and Max, the grey skies, the snow, the frost, the thaw, and again the thaw, and the frost, and the snow, and the cold killing wetness, and I started to shiver. My mother would then quickly change the subject.

After a few days, I was given a bed in the main ward, and I noticed people staring at me. I was a novelty in the ward. All the women there had had operations, whilst I was only there because I had been found at the railway station, nearly at death's door, and had nowhere to go. The nurses must have told the other patients about my journey or, maybe, my mother did, and people kept on asking:

'Did you see the Russian tanks? What were the Russians like? Do you think the German army will beat them back? How far do you think they have come, surely they will never cross the river Oder, or come as far as Greifswald and Stralsund?'

Because I had fled in front of the Russians, I was expected to know the answers! I was glad when my mother came, because then I did not have to take much notice of the people around me, but could concentrate on her talk and her plans for the future.

She was still convinced it would be best for me to marry Hermann, particularly now, where we seemed to have lost everything. When the war was finished he would have a good job, as he had his degree in chemistry and physics and, if nobody else from the family turned up, my mother, too, would stay in Greifswald, to be near me. Of course, she would have her own flat, and I could have the one she was living in at the moment back, because it did really belong to Hermann.

I just let my mother talk, what did it matter? I liked her voice, and the excitement she put into it with her plans but, at the same time, I knew that her dream would not come true, because I could not marry Hermann.

I will have to tell her one day, I thought, but not now. It will only spoil our relationship.

The doctor who looked after me was like a father, or even like a grandfather. He was quite an old gentleman, very kind, and terribly concerned about me. Sister Wanda said he used to come and see me several times in the beginning when I came to the hospital.

'You talked a lot,' she said, 'and the doctor used to listen to what you said. We know what happened to you. Fancy you walking with all those refugees over the ice of the Frische Haff! You are very lucky to be alive. However did you keep warm?'

One day the doctor said I could get up. Sister Wanda produced a dressing gown from somewhere and they lifted me up and sat me on the edge of the bed. I was warned that I would probably be very weak and might not be able to stand. I had two nurses holding me, one on each side. I lifted myself off the bed. My legs had no strength, and I collapsed. I would have dropped to the floor, if the nurses hadn't held me up. I tried several times after that and eventually could stand. The next day I did a few steps, but with help. By doing exercises, and trying to eat more, I did get better and, after three weeks, I could walk about the ward unaided.

I had no clothes. My mother couldn't give me any, because she only had the few clothes she took with her when she went on her trip to see Astra. I was still walking about in the dressing gown which Sister Wanda had given me and the nightgown I wore was from the hospital also. Sister Wanda talked to the nurses and the other patients and suddenly some clothes turned up. I was most grateful as I was now able to go outside.

It was the end of March by then, and the winter had practically gone in Greifswald. The first Spring flowers were trying to come out, and the sun was shining when I made my first steps outside the hospital door.

I was wrapped up warmly, and my mother accompanied me. Everything looked so different, fresh and clean and peaceful. Greifswald had not been bombed, and most people in the town still did not really suffer because of the war, except that their food was rationed. The refugees from the east did not come so far north either. They made their way to the river Oder and, once they had crossed it, they moved towards Berlin and the province of Brandenburg. So Greifswald gave the impression of a quiet and calm university town.

I only had a short walk the first day. I still felt very weak. I had not lost my cough, which troubled me quite a bit. Every day I got stronger and could walk further. My feet, which had been sore from frostbite, blisters, and calluses got better and I started to put on weight again. My muscles were very weak from lying in bed, so I had to do exercises. I still took sleeping tablets, because the doctor said it would prevent the nightmares that I got at night.

Mrs Fassbach came to see me once or twice, but said she found it difficult to get away from her husband. Having only one leg, he needed a lot of help. She brought me a letter from Hermann, who was very pleased to hear that I had arrived in Greifswald (his mother must have written to him), and hoped that I would recover soon. He told me to stay in the flat with my mother, and also to get to know his mother better and, maybe, help her with his father. He said that he didn't think the war could last much longer and if I stayed in Greifswald he would know where I was and return to there.

On April 1st, I decided it was time to leave the hospital, and to move in with my mother. I was not completely well, but I was bored and I felt that it was not necessary for me to occupy a bed any longer. I was surprised when the doctor told me that I was not fit enough to leave. I felt that the old man was over-protective. My mother felt I could come and stay with her. I could do little jobs in the flat, and gradually get used to a normal life again. I asked Sister Wanda what she thought.

'I think the doctor is worried that you could have a relapse,' she said. 'You are still having nightmares. You are only just starting to put on weight, and there are a number of things which you cannot eat yet; you have lived on a starvation diet for a long time. You said yourself, you keep on feeling sick. And there is your cough. If you leave, they won't take you back into the hospital if you get ill again. Beds are very short and you were lucky to get here in the first place. My advice is to stay here, rest, eat, take your medicine, and get really well.'

I stuck it for another few days, but then I made up my mind that I had had enough of hospital life. I also felt that most people did not understand what really was happening outside the hospital walls. They all said that the war would be over soon. Nobody seemed to worry about the Russians, or the other Allied forces. It was much too calm in the hospital and I did not trust this calmness. I could not share the people's belief in the invincible German Army and Air Force, because I had seen what had happened to this great force in the cold winter in East Prussia.

I had no permission to leave the hospital, so I arranged with my mother that I would climb out of the toilet window when it was dark, and I told her to meet me. The patients in the ward, in co-operation with Sister Wanda, had collected clothes and a few other things for me, and somebody had even given me a small bag. I still had my rucksack with some of my belongings. Sister Wanda, not knowing what was in the little phial around my neck, had put this into an envelope and deposited it in my rucksack. She thought it was a good luck charm. I agreed with her, and said it had helped me many times!

I got the rucksack and the little bag together.

I felt guilty for sneaking out of the hospital, so I wrote a letter to Sister Wanda, thanking her for all her devotion and help. I extended my thanks to the rest of the staff, and particularly to the doctors. I put the letter under my pillow. When I thought everything was quiet, I opened the door a little, and looked out. Nobody was there, and I moved quickly into the toilet. I opened the window and climbed out. When I jumped down, my legs and feet hurt and I caught my breath. My throat tickled and I wanted to cough, but I knew I must not do it as somebody might hear me. My mother touched my shoulder:

'Are you alright? Come on, then, I will take the rucksack, because it is heavy; you can take the bag.'

It was a long walk to Hermann's flat. I think my mother, being used to me as a healthy strong girl, never realized that I might find it difficult to walk so far. I stopped, and held on to a garden fence. My mother dropped my rucksack, and touched my arm:

'Come on, it is not far now.'

I could not walk any further and dropped on to my rucksack. I put my head down and pictures of the past came flooding over me. I felt that I was on the long march again and had stopped for a rest, sitting on my rucksack. But I always had had the strength and the will to get up again and to carry on walking.

My mother said:

'It is too cold for you to sit here. Come on.'

I slowly got up and started to walk again and eventually did reach the warm comfortable flat.

I was glad that I had left the hospital. The flat was homely. There was no smell of antiseptic, and no nurses in their white starched aprons, checking up all the time with thermometers and taking the pulse.

Mrs Fassbach came to see us and was pleased to see how much I had improved.

'Now you are better,' she said, 'maybe you could come and help me with my husband. He still needs a lot of attention, and I cannot get any help, or a nurse to attend to him. You have worked in military hospitals, so you should be knowledgeable enough even to attend to his leg, which is still not healed up completely. He has got an infection in the wound. I try and do his dressing every day, and a nurse comes occasionally, but it would be so much better if you could do it.'

I felt sorry for the old man. If he had an infection, the wound would never heal. I promised to come the next day.

'I will pay you for it,' she said. 'I could drop part of the rent for the flat if you like.'

I looked at my mother. I had not realized that she paid rent.

When Mrs Fassbach had left, I asked my mother about the rent of the flat.

'It all started when I suggested that I should pay for electricity and gas, as I did not want Hermann to be out of pocket,' said my mother. 'Mrs Fassbach said, of course I would have to pay this, and also the rent. Hermann does not own the flat. He pays quarterly and, as he had already paid, I have to give the money to Mrs Fassbach. I pay her every week. It takes nearly all my wages, because I only work half day. The only thing I don't like . . .'

My mother stopped and looked at me. I waited for her to continue.

'I did not want to tell you this, but maybe I should. Mrs Fassbach is charging me more for the flat than Hermann pays.'

'Oh no!' I said. 'She must think we have plenty of money. How could she do this! I am sure Hermann would not want that. We have lost everything and she is trying to make money out of us!'

'We are lucky to have the flat,' said my mother, 'and we can stay here as long as we like.'

'I am not staying here,' I replied. 'Have you listened to the news, and heard people talking? I don't know how far the Russians will eventually come but if they get any further, which they seem likely to do, they might even come here. I think we ought to get further west, at least to Hamburg. The town has a big harbour, and I doubt whether the English would like to have it occupied by the Russians. I prefer to be under English occupation.'

My mother stared at me.

'I think you are foolish to move from here. You have only just recovered, and cannot start off again. Where are you going to stay, and how are you going to get to Hamburg?'

'I have made enquiries whilst you were at work. There are still trains going, but one needs to get a permit, which is quite difficult to obtain. There are occasionally open lorries going to Hamburg to collect things. I spoke to a driver, who goes there twice a week and for a small amount he takes people and their luggage with him, as his lorry is empty up to Hamburg. We could go and stay with your aunt and uncle, with whom you lived before you were married.'

It had never occurred to my mother that we should go further west. She felt happy in the flat, and was hoping and waiting for the rest of her family to turn up there. She could see that I was quite determined. Our roles were suddenly changed. I, as her child, told her what we ought to do and she accepted my decision.

I got my map out. We looked at it, trying to guess how far the Allies in the west and south had come, and how far the Russians had moved. It had to be a guess, because I knew that we were never told the truth on the radio or in the paper.

After the war, I discovered how good our guess had been.

Once I had persuaded my mother that it would be best to leave Greifswald and make our way further west, she was prepared to get on with the packing arrangements. We decided to keep our plans secret, not even telling Mr and Mrs Fassbach. I hadn't started to help Mrs Fassbach with the nursing of her husband. My mother made excuses for me, saying that I was still very weak and needed to rest every afternoon.

My mother had her two suitcases, (the only things that she possessed after her aborted trip to my sister Astra), and we found some cases of Hermann's, which we decided to take. My mother had explored all the cupboards in the flat, and discovered two lengths of suit cloth.

'They will make excellent men's suits,' she said, 'but they are also very suitable for ladies' wear. I think we will take them with us. We will also take the few tins of food which are in the cupboards, and there is one bottle of brandy left, which we might need as medicine. If Hermann finds us after the war, he can have the cloth back; if not, we will keep it. We are very poor now, and have to look after ourselves.'

I was surprised by my mother but I had to agree with her. She also packed in a pair of check curtains which she found in a chest of drawers, saying:

'They will make two summer dresses for the girls.'

I arranged with the lorry driver where and when he would meet us, and I also settled the price for the journey. The driver wanted to make a really early start, and we, too, were in favour of this.

It was the 12th of April when we left, and I wrote later in my diary:

'We got up at 5 o'clock. Mamuschka made some sandwiches, closed the lids of the suitcases, and tied them up with string. She then pushed blankets under the string of two cases. I decided not to ask where she had got the two blankets from. We were both dressed warmly, Mamuschka in her fur coat, and I had two pullovers on, as I did not possess a coat. We knew it would be cold on the open lorry. Mamuschka locked the door. She put the key into an envelope, together with a letter to Mrs Fassbach. We struggled along with our heavy cases to the collecting point, stopping only once to drop the letter into a letter box. (Post was still collected and delivered). The lorry was late but, as we were not the only ones waiting for it, we felt pretty sure that the driver would turn up. He had wanted to leave at 6 o'clock, but didn't come until after 7 o'clock. He apologized, saying that he had to collect a trunk, which had to be delivered to Bad Segeberg.'

This meant a slightly different journey, but the final destination was still Hamburg. There were two more elderly couples, who wanted to go to the city, and two women, who wanted to go to Rostock.

The driver opened the back flap of the lorry, and lowered a ladder. I made sure my mother was the first one on to the lorry. I had told her to be quick, so that we could get the position at the front, behind the cab where the driver was sitting. This was the only sheltered part on the open lorry. I handed the suitcases to her, which would be our seats, and climbed on to the lorry after her. We were soon off, but stopped twice to pick up more people and by the time we came on to the open road all the floor space of the lorry was occupied.

It was a cloudy day, and I hoped it wouldn't rain. My mother pulled out the blankets from under the string of the suitcases, and we wrapped ourselves up. It was very cold and draughty. The driver stopped in a wood after a few hours and everybody disappeared behind the trees and had a little walk and stretch.

The journey went from Greifswald to Stralsund and Rostock, where the two women got off. We carried on to Wismar and Lübeck, where more people left. At dinner time we ate our sandwiches, but had nothing to drink, and I could not take my tablets, which I had to have to keep my food down. I don't know whether it was luck, or the great amount of fresh air that we had on the open lorry, but this time I was not sick.

Maybe I am getting better at last, I thought.

The driver made his delivery in Bad Segeberg. The trunk went to a family in a big house. The lady was very kind, and gave us all a drink, which everybody appreciated. We were not many left in the lorry by now. There was the driver, quite an old man, and he had a woman with two young children sitting with him in the front. In the back were just my mother and myself, and the two elderly couples from Greifswald. The two were going to stay with relatives in Hamburg.

It was late afternoon, or early evening and, although it had been cloudy all day, by now the sky had cleared. We had just passed Leezen and were driving towards Gross Niendorf, when I saw the Spitfires. I had not seen Spitfires before. They looked different to the Russian planes but, when they flew over us to have a look, and then turned and came diving back, I knew what was going to happen. I was not going to wait for the attack.

'Spitfires!' I shouted, and banged on to the top of the cab roof to draw the driver's attention to them and make him stop. I grabbed two of our cases and my rucksack, and threw them over the side into the ditch.

'You will have to jump,' I shouted to my mother and the other couples.

I ran to the back of the lorry, pulling my mother along, and released the bolts so that the back flap fell down. The driver had started to slow down, but my mother and I jumped off and rolled into the ditch before the lorry stopped.

I heard the whining noise of the planes' engine, and the bang, bang, bang of the bullets from the machine guns hitting the road. There were three Spitfires, and they came over us one after the other. I buried my head into my mother's fur coat, and I was holding my ears, but I could still hear the noise of the planes and the shooting of the machine guns. I was back on the Haff again, with the Russians shooting at us, and the ice breaking, and people with wagons and horses disappearing into the frozen water.

'No, no, no!' I screamed.

There was a terrific bang and I thought one of the planes had crashed.

I looked up and saw, a little further along the road, our lorry burning. It had been hit, and had exploded.

'One of the suitcases has been left on the lorry', I said, and looked at my mother, who was sitting up now. She was very white and stared at me with big eyes and a completely immobile face. She did not move, but just sat there.

'Say something,' I said, and shook her shoulder.

She is in shock, I thought. If it was a stranger, I would smack her face, but I cannot very well hit my mother.

I shook her several times, quite hard, but she did not react, so I laid her down in the ditch. I looked around and saw that the planes had gone. They looked like little points in the sky. The lorry was burning fiercely. I crawled out of the ditch and made my way towards the lorry.

I found the driver, and the woman with the two crying children, but there was no sign of the two couples who were with us on the back of the lorry. The driver was shaking, and looked very frightened.

'I am glad you banged on the roof,' he said. 'I was at least able to stop and pull the woman and children out of the cab. What happened to the other people?'

We walked back along the road, looking into the ditches on either side. The asphalt was torn and there were holes in the road from the bullets of the Spitfires' machine guns. We came to my mother, who had stood up by now, and I said:

'Let's go back and look for our cases.'

Miraculously they were not damaged, only dented. One of the blankets had holes from the bullets, but we decided it was still serviceable. We had been lucky, our lives were saved, and we had only lost one suitcase.

'I don't think the two couples got off the lorry,' said the driver. 'They were probably afraid to jump.'

My mother started to shake and tremble and then she cried:

'Oh dear, oh dear. The people must have burnt to death on the lorry. We could have helped them. Why didn't we help them?'

She looked accusingly at me and the driver, and I said:

'We got saved because we reacted quickly. If we had tried to help them, we would all have been blown up, or burnt to death. I have learnt that, in these situations one has to be selfish. I would have never survived on my flight from Königsberg if I had helped everybody in need. The rule is: Protect yourself first and, when the danger is gone, go and help others, if you have the strength. So now let's take our cases, and see how the woman with the two children is getting on. She, too, was very frightened, and the children were crying. We can probably help her to keep the children quiet.'

We took our cases, and struggled back along the uneven road until we found the woman. She was still sitting in the ditch, with her arms around the two children, rocking her body forwards and backwards. The children had stopped crying, and the younger one, no more than two years old, was sucking his thumb. His tears had made thin lines on his dirty face, and his nose was running but, even so, he looked like a little cherub with his fair curly hair and his lovely blue eyes. I had tried, until that moment, not to get too upset about what had happened, to keep a distance from everything. It was good to build a wall around oneself, and to say:

'This is me, I will look after myself. The rest is the outside, and that is not going to touch me.'

I often did this, and it helped me. But when I saw this young innocent face, I had a lump in my throat and had to swallow hard.

The woman stopped rocking. She said: 'What are we going to do now? The children are tired and hungry.'

After a few minutes, she added: 'My suitcases were left on the lorry.'

We all looked in the direction of the vehicle which, by now, had burnt out. Only part of it was there, still smouldering, the rest had been scattered in the field.

'We are not far from Gross Niendorf,' I said. 'Let's go to the village, you can see it from here,' and I pointed to it. 'We will go and see the *Bürgermeister*, who will probably help us. We will have to report the death of the two couples also, their relatives might make enquiries. Do you know their names?' I asked the driver.

He shook his head.

We started off towards the village. My mother carried one case and the blankets, and I took the other case, the bag and the rucksack. The little boy didn't want to walk, so the woman carried him, and the other child, a girl, who was a little older, walked quietly next to her mother, holding her hand. We kept on stopping because the cases were heavy, and so was the little boy. The driver helped us occasionally, but he was an old man and didn't seem to have much strength. Of course, if he had been much younger, he would have been in the army.

It started to get dark when we reached the village. There was nobody in the street, and there were no lights because of the blackout. We knocked on one of the doors and asked the woman who opened it where the *Bürgermeister* lived. She looked at us, at our suitcases, the children, our dirty clothes, and her eyes widened in astonishment when I explained what had happened to us.

'We heard the Spitfires,' she said, 'and we could see something burning, but we didn't think anybody would be alive after that. The *Bürgermeister* lives further down the road. I will show you. Just let me get my coat.'

She went indoors to get her coat, and then walked with us to the *Bürgermeister's* house and knocked on his door.

Gross Niendorf was only a small village, with 300 inhabitants, and everybody knew everybody else, or was related. The woman, together with the *Bürgermeister*, soon arranged things for us. The woman was going to put up the mother with the children for the night, the driver was going to stay with the *Bürgermeister*, but my mother and I would have to go and stay on a farm outside the village, at the *Bürgermeister's* sister's place. He offered us a cart to transport our suitcases in. He said that early in the morning we could go to Hamburg in the milk lorry, and his sister could bring the cart back.

He phoned his sister and I could hear that she was not very keen on having people coming to stay with her. She seemed to make some excuses, but her brother wouldn't hear of it. He said:

'You are not all that ill and, in any case, the women can help you. I will bring them along myself.'

This is exactly what he did, and I was glad that he accompanied us, because it was dark outside, and we had to walk for another twenty minutes along a small lane.

When I met Mrs Schraubeneck, our new landlady, I understood why she didn't want the work of bed making, and putting up two extra people for the night. She had fractured her right wrist and her arm was in plaster. Her brother told her that it was only for one night.

Mrs Schraubeneck was about my mother's age and, when she heard our story, she felt sorry for us. She was very nice, telling us to help ourselves to some food from the pantry. Whilst my mother made something to eat, she showed me our room, and asked me to put some fresh linen on the beds.

'My two sons sleep here,' she said. 'They are both in Hamburg in the home guard and my husband is in the army. I am running the farm on my own. My brother is helping me, and so are some of the women from the village, but it is hard work, and now that I have got my arm in plaster, I can only feed the animals. We have some prisoners-of-war in the village, who get allocated to the bigger farms, and sometimes I get two to help me. I am sorry that you have lost everything. At least I have got my home and land. I do hope that the war will be finished soon.'

My mother had made an omelette for me, but I could hardly eat it, I was too tired. Mrs Schraubeneck could see that, so she sent us to bed, especially as we had to get up early in the morning.

I went to sleep straight away and could hardly believe that the night was finished when Mrs Schraubeneck called me in the morning. I got up but, when I touched my mother's shoulder to wake her, she started to tremble and pulled the bedclothes around her as if she was cold.

'I just cannot get up,' she said. 'I have got one of my bad migraines. Maybe we could stay an extra day here.'

My mother did look ill. I realized that it was the after effects from the day before, maybe delayed shock. She had been in a very bad state after we jumped off the lorry, and I remembered her white immobile face when she saw the burning vehicle.

Maybe it is as well to rest a day here, I thought.

I went to talk to Mrs Schraubeneck, who was sympathetic, and felt it was probably a good idea to let my mother rest. I promised to help her as she had one arm in plaster.

My mother stayed in bed for three days and I made myself useful in the house. When Mrs Schraubeneck discovered that I could milk, she asked me to help with the cows. After that, I was shown how to boil the potatoes for the animals, prepare the food for the pigs, and then the vegetable garden needed digging, and suddenly it was time to plant the cabbage plants in the fields, and more and more jobs seemed to be piled on to me.

When my mother got up, she started to help in the kitchen. It wasn't long before she took over the cooking, because all helpers at the farm had to have one hot meal a day. When Mrs Schraubeneck discovered that my mother could sew, she soon produced some materials and a sewing machine and asked my mother to make her some dresses.

We had come for one night, but it turned out that we stayed on. My mother was not all that keen to contact her relatives in Hamburg and live in a city which was continuously bombed. We talked about it, and felt that we were really quite well off on the farm. We had a roof over our heads, good food, and Mrs Schraubeneck seemed to like us. We were allowed to listen to the radio and sometimes in the evening Mrs Schraubeneck would invite us into her sitting room for a little chat.

My mother and I worked very hard on the farm. The only thing we sometimes felt was wrong was the fact that Mrs Schraubeneck never offered to pay us anything. We had our food free, but she also had cheap labour.

Every few days I had to go into the village and collect our rations. It was not much and by living on the farm we had extra things, like eggs, flour, milk, and even butter, which we made secretly.

One day, when I went to the village, I met a column of prisoners-of-war. I had never seen any before. These were walking along the main road, accompanied by only a few guards, old soldiers in thick coats, with a gun hanging from their shoulders. There were English and American prisoners, and they looked well fed, with Red Cross parcels hanging on their backs. Behind them walked a column of Russian prisoners, with dragging and clattering steps, dressed in torn coats and rags, their pathetic clothes tied with a paper cord. The difference between these columns was tremendous.

I spoke to one of the guards and he told me that the English and American prisoners wouldn't have anything to do with the Russians. He said that they even refused to sleep with them in the same barn at night. Seeing this, I could understand why many Germans thought that, in the end, the English and American forces would help them in their fight against the Russian Communist advance.


On May 1st, late in the evening, we heard an announcement on the Hamburger radio that Hitler had been killed in his bunker in the Reichskanzlei, fighting Bolshevism to the last minute, and that he had appointed *Grossadmiral* Dönitz as his successor.

A second announcement came later, this time from Dönitz. It was a call to all German men and women and soldiers of the German army. He said that he would take over this great responsibility as leader in Germany's hour of need. His first task would be to prevent the German people being exterminated by the Bolshevist enemy. This was the only purpose in carrying on with the fighting. As long as the English and American forces prevented this aim, the German army would also have to defend itself against them and carry on fighting.

This was not only a call to the German people, but also a message to the Allies. Dönitz wanted to capitulate to the western powers, but not to Russia, so that the German soldiers could become British or American prisoners-of-war. Montgomery refused; he said he could not accept as prisoners an army who had fought the Soviets, who were their allies in the war. Even so, he did make exceptions with some divisions, but not with the refugees. The troops had to march into captivity, whilst the refugees waited by the roadside. By the time the refugees started to move again, it was too late for a number of them, as the Russians arrived before they had reached the English or American troops.

It was Eisenhower who was the hardest. He would not budge. It had to be capitulation to East and West. German officers sent to talk about a possible capitulation explained that no general could ask his troops to lay down their arms and stop fighting, and become Russian prisoners-of-war. Every German soldier knew that he would not get the same treatment from the Russians as he would get from the Allies. The Americans could not understand this.

Eventually, on May 7th, the surrender was signed in the presence of representatives of the United States of America, Britain, France and Russia.

On Tuesday, May 8th 1945, Churchill broadcast at 3pm, and announced: Victory-in-Europe-Day, "V-E-Day".

On Wednesday May 9th 1945, all hostilities ceased officially, and the surrender of all German forces went into effect at 0001 hours.

Until Hitler died, we were still promised victory and the success of the new secret weapons. It was a shock to hear the truth after the war, see the pictures of the concentration camps, and the terrible destruction of the country. It was then the turn of the German people to suffer under the hate of the enemy.

My mother and I were busy on the farm and, even when Mrs Schraubeneck had her plaster removed, she still relied on our help.

My mother was responsible for the house and the cooking. Mrs Schraubeneck fed the chickens and pigs, and I had to milk the cows. As soon as it rained and the ground was wet, we planted white and red cabbage plants in the fields. I went barefoot because I only possessed one not very strong pair of shoes, given to me in the hospital. I had to preserve them, so that I had some footwear when I went to the village.

On May the 3rd, we heard an announcement on the radio that Hamburg had surrendered to the British troops without fighting. The *Bürgermeister* felt his town had suffered enough from air attacks, and he could not see any point in prolonging the fight until the rest of the city was destroyed. For the last few days we had a number of Spitfires searching our area, often flying quite low. There were no soldiers or vehicles in the village, and the enemy planes did not shoot at civilians like the Russians had done if they realized there was no army. Even so, every time I heard the planes, I threw myself on to the ground and held my ears, as I could not bear the noise they made when they were diving down.

The day after Hamburg surrendered, there seemed to be an ominous silence. There were no planes in the sky, and the noise of the guns had stopped too. Mrs Schraubeneck asked me in the morning to take a note to her sister-in-law in the village, as she needed one or two things for a dress my mother was making for her. It had been raining the night before and, as the footpath was rather wet, I decided to go along the road, although this was a little further. The road was full of puddles, and I jumped over them, not really looking far ahead, as I had to watch my feet. There was a small wood and a sharp bend in the road and I had to look up then to judge my next steps.

I stopped and stared. Just round the bend stood a great big tank in the road, a British tank. The thick long gun barrel swung slowly from the side, and pointed at me.

My heart was beating like mad. I thought: Surely they are not going to shoot at me. I don't want to die!

I quickly lifted my arms up into the air, and then I shut my eyes tightly because I didn't want to see what happened next.

Nothing happened, so I opened my eyes again, and the tank was still there. It looked very big, and was very muddy, and I realized that it must have come over the fields. A foolish thought crossed my mind:

I wonder whether the tank had come over the field where we have only just now planted the cabbages?

Suddenly the hatch opened and a head appeared with a red beret on, looking around quickly, then an arm came up with a pistol, pointing at me. That was enough, I could not stand still any longer. I turned and started to run. A loud voice shouted:

'Stop!'

This is a command that everybody understands.

I had only gone a few steps. I stopped and turned back and watched the soldier climbing out of the hatch, followed by another with a pistol. They approached me, and asked me questions which I did not understand. How I wished my school English had been better. Mrs Lemke, my teacher, had always said that I would never be any good at languages!

One of the soldiers had a map and pointed to it. I realized that they wanted to know where they were. I showed them Gross Niendorf on the map, and also pointed in the direction of the village. I did understand some of the questions. They wanted to know whether there were any soldiers in the village, any guns, or whether there were any tanks. I told them that there were only village people in Gross Niendorf, and that there was no German army near here. I don't know whether they believed me. They talked to one another, and to a third soldier looking out of the hatch, and then climbed back into the tank. At least they had decided that I was not dangerous.

The tank turned and moved into the wood, and I decided to run to Gross Niendorf, and tell the *Bürgermeister* that the British troops had arrived.

The news soon went through the village; people were apprehensive and kept indoors. I didn't stay long, just got the few things Mrs Schraubeneck had asked for, then made my way back to tell my mother the news.

After that, we all waited to see what would happen next. In the afternoon, the British arrived in Gross Niendorf. They just arrived in cars, open jeeps, and motorbikes with sidecars. This was all quite peaceful; not a shot was fired. The *Bürgermeister* was asked to find quarters for the officers and soldiers for a few nights.

Mrs Schraubeneck had to put up two officers and their batmen, so she asked my mother and I to move out of her sons' bedroom. She moved into a small room with a camp bed, and we had to find a place in the barn. She said she was very sorry, but there were not enough beds in the house; we really didn't belong there, but had stayed on as refugees.

My mother and I made ourselves as comfortable as possible in the straw in the barn, choosing a place higher up, only to be reached with a ladder which we could pull up at night. We had our two blankets and

Mrs Schraubeneck gave us some more. I built an L shaped wall around our sleeping quarters with the straw bales, so that we had a bit of privacy. I put nails into the beams by the small window, so that we could hang up our few clothes. The rest of our belongings were in the suitcases. I organised two straw bales as seats, and a third as a table, and covered them with clean sacks. We had our own little corner, our room and, being the month of May, it was already quite warm. When we went to sleep that evening, I heard my mother crying, so I got up and slipped under her blanket, snuggling up to her.

'Don't cry,' I said. 'It will be alright. Mrs Schraubeneck said we can use her bathroom in the morning. She couldn't help it that we had to move out. The British are the victors now, and we have to do what they say. We can probably move back into the house once they have gone.'

'We will never move back,' said my mother. 'Mrs Schraubeneck wants us to go to Hamburg now, you wait and see. What do you think will happen when her sons and her husband return? She needs the bedroom. Why should she keep us any longer? We are no relations of hers.'

She cried again. 'What will happen to us? The war is finished now, at least for us here, but it won't be long before everybody will stop fighting. I keep on thinking about the others. Papa and Hans and Astra and Christel. How are we going to find them? Astra is probably alright, the British or Americans are fighting in the south. But Hans and Christel might be overrun by the Russians, and then we will never see them again, or get any news from them, and Papa - oh dear, I don't know, I always think that he must be dead. Please forgive me, my dear child, I shouldn't cry, and talk to you like this. I have got you, and you are strong in mind, and will be strong in body too, once you have completely recovered.'

She put her arms around me and hugged me and, holding on to one another, we eventually went to sleep.

My mother was right; for us the war was finished when the Red Devils entered Gross Niendorf. They were only the advance troops, and didn't stay long. One lot of troops left, another arrived until, in the end, the occupation forces took over. We never moved back into the farmhouse, but stayed in our little "room" in the barn.

# CHAPTER FOUR

## Occupation - A New Home

All fighting stopped officially on May 9th. The armed forces, the air force and the navy surrendered. Germany's proud fleet had gone in late 1944. U-boats and battleships had disappeared, through bombs, mines, depth-charges, torpedoes and gunfire. The last survivors of the U-boats came, sullenly, to the surface, hoisting black flags of surrender.

The German governmental organization stood until the end of the war, then collapsed. Suddenly there were no trains, no post, no ration books, no stock exchange, no banks. Shops closed, because they had nothing to sell.

Prisons and concentration camps were opened. Millions of uprooted Europeans tried desperately to get to homes and families that often no longer existed. The roads of Europe were full of people, ex-prisoners, freed slave labourers, orphans, widows and old people, all struggling along. Some were fleeing from the Russians, others were trying to get back to Poland or Rumania.

In the cities, the survivors lived in the rubble, poking about aimlessly. The conquerors had to organise a new life for the conquered. Displaced Person camps were established. People were screened, to discover what role they had played under the Nazi regime. The Allied agreement on their post-war policy was denazification, disarmament, demilitarisation, punishment of war criminals, reparations, and dismantling of war industries.

Russia, and the government of Poland divided Prussia between them. The Russians got the frontier between Russia and Poland that they wanted, and moved Poland's western frontier that much further into Germany.

The western Allied commanders had to bring order to their zones of occupation. These one-time soldiers became administrators overnight. They had to rebuild the German administration, restore communications, re-open factories, feed the civilian population and not only demobilize their own armies, but also return the thousands of displaced persons who had been brought in by the Germans, either as prisoners-of-war or forced labour. They had to find homes for the millions of refugees who had recently fled from the east.

Germany was divided into occupation zones with considerable differences between the three Western and the Russian ones, and the way they were handled. The Russians not only looted what was left in peoples' homes, but also what was left in the surviving industry. They dismantled machinery and plant for shipment to Russia as reparation. Much of it was reduced to scrap metal before it reached the war-damaged industrial areas of Russia because of their careless treatment of the equipment. The Soviet soldiery were let loose in the traditional style of the Mongol and Tartar hordes, and a brutal pillage and degradation of people took place in the Russian occupied zone. The most common words were *Uti, Uti* (watch) and *Komm, Frau* (come, woman). Russian soldiers often wore half a dozen watches on each arm and the louder they ticked the greater was the admiration.

The British zone was the largest, in terms of population, and soon displayed some air of order and calm. The British tended to remain aloof and distant from the German people at first and lived apart in special areas. The non-fraternization was not revoked until December 1945.

The French zone contained the best and the worst of the Allied administration. They hated the Germans and were the most stringent and uncompromising of the Western occupation powers. They liked to show that they were the conquerors.

The American way of life, as displayed by the US administrators was in great contrast to the average German lifestyle, most of them on the border of starvation. It was a great hindrance to civil-military relations. The result was the practice of the black market.

Gross Niendorf was in the British zone, and the occupying forces took over the village school for their work. Officers and soldiers lived in private houses, which had to be vacated for them. One of the houses occupied belonged to the *Bürgermeister*, who now, being without a home, asked his sister, Mrs Schraubeneck, to put him and his wife up.

We had to remain in the barn. Not only that but with two women in the kitchen, Mrs Schraubeneck and her sister-in-law, my mother was not wanted there any more. Mrs Schraubeneck suggested that we should enquire about a refugee camp.

My mother decided that we should contact the Swiss Embassy, get in touch with the Red Cross, who had started a list of missing persons, and then try and contact my mother's relatives in Hamburg.

There was no public transport, and there was no post, but the milk lorry went three times a week to Hamburg. I enquired at the dairy, but I was told that nobody was allowed to go with the driver to Hamburg. I soon discovered who the driver was and I stopped him one day in the road outside the village, and had a little talk with him. Being a young girl, and quite pretty, and putting on all my charm, I soon had his promise that he would take me to Hamburg. The only stipulations were to meet him outside Gross Niendorf and not to tell anybody.

My mother was disappointed that she couldn't come with me, but happy that I had found this transport. As I was going to be away a day or two, we couldn't hide this from Mrs Schraubeneck, especially as she would have to take over my jobs with the animals whilst I was away.

I told Mrs Schraubeneck that I was going to make my way to Hamburg, maybe even get a lift but, if not, I would just walk. She was pleased to hear that I wanted to enquire about my relatives, and also go to the Swiss Embassy. She made me some sandwiches and got a bottle of drink ready, even produced a little rucksack.

I left at 5 o'clock in the morning. My mother kissed me, and said:

'Good luck, come back safe and sound, and take care.'

I met the milk lorry as arranged, and the driver, an old man of about sixty years of age, was pleased to see me. I was company for him on his trip.

'We have to pass several security posts, because the curfew is until 7 am but, don't worry, I will tell them that you are my daughter. I have permission to be on the road', he said.

The journey was uneventful. We were stopped twice, and the driver showed his pass. The first time nobody queried my presence but at the second stop the British sergeant wanted to know who I was. My English was good enough to explain that the driver was my father. The sergeant smiled, and seemed pleased that I spoke a few words of English.

I had never been to Hamburg before but, even if I had, I would not have found my way to any particular place. The centre of the city was absolutely destroyed, and all that was left were ruins and craters. There were some houses left, that's what the driver said, but we seemed to travel along rubble and make-shift shacks. There were people about, clearing the rubble from the road with their bare hands, or coming out of the ruins.

Children played in the dirt; old men and women, disheartened and starving, sat on bricks by the side of the road.

The dairy was partly bombed out, but the back yard was still intact. The driver stopped there and told me to meet him in the afternoon at 4 o'clock.

'I must get back before the curfew,' he said. 'I have only got a pass for the early morning hours. If you miss me today, don't come tomorrow, but the day after. I will look out for you every time.' He was very concerned about me. 'I don't know where the places are that you want to visit, you will just have to ask. But take care, there are a lot of rough people about. Not all the people released from the concentration camps were innocent, and the people from the prisons usually had committed some crimes. They are all free now, and the roads are full of them.'

I was not scared. I felt I could cope; I had come a long way on my own. At least it was not cold, and I had had something to eat and, of course, there was the promise of a return trip to my mother on the farm.

I started off, and soon realized that most people didn't know where the places were which I wanted to see. They had not heard about the Swiss Embassy, but they had heard about the Red Cross. Nobody could guide me, as there were hardly any road signs. I did get some advice like this:

Follow this path (which was really a road, now reduced to a path, because of collapsed and bombed buildings), until you come to the burnt out church, then turn right and, after passing the pieces of the monument, you know you will recognize them, there is a horse's head and the rider's arms and legs, you will come to a house which has no front. One can look into the rooms, with their burnt out furniture. After that house, you have to turn left, and then you had better ask again.

Advice like that got me going, and I wandered about for hours, getting more and more disorientated, and worried that I would never come to my destination. I also realized that by walking around like that I would never find the dairy again, from where I had to make my return trip.

Eventually I found the Red Cross place because, the nearer I got to it, the more information I received. I was shocked to see the mass of people queuing up to get in.

The Red Cross occupied a large building, which looked like a school. It was still intact, although some windows were broken and boarded up. The big double doors were closed. People stood in front of them, and then down the steps. The queue continued along the pavement, with people standing three or four deep, and was as far as I could see, stretching until the next corner of the street. Half way along, people didn't stand any more, but sat on the ground. People of all ages were there, old and young, even children. They all stood or sat, silently waiting for the doors to be opened.

'You will have to go to the back,' said an old man to me, pointing towards the corner of the street. 'The queue continues around the corner.'

'How long have you been waiting?' I asked.

'Three days,' he said. 'You must not move away, otherwise you will have to start again at the back. I sleep on the pavement with the others. They come and bring some soup and a piece of bread for everybody in the evening. Nobody tells us to move on.'

Suddenly there was movement in the queue. People got excited, and started talking and pushing forward. The big doors had opened. Two men with Red Cross arm bands allowed some people to come out of the building and after that a number of people were allowed in. The doors closed again, and the crowd settled down for another waiting period, the front ones standing, the rest sitting on the pavement. I will have to wait for days, I thought. Let's hope Mamuschka won't get worried.

Slowly I started walking along the queue of people. Nobody was interested in me. They all looked tired, defeated, old and grey, even the children. I looked at their faces, their thin starved bodies clad in dirty clothes or rags, and their measly belongings - battered cases or boxes. For a moment I was frightened, wondering what would become of all these people, including me and my mother, having lost our homes, and all our possessions.

It was then that I saw the old man, who stared at me with wide open eyes. He touched my dress with a trembling hand. He looked familiar. His face was unshaven. His short white hair was sticking up from the top of his head in an untidy tuft. Tears were running down his face and over his sunken cheeks. He was sitting next to a lamp post, using it as back support. He was dressed in an old jacket and next to him lay a stick, to which a small bundle was tied. He kept on pulling my dress.

I saw his lips moving, but I could not hear or understand what he was saying. He seemed desperate, and his voice got louder, and suddenly I understood the words:

'I had a daughter like you, a beautiful young daughter, and two more girls, and a son, and a wife, but they have all gone, all gone. She was just like you, just like you,' he said, and each time he said "you", he pulled my dress.

'Leave her alone, Grandad,' said a woman in the queue.

I kept on staring at him. My heart beat louder and louder, I could hear the beat in my ears, and I, too, started to tremble. I felt the lump in my throat, and I knew who he was, but I could not believe it. His lips moved, and he mumbled:

'I keep on seeing my children, but it is always a vision. They always disappear again. You are a vision, too, but this time I will hold on to your dress, and maybe you will stay.'

'It is no vision,' I whispered, and I knelt in front of him, putting my trembling arms around him.

'Oh Papa, Papa, I can't believe it is you. What are you doing here? How did you get here? It is just like a miracle!'

I cried and cried and hugged my father. He didn't respond at first, because he couldn't believe that he had found me.

Eventually he realized that I was truly his daughter. Everybody around us was pleased for us, happy to see that two loved ones had found one another. My father broke down and, for the only time in my life, I saw him really cry. His whole body shook and the tears poured down his face. He hung on to me and would not let me go. He laughed and he cried. He tried to say something, but I couldn't understand the words. I, too, could not find proper sentences, all I could say was:

'Papa, Papa.'

Gradually we both stopped crying and laughing. I sat on the pavement next to him, holding his hand and leaning on his shoulder, and we both were quiet.

'How did you get here?' We both asked this, and the reply was the same:

'It's a long story.' But I had to tell him that I was with Mama on a farm. 'I am with Mama on a farm in Gross Niendorf, not far from Hamburg,' I said.

This made him cry again. It was another miracle for him that he not only had found me, his daughter, but also Mama, his wife.

Suddenly he wanted to do something for me. He fiddled in his pocket and produced a piece of dry bread.

'Here, take it, you look so thin, you eat it, I am not hungry.'

'No, no,' I said. 'We do get enough to eat on the farm where we are staying. I will give you a sandwich with sausage on it, I have it in my rucksack.'

I took my rucksack off and unpacked my last sandwich. My father stared at it. There was a hush all around us. I realized that people hadn't eaten a sandwich with sausage for a long time, not even seen one. It made me feel embarrassed. It was my last sandwich, and I wanted my father to eat it. I took the piece of dry bread and gave it to the woman who had tried to stop my father from holding on to my dress.

'Here, you can have this. I want my father to have my last sandwich, I have no more.'

My father took the sandwich and, holding it in both hands, he took a small bite, then wanted to pass it over to me. I shook my head. I knew what it was like to starve, but I had had enough food on the farm. Now it was his turn to have food, not mine. He ate the sandwich very slowly and, when it was finished, he picked up every crumb.

He smiled, and patted my hand:

'Thank you,' he said. 'And now, I could do with a cigarette. I haven't got any, so let's just imagine it.'

He closed his eyes, and gave a good imitation of lighting and smoking a cigarette, making all the appropriate hand movements and shaping his lips to blow out the smoke rings, which he often had done when we were children. It was an excellent mime.

We had nothing to do, except to sit here and wait. My father said he had already slept here for two nights and this would probably be the last night.

'There is a curfew from 10 pm until 7 am,' he said, 'but we just sit here, because most of them have nowhere to go. The English Military Police come at night to look at us but, as long as we don't move about, they leave us alone. They don't know what to do with us; the prisons and camps are overfull, and a lot of people sleep and live in the rubble of the town.'

'Do you live anywhere?' I asked.

He nodded his head. 'I am not talking about it here. I will tell you later.'

A soup kitchen turned up in the late afternoon, organised by the British Forces. We all had some soup and a piece of bread. In the evening everybody settled down as comfortably as they could. Some people had blankets or coats, others had nothing. My father had a blanket, which we shared. We had moved up during the day, but had not yet reached the door of the Red Cross station, and now we were leaning against the wall of the building. We knew that tomorrow we would be able to get in.

During the night, my father told me his story in a whisper. He stopped from time to time, overcome by the memory. Once or twice, he said:

'I can't talk about it. It doesn't matter, at least I am alive, and you are here, and Mama is safe.'

My father had left Tilsit too late; the Russians were already shooting at the town. He had his car and plenty of petrol, and he hoped to get away. As usual, the roads were packed with refugees and soldiers. A car with only one driver and private number plates (not army), looked suspicious. Sure enough, he was stopped by the SS, who wanted to confiscate his car. He showed his Swiss passport explaining that he was making his way to Königsberg, to get to his family. If they could not have his car, he would have to drive for them, they said. It would only be for a day or two. My father felt that this was better than losing his car and having to walk, so he did what he was told. A day or two turned into a week, and then another week, and he was getting no nearer to Königsberg. He then heard that Königsberg was surrounded by the Russians. He did not believe this at first but, being now in the middle of activities, he eventually had to face the truth of the situation. He decided to escape, and make his way to Elbing, where the Swiss Embassy was, and then to Tuchel to be with our mother. One night, he got away unobserved with a couple of cans of extra petrol from the SS. He picked up some soldiers, which made the travelling easier as he was then not so conspicuous. When he dropped them off, he picked up others, some of whom had given up fighting, but all of them in uniform. They shared their rations with him, but many times he had to starve. He did not get to the embassy in Elbing, because he was put into prison.

My father always had good maps. The army, realizing that they had difficulties moving along the main roads because of the mass of refugees, had cleared quite a number of side roads. Somehow, my father got to the outskirts of Elbing, going along these cleared roads. Here he decided to hide his car and make his way as a civilian into the town to find some food, and to go to the embassy. He took only an old bag with him, and his papers. He was able to get two loaves of bread by exchanging them for some cigarettes. He was confronted by the SS again, who were looking for deserters. They took him to the local prison for an interview, confiscated his papers, made him sign a statement and, before he knew what had happened to him, he was locked into a cell with some deserters.

My father was frightened then, because these soldiers were waiting to be shot or hanged or put into a SS suicide squad. Again he explained his position, but his cell mates only laughed, saying that nobody got out of this prison alive.

If it was true that this was the death cell, then my father knew he would have to escape. He had to forget about going to the embassy, even leave his papers behind, if he could get out. There was still his car in the forest, if nobody had found it, which would help him to get further to the west. He waited for an opportunity.

After the third night in prison, my father was the only one left in his cell. Up till now they had hesitated to execute him, because he did have a Swiss passport, but my father didn't trust them. Every day he had a bowl of thin soup and, if he hadn't had his bread he would have been very weak. He had only finished one loaf and there was still the second left. The old soldier, the so-called jail keeper, had told him that there was no food in the town and that he could hear the Russian guns. My father offered him his loaf of bread and asked him to forget to lock the cell in the evening. The old soldier looked at my father, took the bread, but never said a word. My father was very surprised when, in the evening, he heard a key turn in the lock. He waited a little while, then tried the door, which opened. There was nobody about, the prison seemed empty, and my father just walked out. The streets were empty too, but the rumbling of the guns was near.

My father found his car, still covered with branches and snow in the wood. He knew that he was very vulnerable, driving off without his papers, particularly without his passport, but he had to leave. He hoped that by now, dirty and unshaven, he would look an old man who was not capable of doing any fighting in the army or home guard. Again, he picked up some soldiers and only travelled at night. If he was stuck in the snow, he always had help from his passengers. The army was always helpful, said my father, as long as he did some driving for them. They even supplied him with petrol. Several times he took officers to advanced positions, and then others further along and in this way he gradually made his way towards the west. He had to abandon the idea of going to Tuchel; the Russians had advanced too far. Once he crossed the River Oder things went easier and, when he reached the River Elbe and another flood of refugees, he filled his car up with old people and made his way to Hamburg. He had already been in the town for several weeks and knew his way about. He arrived before it was taken over by the British.

'Have you still got your car?', I asked.

He nodded his head and put his finger to his lips. There were too many people about, most of them asleep. We were only whispering but, even so, my father didn't want anybody to hear us.

'I have been to the Swiss Embassy,' he said, 'to get another passport.

I am afraid they cannot give me one, as I have no papers to prove that I am Swiss. There is no post, and there are no trains, but the embassy is in contact with Switzerland by road transport. They gave me a food parcel and, once they have established that I am Swiss, I will get more help. I filled out a lot of forms, also one to search for my family. I always hoped that Mama or you or Christel or Hans would contact the embassy. They promised to notify me if they heard from anybody.'

He stopped for a little while, then he took my hand and said:

'I am so glad I have found you. Tomorrow we will register at the Red Cross and after that make our way to the farm where Mama is and try and find a place where we three can live together.'

He whispered even more softly:

'I have got some money. I took it all out of the bank before Germany completely collapsed.'

'Mama did the same,' I said.

I tried to catch some sleep, but kept on waking up, and often my father was awake too. After midnight, the British Military Police turned up in three jeeps.

'Pretend to be asleep,' whispered my father, 'and cover your face.'

I curled up, and pulled the blanket slowly over my face. With my father next to me, I felt protected.

The police in their grey uniforms and white helmets walked along the sleeping queues of people, shining their torches at us. I was glad that I had covered my head. I heard them talking, but only understood a little. They were concerned about the number of people there. What were they going to do with us? The camps were full, and they would have to have lorries to transport us. In the end, they just drove away.

We were both stiff in the morning after a sleep on the hard pavement.

I was surprised because I had travelled from Königsberg to Greifswald, sleeping rough all the time. Now, only a few weeks later, my body was already soft again, and unaccustomed to a hard bed. Even my bed in the hay loft on the farm was softer.

We had nothing to eat, and neither did anybody else. My father said that he knew of a few soup kitchens, but they were too far away and, as we were already quite near to the main door of the Red Cross Headquarters, it would be better not to go away as we might lose our place.

It was an anticlimax when we eventually got through the door. All we had to do was to fill in a card, then take this to a clerk, who checked it, and said he would inform us if they found some members of our family.

My father walked with me to two soup kitchens in the afternoon, and we had a good meal with the soup and bread. After that, we were able to walk to my father's so-called "home".

Once we were away from people who could hear us, he told me that he still had his car and that he was living in it.

'I have to keep things quiet and secret,' he said. 'Only the British occupation forces are allowed to drive vehicles, or people with permits. All private cars are confiscated if they are in drivable condition, so it is better to hide the vehicle. I have got some people who have helped me to hide the car. They live in their little summerhouses in their *Schrebergärten* (allotments), because they are bombed out. I have taken out the rotor from the car, so that nobody can drive it away.'

It was quite a long walk to the allotments. I was surprised how well my father knew the town, as most of it seemed rubble to me, or houses with boards over the windows, and no street names anywhere. Some roads had names, written on pieces of wood and propped up at the pavement, or nailed to a charred tree, or the remains of a house. There were also pieces of paper stuck on to remaining fences, trees, buildings, and upright ruins. I read some of them. These were messages for people who had lived there and had disappeared. People who had survived the fighting and the bombing came back every day to sit on the ruins, hoping that a relative would turn up. Everything looked grey, dirty, and broken down. The people were unshaven, thin, frightened-looking, with hungry eyes, and rags for clothes.

'Not all parts of Hamburg are like this', said my father, when he saw how I looked at everything. 'Only the centre, and the dockyards are so destroyed. The villa part, Wandsbek, the pretty part of the town, has still got a lot of big houses intact. The British have taken over a number of them as living quarters for officers, and for the administration.'

We reached the allotments late in the afternoon. There were quite a few children and people about. Some of them seemed to know my father, because they smiled and waved to him. We walked along a wide path which had a fence on either side, with little gates which led to the different gardens. They were all the same size, and there was a small summer house in each of them. Some of the houses had extensions or a lean-to and, in some of them, were tents, makeshift accommodations, made from posts of wood or metal and waterproof canvas. Towards the end of the path, the allotments became bigger, and some had two summer houses in them, plus a lean-to. My father stopped in front of one of the larger gardens with a summerhouse, and a lean-to with pieces of canvas hanging down on the sides.

'Here we are', he said.

He opened the gate and walked along the path towards the lean-to. He lifted up the canvas and pushed me inside.

'This is my home. Here is my car, my belongings and all that I have in this world. Please enter my palace.'

It was dark under the canvas, but I could see the outline of a car. My father rolled the canvas up on the side of the hedge and tied it to the roof.

'I keep this side open when I am here, it is not so obvious. The name of the man who owns this garden and summerhouse is Maierhofer. He lives in a flat in the town with his wife, three children and handicapped mother. They used to live here quite a bit when Hamburg was bombed, because it is away from the centre, the docks and the industrial parts. The trouble was that they could not bring the mother to live here; she is crippled and walks on crutches. They are living in their flat again now, because this place here is really too small. The sister-in-law lives in the next garden. She was bombed out and had nowhere to go. She has two children, and they keep an eye on everything around here. The allotment people all hold together and try and help one another, at least here, at the bottom of the lane.'

My father had been very lucky to get to Hamburg. He looked thin and old, because of lack of good food, but he was alive, and I had found him. He had a suitcase with some dirty clothes, never having had the time or the knowledge of how to clean them, a featherbed, and a large radio, a Telefunken, which he had taken from our home.

We both had a good night's sleep and in the morning we made our way north, trying to get out of Hamburg. We had decided that there was no point in trying to find the dairy where I was dropped off by the milk lorry. The allotments were near the airport in Fuhlsbüttel, and this was already towards the northern part of Hamburg. We found a soup kitchen in Fuhlsbüttel, and the British sergeant was very kind to us and gave us a double ration of bread, which we quickly hid in our clothes. After that, it was just a matter of walking along the main road which led eventually to Bad Segeberg. Gross Niendorf was about 15 km before the town. We were lucky and got a lift from a farmer with a horse and cart for a while. The cart was not very clean, the farmer had transported sacks of potatoes, but the dirt was only earth and dust and it saved our legs, and our shoe soles. We ate our piece of bread at dinner time, and asked for a cup of water in a village.

It was well after dinner when we arrived at the Schraubeneck's farm. I felt it would be better to prepare my mother for the fact that I had found my father. I asked him to sit down behind the barn and wait for me.

I found my mother in the vegetable garden, where she was busy with some weeding. She was overjoyed to see me. We sat down on a grass patch and I started to tell her about my trip. She kept on interrupting me with the question:

'Have you got any news?'

'Yes, I have good news', I said.

'You have heard from somebody, haven't you, tell me, tell me, is it about Hans?' she said.

'No, I have not heard anything about Hans', I replied, and my heart sank. Hans had always been her favourite. The little premature baby had always remained her baby boy. She was not really interested in how I had made my way around Hamburg. All she wanted to know was whether I had any news about Hans. I nearly cried when I saw her disappointed face. We were both silent for a few minutes, then I said:

'I have no news about Hans, but I have news about Papa.'

Her head came up with a jerk. 'Papa! - Papa! - Is it true? I always thought he was dead!'

I took a deep breath. 'I have brought him with me, he is sitting behind the barn.'

She looked at me in disbelief, then jumped up. I held on to her dress.

'He is an old, weak and fragile man,' I said. 'Don't push him over in your excitement', and I smiled at her. I had already forgiven her for the hurt of a few minutes ago.

She ran along the garden path and out into the yard, and disappeared behind the barn. I left them alone and went to find Mrs Schraubeneck, as I wanted to tell her that we had an addition to the family now.

They all seemed genuinely pleased that my father had been found, until Mrs Schraubeneck realized that another mouth had to be fed.

'There are three of you now,' she said, 'and I have no work for you. You will have to move on, as I cannot feed you all. They have opened a displaced persons camp in Bad Segeberg, and it would be best if you tell your parents that.'

My parents eventually came indoors, and my father soon got on the good side of Mrs Schraubeneck with his charming ways. He always had been a lady's man, and seemed to find the right words to flatter her. Soon we all sat down around the big dining room table, and my father kept everybody enthralled with the story of his escape. He told Mrs Schraubeneck that, of course, we couldn't and wouldn't stay here, he was sure he would find another place for us soon.

My father felt that it would be a good idea to live in Hamburg, as we would then be near the Swiss Embassy. Once they had proof that we had Swiss nationality, we could get a passport, would be entitled to some food parcels and maybe also get help from the embassy for accommodation. He also felt that it would not be a bad idea to return to his homeland as starting a new life in Switzerland might be easier than starting it in a defeated Germany.

My mother was more practical. She thought life would be easier in the country than in a town of ruins.

After a lot of discussions, it was decided to do what Mrs Schraubeneck had suggested and go to the camp in Bad Segeberg. There was only one big question - what about the car? My father told Mrs Schraubeneck about it, and also confided in her brother. Both felt it would be a good idea to hang on to the car, as there were hardly any about. Nearly all of them had been confiscated, towards the end of the war by the army. My father felt uneasy about leaving the car in the allotment, whilst staying in a camp in Bad Segeberg. Mrs Schraubeneck then suggested that my father could put his car into the barn.

Who had the courage to drive the car? There was a curfew at night and, to drive the car in broad daylight might be dangerous. On the other hand, my father and I had seen a few cars in Hamburg, driven by civilians who must have had permits. There were no cars about in the country, only the milk lorry, and the farmers used their horses and carts. Thinking of the farmers, my father suddenly said:

'We will have to have a horse to pull the car. People will think the motor is faulty and won't bother about us.'

Although this was a good idea, it was much too far for a horse to pull the car all the way to Gross Niendorf. My father then said that if he could get a horse, he would dare to drive the car out of Hamburg, and then be towed for the rest of the way.

Mrs Schraubeneck, who desperately wanted to get rid of us, promised to find out in the village whether somebody would sell us a horse. My mother felt we were all crazy.

To everybody's surprise, Mrs Schraubeneck was successful in obtaining a horse. The animal looked terrible. He was light brown and thin, and his bones on his ribcage were sticking out. I thought that he could just about walk and must have been very old. He would never pull the car. Mrs Schraubeneck assured us that it was a very tough horse, and only needed some food. She had some oats and would also let us have a fodder bag. We didn't know much about horses, but could see that this was not a good specimen. Still, we had no choice, beggars can't be choosers. My father paid her the asking price, and the horse was then taken into a fenced-off field, where he seemed quite happy. We now had to make our plan.

My father and mother would go to Hamburg and get the car, driving it to the outskirts, where I would meet them with the horse. I was given a map and in two days I had to be at the Underground station which my father marked in. It was the last station on the Underground. I was also told that if they didn't turn up, I would have to return to the farm.

'If they confiscate the car whilst I am driving,' said my father, 'they might imprison me again, but I am sure they will let your mother go, and then you both will return to Mrs Schraubeneck.'

My parents made their way to Hamburg the next day. They slept one night in the car and then, the following morning, they pushed it along the allotment path and drove to the Underground station. Nobody stopped them; it all seemed so easy. They waited for me in a little side street.

My journey was not so easy. The horse, I called him Hitscher, did not want to walk. I tried to ride him but I had no saddle and kept slipping off. Even so, we did quite well, especially when I could get him off the road, which he did not like. I could then ride him along the field. I met my parents in the evening, just before the curfew and, of course, we could not go much further the same night. The area around the Underground station had been bombed. I tied Hitscher to a strong tree, which was black from a fire, and the three of us tried to make ourselves comfortable in the car.

As soon as daylight came, my father fixed up a rope onto the car. He then tried to teach my mother how to steer the car.

We fed our horse and tried to tie the rope to him. Mrs Schraubeneck had lent us a harness, and shown us how to fix things up. Hitscher did not like the car. Every time we got him near to it, he refused to go any further, and tried to get away. In the end, we turned the horse round, so that he couldn't see the car, and pushed the car towards the horse.

The poor animal did not have much strength, but he started walking; we tried to help him, by pushing the car. My mother was told how to use the brake, so that she kept the ropes tight and didn't let the car run into the horse. She was quite good at steering the vehicle. It was my job to guide Hitscher, and to encourage him to pull.

We met a few people, who just stared in disbelief but accepted that this was another way of transport for refugees. Everything went fine as long as the road was straight and level, but then we came to a hill. My father decided to unhitch Hitscher, and let the car roll down, hoping to get a good swing up the other side. This time he did the driving.

My mother and I, with Hitscher, walked down the hill. The horse, feeling suddenly free, started to gallop, and I had to follow, leaving my mother behind. My father did quite well with his freewheeling, and got about half way up the other side. Hitscher was not very happy to be tied up again, especially as this time he had to pull uphill. Still, he did eventually reach the top, and we let him rest a little, getting him some water from a farm. The farmer and his wife came to have a look and laughed when they saw the old horse. The farmer offered to buy the car, but only intended to give a pittance, as it was not a drivable car. My father didn't tell him the truth.

We somehow got to Ulzburg, and then to a little village called Kisdorf. By now it was evening and Hitscher just wouldn't go any further. In any case, we realized by now that we would not get to Gross Niendorf until the next day. My father went to see the *Bürgermeister* of the village and explained our position. He did not tell him about Mrs Schraubeneck, and that we had a place on the farm there, but told the *Bürgermeister* that we were refugees making our way to the displaced persons camp in Bad Segeberg because we had no home. My father also told the *Bürgermeister* that we were Swiss, but had lost our papers, and were waiting for the embassy to supply us with new passports.

The *Bürgermeister* came up with a wonderful idea.

'There is an empty *Funkstation* (radio station) just outside the village. It is the highest point in the district of Segeberg,' he said. 'It was occupied by the army during the war. When the war finished, the soldiers and officers destroyed all the equipment in the two barracks. There are two more barracks, one for the officers, and one for the men. They lived up there in isolation. I think the bunks are still there, the stove to cook on and maybe some furniture. If you want to go and stay there, I am sure nobody will stop you. The British occupation forces go and have a look at it every time a new unit comes to Kisdorf but, as everything is destroyed, they leave it alone. If you are Swiss, I am sure the British commandant won't object to you moving in. We have a very nice one here in the village at the moment. You can ask him in the morning.'

The three of us looked at each other. It sounded marvellous, it was a roof over our heads, a home of our own, even if it was only a barrack.

'Where are we going to stay tonight?', asked my father.

'You can sleep in my barn,' said the *Bürgermeister*, 'and the horse can go into one of my meadows. The poor thing looks worn out!'

I took Hitscher to the meadow and let him loose there. He looked at me and slowly moved away. He did not run, just quietly dragged himself along, tired and worn out. I felt sorry for him. We had asked too much of him. He had really finished his working life, and now he was being asked to pull a car.

We spent the night in the barn, something my mother and I were used to. My father slept in the car, his home for a long time. The *Bürgermeister* gave us some soup and a piece of bread each, and we were grateful, because food was short everywhere.

The next morning, the three of us went to see the commandant. I tried, with my school English, to explain what we wanted, but I didn't know what *Funkstation* was in English. Still, I did make it clear that we were Swiss, not German. This seemed to help, because the commandant got an interpreter. They seemed to know about the radio station, and felt that it was probably quite a good idea to have somebody living up there. We got permission to move in and even received it in writing.

So now we had a new home on top of a hill, and we hadn't even seen it.

I collected Hitscher, who looked quite perky after a night's rest. He didn't seem to mind having to pull the car again. The only trouble was that this time we had to climb a hill straight away. Half way up, we could already see the barracks, and some very tall masts. Hitscher seemed to like my cheerful call of:

'Hü, hü, hü, Hitscher', because he neighed once or twice, and slowly made it to the top of the hill.

The barracks were surrounded by a large piece of land, which was fenced in. From the main road, we turned off onto a small cart track leading to some unlocked gates. There was a small pedestrian gate, and a larger one to let carts or cars through. Hitscher pulled the car through the large open gate and after we closed it we unharnessed him and let him free. A wide road led to the barracks with the equipment, and a smaller path to the living quarters.

One of the barracks was completely empty. There was nothing in the different rooms except dust and spiders and cobwebs. The second barrack had a kitchen, with a *Kanonenofen* (iron stove) and one large saucepan. There was no china, no cutlery, no table and no chairs. There were three more rooms, one with a bed and a palliasse on it. In one of the other rooms were a few more palliasses, some of them torn, with the straw coming out of them. There were even some pillows, stuffed with straw.

My mother looked into every room, then sat down on the bed and started to cry.

'Oh no, no, no,' she said. 'We cannot live here. Hans, you cannot make me live here. There is nothing in the rooms. How am I going to cook? Where are we going to sleep?'

Gradually my father calmed her down, promising to see whether he could get some furniture and some china. He also pointed out that this place, because of its isolation, would give us complete privacy. He painted a terrible picture of the camp in Segeberg, exaggerating all the bad points. Then my father turned round to me and said:

'You can walk back to the village and see the commandant. Tell him what it is like here. I am sure the farmers in the surrounding district have helped themselves to the furniture and china, maybe he can get it back for us.'

I was not at all pleased to go back to Kisdorf, and I certainly didn't like to speak to the commandant. I never liked begging for things.

'You will have to do it,' said my mother suddenly. 'The commandant won't do anything for your father, but he might do it for you. Just use your charm and make him feel sorry for us. We have no choice today. We are beggars. Your father is right, this could be made into a home, a place which we do not have to share with strangers.'

I looked at my mother and I remembered how she had pushed me to see Dr E. in Königsberg, so that Christel could get a job with the Red Cross. She was doing the same again, using me and my youth. I had been successful before, and I felt that I would probably be successful again. The commandant and his interpreter had been very nice to us, but especially nice to me.

So I went to Kisdorf to talk to the commandant. He wasn't there, but I met the interpreter, which was even better. He was quite sympathetic, and promised to help. I found out from him that he had studied in Berlin before the war, and that's where he had learnt German. He took me back to the radio station in his jeep, so that I didn't have to climb the hill again. Before he drove off, he gave me two packets of cigarettes for my father.

Late in the afternoon, my new friend Jim arrived in his jeep, and produced blankets, a few chairs, a rickety table, some china and cutlery, saucepans, buckets, and a few other odds and ends. He even produced a few tins of food, and a loaf of bread which was very white.

I had never in my life seen such white bread. Then, with a big smile, he gave me a bar of chocolate.

'I have asked my sergeant to come with me tomorrow, to find a few more things for you,' he said. 'He promised to put the fear of God into the farmers for stealing things from the station, and hopes that they will give them back.'

After Jim left, my father and I went to find some pieces of wood, so that my mother could light the iron stove. She soon had some water boiling, which she mixed with a tin of soup which Jim had given us.

'We will have to be careful with food,' said my mother. 'I must thin the soup down, so that it lasts for the three of us. Tomorrow one of us will have to go and see the *Bürgermeister*, and ask for some ration cards. We won't tell him that we have got some already. Nobody knows us and if we shop in different places we can use our two lots of cards. Most people have some food in their store cupboards. We have to start from nothing and this will give us a better start. The other thing we will have to talk about is how to get our things from Mrs Schraubeneck.'

We had our soup and bread, but I still felt hungry, and I am sure my parents did too, but nobody said anything.

The allocation of food for each person for one week was: 150 grams of meat, 1000 grams of bread, and 50 grams of butter. Even when this was doubled, it was not really enough.


It took a week before we eventually got to Mrs Schraubeneck. There was a lot to do at the radio station. One of the first things that my mother insisted on was that everything had to be cleaned. Jim and his sergeant turned out wonderful helpers and organisers. We only had to mention things and they were able to get them. They produced soap and soap powder, flour, tea, coffee and sugar, taken from the army kitchen. They seemed to like to sit in our primitive kitchen, with the saucepans and china on the floor, and join us in a cup of coffee or tea. This, for us, was luxury. Coffee and tea were so scarce that we hadn't had any for weeks. We started to like the English tea, after Jim showed us how to brew it in a saucepan as we had no teapot.

I had been to the *Bürgermeister* and got our ration cards. On the way back, I met a milk cart, and made a new friend, Hans-Detlev. He had been in the unit which was stationed at the radio station and, when the British came, he had helped to destroy all the equipment. He didn't want to be imprisoned, so he went as a farm labourer to the nearest farm, saying to the occupation forces that he had always worked there. The farm was behind the radio station. A path led from the road, along the fence of our so-called property, to the farm. The farmer, getting cheap help in this

***On Radio Station with Hitscher***

way, was only too willing to back Hans-Detlev's story. My new friend gave me a lift in his cart, and we organised that he would leave me some milk every morning if I put a jug in the hedge.

We had no running water, no toilet, and no light. There was electricity, but it was disconnected. It was Hans-Detlev who knew how to connect the electricity. He came to see us one afternoon and took my father and me to an electricity sub-station, which was in the middle of the neighbouring field. He seemed to know quite a bit about the different wires, and what to do with them. He sent my father back to the radio station, and asked him to wave to him when the lights came on. He joined different wires, but my father did not wave. He joined some other wires, and suddenly my father waved excitedly. We had light! From now on we were connected to the electricity, we had light, and we could use the Telefunken wireless. But the best thing was, we had no electricity meter and, as long as we lived on the radio station, we never paid a penny for electricity!.

We had to get our water from a well. We had to let down a bucket on a rope, and then pull it up again. The water was fresh, cold and clean, and the top of the well was covered with a large round wooden board, which was cut in half. We had to move half of it to let the bucket down.

The toilet was in a little wooden house behind our barrack. Inside was a wooden box with a round hole, which was covered with a wooden lid with a handle. Inside the box was a bucket which had to be emptied from time to time. To do this, one went outside to the back of the hut and lifted a flap at the bottom of the back wall. The bucket was taken out and carried to the furthest corner of the station, where it was emptied into a hole. It then had to be rinsed out with water from the well, and put back into its place again. It was not a very pleasant job and nobody needs to guess who was allocated to see that this work was done. Whenever I was there, the bucket seemed to be full, and I had to empty it.

Jim organised us two more beds, and we were able to put the palliasses on to them. I had my own room, with my bed, one chair, and everything else laid neatly on to the floor boards. I also had a spare palliasse, which I covered with a blanket which Jim had given me.

My father and I went to see Mrs Schraubeneck. She was genuinely pleased to see us, as she had been very worried. It was over a week since we had started our trip to Hamburg and she thought that we must have been caught driving the car. She had already visualized us all in prison. She suggested that we ask the driver of the milk lorry, who went to Hamburg, whether he would take our suitcases. She didn't know that he had already taken me to Hamburg and that I was quite friendly with him.

I went to see him and he promised to pick the cases up the next morning. As my father and I had walked to Gross Niendorf, quite a long way, we decided to sleep in the barn, and go early in the morning with the milk lorry. The driver picked us up at 5 o'clock with our cases, but told us that we would have to sit amongst the milk churns.

'I am sorry about this,' he said, 'but I am not really allowed to take anybody with me and if I get stopped because of the curfew they won't see you in the back.'

My father and I were glad that we had my mother's two blankets with her suitcases, because it was quite cold on the open lorry so early in the morning. I could already see the masts of the radio station, when suddenly a British jeep came along the road and stopped the lorry. Papa and I crawled between the milk churns, trying to hide. We heard voices. The driver said that he had a permit and probably showed it, but then I heard a voice saying:

'Let's look in the back.'

Somebody climbed on to the back and pushed the churns about, and I suddenly looked into Jim's sergeant's face.

'Well, well, well,' he said quietly under his breath, 'who have we here.' He looked at my father, then at me, then turned round and jumped off the lorry, calling out:

'Everything O.K., Sir.'

The milk lorry moved off. The driver stopped eventually on the road opposite the path to the radio station and unloaded us with the cases.

'That was a near one,' he said. 'I am glad he didn't see you. You must have made yourself very flat and thin between the churns.'

We carried the suitcases up the path and then to the gate. My father had hung a bucket upside down on to the gate, and also a short iron bar next to it. This was our bell. We had to take the iron bar and bang it

*My Mother with Hitscher*

against the bucket, to tell my mother that we had returned. She had been worried, and had had a fretful night and was now overjoyed to see us.

At last my mother could change her clothes and underwear, and I, too, was glad to have the few things which I possessed with me.

In the afternoon, the sergeant turned up and wanted to know why we were on the lorry that morning. I told him that I still had had a rather heavy suitcase on a farm, and that the lorry driver had said he would transport it for me. My father was there to help me. He accepted my explanation, which was very nearly the truth.

We had moved on to the radio station on May 13th. Two to three weeks later we were quite established in our new home and had got used to living there. The weather was warm and sunny, and the roses in front of our hut entrance had started to shoot again. On one side of the front door was a solid wooden table and a bench in permanent position, and we had a lot of meals outside. My mother was marvellous the way she managed our rations. We had also been very fortunate in getting tinned food from Jim, and the milk which Hans-Detlev left every day was a great help. Having the two ration books also helped. The only trouble was that I had to walk to the next village with one set of ration books, which was very tiring, as I was not particularly strong from the little food we ate.

There was not much wood on the station, so my father decided to cut down one of the tall radio masts. He had tied a rope to the mast, which I had to pull, so that when the mast started to fall, my pulling would be in the opposite direction to the hut. He chopped away. Suddenly the mast swayed.

'Pull!' shouted my father to me, but it was too late.

I saw the great mast fall, and knew that no pulling would help, so I ran to my mother. With a tremendous "swish", the mast fell, just missing our hut. He then chopped up the mast into small pieces for our stove.

My father decided to dig up a patch of garden behind the hut, where my mother wanted a vegetable garden. We had been able to get some seeds, and soon my mother had a very nice vegetable garden laid out, which I had to water every day. We now waited for the first little plants to come up.

There was great excitement when the first shoots could be seen, and my mother was already planning what she was going to do with the vegetables. Unfortunately, things never went smoothly with us. Disaster struck my mother's vegetable plot. I was just coming back from the village with some shopping, when my father whispered to me:

'Come outside quickly, don't let Mama see you.'

He took me to the back of the hut and pointed to the vegetable plot. I couldn't believe my eyes. Hitscher had galloped all over the plot, trodden everything down, even the little fence my father had erected all round it.

'I couldn't get him out,' said my father, 'the more I pulled him, the more he trampled about. He even tried to kick me.'

'You should have just thrown a stone at him, or offered him something to eat at the edge of the plot to get him out,' I said.

'Never mind what I should have done. The thing to decide is what are we going to do now? We cannot plant everything again, and to start with the seeds, if we are lucky to get any more, is much too late.'

'It will break Mama's heart,' I said.

'I know, I know. That's why we have to do something. You go indoors and keep her occupied, and I will try and smooth things over. Some of the plants must be still alright.'

I did what he suggested, and went and talked to my mother. Whenever we were alone, she always talked to me about Hans, my brother, about Astra and Christel, wondering what had happened to them, and what we could do to find out where they were. She felt that it was time to go to Hamburg again and enquire at the embassy whether they had any information. One of us should go to the Red Cross and tell them our new address. It was time to go and see her aunt. We had made several attempts, but had never gone to her.

She said: *'Aufgehoben ist nicht aufgeschoben.'* (To put it at bay does not mean it is never done.)

I agreed with everything she said, and even elaborated on the different suggestions, so that she wouldn't go outside. My father came indoors eventually, and gave me a little sign that he had finished.

My father had done his best, but it was obvious that the garden was destroyed and that somebody had tried to resurrect it. At first, my mother didn't say anything. She bent down and straightened one or two plants, stretched the wobbly fence a little and, suddenly, she said:

'Was it the horse that destroyed all this? I thought something had happened, when Papa didn't come in for such a long time.'

Without another word, she went indoors. She did not say anything to my father that evening, but I told him that she knew what had happened.

I was worried about my mother. I would have liked her to cry, or say something. The next morning, she came indoors, very agitated and upset.

'That horse has to go,' she said. 'I had grown fond of the animal. He had worked so hard when we needed him, and I felt that I was making up for it by giving him an easy life. But now he has become too familiar, wanting to come nearer to us. He has been on the vegetable plot again. Hans, take that horse, and go to the village. Sell it, or get something else in exchange. I don't care what it is, but just go. I don't want to see that horse again.'

My father and I went outside. I found Hitscher and put the reins on him. He was quite docile, as if he knew that this would be the last time. I felt sad. I loved that old horse. He had put on some weight, his ribs were hardly visible. It had done him good to have no work for weeks.

'Make sure he has a good home,' I said to my father.

It seemed a long time before my father returned but when he did he gave us both a great surprise. He could have easily opened the gate and come in, but he banged the bucket and my mother and I both walked up to the gate, wondering who was there. My father stood outside, smiling all over his face, and next to him was a bicycle. I opened the gate and, without a word, he swung himself, like a young boy, on to the saddle, and rode the bike along the path to our hut.

We found out that he had exchanged the horse for it. He had to do quite a bit of bargaining and talking, because bicycles were the only useful vehicles, there being no petrol for cars.

The bicycle certainly had seen better days, but it would be a help for my shopping. I used it the next day, but already had a puncture on the way home. I was nearly at the radio station, so I decided to lift the back wheel with the puncture and push the bike home. I had always mended my own bike and I soon had the tyre off. There seemed to be more patches than tube. I mended the puncture and, after that, the bike was alright for a few days. The next time, the front wheel needed mending, but that tube did not have so many patches.

Two things happened very quickly together. Firstly Jim and his sergeant came to say goodbye. They were both looking forward to going home and would now be leaving the army. They brought us some food again, anything they could spare, and we all said a sad farewell. We knew that we would never see them again. They had their families in England and, if all went well, we would one day return to Switzerland. They told us that a new unit would take over, but even they would not be permanently based in Kisdorf.

The other person to leave was Hans-Detlev. He came to see us in the evening, something he seldom did, and told us that he would leave in a day or two.

'The farmer would like to keep me,' he said. 'I am cheap labour for him. He hardly pays me anything. When I mention that I would like to start the trip home, he threatens to tell the British authorities that I was never in a prisoner-of-war camp to be screened. So I will just have to disappear one day. I have never told anybody where my home is so even if the farmer squeals on me, they won't find me. I want to go home, see my parents, and my sister and brother, and only hope that they are all still alive. Thank you for being my friends. I am sorry that you won't have your milk any more in the mornings, unless you, Helga, offer to drive the milk lorry!'

We said goodbye, and wished him luck. Two days later, my jug in the hedge was empty and I knew that he had gone. We missed the people, and we missed the extra food.

A new commandant took over in Kisdorf and a day or two later two British cars turned up at the gate with an officer, a sergeant and some men. They didn't bang the bucket, just opened the gate and drove in. They seemed to be surprised to see my father and me coming out of one of the huts, with my mother following behind.

'What are you doing here?' shouted the captain.

'We have had permission from the commandant,' I said, and I turned to my father and told him to get the piece of paper which we had been given by the last commandant.

The captain, in the meantime, turned round to the soldiers, and gave them some orders. They disappeared into the other huts. I knew they would only find destroyed equipment.

My father returned and showed the piece of paper with the permission but the captain was not impressed. I couldn't understand what he said, but his face showed disapproval. He told the sergeant to search our hut.

'You have no right to go into our hut,' I said. 'This is our home, and the war is finished.'

The sergeant hesitated, but the captain again told him to go.

The soldiers returned, and reported that everything was broken, that nothing was in working condition. The sergeant said that the living accommodation was very primitive, with no running water and an outside toilet with a bucket. It suddenly occurred to me that the captain was inspecting the station for the possibility of taking it over for accommodation for his men. I was glad at that moment that it was too primitive.

One soldier reported that there was a car. The captain walked off to inspect it. My father and I followed. They tried to start it but, of course, it wouldn't go. It looked dusty and dirty, my father having left it like that on purpose. One could see that it had not been used for ages. The captain never asked us about it, and we did not volunteer any explanations. He just ignored us, but did not stop us from following him. He also went to look at the other huts, but not our own quarters again.

'Make sure nobody starts anything here again', he said, turning to my father.

Then he ordered his men to leave, and got into his car. They all drove off, leaving the gates open. We closed the gates, and walked back to our hut.

Even the new group of British occupation forces didn't stay long, and another commandant arrived. From time to time, somebody came to inspect the station. Most of them were polite, but reserved. If they were a little friendly, my father always told me to ask them for cigarettes.

I did not like to do this, but my father would push me forward, and whisper quite loudly, so that they could hear:

'Ask for some cigarettes, they have got plenty.'

They normally gave me some, often more than one packet. My father loved his smoke and, as cigarettes were so short, he had the idea of drying rose petals when the roses were in bloom. He chopped them up fine then rolled them into paper to the shape of cigarettes. My mother would only allow him to smoke these rose cigarettes outside, because they burnt with a lot of smoke, and the smell was terrible, not at all like roses.

***Outside the Hut with my Father***

*My Journey South*

# CHAPTER FIVE

## Journey South

Ever since my father had brought the bike home, my mother kept on talking about the rest of the family. She suggested that, as there were no trains, I should make my way south by bike. At first it was said in jest, with a little laugh, but gradually the thought took possession in my mother's mind. I, too, started to think about it in the evenings when I went to bed.

Sometimes I would toss and turn on my palliasse and, several times, I was sure I could hear little noises in my straw pillow. I started to worry, thinking there was something wrong in my head. In the end, I decided that there must be something in my pillow. The straw was covered with sacking material and, as I had no pillowcase, I laid my towel over it every evening. We only had one towel each. My mother had packed those in in Greifswald, taking them from Hermann. The sacking was split on one side, so I opened the stitching further and took out the straw.

Suddenly I screamed, and my mother came rushing into my room.

There, in the centre of my straw pillow, was a nest with little pink mice in it. They had never seen daylight and were squeaking and wriggling about.

'I slept on them,' I shouted. 'I slept on them, they could have crawled all over me. And what about the mother. She must have crawled around my bed!'

My father had entered the room by now and, taking the pillow with the nest, said to my mother:

'You calm her down. I will go and destroy these.'

He went off, and my mother took me into the kitchen.

'I hate mice,' I said. 'I have always hated them. I used to be afraid of them in Königsberg when I had to go into the cellar, but I was never allowed to say anything.'

When my father returned he said he had destroyed them, and he had also examined my palliasse. He assured me that there were no more mice in the room.

It was at that moment, that I made up my mind to take the bike, and start the journey south. The next time my mother mentioned it, and she usually did it two or three times a day, I said that, maybe, I would go. My father suddenly got very cross with my mother.

'I cannot understand you,' he said. 'You ought to be glad that you have one daughter. Sending her off on a trip to Mainburg, where Astra is, is irresponsible. Firstly, she could never cycle all that way, it is much too far, and secondly, it is very dangerous. I forbid you to mention this journey again, and you, Helga, are not going. I will not allow this. I will go to Hamburg again, and tell them at the Red Cross that they can add the address of the radio station to our cards, and I will also go to the Swiss embassy again. You can come with me, Mama, and visit your relatives at the same time.'

In the evening, my mother said to me:

'We must not talk in front of Papa any more, we will just have to organise everything in secret. I will start making you some summer dresses from the curtain material which I took with me from Hermann.'

She had not given up the idea then, I thought. I was surprised as I couldn't remember that she had ever disobeyed my father before.

My mother cut out two dresses and started to sew them, having to do everything by hand as she had no sewing machine. We made our plans in secret. I found a map in my father's car. I got the bike ready, cleaning everything, and straightening out the luggage carrier, which was over the back wheel. We all made a trip to Hamburg and registered again at the Red Cross with our new address. This time there was hardly any queue. We visited the Swiss embassy, and my mother went to see her aunt. At the Swiss embassy we were told again that we had to wait for confirmation from Switzerland that we possessed the Swiss nationality. There were a great number of people who claimed they were Swiss, because all Swiss people in Germany were entitled to food parcels from Switzerland, and transport back into the homeland. The confirmation had not come yet.

My mother's aunt and uncle were pleased to see her, and to hear that we were still alive, but they could not offer any help, as they were short of money and food. My mother said they were glad when she left, as they were afraid that she wanted to ask for accommodation.

Hamburg was occupied by the British, who used the harbour to bring in supplies for their forces. Bremen, with Bremerhafen, was given to the Americans, so that they had a harbour for their supplies, which they then transported by road to the south to their occupation zone. It was forbidden to travel from one zone to the next without a permit. I discovered that one could- already get a permit in Bremen to enter the American zone. Because of this, I decided to make Bremen my first stop.

I left the *Funkstation* on July 7th, four days before my 21st birthday. At the last moment my mother was worried about me, and I was worried about her, as she would have to face my father.

I started at 6.30 am, half an hour before the curfew was finished and before my father was awake. My mother accompanied me to the main road and hugged and kissed me.

'Take care,' she said, 'and I do hope you come back safely. If you find you cannot get to Astra, come home. I will stay here until you come or send me some news. I am sorry that you won't take your ration book; at least you could get some food then, if nobody helps you.'

I had refused my book, as I wanted to turn up in occupied Bremen as a refugee, pretending that I had come from the camp in Hamburg. My ration book would only give away the fact that I had been registered in Kisdorf.

'I will be alright,' I said. 'At least it is summer time and warm, and not the cold frosty winter like the last time when I travelled.'

'I do hope Papa won't be too cross with you.'

'Don't worry, he will forgive me in the end.' After a few moments, she added: 'Have you still got your little phial?'

I nodded and showed it to her hanging around my neck.

'Please don't use it, I don't want to lose you.'

'Would you like it back?'

'No, I trust you. I suppose it gives you mental support.'

She was right, I thought. It had always given me mental support. It was like a talisman.

I swung myself on to my bike, waved to my mother, and then rolled down the hill to Kisdorf. My journey had begun.

In Hamburg, I went to the refugee camp to stay the night. Camps were usually crowded, dirty, noisy, and the people in charge of them overworked and bad tempered. This place was no exception, but one could get a palliasse for the night, food, and primitive toilet facilities.

I was interviewed by a British sergeant, to whom I told my sad story. I was a refugee from Königsberg, I showed my university card, with my photograph, the only certificate in my possession. I had come to Hamburg as I had an aunt there, having lost my parents, only to find that she was bombed out. I now wanted to go to Mainburg in Bavaria, which was in the American zone, to find my sister. I only wanted to stay for one night, and then make my way to Bremen to get the relevant permit from the Americans to enter the Bavarian zone. Of course, the greater part of my story was true and being able to speak a little English, was helpful. The sergeant felt that he could give me permission to stay for one night, without confirmation from the commandant. I got a piece of paper for barrack No 14 for a palliasse, and two coupons, which entitled me to supper and breakfast.

The supper was some funny-looking soup, with big pieces of half-cooked potatoes, beans and carrots in it, and two pieces of quite tasty brown bread. I only ate one piece of bread, so that I could keep one for the next day for dinner.

I untied my bag from the carrier, and put it on the palliasse as a pillow. Then I laid the bike on the floor and pushed the front wheel under the palliasse. If anybody wanted to steal the bike, they would have to pull pretty hard to get it, and I would wake up. It wasn't long before I went to sleep.

I woke very early in the morning when it was just getting light. There was no point in getting up and leaving, because curfew was until 7 am. In any case, I wanted some breakfast and, maybe, some extra food for the day. I lay there thinking, wondering whether it was such a good idea starting again on my own to make this trip. I could have stayed on the radio station like my father wanted me to do and in a month or two there would probably be the postal service again, and maybe the train service also, and Astra would write to my aunt in Hamburg.

I was not frightened, but I felt apprehensive and uneasy. I got up at 6.30, and tied my bag to the carrier of the bike. I found the primitive toilet and even there I took my bike with me.

I didn't like the thought of having to stay in camps. I had found my parents, and we had started a kind of home on the *Funkstation*. How right my father had been, when he persuaded my mother not to go to the camp in Bad Segeberg. It would have killed my mother to live in those conditions.

After my breakfast, I left the camp site, and made my way to Bremen.

I cycled on and off all day. Late in the afternoon, I got a lift from a farmer, who came along the road with a horse and cart. I told him my story, and he said I could sleep in his barn, and maybe his wife would find me a plate of soup. She did, and also some bread and *Räucherspeck* (cold smoked streaky bacon).

The next day I reached the outskirts of Bremen. There was a barrier across the road, and American soldiers were controlling everybody who went in and out of the town. I noticed this too late, otherwise I could have walked over fields, avoiding the road. By the time I realized what was going on, the Americans had already seen me.

'Have you got a permit?' asked the soldier at the barrier. 'No', I said. Again I told my story, stressing that I wanted to travel to the south to my sister in Mainburg, which was in the American zone.

I said that I had come to get a permit.

The soldier looked at me, and seemed to like my effort at speaking English. I did not understand him as well as the British soldiers, but I got by. He called the sergeant, and repeated part of my story.

'You cannot get a permit here,' said the sergeant. 'You will have to go into a refugee camp to be screened.'

I told the sergeant that I was Swiss. I think he believed me, because he told me to wait whilst he made some enquiries. He came back after a time, and told me that I would be taken to the camp, together with some other people. They would not let us find our own way to the camp, in case we disappeared in the city.

Sure enough, a lorry arrived, and we were all packed in, including my bike, from which nobody could part me. We were driven to the camp, and were told that the screening of all of us would start the next morning. We were allocated night accommodation in huts, in bunks with palliasses and a rug, which were reasonably clean. I took my bike with me and tied it to the bedpost. Nobody stopped me from taking it into the hut. Supper was quite good, goulash with potatoes, a piece of bread, and water. The camp site was reasonably clean, quite well organised, and did not seem as crowded as the one in Hamburg. I had a good night's sleep, waking up occasionally, and checking whether my bike was still there.

Breakfast was a surprise. We had coffee, and snow white bread with jam. What luxury! We were all collected and led to a larger hut, where we were told to wait. Everybody looked at my bike, but nobody said anything. Then we were called in, one after the other, into different rooms.

At last it was my turn, and a sergeant fetched me. I took my bike. The sergeant raised his eyebrows, but didn't say anything, and the two of us entered the interview room. An officer sat behind a desk, the top of which had a lot of papers strewn about.

'Whatever is that bike doing in here?' called the officer. 'Sergeant, take it outside!'

'No,' I said. 'This is my bike, if you take it outside, it gets stolen. I like it to be where I can see it.'

The officer was surprised. Firstly, because I spoke a little English, and secondly, because he had some opposition, which he probably hadn't had before.

'Sergeant! Take that bike outside, and put it in a safe place. I am making you responsible that nothing happens to it. And now let's get on with the interview.'

The sergeant took my bike, and whispered:

'It will be alright,' and the officer pointed to a chair.

When all the forms were finished, I had to sign them, and was told that I would be informed. I was surprised about this, having hoped to receive the permit straight away. What was I going to do in the meantime?

'You will be staying in the camp until you hear whether you are permitted to enter the American zone', said the officer.

'I would like my bike back', I said to the sergeant.

'You had better make some arrangement about this bike,' said the officer. 'She can't very well walk about the camp site pushing a bike all the time.'

The sergeant came with me, and showed me that he had locked the bike into a store room. He assured me that it was perfectly safe there, and that I could leave it there until I left the camp. I just took my bag from the carrier, which was now the only thing that I had to look after. I walked around the camp for the rest of the day, talking to people.

When I woke up the next morning it was raining, and I realized that it was my 21st birthday. I felt awful, lonely, and full of pity for myself. I remembered Königsberg and how when somebody was 21 they were happy and that they had a party. At last they had got their freedom - the key to the door - being grown-up now, and not needing parental permission for anything. So what about me?

I was not happy, and I had no party. Freedom - that was something I had had for a long time. The key to the door - what key? The key to unhappiness, to poverty. I didn't really want that and, being grown-up, and not needing parental permission - well, that was something that happened to me a long time ago.

I watched the rain beating on to the barracks windows, and just sat on my palliasse. I never cried, and I was determined not to cry on my 21st birthday. I would have liked somebody to say to me:

'Happy birthday!', but nobody did, because nobody knew, and nobody cared, because everybody only cared for themselves.

I touched my little phial on my neck, it gave me comfort, but I also knew I would not use it. I was lonely, but I was in no danger.

By dinner time, the sun came out, and I decided that I had felt sorry for myself long enough.

In the afternoon, I met the sergeant who had locked my bike away and he whispered to me:

'I think you might get your permit tomorrow morning.'

Well, I thought, if this is true, and I can be off in the morning, I will remember this as my 21st birthday present. I said loud to myself:

'Happy birthday, Helga, happy 21st birthday.'

It was true. I was called by the sergeant the next morning. The officer who had interviewed me gave me my permit, but pointed out that it was only valid to enter the American zone. The sergeant gave me my bike. I tied up my bag again, and was off.

The next night I stopped near Nienburg, because my bike had a puncture. I called at a farmhouse, and asked for some water, and permission to mend my bike in the yard. The farmer looked very suspicious. He kept on looking at me, and then along the road where I had come from.

'I am alone,' I said.

He allowed me to use the water from the pump. By the time I was finished it was late, so I asked the farmer whether I could sleep in his barn.

'No,' he said. 'You had better be off. I don't like vagrants.'

'You are very lucky to have kept your home and land,' I said. 'I have lost everything, even my family. All I have is this old bike and the few clothes I have on. You are most unkind. All I have asked you for is some water and a space for the night in your barn. You would not even notice if I slept there.'

'Get off my land, you strumpet!' he shouted in reply. 'And be quick about it, or I will set the dog on you. I should have never let you mend your bike in the yard. You are all the same. Give a little finger, and they take the whole hand.'

He turned round, and whistled to his dog.

I swung myself on to my bike, and cycled off.

Near Schessinghausen, I found a large haystack in a field and decided to sleep there. I covered my bike with hay, after tying a piece of string to the front wheel. I had had nothing to eat, so I just drank my water which was still quite cool from the well. I tied the other end of the string from my bike to my foot, and crawled into the hay.

I had a fretful night. I got too hot under the hay and it was also rather prickly. In the end, I just sat by the haystack, waiting for the time to go by and the curfew to finish so that I could be off.

After I started again, I looked for a stream and, when I found one, I had a wash. The water was very cold, but fresh. Again I called in at a farm and the woman there was quite kind. She had just boiled some potatoes for the chickens, and let me have some. She also gave me a cup of cold buttermilk, and this, with the hot potatoes, was a lovely meal.

I thanked her for her kindness, and told her that God would reward her for it one day.

The next day was again very hot and I was sweating, cycling along the road. In the afternoon, I had another puncture. I got off the bike and pushed it. I certainly could not mend it by the roadside, it was much too hot, and there was no shade. I pushed my bike, and walked and walked. By now I was the other side of Hannover. I always kept to the smaller roads.

Suddenly I saw a lorry coming towards me. It looked like a German army lorry. The British had confiscated or taken over a number of them, and used them for their own purposes, sometimes to transport prisoners-of-war. I waved, because it didn't matter to me who they were if they were prepared to give me a lift. The lorry passed me and, to my great surprise, stopped. The back was open, and I could see that it was full of German soldiers in uniform, with their caps on but with all their insignias and evidence of rank taken off. They were laughing and shouting, and waving to me:

'Come on then, come on then, get in if you want a lift!'

'And where are you going, my pretty girl', said one of the soldiers, who looked a little older than the others.

I told him my story, that I had nobody as I was a refugee from the east, and had walked in front of the advancing Russians, and that I was making my way to Mainburg, to see whether I could find my sister. There was silence when I finished.

'You shouldn't travel alone on the roads,' said one of the soldiers. 'It is not safe.'

'Why are you all travelling together in this lorry?', I asked.

'We are not going far,' said one of them. 'We are a working force, chosen by a British commander to mend the telephone lines which were cut at the end of the war. We are stationed on a farm and when we have finished in this district, which will be in a few days, we will be moved to the next district. We are telephone engineers, and the British are making use of our skills.'

'Our own people can then use the telephone lines too', added one of them.

'Things have to be repaired', said another one.

'I would rather go home', said the next one.

After the last statement, none of them seemed to want to say anything any more. A little while ago they were all laughing and joking, and helping me into the lorry, and now they all looked sad, and one could see that they were homesick.

'Do you think I could stay on the farm for the night?', I asked. 'My bike needs mending again and by the time that is done it will be curfew time.'

'We will have to ask the cook. He is very friendly with the farmer's wife. They do food exchanges. She gives him eggs and milk, and he gives her sugar and coffee which he gets from the British,' said one of them. 'I will introduce him to you, and then we will see what he can do.'

It was not long before we got to the farm. There were British and German soldiers, and quite a free and easy atmosphere prevailed. I was introduced to the cook, who said that he would ask the farmer's wife whether she could put me up for the night. He came and fetched me after a little while, and said that the lady of the house wanted to meet me first, before making a decision.

'I told her that you are alright, but she said she doesn't believe that a young girl would travel alone these days. She is afraid that if she lets you sleep in the house, you might have some undesirable friends hiding somewhere who you could let in at night.'

The farmer's wife approved of me, and showed me a room where I could sleep. It only contained a camp bed, but I had a feather pillow and a rug. The cook said I had better come and join the others for some food.

I wanted to mend my bike first, but he wouldn't let me, saying that that was a man's job, and he would find somebody to do it for me.

I had an excellent meal, goulash, with potatoes and vegetables, and even a glass of beer, although, as a rule, I am not fond of beer and don't drink it. I must have been eating like a glutton, because one of them asked me:

'When did you eat last?'

'I had some potatoes and buttermilk for dinner,' I said, 'but I didn't have much yesterday.'

'Food is no problem here, so just eat as much as you like,' I was told.

After our meal, cook came to see me, and said that my bike was mended.

'It could do with a new tube', he said, 'but I suppose you cannot get one.'

'I have tried, but nobody sells anything for money these days, and I have nothing to barter with.'

He gave me a hard smoked sausage, Cervelat, which keeps for weeks, and said that I could either eat it myself, or maybe use it as barter for a new inner tube for my bike.

There was a little garden behind the house, and the farmer's wife said that I could sit there in the evening in the shade, as it was still quite hot. Two of the soldiers came and joined me, and one of them started to talk to me:

'We would like to tell you something; it is in strictest confidence. We would like to suggest something to you, but if you don't want to do it, then that is alright too, and you just forget what we have said. We trust you and hope that you will not break our confidence.'

He stopped and looked at me, then continued:

'Firstly, let me introduce myself. My name is Joachim, but you can call me Achim, everybody else does, and now I will tell you what we have in mind. Four of us and a young boy have decided to leave and go home. There is no post and we are not able to tell our people that we are alive. We have already been in a prisoner-of-war camp, and have passed the screening. We thought then that we could go home but, instead, we were collected into this group as telephone engineers. The four of us live close together near Warburg, and the boy, Friedrich, lives in Kassel. He might have difficulties, because he has to cross into the American zone. We have repaired a lorry, which is hidden at the back of the farm. We have plenty of petrol, and tomorrow morning we are off. I know the district, and all the little roads, and I will use them. When we get to my home, I will hide the lorry. Cook knows what we are going to do and, if the commandant presses him, he will eventually tell him the truth. If they want to come and fetch us back, that's that. At least then we have met our families, and they know we are safe and alive. I doubt if they will imprison us, they have too many people without homes. Now, if you want

318

to come with us, you are very welcome. It will get you a little further on your journey. We start at 4 am.'

'You have a lot of courage,' I said. 'Not only for breaking the curfew, but particularly for taking a lorry and escaping. You might all be imprisoned for this. If the British stop us, I could just say that you gave me a lift, but I never knew who you were.'

'Does that mean that you are coming with us?' asked Achim.

'Yes, I think it is a good idea. It will get me further on my journey. My bike keeps on breaking down, and is not very reliable, so transport on four wheels is always welcome to me.'

'I am not going to tell you any more about our trip, the least you know about it the better. Your prepared answer to any British patrol is quite good. It won't be an easy drive, because some of the small roads we are going to take will be very bumpy, and we can only give you a seat in the back of the lorry. I will be driving. There is going to be another friend next to me, and then two in the back, with Friedrich the young boy. He is only sixteen years old, and frightened and homesick. He needs looking after, so be kind to him.'

'Alright then,' I said. 'How am I going to wake up at 4 o'clock? And what about the farmer's wife. She was kind in letting me have a camp bed. I don't want her to feel that I have made use of her, disappearing early in the morning.'

'Leave your window open a little bit,' said Achim. 'I will call you, and give you ten minutes to get ready. We will put your bike into the lorry, and I will help you to climb out of the window. Cook will explain things to the farmer's wife.'

I looked at him, then I said: 'Leave the window open . . ., well . . .'

I just looked at him. I was a young girl, and here were all these soldiers who had been without wives and girlfriends for a long time, and two of them were sitting with me in the garden. Achim smiled, a little crooked smile, then he said:

'I know exactly what you are thinking. But you either trust us or not.'

After a few moments, he added: 'We are all going home to our wives, except Friedrich, who hopes to find his parents still alive in Kassel.'

'I think I had better have an early night,' I said. 'Please don't forget to call me.'

Achim smiled again, and then said: 'I won't forget.'

I told the farmer's wife that I wanted an early night, as I was extremely tired, and got into my room. I pushed the camp bed nearer to the window, so that I could hear Achim when he called me in the morning. I left the window slightly open. I was lucky that I slept downstairs. When I was in bed, I suddenly realized that I had a feather pillow. The last time that I had slept on a feather pillow was in Greifswald, in hospital, and in Hermann's flat and, before that in Königsberg, seven months ago, - an eternity.

I was soon asleep, too tired to think any more, as I had cycled a long way during the day. I could not have been too fast asleep, because I heard Achim calling my name in a whisper. He had opened the window wide, and was leaning into the room. He stood on one of his friends' shoulders.

'Come on, you have five minutes', he said, and then disappeared.

I got up, and dressed quickly. I even folded the blanket, and laid it on to the camp bed. I looked out of the window. It was only just getting light, still too dark to see far. Achim came back with his friend. I threw my bag out, and then lowered myself from the window, and slipped into his arms.

We reached the lorry at the back of the farmyard behind the barn. Achim got into the driving seat. His friend threw my bag into the lorry, which, to my delight, had a canvas cover. I knew now that I would not be too cold travelling in the back.

'Come on, push', said Achim's friend. 'We cannot start the engine, it will make too much noise. We will have to push for the start.'

We all pushed, Achim's three friends, Friedrich and I, with Achim steering. We seemed to go over a field but there was a narrow path which a tractor had made. The lorry had no lights on, so Achim had to watch where he was going. He seemed to know his way, it was slightly downhill, and the lorry rolled along easily.

We came to a road, Achim started the engine, and we all climbed into the lorry. I had no idea which roads Achim was taking. Gradually it got light, and I noticed that the road that we travelled on was not asphalted, but a cart track.

At about half past six, Achim stopped in a wood, and we all had something to eat. Cook had packed food for everybody.

'Now comes the dangerous part,' said Achim. 'We have to go on to the recognized roads for a while, until we come nearer to my home. Round here, I do not know the very small roads. We are not going on to a main road, and we are not going through towns. If we are stopped, I will say that we are looking at telephone lines and repairing them, so please, Helga, keep low, and sit behind the cab, or lie on the floor when I suddenly slow down. I will make it quite obvious when this happens.'

We were lucky, nobody stopped us. We had another stop at dinner time for some food and late in the afternoon we stopped in a wood. Achim drove completely off the path and into the thickest part of it.

'We will leave the lorry here,' said Achim. 'I dare not take it into the village.'

'I thought that you lived in Warburg,' I said.

'No,' he said, 'not in Warburg, but near it. This is my village. My wife and I have got a smallholding. I also had a small petrol station and garage before the war, which had to be closed because my wife couldn't look after that. In any case, there was no petrol, and no cars to repair. I know the people in the village, but I don't know whether I can trust them all, so it will be better if I leave the lorry here. Let's cover it a little more with branches.'

The lorry was soon covered up, and Achim said goodbye to his friends. From here they had to make their own way home. Only one soldier stayed with Achim, apart from Friedrich and myself and, pointing at him, Achim said:

'He lives in my village. We have always been together.'

Friedrich looked frightened and kept close to Achim. He had not said much in the lorry, just sat there staring out of the back. Each time I said something to him, he had jumped, and then only replied with 'yes' or 'no'. I wondered whether he had shell-shock. I thought he was rather young to have been in some fighting, maybe only the Home Guard, but even those were used in the fighting in the end.

We started to walk away from the lorry, and soon one could not recognize that there was something covered up in the wood. We came to a road, then turned off along a small path, and suddenly we were at the end of the wood and there were houses close by.

'Are you coming with me, or are you making your own way home?' Achim asked his friend.

'I think I will make my own way home. I will come and see you tomorrow.'

The two of them said goodbye, then Achim turned to Friedrich and me, and said:

'I must ask you to wait for me here. I will make my way to my house and come back for you. I don't want to give my wife a shock by bringing a young girl and a boy home. I will also leave some of my things here.'

He put one of his large bags on the grass. He looked at Friedrich, then continued: 'You will be alright. I promise I will come back to fetch you. You know that I have always kept my promises.'

Friedrich nodded and sat down on the grass. I sat down beside him, after I had laid my bike down, and we both watched Achim walking towards the houses, and disappearing behind them.

It seemed a long time before Achim returned, and Friedrich started to get worried. At last, we saw two people coming up towards the wood, one tall, and the other small. It was Achim and his son, who was about eleven years old. Achim looked very happy, and was smiling all over his face.

'Everything is alright', he said. 'The whole family are alive and well. I certainly gave them all a shock when I turned up. I hadn't seen my wife and children for over a year, and young Achim just wanted to come with me.'

Young Achim stepped forward and shook my hand in greeting, and did the same to Friedrich. I picked up my bike, Friedrich took his bag, and Achim and his son carried the other bag. All four of us walked towards the village. We didn't meet anybody until we got to Achim's house, where his wife made us very welcome. She had prepared some supper, and we all sat round the big kitchen table eating it.

We had not finished supper when the first visitors arrived. People just kept on coming in to greet Achim, and all were pleased to see him. I felt that I was in the way, and so did Friedrich. I quietly went outside and sat down on a bench in the yard. I took my diary out and caught up with the latest happenings. Friedrich came and sat close to me.

When I had finished writing and was just putting everything back into my bag, Friedrich said:

'Will you help me to get to Kassel? Achim said you might, if I asked you. He is home now and will stay here, and cannot help me any more.'

These were the longest sentences that he had spoken to me, and I could see that it was a tremendous effort for him.

'If I can help you, I will,' I replied, 'but I don't know how. I have also got to make my way to Kassel. I have an entrance permit for the American zone. Have you got one?'

'No. I have also never been a prisoner-of-war, and got screened. I only have my army papers. I told them that I was eighteen years old when I joined.'

He stopped, took a deep breath, and then said: 'I left home because I didn't want to go into my father's business. He has got a butcher's shop. My parents didn't want me to go into the army. I told the recruiting officer that I was eighteen years old and, after four weeks training, I was posted to the army in the west. There were two battles and a lot of us got killed. I lost all my new friends, so I just lay down and hoped to die. They found me, and said that if I didn't fight I would be hanged as a deserter. They put me into another company. Achim was my officer. He has taken me with him from then on, but now he is home, and I, too, would like to go home and tell my parents that I am sorry that I left without telling them.'

It was quite a story that Friedrich had told me. I could understand now why he was so frightened and disturbed. It was good of Achim to take him under his wing. Although I was prepared to help Friedrich to get to Kassel, I could not see how he could get into the American zone without passing through a camp. That was what he was frightened of; he only had his army papers, and they stated that he was eighteen years old, and a fully fledged soldier.

'I don't know how you can get into the American zone without a permit,' I said, 'unless you can cross the demarcation line somewhere in the wood, or on a field, because the roads are apparently manned by the occupation forces.'

Achim's wife came to look for us and said that she was sorry that Achim had left us to fend for ourselves, but he had always been a popular man in the village, and now everybody wanted to meet him.

'I am sorry that I have not got a bed for both of you,' she said. 'The house is not very big, but you can sleep in the attic. I will show you where we keep the straw, and you can take some up there. I will give you some rugs and clean sacks to lay over the straw, so that it is not too prickly.'

She showed us how to make up our beds, also where we could wash, and said that I could have a bath if I liked. This was absolutely heavenly. I hadn't had a bath since leaving Greifswald.

I only saw Achim fleetingly to say good night and he said that he would see me in the morning, to talk to me. I had a very good sleep. My bed was quite comfortable; it was quiet up in the attic, and I had been up since 4 o'clock in the morning.

Achim looked different in civilian clothes, when I met him for breakfast. Friedrich was still asleep, but the family said they would leave his breakfast on the table.

'I am glad that I have the opportunity to talk to you,' said Achim to me. 'Did Friedrich tell you his story? I told him to speak to you.'

'Yes, he told me that he had left home, because he didn't want to go into his father's business, and also that he wanted to join the army.'

'Friedrich was a leader in the *Hitlerjugend* (Hitler Youth). He adored, admired and believed in Hitler, until he saw what it was like to fight. He

323

wanted to give his life for the *Führer* and for his *Vaterland*. He had a terrible shock when it came to the actual fighting, when all his new friends were killed, and he saw their torn bodies. He was accused of being a deserter, and threatened with a court martial. When the war finished, and he heard about the sufferings and killings in the concentration camps and the persecution of the Jews, his faith and belief in Hitler was destroyed, and the reason to volunteer to fight taken away. He thinks that he has nothing left to live for. His only thought now is to get home, to the place where he was happy as a child, so that he can get the comfort and love which his parents can give him. He is young, he will recover, but it will take time.'

He stopped, and looked at me searchingly, then he continued:

'He cannot go into a prisoner-of-war camp to get his official release papers. Once they start questioning him, he will have to admit that he was a leader in the Hitler Youth, and they will keep him in the camp. This will destroy him mentally. I am not a psychiatrist but, in my opinion, it is important for him to get home, so that he can find himself again. Once he is home, he doesn't have to say that he was already a soldier. He could have been away for a time. In any case, I doubt whether anybody would tell the occupying American forces what really happened to him. - You can help him to get into the American zone, and that's why I have told you all this. Last night, when I met my friends and neighbours, I found out a few things about the Americans, and I think I know a way of getting Friedrich from one zone to the other. Approximately 10 km from here is a small bridge leading over a railway line. It is supervised by the Americans, who check everybody for permits to enter Kassel. No permit, no permission to cross the bridge. People from concentration camps, with their number tattooed on their arms, are permitted to go anywhere, so are foreign workers if they have an identity card. To get a permit, one has to go into a camp, and you know why Friedrich cannot do this. But - and now I come to it - you have already got a permit. The plan now is for you to keep the American soldiers talking; they are bored and you are a pretty girl. They are much more talkative than the British and like to be sociable. In the meantime, Friedrich will slide down the embankment, get over the railway line, up the other side, and meet you in the wood there. He won't cross the rails by the bridge, but a little further. At 12.30 dinner time, some of the guards go off for their lunch break, and often only two are left behind. At that time, they only control the bridge and not further along the railway line. It should not be too difficult, it has been done quite successfully before. I will keep an eye on Friedrich, and tell him where and when he can cross. If anything goes wrong, you are not involved, you just don't know Friedrich, but I hope things work out alright. - What do you think?'

'I will do it,' I said. 'When do you want us to make our way to Kassel?'

'Maybe tomorrow. It will probably be too late to do it today, as it has to happen around 12.30 at dinner time. We will have to get there early to explore the land. We might even cycle over this afternoon to take a look.'

That afternoon Achim supplied Friedrich with a bike and we cycled to the railway line. We stopped in a wood and, with binoculars, we could see the soldiers on the bridge.

We cycled back to Achim's house and I spent another night in the attic. The next morning, we went through our plan again. After that, Achim helped me to tie Friedrich's bag on to my carrier, and my smaller bag on to the handlebars. We cycled off in good time, and parted well before the bridge, with Achim and Friedrich cycling over a field towards the wood, and me cycling along the road.

I had to have perfect timing. As I was too early, I got off my bike and walked, pretending that I was too tired to cycle any more. I noticed there were two soldiers waiting for me at the entrance of the bridge. They were watching me, so I stopped and emptied my shoe of imagined little stones. I saw them laughing, and hoped that they were so interested in me that they would not look along the railway line, because it was time for Friedrich to slide down the embankment. I reached the bridge and the guards. I smiled at them, and said:

'I had some stones in my shoe.'

'She speaks English,' said the taller soldier to the other, 'how marvellous.'

The other soldier felt he ought to be more businesslike. He stopped smiling, and asked me in a more serious voice whether I had a permit to enter the American Zone.

'Oh yes,' I said, 'I will find it.'

I untied my bag from the handlebars, undoing every knot, to gain time, and then started to rummage in it.

'I don't think she has got a permit,' said the first guard. 'Where are you going anyway?'

I told them my story, beginning with when I left Königsberg. They had no idea where that was. I mentioned that I had already been to Bremen to get a permit. Then suddenly I found it. They both looked at it, and saw that it was genuine. I explained that I was on my way to Mainburg to find my sister. All this, of course, was told in my limited English, and the two guards were fascinated with my story. They enjoyed talking to me. As there was no other traffic, they were glad to have some distraction. I hoped Friedrich had succeeded in crossing the railway line. I had not been given a time limit by Achim, as it all depended on how long I could keep the guards' attention.

'I think I'd better empty my other shoe too,' I said, and sat down by the side of the bridge, and took my other shoe off. The guards were watching me again, making little jokes, and laughing. We were at the left hand side of the bridge, and Friedrich would cross on the right hand side. I realized that the guards could only see the right embankment if they stood on that side of the bridge so, as long as I kept them interested in me, Friedrich was safe. The soldier who was more businesslike went into the guard house and came back giving me my permit saying:

'I have stamped it, you may pass.'

I still prolonged things by joking about their job here, as there was nobody on the road. I shouldn't have done this, because it reminded them that they should look along the railway line with binoculars. One of them said so and stepped on to the bridge and looked to the left. I helped him to look, saying that nobody would cross the railway line because of possible trains. I wanted to keep him on the left and, when he started to move to the right, I called out:

'Oh dear, oh dear,' and smacked my leg.

'What is the matter?' he said, and came back.

'I think something big has stung me,' I said. I didn't know the word for *Wespe* (wasp), but it did the trick.

'It hurts, oh it hurts,' I said.

'Let's get the First Aid Kit,' said the other one. 'It is probably a wasp sting. We can put something on it.'

Whilst he went into the guard house, I quickly pinched my leg hard, so that there was at least a red spot.

It took some time to put on the liquid which the guard produced, I think it was something like TCP (disinfectant). The pain was terrible, and the two men were very sympathetic. In the middle of all this, a couple arrived with permits to cross the bridge and, after they had left, I decided that the pain had eased and it was time for me to cross the bridge. I looked back along the road, and saw, in the distance, somebody standing with two bikes who looked very much like Achim.

I tied my bag to the handlebars of the bike, and thanked the two Americans for their help with the "sting", then cycled off. The road on the other side of the bridge had a cycle path, which I used. Soon I could not see the bridge any more, as the path was quite winding. When I came to the wood, I found Friedrich behind some trees, calling me in a hushed voice. From now on we had to walk, as Friedrich had no bike, Achim had taken it back. Friedrich seemed to be happier, and not so frightened any more. He probably felt that the biggest hurdle was passed.

We got to Kassel late in the afternoon, and Friedrich had to enquire how to get to his road, as there had been quite a bit of bombing since he had left. Once we got nearer to the district where he lived, he knew his way, and started to walk faster. And then he suddenly called out:

'There is our house, and the shop, I am home! I am home!' and he ran off. I followed slowly. I wanted to give him the chance to greet his parents, without a witness. He might cry and then be ashamed of it. When I reached the shop it was closed, and so was the entrance door to the house.

I didn't like to go to the back, not knowing my way, so I just leaned my bike against the shop window and sat down on the step. I was very tired, having walked all the way from the other side of the bridge to Kassel and Friedrich's house. I also had my monthly tummy ache, which made it most uncomfortable to ride a bike.

Friedrich seemed to have forgotten all about me, because he didn't come back. I was surprised about this, as I still had his kit bag on my bicycle. I started to undo the string which held it to the luggage carrier, intending to leave it at the shop door and go off to find a place for the night, when I heard voices, one of them Friedrich's.

'I must go and look for her,' he was saying. 'I told you, she helped me to come home. I should not have left her. She even carried my bag on her bike.'

Saying these last words, he came out of a small passageway a little further along from the shop, accompanied by his mother and father. I could see he had been crying, and so had his mother. Friedrich looked and saw that I had just put his bag in front of the shop door.

'You can't leave yet,' he said to me. 'Mother, you must not let her go, she has nowhere to stay the night. Please ask her to stay with us, we have plenty of space.'

Mrs Grau came towards me and took my hand: 'Friedrich is right, please come indoors, you can stay the night with us. We just cannot believe that Friedrich is here. We thought he was dead, we didn't think we would ever see him again. Please, please come indoors, we cannot stand out here in the street.'

Mr Grau stood by, and nodded to everything his wife was saying. He was so full of emotion, that he couldn't speak. When his wife let go of my hand, he took it into his two big hands and kept on shaking it, trying to say something, but no words would pass his lips. I, too, felt very emotional, looking at these two people who had found their only son again, and I hoped that I, too, could return to the *Funkstation* at the end of my trip, and bring Astra, Christel and Hans back, so that my parents would be as happy as Mr and Mrs Grau.

Mrs Grau produced a lovely supper, and showed me my bedroom on the first floor. I had a soft bed, with sheets, two pillows and a featherbed. I hadn't slept with sheets since I was in Greifswald. This was absolutely heaven! I was also told to sleep as long as I liked in the morning, which I did.

When I came downstairs in the morning, I didn't see anybody. Eventually I found my way into the shop, and there were Mr and Mrs Grau with some customers, and they were telling them that Friedrich was alive, and home. Mrs Grau saw me, and told her husband that she would go and give me some breakfast. She also wanted to have a talk with me.

Whilst I was eating my breakfast, I told her my story, how I had met Achim, and what he had told me about Friedrich, and then finished off by telling her how Friedrich got into the American zone.

'Friedrich cried a lot last night,' said Mrs Grau. 'He keeps on saying that he is sorry that he left us. He must have had a terrible experience. We are most grateful to you for helping him to come home. Please stay a few days with us, and have a rest. You have no home, we still have our house and our business, and we would like to repay you for your kindness to our son.'

'Achim is the one who saved your son,' I replied. 'He was, and still is very fond of him. He said that what Friedrich needs now is a home and his parents' love, and gradually he will forget the horrors of the war. Once the barriers between the different zones are removed, you will be able to meet him and Friedrich, too, would like to see him again, I am sure.'

I finished my breakfast, and Mrs Grau said again that she would like me to stay, so I accepted her invitation. I told her that I had my monthly "inconvenience", which made cycling no joy. After this confession, she was most kind to me. When she discovered that I only had my little bag, having lost everything else, she produced all sorts of presents for me.

First of all, I had to have a nightgown to sleep in, and a few toiletries and handkerchiefs. She also gave me towels, some underwear, and a summer dress. The weather was still very hot and she produced a two-piece swimsuit for me, saying that, although I could not swim at the moment, I might be able to do so in a few days. She pampered and spoilt me, and so did her husband. The food was excellent, plenty of meat, and vegetables from the garden. There was no shortage in the household of a butcher!

I stayed two whole days with the family, and left early in the morning after the third night in a soft and comfortable bed, loaded with presents and plenty of food, which included tins of meat, and the long lasting smoked Cervelat sausages. Mr Grau had discovered that a lorry was going to Feuchtwangen in the south of Germany. The driver was prepared, for a certain payment, to take a few passengers.

'They hope to get to Würzburg in a day,' said Mr Grau, 'and to Feuchtwangen the next day. I have reserved a place for you and your bike, but I don't know where you could stay in Würzburg. Still, it will get you a good bit further and maybe you could ask them to drop you off in the country, so that you can stay on a farm again.'

After a few moments, he added shyly: 'I have paid for it, and please don't object. Every time I look at Friedrich, I feel grateful. I am not very good with words, my wife is better, but I, too, wanted to do something for you. Actually it was Friedrich who heard about the lorry, and I went to see the driver.'

I was very grateful, and said so.

The lorry was supposed to leave at 6.30 am, and the family accompanied me to the meeting place. Quite a number of people were already waiting when we got there, and I thought: The driver is going to earn a good bit of money!

'I hope they all get in,' I said to Mr and Mrs Grau, 'and my bicycle.'

'Don't worry,' said Mr Grau, 'you will get in. I promised the driver some meat. That is more important than money these days. My wife has got it in her bag.' He smiled and chuckled, pleased in the knowledge that he would succeed.

When the lorry came, the people started to push, as everybody wanted to be first. Mr Grau eased himself forward, and touched the driver's arm.

'Ah, Mr Grau,' said the driver, 'where is the young lady with the bicycle? You were the first one to book, so she will be the first one on the lorry.'

Mrs Grau put her arms around me, and kissed me, so did Friedrich, and even Mr Grau gave me a peck. They pushed me towards the steps, and I climbed in.

'The bike can go in at the back in the end,' said the driver. 'I will see to it, don't worry.'

It was not long before everybody had climbed in, and my bike was handed in also. There was no delay; it was already getting on for 7 am, when the curfew finished, and everybody hoped that the Americans were not too strict about the time. The lorry set off, Family Grau waved, and called:

'Don't forget us, come and see us one day!', and then I couldn't see them any more, as the lorry went round a corner.

# CHAPTER SIX

## Imprisoned - Finding Astra

I had no idea which way we were driving. Sometimes I saw the name of a village, but we never seemed to go through big towns. By dinner-time, we stopped in a small town and some people left us. After that, we stopped in a wood, where we were allowed to get out and have a walk and a stretch. We stayed in the wood for about an hour, and everybody had something to eat.

It was evening when we got to the outskirts of Würzburg. The last people had left the lorry, and I was just going to take out my bike, when the driver approached me, saying:

'I understand you want to go further. My partner and I have decided to carry on driving. We hope, by keeping to the small roads that nobody will stop us because of the curfew. If they do, you can make any excuse you like. So, if you want to carry on, you are welcome.'

'I think I will come with you. I have nowhere to sleep, and I prefer to be driven than to cycle.'

I climbed back into the lorry and we drove off. We got through Würzburg and were soon on a country road, because there were no more houses. The driver chose rather small and rough roads from now on, because it started to get dark, and curfew was at 10 o'clock. When it was completely dark, I noticed that the lorry only had sidelights on. We were going much too fast for the small, bad roads that my companions had chosen. I was rocked about in the back, and kept on sliding off my bag. My poor bicycle was jumping up and down, and everything loose on the lorry rattled. My hands got cold and stiff from holding on to the side of the lorry and, although I had felt alright all day, I now started to feel sick. I took deep breaths, to prevent me from vomiting, but we must have been travelling along an untarred road, because I nearly choked from the dust I was inhaling.

Whenever I was in an uncomfortable and frightening position, I would think back to the time when I crossed the Haff in that bitter cold winter, and say to myself:

'That was worse, that was much worse.'

I did the same now, and tried to comfort myself with the thought that it wouldn't take long before we stopped.

Suddenly we did stop, with screeching brakes and wheels which slid over stones and gravel, and there was even more dust coming into the lorry.

I slid off my bag, and rolled towards the back of the vehicle. There seemed to be a lot of lights on the road.

I crawled towards the side of the vehicle, and carefully lifted my head to look out. There were a number of vehicles on and at the side of the road, with big headlights on, and American soldiers with guns. My heart started to beat faster.

It couldn't be another war, I thought, and crawled back to my bags and sat down again. There was shouting, orders were given, the cab door was opened, and somebody commanded in a loud voice:

'Get out!'

I assumed that the driver and his partner got out. Somebody climbed up at the side of the lorry and a torch shone into my face, blinding me. I put a hand in front of my face.

'There is a girl in the back here,' called the soldier who had climbed up, 'a bicycle and two bags.'

'They belong to me,' I said quickly.

'She speaks English,' the soldier shouted.

'Clear the lorry, everybody out!' came the reply.

I got up painfully. Everything in my body seemed to hurt after that rough drive and the sudden stopping of the vehicle. I climbed over the side of the lorry, but then realized that I was still quite high up and hesitated to jump. I had previously had steps to get in and out of the lorry. I looked around, but the big lights of the vehicles were blinding me.

'Come on, then,' said a kind voice, and I looked into a smiling face, with kind brown eyes. I took the outstretched hand, which helped me down.

'Hands up!' shouted somebody.

I put my hands behind my head. I saw the driver and his partner with their hands on the bonnet of the lorry.

'Search them!' shouted the voice again.

Two soldiers searched my companions. The soldier who had climbed on to the lorry came towards me and I thought that he was going to search me too.

'Do not touch me,' I said. 'Only a woman can search me.'

'Leave her alone, she is alright,' said the kind voice of the man who had helped me down. He was a sergeant.

I looked around and noticed that, in front of our lorry stood a big tank. There were two jeeps, a car in the field, and all vehicles had head lights on.

We were told to get into a small lorry. My two companions climbed in from the back, where some steps were folded down. I looked around and realized that my bike and bags were still in the big lorry, so I walked towards it, when a heavy hand pulled my back.

'I only want my bicycle and my bags,' I said.

'Get the bicycle and the bags into the lorry,' said the sergeant with the kind voice. He put his hand on my shoulder, and pushed me gently towards the American vehicle. I climbed in, somebody handed me my bags, and then my bike was also lifted in. The tank moved from the road into the field, and the lorry, accompanied by one of the jeeps and the car, moved off along the road. We soon stopped at some houses, and the driver and his partner were ordered to get out of the lorry.

'I hope you will be alright', he said to me. 'I am sorry that we have got you into this, but you have done nothing wrong. The Americans are supposed to be quite decent to women, so don't worry. We will probably see you again in the morning, when they get an interpreter to interview us.'

I felt a little frightened and lonely after that. I had not seen the kind sergeant again, and I had no idea where I was going to spend the rest of the night.

The vehicle set off again, the houses disappeared, and we were on the open road. There was no cover over the lorry and I got quite cold. The road was bumpy, so I had to hold my bicycle. I had an American guard soldier with a gun opposite me, and he, too, seemed to get cold, but didn't say anything. It seemed ages before we came to the next village and stopped in front of a big house. There was a light over the big front door and, underneath, were some letters which read:

*Gefängnis* (prison)

Oh no, I thought. Surely they won't put me into prison!

My guard told me to get off the lorry and pointed to the door, which was now open. I looked at him, at the open door, the lorry, and then I turned round to get my bags and bike again.

'No,' he said, and pointed to the door again.

I was not going to leave the only things which I possessed behind. I climbed back into the lorry and took my bags. He tried to pull me out again, saying that I must get inside the prison.

'I want my bags and my bicycle,' I said in English. He was surprised; he had not realized that I spoke a little English. He stopped pulling me and let me have my bags, even helped me to get my bike off the lorry. When I got inside the prison, I met my kindly sergeant and the warder and his wife, who was in her dressing gown.

'So you are the prisoner,' she said. 'The sergeant kept on saying *'Frau'*, and I couldn't make out why he wanted me to accompany my husband. We don't have women prisoners very often. Whatever have you done, girl, to finish up here, and so late at night, too?'

I told her that I had had the misfortune to be on the back of a lorry after curfew.

'We had better get upstairs,' said the warder.

Upstairs was reached by a spiral staircase. I got hold of my bags and bike, but realized that it was not going to be an easy climb because of the winding steps. The sergeant said something to the guard. American is not always easy to understand, so I didn't know what he had said. The guard didn't like it, he frowned, but suddenly he took my bike and carried it upstairs. The four of us followed him, and came to a landing, with four doors on each side. The warder unlocked the last door on the left and said to me:

'This is the best and cleanest cell we have got, you had better get in.'

I stepped inside, put my bags down, took a deep breath, and bit my lip to keep quiet. I couldn't believe what I saw. It was a small whitewashed room with a concrete floor, part of it raised with a rim around it. The warder pointed to it and said:

'That is the bed. We usually have straw on it, but we didn't expect anybody, so we have not got anything prepared.'

The warder's wife looked at me with pity in her eyes. The guard brought my bike in, adjusted the gun which was hanging over his shoulder, and stepped outside again. My kindly sergeant looked embarrassed. I looked at him and at the bed. I did this several times, then I laid my bags on the floor by the wall and sat on one. I pulled my knees up and folded my hands around them. My head dropped down, and I just cried. I had slept in all sorts of places, even on the street and in doorways, but I had never slept on a concrete bed, in a prison with barred windows. The warder's wife put her hand on my head, and whispered:

'I will try and find you a blanket.'

They all left me and the door was locked from the outside. After a little while I stopped crying. They had left the light on, a single bulb in the centre of the room. There was no switch, so I couldn't turn it off.

I sat and waited and waited. I was just dropping off to sleep, when I heard footsteps and voices. The door opened, and the warder and his wife stepped in, smiling all over their faces.

'You have made a conquest,' said the warder's wife. 'The sergeant felt very sorry for you. He has produced a camp bed and some food, and I have got you some blankets.'

They opened up the bed and laid the blankets on top. There was also a tray with bread, butter and sausage, and a bottle of beer. I gave the beer to the warder, and he was pleased. They left me then, saying that the light would go out in twenty minutes.

I ate the food and went to bed, rolling myself into the blankets. I did not get undressed, because of the American guard outside on the landing. The bed was quite comfortable, and I was soon asleep.

It was light when I woke up and the sun was shining into my cell. I had to go to the toilet, so I knocked on to the door. The guard came, and looked through the little barred viewing window. I told him what I wanted and he unlocked the door. He pointed along the landing to another door and, when I walked off, he followed me. I stepped through the door into a small room with a washstand and two toilet cubicles without doors. The guard followed me into the conveniences. I stared at him, hoping he would leave me alone. When he didn't move, I opened the door again and said:

'I want to be alone.'

He hesitated, a little embarrassed, but then stepped outside. When I had finished, I returned to my cell, with the guard following me again, his heavy boots making quite a noise, marching along the landing. I didn't know whether the other cells were occupied, I didn't hear or see anybody. I had hardly returned to the cell when the warder's wife turned up with a jug of hot water and a bowl so that I could have a wash.

'I will wait outside,' she said. 'You can knock on the door when you have finished and, after that, I will bring you some breakfast.'

I did what she told me and she brought me some breakfast, which was a great surprise. This certainly was not prison food! There was a jug of real coffee, milk and sugar, fresh rolls, an egg, butter, marmalade, sausage and cheese, and two roses in a little old milk jug. The woman smiled and waved her finger at me.

'What have you done to the sergeant? He has brought us other prisoners, but never supplied them with a camp bed and food. Maybe it is because you are the first female prisoner he has brought here. He turned up early this morning and brought the food for you, and also gave us something. I must say, I am glad to get the coffee, I have not drunk real coffee for ages. He only speaks a few words of German, but he said he would collect you at 10 o'clock. Still, you have plenty of time.'

'Did he send me the roses too?' I said.

'Yes,' she replied. 'I don't know where he pinched them from, maybe even from our garden.'

We had a little chat whilst I ate my breakfast, sitting on the camp bed.

I discovered that the village was called Gerabronn, and that the prison served quite an area of villages. Her husband had been the warder here since before the war. She said that the prison was hardly occupied at the moment, often only for one or two nights, until people were interviewed. Anybody sent to court and convicted, would finish up in the bigger prison in Crailsheim. She lived with her husband downstairs in a small flat, and they also had a garden, where she grew flowers and vegetables. I had to tell her my story, and she was very astonished when she discovered where I had come from.

She took the tray away and just before 10 o'clock the door opened again. My guard stood to attention and the sergeant came in. He looked very official, and informed me that he had come to collect me for the interview in Crailsheim.

That's where the big prison is, I thought.

I had already tied my two bags to my bicycle, so I pushed it on to the landing and, as it was rather heavy, I bumped it down the winding stairs, scraping the wall occasionally.

A jeep with a driver stood outside the prison. There were some children on the other side of the road, watching what was going on. The sergeant was not quite sure what to do about my bike, but he probably realized that I wouldn't leave it behind. He said something to the driver, who got out and lifted the bike into the back of the jeep. The driver got behind the steering wheel, the sergeant helped me into the jeep, and then sat next to me and we drove off. At the last moment I remembered the warder and his wife, and looked round. They were at the window of their flat, so I waved, and they waved back. Neither of us knew whether we would see one another again.

I glanced at the sergeant. I would have liked to thank him for his kindness, but I was not sure whether I should do this in front of the driver. He looked at me, smiled, and put a reassuring hand on my knee. It was a hot hand and, as he left it there, squeezing my knee once or twice, I decided that I did not like this. I took his hand and put it firmly back on his own knee. He looked at me, surprised. I also felt that it would be wiser to distance myself from him, so I moved gently away towards the side.

Did he expect payment for the food and the camp bed? I wondered. We were in an open jeep, and the driver was in front, so nothing could happen, but I did not want him to get the idea that I was the type of girl who paid with sex for favours granted and for favours to come. I still had the interview in front of me, and it was possible that he could help me, but any help from him had to be given on my terms, not on his. Even so, I looked at him, and smiled a little, giving him to understand that I was not really cross. He just looked at me, not saying a word.

'Who is interviewing me?' I asked.

'Our commanding officer, Captain S.' he replied.

This did not help me at all, I didn't know Captain S.

'I have done nothing wrong,' I said again.

'That is up to Captain S. to decide,' he replied.

After that we were silent. It was quite a pleasant drive. The weather was good and the countryside pretty and peaceful. There had been no fighting here, and there was barley and oats and wheat in the fields, and cows in the meadows. Even so, I shivered a little, probably in apprehension of what was coming.

'We are nearly in Crailsheim,' said the sergeant, and I had the feeling that he had noticed that I shivered, and wanted to ease the situation. We stopped at an impressive large building in the town with an American flag on the roof, two guards outside the entrance, and several cars and jeeps parked outside. Again I wanted to take my bike and luggage with me, but I was told to leave it in the vehicle, as the driver would keep an eye on it.

The sergeant guided me towards the guards, produced a piece of paper, and then we were permitted to enter the building. We had to go up one flight of stairs, and then he knocked on a door and entered, pushing me in front of him. He greeted another sergeant at a table, piled high with folders and papers and a telephone, and spoke too fast for me to understand. Even so, I knew it was about me; they kept on glancing at me, even having a little laugh. The other sergeant went next door and, when he came back, he told us to wait.

We sat down - there were two empty chairs - and we waited. The telephone rang a few times and, each time, I thought it was a message for us to come in. Eventually we were told to go into the next room, where a Captain was sitting behind a table. There were only a few papers in front of him, but two telephones.

The Captain was very polite, very correct, but rather stern looking.

'Sit down,' he said to me, pointing to the chair opposite him. He then looked at the sergeant, who reported to him the happenings of last night.

'I understand you speak English,' said the captain. 'I would like to see your papers.'

I handed him my university pass and the permission to enter the American zone. He looked at them.

'Why were you in the lorry? Where do you live? Where are you going to?'

These were plenty of questions, all of them said in short sentences. My English was not very good, and it was a struggle to answer all the questions. I tried to explain that I had got a lift so that I didn't have to cycle or walk, as I had to travel a long way to my sister. I explained where I originally came from, that I had already had a terrible journey through ice and snow, fleeing in front of the Russians.

I suddenly realized that the captain wouldn't understand, because the Americans and the Russians were Allies. It was also such a struggle to find the English words, so I just said in German:

*'Keiner kann es verstehen der nicht durch diese Hölle gekommen ist.'* (Nobody can understand it who hasn't come through this hell.)

With that, I stopped talking, and looked at my hands on my lap, which were shaking slightly.

The Captain suddenly said in German: 'You can carry on in German, I do understand the language.'

He didn't say where he had learnt it, and I was cross that he had let me struggle along with the little vocabulary I knew so, in reply, I remained silent. I think he realized my feelings and, after a little while, he carried on questioning me in German.

In the end, he was satisfied with my tale, and my explanations as to why I was in the lorry. He had already interviewed the driver and his partner, and they had corroborated my story.

'You may go,' he said. 'But don't break the curfew again.'

He signed some papers and handed them to the sergeant.

338

'I hope you find your family,' he said, and then added with a smile: 'Good luck.'

'Thank you', I replied, and walked towards the door, down the stairs, and outside as quickly as I could. I looked for the jeep with my bike, and saw it parked a little further from the outside door. I rushed towards it and tried to take out my bike, when the driver stopped me. He thought I wanted to run away. I told him that I could go, but he would not let me lift out the bike until the sergeant arrived and said that I was free to go. After that, they both lifted the bike out of the jeep, and the sergeant pushed it towards me.

'It has a puncture again!' I called out in German. The back tyre was flat. It must have happened when I bounced it down the stairs in the prison.

Both men, although not understanding what I had said, could see what I meant. They looked at the bike, felt the flat tyre, and sympathized with me.

'I can mend it for you', said the sergeant, 'but you will have to come back to Gerabronn.'

There was really no point in rushing off with a broken bike, if I could have it mended, so I said: 'Thank you, that would be nice. I really need a new tyre.'

I didn't know the word "tube", so I said tyre.

'I might be able to get that too,' he replied.

He took the bicycle, and put it back into the jeep. I climbed in, he followed, and the jeep drove off. We stopped again in front of the prison in Gerabronn, unloaded my bags, and the sergeant said:

'You can wait with the warder and his wife.'

He drove off with my bicycle, after telling the driver where to go. The warder's wife was surprised to see me. I told her what had happened, and that my bike had a puncture again.

'I am sure the sergeant will have it mended,' she said. 'He is very resourceful. Why don't you go and sit in the sun in the garden. I will come and join you in a little while, and bring something to eat. There is plenty of food left from what the sergeant brought me this morning.'

She came and joined me in the garden after a little while, and brought some sandwiches which were delicious.

After about an hour, the sergeant arrived without my bike. He said that it would take longer than he thought and that I would have to wait. He sat down next to me and started to ask me questions about Königsberg. He had brought a map, and wanted to know more about my journey, and about the Russians. The warder's wife got up and said in German:

'I think he wants to be alone with you. In any case, I have things to do in the house.' She smiled in a conspiratorial way, and walked back to the house.

Sam, that was his name, was very interested in my story. He had heard tales about the Russians, and their treatment of the Germans, but didn't believe them, and now here I was, giving him a first-hand description. He didn't seem in a hurry to go and get my bike. He produced a pack of cards, and we played a game he taught me. When we had finished, he pointed to the pack of cards. They were called: Uncle Sam.

He said I could keep the cards, because his name was Sam. He left at about 4 o'clock, to see whether my bike was ready. It took quite a time before he returned, and he informed me that the tube (a new word for me) was so bad that it could not be mended. He also assured me that he could get a new one the next day. So now I would have to stay another night. He smiled all over his face, and I could see that he was very pleased about this.

'And where will I sleep tonight?'

'In the prison.'

'No, I am not going to sleep there again. I am free now, not a prisoner any more.'

'We will ask the warder.'

The warder's wife said she wouldn't mind having the camp bed in her kitchen. She also cooked dinner, with food supplied by Sam, but he did not join us for it, as he was on evening duty.

Before dropping off to sleep on my camp bed in the kitchen, I thought about Sam. He had been very kind to me and was obviously starting to fall in love with me. I guessed that he was about twenty-eight years old, seven years older than myself. He had a dark complexion, nearly black hair, and soft brown eyes. He was a good listener, very inquisitive, but in a gentle quiet way, trying to speak a slow and simple English, so that I could understand him. He had studied law and had been in the infantry for over a year. Now he was looking forward to going home soon. I liked him and, in a way, I was sorry to have to leave the next day.

Sam turned up after breakfast and told me that he had not succeeded in getting the inner tube for the tyre, but had ordered the driver to go to Crailsheim in the afternoon, with strict instructions not to come back until he had found one. He looked at me quite mischievously and said:

'You will have to stay here another night. I have the whole day off. We can go for a walk in the woods. Now you are my *Fräulein* (Miss). Lots of my friends have a *Fräulein*. I have never had one before.'

What was I supposed to reply to all this? Last night I had been sorry to think that I would have to leave, and now he had manoeuvred things in such a way that I had to remain there a little longer. I wasn't sure whether I could believe his story about my bike. On the other hand, it was marvellous if I could get a new inner tube. It would also be rather fun to have a day with Sam. I didn't like the expression *Fräulein*. I knew that there was a lot of fraternizing going on between the young soldiers of the occupying forces and German girls, who took food and cigarettes as payment. I did not want to belong to those types of girls.

'If you promise that I will have my bike back by this evening, I will stay another night, but you must promise it.'

He stopped smiling and looked at me searchingly, then he said very calmly and quietly: 'I promise.'

We went for a walk in the woods, and I teased him, by hiding behind a tree, running away, flirting with him and, all the time, I felt light-headed and happy. We kissed, we laughed, and we said silly things, and I thought life was happy after all. It was worthwhile to exist, and to be there in the coolness of the wood, with the sun shining through the treetops.

We returned in the early afternoon, and the warder's wife made us some sandwiches and brought them out into the garden. We sat on the bench by the table and talked and played cards, and we both forgot about my bike. Suddenly it was evening and the day nearly gone.

'What about my bike?' I had remembered why I was here.

'Never mind the bike. You cannot leave. You will have to stay here, otherwise I won't see you any more.' He was so sure of himself, and so sure that I wouldn't leave him, and go away. 'I will give the warder and his wife some food, and I will pay them for your stay. I will come and spend all my free time with you. You are in love with me, aren't you?'

Was I in love with Sam? I was very fond of him, he had shown me happiness again and let me forget the harshness of life for a day, but there was no future in a relationship with him, and I was not going to be a kept *Fräulein*, however much I liked him.

'You promised to let me have my bike by this evening,' I said.

His smile vanished; he looked at me, then tried to pull me towards him.

'No, please, let me have my bike back. I will have to leave tomorrow morning. We have had a lovely time together, but there is no point in my staying on; we will only get hurt in the end, both of us.'

He just sat there, looking at me, trying to read in my face whether I really meant what I said, not wanting to believe it. With a jerk, he got up:

'I will be back, don't go away.'

Sam returned with my bike, and a bag with some bulky things in it. He leaned the bike against the table and went into the house, returning again with the warder's wife.

'Please explain to her in German that I would be grateful if she could cook us a meal. I have brought some food and put it on to the kitchen table. It is a lovely evening, and we could have it outside, so we won't disturb her and her husband.'

I translated everything and the warder's wife was only too pleased to do what she was asked, as she knew that there would even be extra food for her and her husband.

We had a very good meal and even a bottle of wine, and when we had finished, I took the dishes and the tray indoors, but was not allowed to help with the washing-up. We had not spoken much during the meal. I had thanked Sam for the repair of the bike, particularly as I now had a new inner tube. Sam seemed to try to work something out. He was preoccupied during the meal with his thoughts. He took my hand.

'If I say I will marry you, will you stay on? I have never met anybody like you. I don't want to lose you. I want you to come back with me to America. My parents will be your parents, my brother your brother, and I know you will like my sister.'

I could see that he meant every word he said. He meant it today, he would mean it tomorrow and maybe next week, but would he mean it in a few months time, when he had returned to his homeland and I was still here waiting for permission to follow him? I felt suddenly older than him, and wiser, because I knew the answers. Life had taught me to be careful.

'Sam, I must find my family first. If you still want to marry me when you are back in America, you can contact me. As soon as I have an address, I will let you know and you can write to me.'

He tore a page out of his diary and wrote down his home address and gave it to me. After that, he pulled off a ring that he wore on his little finger and handed it to me.

'This is all I have to give you, I have no picture of myself, or a present for you, but it is something that I have worn for a year, ever since I joined the army. It is not very valuable, but it will remind you of me.'

It was a heavy silver army ring, decorated on the sides with the stars and stripes and USA initials. In the centre was a black oval shape, with two crossing guns encircled with the words INFANTRY U.S. ARMY. It was probably not a very valuable ring, and I later saw other soldiers wearing similar ones but, at that moment when he took it off his finger, and gave it to me, that was the valuable part for me. The ring is still in my possession today, and so is the pack of cards with "Uncle Sam" on it.

After that we didn't talk very much, but just sat there looking at the moon and the stars. When the midges became too irritating, we went indoors, and sat for a while in the kitchen, until it was time for Sam to get back to his unit. He said that he would try and arrange that he could take me in a jeep to Crailsheim in the morning, maybe a little further, if he had the time.

Sam turned up at 9 o'clock, and said he would take me to Crailsheim and, from there, I would get a lift to Ansbach on an army lorry with a friend of his. This time he had no driver. He put my bike and bags in the back, and told me to sit in the front next to him. I said farewell to the warder and his wife, and thanked them both for helping me. I was particularly grateful for the meals I had had there. Sam was a good driver, avoiding, if possible, the holes in the country road, so that I had a smooth drive. He turned off on to a small winding road in the wood, and said he wanted to say goodbye now, as he could not do this so thoroughly in the town of Crailsheim with everybody watching. He kissed me and told me again that he wanted to marry me, and stressed that I must forward him my address, otherwise he could not contact me. He also gave me some food and cigarettes to barter with, and produced a plain kit bag, which was bigger than my bags. I still had some tins and sausage from Kassel, so I put all the food together in the kit bag, and kept the bigger bag for my clothes and all the soft stuff.

In Crailsheim, Sam stopped at the church, where a covered army lorry was already waiting with the back flap down. My bike was quickly lifted into the back, and so was I. The driver smiled at me, and returned to the front, whilst Sam quickly climbed into the back.

'Please don't forget me.' He held my face in his hands, and looked at me with his soft brown eyes, which made me feel I wanted to cry.

'I will never forget you,' I said, and I never have.

He jumped out of the back, banged on the side of the lorry, and the driver started off. I sat down on my soft bag, and wondered whether I had made the right decision after all.

When the driver stopped, it was on the outskirts of Ansbach. He explained that he was not really allowed to have civilians in the lorry, so I would have to get out here. He wished me good luck, after unloading my bike and bags, and drove off. I tied the kit bag to the carrier, and fastened the other bag to the handlebars. I got out my old map to orientate myself, and discovered that it was not such a good idea to have come to Ansbach. I had moved east by getting the lift, and must now concentrate on going south again. It was a dull day and looked like rain. I cheered myself up by saying that this type of weather was better for cycling than a hot day, and swung myself on to the saddle. I pedalled in rhythm on the flat road, seeing a smiling face, with kind, brown, soft eyes in front of me, and got further and further away from Ansbach.

I woke up from my daydreaming when big drops of rain hit me. The road was empty, but there were a few trees further along. I pedalled fast but, by the time I reached them, I was pretty wet. I sheltered under the biggest one, resting my bike against the tree trunk. A farmer passed me, with horse and cart, but I was not interested in getting a lift from him, I would only get wetter sitting on the cart. The figure holding the reins was unrecognizable, a shrunken body, wrapped in a thick coat, holding an umbrella. I doubt whether he even noticed me under the tree. The rain changed to drizzle, and I was just wondering whether to chance it and carry on to the next farmhouse or village to look for shelter, when I saw a German army lorry coming along. I stepped forward and waved, but the lorry passed, then it stopped and reversed. Somebody opened the steamed-up window, and I saw two faces. One belonged to an American soldier, and the other one to an ex-German soldier, still in uniform, without insignia. It was the latter one who asked, in German, where I wanted to go to. I told him that my final destination was Mainburg, but I would be grateful for any lift further south, especially as it was raining. He looked at the American, and said:

'*Fräulein*?' like a question, and I realized that he didn't speak English. So I asked the American whether I could have a lift. He was pleased that I spoke English, and said that I could come with them. The driver got out, and opened the back of the lorry to put in my bike and my luggage. I noticed that there were boxlike seats along the sides of the lorry, and behind the cab, whilst the centre was empty.

'You can come and sit in the front with us. The engine is warm, and your clothes will dry better. In any case, Jo will like it, he can talk to you in English. His German is not very good, and he gets bored, sitting there all day.'

He gave me a helping hand into the cab, and I sat between the two men. Soon we knew each others' names. The American was Jo, a non-commissioned officer, and the driver was Heinz. We were on our way to Ingolstadt, where Heinz lived, and where they would spend the night.

'Do you go as far as Hamburg?' I asked.

'Oh yes,' said Heinz, 'I have been there once.'

I decided that this time I had better alter my story a little, and say that I had left my mother near Hamburg. There might be the opportunity to use this transport for my return trip. I told my story, and Heinz, in particular, was very sympathetic. Jo didn't understand what it meant to be a refugee, and why so many Germans had left their homes, to get away from the Russians.

I was able to stay the night with Heinz and his wife. The next morning we were quickly off after breakfast. I sat again between the two men. This time we went on the autobahn, because Heinz and Jo had to get to the other side of Munich. I think that Heinz hadn't looked at the map properly to see where Mainburg was, because he took me too far south before he turned off the autobahn to drop me off. He stopped near Pfaffenhofen on a small road, because bicycles are not allowed on the autobahn. Jo stressed that I could contact him if I needed help, and Heinz hoped that I would visit him again in Ingolstadt. I waved to them when they drove off, and then swung myself on to my bike and pedalled away.

I had a long way to go and I wanted to get to Mainburg in one day. The road was hilly but, whenever I went down hill, I made sure that I had a good swing, which helped me half way up the other side. Once or twice I had to push the bike, because the last bit of the hill was too steep to pedal up. It was a dull day, the sun trying to break through once or twice, and I was glad that it didn't rain. At dinner time, I stopped and had something to eat and, after that, I was very thirsty. I found a lonely farmhouse, and asked for some water, and the farmer's wife gave it to me.

It was late in the afternoon when I got to Mainburg. I found the house where Astra was supposed to live, but the woman who opened the door said that she was not living there any more. She was very guarded, as if she didn't really want to talk about Astra. I explained to her how far I had come to find my sister and after that she became a little friendlier.

'I think she is working for the Americans,' she said. 'They have a canteen in the school hall. You could enquire there. The Americans will probably be having their evening meal by now and your sister should then be there.'

She told me where the hall was and I set off again. I was very disappointed that I hadn't found Astra.

When I got to the school building, I saw a number of Americans walking in and out, so I looked for the back entrance. It was only a small door, but it had a window at the side. I looked through it and saw some women dishing up food, so I knew that I had found the right place. One of the women looked up, I beckoned to her and she came outside. I asked her whether she knew my sister Astra and she said:

'Yes, I know her. She is serving meals. I will tell her to come outside and see you.'

It wasn't long before Astra arrived at the door. She stared at me as if she could not believe that I was there. Then we both hugged one another, and kissed and cried. I had never been overfond of my sister, but at this moment we loved one another, and were glad to meet again.

'I must get back to work,' said Astra. 'I will be finished in an hour and then we can talk. Just wait here, or come back in an hour. If I don't go back, I might lose my job, and I need it, otherwise I will have no money to live on.'

She kissed me once more and ran back inside. There was a strip of grass by the side of the building, so I laid my bike down and sat next to it on the grass. I had cycled a long way and was extremely tired. Before I knew what had happened, I had dropped off to sleep. Astra woke me, shaking my shoulders. She had finished her work.

'Come on, let's go,' she said. 'I don't want people to hear what we are talking about. I am afraid that I have no accommodation or home, but I will show you where I sleep and live at the moment.'

Pushing my bike, we walked through several streets until we came to the outskirts of Mainburg. Astra stopped at a big house with an open archway in the centre. I could see a small courtyard in the back with a well and a pump. Inside the archway was a door on each side. Astra opened the left one, and we were confronted by a rough wooden staircase.

'You had better take your bike with you, you cannot leave it down here,' she said.

I looked surprised at her. One doesn't usually take a bike into living accommodation, but I did what she told me. It was a struggle to carry the bike with the kitbag and the other luggage on the handlebars up the stairs, but I succeeded. Astra didn't help me. A surprise was awaiting me when I came to the top of the stairs. This was not a house, but a barn, full of straw and hay.

'I thought this was a house. Do you live here?'

'Yes. This is the easy way to get up here. The straw is pushed into this loft from the street side through a hatch. I sleep here and you can sleep here too. The farmer has given me permission. I can use the pump downstairs for my washing. I don't need to cook as I get my food from the Americans where I work. In any case, when Otto comes back, we will move away. People in the town never liked us. They still don't like me. I suppose they have told you this already.'

Nobody had said anything to me, but I kept quiet. Everything sounded rather mysterious and if I agreed with her she would probably tell me more.

'You had better start at the beginning,' I said. 'The last we heard from you was in a telegram, telling us that you would get married. The message arrived a day or two after your wedding day. Did you do that on purpose?'

Astra laughed: 'How did you know that? Let's sit down, and I will tell you all about it.'

I leaned my bike against a post holding the roof and Astra spread out some blankets, so that we could sit down. The last time I had seen her was when my mother and I had taken her to Oberstdorf. She was then thin and pale. She looked very much better now. She had put on weight; actually, she had quite a tummy. She even had some colour in her face and looked fresh and alert. It might, of course, have been the excitement of seeing me, but she certainly had put on weight. She then told me her story:

At first she was quite happy in Oberstdorf receiving her treatment in the sanatorium, but gradually she got bored. She didn't like the people there. Some of them were very ill with tuberculosis and she was afraid that she, too, might catch it. She decided to leave the place and get a job. She looked at the papers and found an advertisement for a second cook in a diet kitchen in a hospital in Mainburg. She went for an interview, taking her certificates and she got the job.

She told everybody in Oberstdorf that she was leaving, asked them to post on any post to her new address, and then left. In Mainburg, she met Otto and fell in love. He was older than her, had Austrian nationality and was in the process of being divorced. His wife and two teenage children were still living in the little town. Because Otto was so lonely, he moved in with her at the address I had called on before. This was quite a sensation. Couples didn't live together in those days, and Otto wasn't even divorced yet! She was ostracized straight away. As soon as the divorce came through, they got married. She made sure that the telegram to my mother with the announcement of the wedding arrived late.

Once she was married, she gave up work in the hospital and only looked after Otto. She said that she was very happy with him. He was a forest warden, and responsible for a large section of the local woods. He had not been accepted to fight in the war because of his health, and also because he was Austrian.

Towards the end of the war every man was asked to come forward and fight. Otto did not volunteer. Two days before the Americans entered Mainburg, the SS arrived with a lorry and collected Otto and a number of other able-bodied men who had not volunteered and drove them away. Nobody had seen the lorry again.

'People say that they have been shot and that there should be a grave somewhere in the wood, but it has not been found,' said Astra. 'I don't believe this I think Otto will come back to me.'

The Americans came and, after a while, when Astra couldn't pay her rent because Otto, the breadwinner, was not there, she was given notice to leave. She didn't know where to go, so she asked her landlady whether she could store the few pieces of furniture which she possessed in her attic. She permitted this and after that Astra moved into the hay loft. She now had the job in the canteen, working for the Americans. Nobody would let her rent another room, although she had the money for it. But, as she said, people just didn't like her.


She talked very bravely and defiantly, but I could feel that she really was hurt and unhappy, and I felt sorry for her.

'You will have to come back with me to Mama and Papa. You cannot live here all alone. What will you do when the winter comes? You cannot live in the hay loft then.'

'I have to wait for Otto here. Did you say you know where Mama and Papa are?'

So now it was my turn to tell her what had happened to us. She was very happy to hear about Mama, and that she was alive. She was fascinated with my description of the *Funkstation*. I did not go into too many details about my flight from Königsberg. She was not all that interested in it either. She had no news from Christel or Hans, or from Hermann, to whom I had also given her address. We all had Astra's address in Mainburg, and had given it to others, too. We always felt that the Russians would never get so far south, and that she would be the one who was safe. Although she was alive and well, I had found her in a hay loft.

In the morning, Astra showed me where her things were. She had two suitcases and a large box hidden in the back of the loft under some straw. By now, I had to do some washing, because I had been sixteen days on the road. I left on July 7th and it was the 23rd when I found Astra.

We went downstairs into the courtyard, where Astra said that there were primitive washing facilities. They consisted of a concrete trough, with a shiny big flat stone next to it. Astra stuffed a piece of old cloth into the hole at the bottom corner of the trough. She got a bucket, filled it up with water from the pump, and poured it into the trough. She did this several times, until the trough was full. After that, she produced a piece of soap and a scrubbing brush, took my dress, which I wanted to wash, wet it in the water, laid it on to the stone, and scrubbed it with the brush and plenty of soap.

She watched me start, and then said: 'I will find us some breakfast. I am on duty again at dinner time and in the evening, but I am off this morning, because of you. Even so, I am entitled to breakfast.'

With that, she walked off, and I did my washing, which was a cold and hard job. The water from the pump was very cold, and the soap strong, and it was not long before my hands were red and sore.

When Astra returned we had breakfast, which was very good; she had brought fresh rolls and butter and jam. I supplied some sausage from my kit bag. I had told her that I got food in Kassel, and that I had been in prison, also that Sam had helped me, and that he had given me food.

I did not tell her that Sam had proposed to me, this was my secret. Astra and I had never been close. I never told her anything except the facts. I would most certainly never confide in her. Christel, on the other hand, was different. One could talk quite openly to her. She always understood, and was sympathetic. Astra never gave sympathy, she only craved it for herself.

After our breakfast, I finished the washing, and we hung it up in the loft, and then it was time for Astra to go to work. She came back at 3 o'clock for two hours, and then had to help with the evening meal again. She said that she had arranged that she was off the next day. She was entitled to one free day in the week. Maybe we could go into the wood, if the weather was fine. She knew lovely places there where Otto had taken her, and she said that, late in the afternoon, one could see rabbits and deer there.

Whilst I was left alone, I caught up with my diary, then explored the town a little. There had been no fighting or bombing here, and the buildings looked clean and pretty with their flower boxes. People resented the occupation forces because it was a reminder of the war, which had hardly touched them.

They will never understand, I thought. They have no compassion. They are cruel. How can they let Astra live in a hay loft, although she is prepared to pay for her lodgings?

The next day was beautiful, and we did what Astra had suggested and went into the wood. We took a picnic, and had our dinner in a little hut, deep inside the forest. It belonged to the forestry commission, and Astra told me that Otto sometimes stayed the night there. The hut was very small. It had a wooden sleeping bunk, a solid wooden table, and a bench. We spread our food out on the table, and my sister told me about her work in the hospital, about Otto, and about the Americans.

At first I had thought she had changed, but I soon realized that this was not the case. She criticized everybody and everything, except Otto. He was good and kind, and never did anything wrong. I was not a bit surprised that she had never made any friends in the town, if all she could do was to find fault with people.

In the late afternoon she showed me a little stream, and a hiding place where we could wait for the animals. We saw a stag and one or two deer coming to the water to drink, but no other animals. On the way back, we disturbed a hare, which chased across the field in zigzag jumps. Before returning to our hay loft, Astra collected some supper for us from the American canteen. She explained that the reason she put up with this menial job was that she got all her food free, even on her day off and, on top of that, she was still entitled to her ration cards. I agreed that from that point of view she was quite fortunate but, even so, I still would have liked her to have some lodgings.

'Have you talked to the *Bürgermeister*?' I said. 'I would insist that he gets you some kind of accommodation. Threaten him that you will tell the American commandant about it. You could say that because you are working for them, you meet him occasionally. Even if it is not true, he might believe you.'

She was not going to do this, so I said that I would go and see him myself. Astra told me where the *Bürgermeister* lived, and also at what time he would be at his office in the *Rathaus* (town hall). I had a look at his house. It was quite large and I was sure that he had space there for a refugee.

The *Rathaus* was occupied by the Americans, but the *Bürgermeister* had a small office for himself. When I got there, people were already queueing up to see him and I had to wait. Eventually it was my turn. I told him who I was, asked him whether he knew my sister, and where she lived. He knew Astra, but had no idea where she lived. So I told him:

'She lives in a hay loft, with two suitcases and a box, and does her washing in a cobbled courtyard, with cold water from a pump. There is no toilet and, as she is working for the Americans in the canteen in the school building, she is forced to use the toilet there. This is a long way to go, in the middle of the night.'

He looked a little embarrassed at me, and explained that empty accommodation was non-existent in the town. I told him that something would have to be found for her, and quickly, too. I even suggested his own house, saying that it looked quite big. He said that he had some American officers living with him. I threatened to expose this situation to the commandant, as Astra was working there. He looked at me searchingly. He was not only embarrassed, but I could see that he was uncomfortable, and that there was more to it than just shortage of rooms.

'Your sister is not popular in the town', he said. 'We are a strong catholic community here. She lived quite openly with a married man, who eventually got divorced, something which the church does not recognize. His ex-wife was born and bred in the town and still lives here with the children, and so do a lot of her relatives. I am telling you this, so that you understand. Your sister knows all this and it would be much better if she moved away.'

So that was the reason for Astra not getting rooms. She had told me that she didn't want to leave in case Otto came back and looked for her. I had not realized the strong feelings in this little town about what people thought was right and wrong, and the punishment they would inflict on wrongdoers. I was not very religious, but we read the Bible at school, and I remembered what Jesus said about adultery, so I replied:

'If people are such good Catholics, then they also should know their Bible. Jesus said, when a woman was brought to him who was caught in adultery: "Let him who is without sin amongst you be the first to throw a stone at her".'

He didn't like what I had said, but I carried on: 'And what about Otto, what happened to him and the other men who were taken away? Have you done anything to find them, or enquired where the lorry went to? A vehicle cannot just disappear, and neither can the people who were responsible for it, like the driver, or the SS. The nearest concentration camp was Dachau by Munich. People disappeared there, but somebody would have to take them there first, and it is up to you to find this out. Maybe you know more than you like to say, or maybe you are shielding somebody. There were a lot of witnesses when the men were collected and driven away, and I am sure somebody would recognize the SS men again.'

The last part was a shot in the dark, but it unsettled him, and he became cross. He assured me that he had done everything possible to find the men; they must be dead, or at least one of them would have returned by now. I told him that this was probably true but, even so, people ought to know how they died and where their bodies were. It only happened two days before the Americans entered Mainburg.

After that, I changed the subject again, and came back to Astra, telling him that I would take her back to Hamburg if I could arrange transport. I did not say how I was going to do it, only that I had to go away for a few days to try and find some friends near Weilheim (I had looked up this place on the map, as I didn't want to tell him that I really intended to go to Habach.) He admitted then that if the accommodation for Astra was only for a short time, he might be able to find something. I told him that I would call at his house in the afternoon to find out how successful he had been, as I intended to leave the next day, and didn't want to travel with the thought of having left Astra behind in the hay loft. I could see he didn't like the idea of my calling at his house, I don't know why. He said that he could not arrange things so quickly, I must give him time.

'I will call at your house at 5 o'clock, that should be time enough, and I will bring Astra with me, so that both of us can look at the room you have found for her,' I said.

Now he really looked uncomfortable.

'I prefer this to be an official visit. Please come to my office at 5 o'clock, when I will be able to tell you how successful I have been', he replied. Then he added: 'Is your sister able to pay the rent of a room?'

'If it is reasonable, yes, otherwise she will have to ask the Americans for an increase in her wages.'

With these words, I warned him not to let Astra be overcharged because if she asked for more money and gave the reasons, everybody would know it. He shook hands with me when I left, a sign that he understood that I was right in what I had said and done, and also in relief, because he knew now that Astra would leave soon. I was wondering whether he, too, was a relative of Otto's wife.

I told Astra about my visit, but she didn't think that the *Bürgermeister* would find any rooms for her.

'They are all related, and nobody wants me. Even Otto was never completely accepted here, because he came from Austria. You shouldn't have told him that I will come back with you, I have not yet made up my mind.'

My sister was wrong because, when I turned up in the afternoon at the *Rathaus* (Astra had gone to work), the *Bürgermeister* smiled, and said that he had found a room for her.

It was a good sized room on the first floor of an old house, not far from the school where Astra worked. There was a bed in the corner, covered with a colourful blanket, a small faded settee with some cushions on it, a table under the window, two hard chairs, a wardrobe with a mirror inside, and even a thin carpet in the centre of the room.

The lady of the house was a war widow, and her only seventeen year old son was apprenticed at the local carpenter. She said that he would help Astra with her cases and the box, probably borrowing a small cart from a neighbour. The price, too, was reasonable and, as the room was clean and the lady quite nice, I accepted it straight away without asking Astra. I also said that I hoped it would be alright for me to sleep on the small settee.

Before leaving, she showed me the bathroom, which Astra could share and, although she didn't like Astra to cook in her kitchen, she would permit her occasionally to do so as long as it was not too often. I told her that I didn't think this would be often, as Astra received all her meals already cooked from the canteen where she worked. I thanked everybody, and said that I would bring Astra after work, and was glad to hear that the son was free that evening, to help with the move from the hay loft.

I met Astra, and told her my news. She seemed pleased, until she saw the room. She didn't like the faded settee, thought the bed with the coloured blanket looked awful, and also made a remark about the thin carpet. I told her off and said that she could get back, and live in the hay loft, where she had so much luxury! Her reply was that she didn't have to pay for that accommodation.

I wasn't a bit surprised that nobody liked my sister, she had a genius for putting her foot in every time.

The landlady had not heard her remarks, as Astra had only said all this to me. So I warned her to keep quiet, and just enjoy sleeping in a bed again. The son came and helped us with Astra's luggage and, once we got it all into the room, she was able to hang her clothes into the wardrobe. I made sure that she paid her rent for one week. I told her that I would leave in the morning, and see whether I could arrange the transport for her to come back to Hamburg with all her things. She still insisted that she had not made up her mind, but felt it was a good idea to find out the possibilities.

We both had a good night's sleep. The settee was quite a good bed, especially as I could use the cushions and the colourful blanket from the bed.

# CHAPTER SEVEN

## Habach - Christel - Back to the Funkstation

I left early in the morning for Habach, the camp where the lorry with Jo and Heinz had come from. I had three lifts during the day, two from the Americans, and the last one from a German driver. He knew about Habach, and said it was a big place.

'It is not really a prisoner-of-war camp, rather a collecting place for *Wehrmacht* (army) personnel, in order to release them officially, and transport them home,' he said.

I told him that I wanted to return to Hamburg, but I did not mention Astra. He thought that I wouldn't have difficulties, but might have to leave my bike behind. He turned off the autobahn, and took me to Iffeldorf, pointing out that I only had about 8-10 km to Habach.

In Mainburg, I had learnt what one could achieve by going to the *Bürgermeister*, so I did the same in Iffeldorf. The *Bürgermeister* looked quite surprised when I told him that I wanted some night accommodation.

I don't think anybody before had ever asked him for it.

I explained what I intended to do, travel to Habach to get a transport to Hamburg. I told him that I had been a nurse, but wanted now to return to Hamburg, where I had an aunt, in the hope that my parents had made their way there too. I had, by now become a good story-teller, changing my tale to suit the situation. I said that I didn't mind sleeping in a barn in straw or hay, as long as it was dry, clean and safe.

He had a talk with his wife, and then offered me a camp bed in a store room, where the reins and tackle for the horses were kept. It smelled of leather and polish, but it was dry, and the bed, with the blankets, was comfortable. I also could have my bike there. His wife even gave me a bowl of soup and a piece of bread for supper and, in the morning, I had a mug of milk, and again some bread.

I cycled the last part to Habach, and there was no need to enquire where the camp was. There were some tents in a field, and a number of lorries in another. The big farmhouse seemed to be occupied by the Americans whilst, in the yard and the barn there were a great many people walking or sitting about. It all looked a terrible muddle, as if nobody knew what to do.

At the entrance of the house sat an American guard with a gun between his knees, chewing gum. He grinned at me. I had never seen a guard sitting on a chair and it gave me quite a jerk. Somehow it didn't look right, but he must have had permission to do this, otherwise he wouldn't sit there so brazenly.

'Hi', he said.

'Hi, can I go in?'

'I am sure you can, but you may not, unless you tell me why you want to go in. - Nice of you to speak English.'

'I want to apply for my release papers and get transport to Hamburg. I am a nurse, and have worked in military hospitals.'

He looked me up and down. 'Where is your uniform? Have you got papers?'

I could see that it was not going to be as easy as I had thought. I had no uniform, and I had no papers to prove that I had been nursing, only my university identity card, with my photograph. Well, that would have to do. I produced it, and showed it to him.

'University Hospital, sounds a good one. They might not let you go with a transport but put you to work in the hospital', he said.

I then asked him about Jo, giving his full name and rank.

He knew Jo, but had not seen him lately, it could be that he was on a transport at the moment. He then told me where I had to go to fill in a form and be interviewed. He said that he would look after my bike, so I left it behind.

It was not difficult to find the interviewing room, because there was a queue outside. Several men and women waited in front of a closed door, sitting on the floor.

Eventually it was my turn to go in. I met a captain and a sergeant, the latter sitting in front of a typewriter, at a large corner table. He did not even look up when I entered, because he was so busy typing away. The captain sat behind a desk, and was speaking to somebody on the phone. There was a chair on the other side of the desk, and he pointed to it when I entered, motioning to me to sit down. When he had finished on the phone, he asked me whether I spoke English and, when I said that I knew a little, he seemed relieved. Actually his German was as good as my English, and the interview went quite well. He just couldn't get over the fact that I came from Königsberg, and had done that terrible journey all on my own.

I told him that I had come to Greifswald, and then made my way south to Munich. I had already been in that big town with my bombed-out relatives but, since I knew that my parents were in Hamburg, I wanted to get to them there. He said that he had nothing to do with the transport side, he was only doing the interviewing, but he would recommend that I get on to a transport as soon as possible. In the meantime, I could have some accommodation, either in a tent, or in the barn but, for this, I would have to see the sergeant, the one who was typing away in the corner. He also said that I could get meal coupons from him, as there was a soup kitchen, run by the army.

Having received my tickets and form, I was now at liberty to walk around the farmhouse and yard. I found out that the farmer still lived there in some of the rooms, with his wife and children. Only the rooms on the ground floor were taken over by the military.

The store room was in one of the sheds outside. There I received my blankets. After that, I took my bike and found my allocated tent, the front of which was closed. I laid my bike on to the ground, and opened the tent. I stared in disbelief . . . . On one of the camp beds was a couple making love. They were nearly naked and completely unaware of their surroundings.

There was nobody else in the tent; all the other beds were unoccupied for the moment. I was so shocked, that I just dropped the door flap of the tent, picked up my bike, and walked back to the farmhouse. I was young and inexperienced, and I had been brought up in the belief that sex was strictly forbidden until after the wedding ceremony, and here was a young couple making love unashamedly, in broad daylight.

I felt that I could not go back to that tent, so I went and looked in the barn. Here, too, were people sleeping and living, but it was not crowded, because there were no camp beds, only straw and hay. I decided to find a place there. The only thing that troubled me was that there was no segregation. I thought that I would not get undressed at night and hoped that I only had to stay there for a night or two.

I took my bike with me everywhere, even when I went to the soup kitchen. There I met Karl and Josef. They both had been in a concentration camp and had a number tattooed on their arms. Karl was quite a bit smaller than myself. He had hardly any hair, as that was usually shaved off roughly in the camp, often even pulling the skin off. When he smiled, one could see that he had some teeth missing in the corner of his mouth. He wore a leather cap, and a thick leather jacket, which seemed to have a great many pockets. He never stopped talking, and always seemed happy. Josef was taller and thin, with insignificant features, the sort of person who disappears in the crowd. He was the opposite to Karl, quiet and unhappy-looking.

Karl offered to hold my bike so that I could collect my soup and bread. Somehow I trusted him, and let him have it. When I returned with my food, he had laid the bike on to the ground, and sat next to it. Josef had gone away. I sat next to Karl and my bike and started to eat, when I realized that he had nothing to eat.

'Haven't you got any food tickets?', I asked. 'You can share my bread and soup if you like.'

He laughed: 'Don't worry, I have plenty of food, I can give you some if you like.'

'No thank you, I am alright.'

He watched me eating my soup and bread, then he asked:

'Where do you sleep? Have you got some accommodation?'

I wasn't quite sure whether I should answer him. Why should I tell him where I was spending the night? I had learnt to be careful.

'You don't need to worry', he said. 'I won't molest you. There are a lot of comings and goings here at night. I was going to warn you to take care. You don't belong here.'

'I had been allocated a camp bed in a tent', I said, 'but when I went there, I found two people making love. I decided that I would prefer to sleep in the barn. I had a look at the place. It is not crowded. I also can keep my bike with me there, and I prefer to do that.'

Karl looked at me, then he said:

'Josef and I sleep in the stables. The farmer used to have horses but during the war they were taken away from him, and now the stalls are empty. We have cleaned one out, put fresh straw in it, and it is quite comfortable. Do you want to have a look at it?'

I said that I would be pleased to see it, and went with him to the stables. There were four stalls in a row, divided by wooden partitions, and every one had a door. One could easily imagine the horses in the stalls, with their heads hanging over the wooden walls. Karl's place was the corner one and, when he opened the door, I saw that he had made it quite comfortable.

'Josef and I sleep here,' he said. 'It is comfortable and warm. If you like, we can clean out the next stall for you, so that you can sleep there.'

I was surprised at his offer, but I accepted it, and said that I would help to clean it up. Karl went off to find Josef. I rested my bike against the wall of the stable, and started to sweep the stall, borrowing his broom.

When Karl and Josef returned, they told me to go away for a while, so that they could get on with the cleaning and preparing of my new accommodation. Karl just took the broom away from me, saying that it would be much too dusty for me to be there whilst they swept everything. So I went off, looking around Habach for a while.

When I got back, my stall was clean. I had new straw, and my blankets were laid out ready for my night's sleep. Even my bike was put into the little room.

I was most grateful, and told Karl and Josef that I wanted to go to sleep straight away, as I had cycled rather a long way over the last two days. They quite understood, but said that they would like to invite me for breakfast. I laughed, because it sounded so grand, and I didn't think that they had much to offer me.

Breakfast was a surprise. There were fresh rolls, fresh butter, jam, sausage, cheese, and deliciously smelling coffee. Karl grinned like a schoolboy who had performed a mischievous joke, and enjoyed my surprise. When I asked him how and where he had got all this food, he said that he had stolen everything, and then he laughed again. I didn't believe him, although I knew that he had been in a concentration camp, and realized that there must have been a reason why he had been imprisoned there. He was not Jewish, neither was Josef, I had asked that already. Neither of them had told me why they were in the concentration camp, so it was possible that they were thieves.

Both of them had a special identity card, with their photos, showing that they had been released from a concentration camp. Favours and privileges were granted to them because of this. They never needed to queue up, but could go straight to the front of a row of people, whether it was at a food store, or to receive some kind of permit from the authorities. Karl said that people felt very guilty about the concentration camps, and did their utmost to help the released inmates. They believed everything that he told them. He had gone to the *Bürgermeister* in a village, and told him that he was the leader of a group of twenty people, and would like the ration cards for them, as they were living and travelling together. In this way, he and Josef had a very good allocation of food. He had also asked for monetary aid for his group. The food which he didn't use, also the cigarettes, because he didn't smoke, he sold on the black market, which gave him quite a bit of money.

I got my papers on the third day, stamped July 31st 1945, and I now had a right to be transported to any town I named. By now, I knew Karl better, so I told him about Astra, and that I wanted to take her with me to Hamburg. I told him about my parents on the radio station, and how I had made my journey to Mainburg. I did not tell him about Sam, only that I had been imprisoned, but I told him about Jo, and asked him whether he knew him. Karl said that he might have met him, he would only know this if he saw him again. He thought it would be a good idea to bring Astra to Habach, and then approach Jo for some help.

'If you like,' he said, 'I will come with you to Mainburg, and help you to get transport to Habach for your sister and her suitcases. I will find out from the German drivers who travel north of Munich. They could pick you and your sister up on the way back.'

Karl was a good organiser. It took another two days, and then he told me that he had arranged everything. He wanted me to return to Mainburg, and wait there for him. I had to give him Astra's address, and then he told me his plan:

'I have talked to the drivers. Some of them can go on their own, without being accompanied by an American soldier, as long as they are back on the same day. I have found somebody who will go like that to Nürnberg on the 9th of August. I have to give him a bottle of brandy and some cigarettes. He promised to drop me off at the autobahn turning to Mainburg, from where I can make my way into the town. He will pick us all up on his return journey in the afternoon, when he is empty. Mainburg is not very far from the autobahn. I will come on the 9th, and help you and your sister with her luggage, and bring you to the meeting place at the autobahn. Your task now is to make sure that your sister agrees to come with you, and to make sure she is ready when I come. She must not have more than two suitcases, because there will be limited space in the lorry to Hamburg later. We won't have much time to get to the autobahn and, if we are late, the driver will not wait. He is already making a detour, by going towards Mainburg and, if he gets back to Habach too late, somebody might get suspicious. You have a whole week to get to Mainburg and to organise your sister. This should also give her plenty of time to dispose of her furniture.'

'I have just two questions. One, what about your friend Josef? and two, what if my sister refuses to come with me?'

'Josef will stay in Habach until we return. He has got himself a girlfriend, and is quite happy to stay here at the moment. If your sister doesn't want to come with you, you will just have to come back to Habach on your own, if you want transport to Hamburg, if not, you can stay with her, and I will return alone to Habach.'

I thought about these arrangements. Karl certainly had organised everything, and now he was even prepared to help me in person. How was I going to pay him for his kindness? I did not want to be under any obligation to him. Josef had a girlfriend, I had seen him walking about the camp with a young woman, and I also had noticed that he didn't sleep in the stable at night any more. Some ex-soldiers had tried to come near me, but Karl had made sure that they didn't touch me, and everybody thought now that we belonged together. I felt uneasy about Karl at times. I had tried to find out why he had been put into a concentration camp, but his reply was that, if he told me the reason, I wouldn't like him any more.

'Why do you do all this for me?' I asked him. 'I can't give you anything in return.'

'I have nothing else to do, so I might as well do something for you. I have done many things wrong in my life, for once I am happy to do somebody a good turn.' He laughed, he always did this, he was never serious, always joking. I kept on looking at him, wondering and thinking. Suddenly he stopped laughing. He put his hand on my arm, and said quietly:

'I will tell you the truth. I am only a simple man, not good looking, with a bald head, and only a few teeth left. Look at me, a small chap, with crooked legs, and short arms. My hands have fingers like sausages. They say I am clever, but I am also ugly. You are a beautiful tall girl, and you don't mind being seen with me. You walk around the camp with me and treat me as an equal, and that's what is so important to me. We were treated worse than animals in the concentration camp and when I was free again there seemed no purpose in anything. I suddenly have got something to do, a goal, so just go ahead and trust me. If you want my advice, then it is this: Make sure your sister comes with you. I am convinced her husband is dead. There is no need for her to wait for him. She will be much better off with you and your parents. At least you are all together then. It can be damned lonely if one has nobody. I know, I have experienced it.'

Karl had never talked like this, and I could suddenly see another side to him. All his laughing and joking was a cover. He was a lonely person, trying to forget the past. He was right about his looks, and I knew that he would find it difficult to get a girl. He was very kind, often helping other people. I decided to accept his help, and go along with his plans.

I left after dinner, supplied with food by Karl, and the promise to pick me up on the 9th in Mainburg. I did not have to cycle very far before I got a lift to Starnberg. I remembered suddenly that Hermann had told me that his sister was working in the laboratory in a hospital in Starnberg. As I had a whole week before I had to leave Mainburg with Astra, I decided to see whether I could find Lotti.

There were two hospitals in the town, so I made my way to the bigger one first. I was in luck. Lotti Fassbach worked there, but she was off for two days, and nobody seemed to know where she lived. As I didn't want to spend too much time in Starnberg, I left her a note. I just wrote that I was sorry to have missed her, asked whether she had heard anything about Hermann, and gave my address from the radio station.

Just outside the town, I asked a farmer whether I could sleep in his barn and, early the next morning, I was off again, on my way to Mainburg. I got a lift, and arrived at Astra's place in the evening. She was not there, and neither was her landlady, so I went to the school where she had worked before for the Americans. To my surprise, I was told that she had left the job, and nobody knew where she worked now. Astra had no friends in the town, and I was at a loss to know where to look for her. Then I remembered my sister's old address and, knowing that she still had some furniture there, I thought that maybe they would know whether she had moved again, or had a different job. I found the place, and rang the bell. A woman opened the door, the same one to whom I had spoken before. I asked whether she knew where my sister was.

'Which sister?' said the woman.

'My sister who rented rooms from you before.'

'Oh, that one,' she said. 'I thought you meant the other one. She, too, was looking for her.'

I stared at the woman. I really couldn't make out what she was talking about. She had said the other sister, what other sister? I had enquired after Astra. My other sister Christel was not here, or was she?

'Tell me, did somebody else look for Astra? Is that what you are saying? Do you mean my other sister has turned up? She is small and blonde.'

'Yes, she was blonde, and she said she was Astra's sister. I told her where she lives. The *Bürgermeister* had found her some accommodation for a short time, as she is going to leave soon.'

So everybody knew about the room I had got for Astra through the *Bürgermeister*. Astra must have gone out when I called, she would probably be back by now. I thanked the woman for her information and made my way back to Astra's last lodgings. I met the landlady, who was quite excited when she saw me.

'Come in, come in,' she said. 'There is a big surprise waiting for you. Just go and see your sister.'

She smiled all over her face, then she knocked at Astra's door and said: 'Your other sister is here!' and, with that, she opened the door and pushed me gently in.

My surprise was sitting on the settee - Astra and Christel - holding hands.

'Oh Christel, Christel,' I whispered. The lump in my throat did not let me speak loudly. I felt hot and cold, and I wanted to sit down, but I could not move. Christel got up and came running towards me. She threw her arms around my neck, and cried, and sobbed, and laughed, and stumbled over words which I did not understand. Her small body was shaking. As usual, I felt I had to protect her and comfort her.

'Sh, sh', I said. 'It is alright. You are safe now, come, come, you must calm down.'

I guided her back to the settee, and sat next to her, hugging her and holding her hands until she got quiet again. Astra had already told her that I had been to Mainburg, and had left to find out whether I could arrange transport back to Hamburg.

Christel had a long story to tell; she was working in a military hospital in Königsberg, which was on the outskirts of the town, in Maraunenhof. Although we both had agreed to leave the town together if it was necessary, somehow things did go wrong, and now I got the explanations:

In January, it was decided at Christel's hospital to take as many wounded as possible to Pillau, the harbour, and try to get them on to ships to the west. A number of nurses were chosen to accompany the more seriously wounded soldiers and officers, and Christel was one of them. The wounded were transported in ambulances, cars, even lorries, anything that had wheels, and was motorised - these were desperate times. Christel tried to contact me, but there were only a few telephone lines in operation, and she could not make contact with my hospital. She was ordered to accompany a lorry. Just before it started, she slipped off, and tried once again to phone, but could not reach me. When she returned to her allocated lorry, it had gone.

Eventually Christel was able to contact my hospital, and was told that I had left, or must have done so, as I didn't return to duty any more. She could not phone our home number, as no private calls were allowed or connected. Phoning from one hospital to another was a duty call. Christel then went to find her friend Dorothea, who was surprised to see her, because she had thought Christel had left with a transport to Pillau. Dorothea informed my sister that I had phoned, and that one of the nurses had told me that Christel had left. Christel was now frightened. She had no protecting sister and no transport. It was Dorothea who suggested that they should both try and get away.

Christel stayed with Dorothea for another night. The next day they were able to get on to a lorry, with wounded who were unable to walk. The roads were full of snow and ice, and the lorry got stuck again and again on hills, but they arrived in Pillau on January 25th, together with a mass of refugees. It was later said that 28,000 people arrived on that day. The next day, January 26th, the ammunition depot was blown up by saboteurs, probably foreign workers, which absolutely devastated the old town.

'It was a terrible picture, which I will never forget', continued Christel. 'Dorothea and I were lucky to get away with our lives, because we were not near the depot. When the explosion came, a great number of people and animals who were waiting for the ships were torn to pieces and thrown high into the trees. There is nothing left of the town because the next day Russian planes arrived again, bombing the refugees and the town. The houses which were left after the explosion were made into ruins.

Dorothea and I didn't know at first what we should do. There were ferries that went between Pillau and the Nehrung. Nobody knew how long this would carry on, because the Russians were now not only bombing and shooting these ferry boats, but also the people who queued up for them. Dorothea and I only had one small suitcase each, and felt that it would be better to try and get on to a ship that went across the Danziger *Bucht* (Gulf of Danzig), and the Baltic.'

'I heard that a number of ships were sunk, and a lot of lives lost,' I interrupted Christel, then I added. 'I walked along the Nehrung.'

'Yes, you are quite right about the ships', replied Christel. 'Of course, at the time, nobody thought about it, everybody wanted to get away. We all felt that it was better to die in the sea than to be prisoners under the Russians. There were several passenger liners in the harbour, the Hansa, Hamburg, Deutschland and the Wilhelm Gustloff. All were ordered to leave the harbour in the Danziger *Bucht*, taking Marine personnel, materials, and supplies for U boats with them. Any spare space on these boats was given free for refugees. We could not get on to the Wilhelm

Gustloff, which was quite well equipped, as it was a luxury liner before the war. This was as well because, when it set off to sea, it was crammed with 7,000 people, 5,000 of them refugees. The liner had no escort when it left on January 30th. It was torpedoed by a Russian U boat the next day and, seventy minutes after being struck, the liner sank. Only 950 people were plucked from the sea and some of them died later from exposure. We didn't mind where the ships went to, whether it was Swinemünde, Lübecker, or Kieler *Bucht*, as long as we could get on to a ship. Somebody suddenly gave an order that people with children would get a place on the ships. Whoever organised this did not realize what would happen. Children now became a ship's ticket. Some mothers wrapped them up into bundles and, once they had entered the ship, they threw them back to their relatives, to their grandmothers or their sisters, so that they, too, could get on board. Sometimes these children fell between the ship and the pier, or amongst the crowd of people who tried to get on to the ship, and the excited crowd would fight over the possession of the child, or tread on it. In this way, children got hurt, or even killed. At night, children were stolen, sometimes even by soldiers who had changed their clothes and tried in this way to get away. Pillau was the first hell that I went through.

Dorothea and I had part of our Red Cross uniform on. A thick coat with the Red Cross arm band, a scarf over our heads, and the Red Cross triangle cap over it, boots and gloves, so that everybody could see who we were. We made ourselves useful with the wounded, hoping in this way to get on to a ship. Wounded did get preferential treatment if there was a space on a ship. The authorities soon got to know us, and we were allowed to help the wounded over the gangplanks, on to the entrance of the ship, but not into the ship.

Dorothea and I were working in one of the makeshift hospitals by the harbour. One of the doctors was impressed with our efforts, and promised to try and get us on to a ship accompanying severely wounded officers. He succeeded in getting our suitcases on to a small merchant ship called Taube. All the morning we had to carry and wheel the wounded over the gangplanks to the door of the ship. By dinner time, Dr Sauerbach accompanied us whilst we were carrying a stretcher case. After crossing the gangplank, he insisted that we brought the wounded officer who had just had an operation into the ship. Nobody objected; we had carried many wounded before, and the sailors knew us. Dr Sauerbach showed us where to deposit the patient, and then told us to go round the corner into the toilet, lock the door, and stay there until the ship had left the harbour.

We were not officially allocated a place on the ship. There were no refugees.

We stayed in the toilet until the Taube was out at sea. It was a rough trip, and I was sick all the time. Dorothea was a much better sailor than I. We met Dr Sauerbach who told us that we were now on his staff, and had to help to look after his wounded. Do you know, I don't even know how long we were on the ship; all I remember is being sick, feeling awful, mopping up sickness from the wounded, feeding them, and giving them drinks. The ship was overloaded. There was nowhere for us to stretch out and sleep, so we huddled in a corner when we were off duty, and dozed or slept. I preferred to be on deck in the fresh air, although it was bitterly cold, because the smell of the wounded and the sickness made me retch again and again. I call this journey hell number two.

Dorothea said that we were four days and nights on the Taube, before we landed in Swinemünde. Merchant and warships, liners, big and small boats all queued up at the harbour, and I was glad to get off the ship.'

Christel and Dorothea stayed with Dr Sauerbach and his team, and eventually got all the wounded further down into Germany to Sachsen/Thüringen (Saxony/Thuringia). They both worked in a hospital near Leipzig, until the end of the war. It was the Americans who arrived in Sachsen/Thüringen and, on April 21st, met the Russians in Torgau, on the river Elbe. The two girls felt safe with the Americans. They stuck to the Geneva convention, and did not molest the wounded in the hospital, or the staff. On the contrary, when Dr Sauerbach mentioned that they were short of medicine in the hospital, he got a supply from the US army.

Unfortunately, the new-found peaceful life did not last. There was suddenly a whisper that the Americans would move out, because Sachsen/Thüringen was going to be occupied by the Russians. Somebody had made a vague agreement with the Soviets, and the Americans had to evacuate Sachsen/Thüringen, which they had conquered. It was Dr Sauerbach who told Christel and Dorothea the news, and it was Dr Sauerbach who helped them to escape again.

'Dr Sauerbach told us that he had not fled so far and so long from the Russians to be caught by them now, when the war was finished,' said Christel. 'He decided to get out this time, leaving the wounded behind, and only taking some of the staff. He told us that he had organised an ambulance, and anybody who wanted to come with him was welcome. He warned that it could be dangerous, because there were already border posts established on the roads, and people were not allowed to leave, and move into the American or British zones. He was going to drive the ambulance at night, hoping that nobody would stop him, and at the border he would just drive through, even if they shot at the vehicle.

'We were quite a crowd in the back of the ambulance,' continued Christel, 'and everybody was apprehensive. Dorothea sat next to Dr Sauerbach. She is a big girl, and always looks like a very efficient nurse. The ambulance went pretty fast until we got near the so-called border. One of the nurses looked through the little window connected to the driver's seat and told us that there were big lights on and that the barrier was down.

Dr Sauerbach slowed down, then shouted to us to duck and to hold tight. The ambulance siren roared, the vehicle speeded up, lights flashed through the side windows, and then there was a tremendous crash. The vehicle started to rock and slide and bump, as if out of control. There were shouts, and then there were shots. The windows in the back door shattered, and then there was a bang. A nurse said:

'They are shooting at the tyres. I think they have hit one.'

But the ambulance kept on rolling and bumping along, and Dr Sauerbach shouted again, telling us to hold tight. Eventually the vehicle stopped, and there was silence. Nobody moved, or said anything.

I don't know how long we stood there. My body ached, because one of the nurses was lying on top of me.

Nobody seemed to be hurt. 'What about Dr Sauerbach and Dorothea?' asked somebody. And then we heard a car approaching, and another and another. The back door was opened, and a torch shone over us. An American voice asked:

'Are you alive?'

We started to climb out of the ambulance. There were two American cars, and a lorry with soldiers and officers. Guns were pointing at us, but were dropped when an officer shouted something. I think they could see that we were nurses, because we were all in uniform. Dr Sauerbach walked towards us with his hands raised and, behind him, two American soldiers with guns. He looked very white and I thought that he was going to collapse at any minute. Dorothea was next to him, and suddenly took his arm, because he swayed. Another nurse ran to him and held him on the other side. The two of them could not hold him, so they sat him down by the side of the road.

The sun was just coming up and everything looked very eerie in the dim morning light. I looked at the ambulance, and realized what Dr Sauerbach had been through. We had two flat tyres at the back and the windows in the back door were broken. The front was bashed in, and the windscreen shattered. There were also some small holes from gun shots.

I was surprised that nobody was hurt, unless Dr Sauerbach was shot.

'Are you hurt?' said the officer to Dr Sauerbach, who was sitting hunched, with his head between his legs. He slowly lifted his head and said:

'No, this is only the reaction from driving through the barrier and being shot at.'

I was surprised at how good his English was.

'You are a brave man,' said the American. 'We didn't realize that you had so many nurses in the ambulance. The Russians shot at you because they were told not to let anybody across the border. We thought that you had somebody very ill and important in the back because you sounded the siren.'

'That was what you all were supposed to think, so that you could open the barrier but, in the end, I had to drive through it. You can make me a prisoner-of-war, but please let the nurses go. They have done no harm to anybody.'

'You know,' said Christel, 'Dr Sauerbach was a marvellous man, and a wonderful, kind and considerate doctor. Dorothea and I owe him our lives.

Anyway, the Americans took us all back to their quarters. Dr Sauerbach was made a prisoner-of-war, but he didn't mind, knowing that he would get good treatment, and we nurses were told that we could leave. Dorothea had some relatives in Friedberg, near Augsburg, and told me to come with her. We had no money, no job, no food, and I didn't know where to go except, maybe, to find Astra. I went with Dorothea and, when we got to Friedberg, she found her parents with her relatives. They all made me very welcome, and offered me a home, if I couldn't find any of my relatives. Dorothea and I started to work at the local hospital but, after a time, I decided that I ought to try and find out what had happened to Astra, and I made my way to Mainburg, walking, and getting lifts, and sleeping on farms. I arrived yesterday afternoon, and had the greatest difficulty in finding Astra. Still, I am here, and I am so glad that I have found you, too, and that you have found Mama and Papa. Now only Hans is missing.'

By the time Christel had told her story, it was too late to tell mine. I asked the landlady whether all three of us could sleep in the room, and she didn't object. She even gave us a couple of blankets. Because Astra had given up her job with the Americans, she was short of food. It was a good thing that Karl had given me some, so now I could share it out.

I was surprised at Astra's decision to leave her job, but she said that she had made up her mind to come with me to Hamburg.

'I haven't been very well lately,' she said. 'I must have eaten something which upset me, or I have got a virus. I keep on being sick.'

I was not sure whether this was true, but she was sick again the next morning. I only hoped it was nothing serious, because an upset tummy didn't last a long time as a rule, and she had said that she had had this sickness already for several days.

Christel decided to stick with us, and not to go back to Dorothea's family. She said that she would come with me to Habach, and could get her release papers there which would entitle her to transport.

'I have told Dorothea that I might not come back,' said Christel. 'When the post is going again, I will write to her and explain everything.'

I told Astra and Christel what I had arranged in Habach with Karl, and that we had to be ready by the 9th. I explained to Astra that she could only take two suitcases, and that we ought to try and sell her furniture, as I doubted whether she would come back here again.

'I am not selling the furniture', she replied. 'Otto might come back, and will need everything. I have two suitcases and a box with my own things in them, and must take it all with me, otherwise I will not come with you.'

'What have you got in all your cases, and in that box? Maybe we can sort things out. I will help you. You can leave some of your nicknacks behind with your furniture if you are not selling any. The trouble is that you have to be smuggled on to a transport to Hamburg. The lorry will already be full of people and cases, there is never much room left.'

'I told you that I will take two suitcases and the box. You are not looking through any of them. If I cannot take them, I will stay here. I didn't want to go in the first place. You persuaded me.'

And that was that. Christel tried to change her mind, but was unsuccessful. At one time, I felt like leaving her behind but I could not return to Hamburg and tell Mama and Papa that I had not brought Astra because she refused to leave part of her belongings in Mainburg.

As arranged, Karl arrived on the 9th, during the morning. I explained to him about Astra's extra luggage. He told her to leave the box behind. She just looked at him, shrugged her shoulders, and walked away without replying. Later she whispered to me:

'I don't like him, he is common.'

Karl was pleased for me that I had also found my other sister. She, too, could get her release papers in Habach. He had organised a small pick-up truck to take us to the autobahn with all our luggage. Astra insisted that her box went in first, and then her cases. (I think she was afraid that I would leave the box behind). After that came Christel's case, my bag, and my bicycle. Although Astra supervised the loading, she did not help to carry anything, but went and sat in the truck next to the driver's seat. I made Christel sit next to her, she was only a small person, and Karl and I went into the back.

'I can see what you mean about your sister,' said Karl. 'She also made sure she got the best seat in the truck.'

Everything went as planned. We met the lorry at the autobahn, and arrived in Habach in the evening. Christel thought that my accommodation in the stable was fun. Astra didn't like it, but she had slept in a hay loft before. I pointed out that at least it was clean.

The next day, Christel went for her interview, and was promised her release papers. We now had to see how we could all get on to a transport to Hamburg. Karl had decided to come along, and Josef didn't want to part from his friend, so he would come too. The four of us were alright. We would get official permission. It was only Astra, with her cases, who had to be secretly put on to the transport lorry.

'I can bribe the German driver,' said Karl, 'but, on the long journeys, the transport is accompanied by an American sergeant. I think you had better find out what happened to Jo, and ask for his help, otherwise I cannot see how we can take your sister and her luggage with us.'

I found out that Jo was not on the transport run any more. He was stationed in Altenstadt by Schongau and, as it was quite a large American base, I was able to get a lift to the place. This time I left my bicycle behind and only took a bag with some food with me.

I found Jo, who was very pleased to see me. He had different duties now, but knew a number of sergeants who had been allocated as escorts for the different transports. There was no rota. As a rule, they got two days notice for a long journey, and often only one day's notice for a short one. Everybody promised to help me if they could, and said that I should look out for them in Habach.

Back at the camp Christel received her papers and was put on the list for transport to Hamburg. We were told that there would be a lorry in two days time to take us, where to assemble, and at what time. I had now to find out which American sergeant was escorting the German driver, and

Karl had to find the driver in order to bribe him. The sergeant was not one of the friends to whom Jo had introduced me, but he knew Jo. I asked him, in my broken English, whether he would also take Astra, explaining that we two sisters couldn't very well leave our third sister behind. He said that he would have a talk to Jo, and think about it. He also felt that the German driver would have to be told, to which I replied that I already had his agreement.

The next day, he said it would be alright, as long as Astra only had one suitcase, because the lorry was rather full. I did not reply to this, knowing very well that Astra wouldn't part with any of her luggage. Even so, I told her about the stipulation, and wondered again what she had in the box and the cases.

This time Astra didn't threaten that she wouldn't come with us if she couldn't bring her luggage. She just cried and, looking at Karl, she asked him pleadingly to help her. She had forgotten that she didn't like him! Karl said that he would find a way, and he did. Josef only had a small bag, so suddenly the box belonged to him and, as Karl only had one small dilapidated suitcase, he decided to adopt one of Astra's cases. My sister had got her way and soon smiled again.

We arrived in Hamburg in the afternoon. The driver stopped the lorry near the centre of the town, and unloaded everybody and everything in front of a bombed-out church. From now on we had to make our own arrangements. Our fellow travellers only had one suitcase, or a rucksack, and they were soon off, wishing us all the best. If it hadn't been for Astra, and her two big suitcases and the box, and my bike, we, too, could have made our way to the underground, which was close by.

Karl said that he would try and find some transport for us, and walked off. Josef walked towards the ruined church, to have a look, and Christel and I sat on the box. Astra had to sit on one of her cases. Nobody said anything, and we just sat there waiting.

Karl turned up at last in a small van with a driver.

'Sorry to be so late,' he said. And then he whispered to me: 'The driver wanted an awful lot of money. I had to do quite a bit of bargaining. It's a good job that I have got a bottle of brandy in my case.'

I explained to the driver where the radio station was. We got to Kisdorf without trouble, then up the hill, and I remembered how we came along there with Hitscher, our horse, pulling the car.

I got quite excited, the nearer we got to the radio station and the reunion with my parents. I felt that I had done rather well to achieve all this, and was a little proud of myself. My heart was thumping when we turned off the main road into the long drive up to the gate of the radio station. We stopped, and there was the bucket, our big bell. I banged it really hard, because I wanted both of my parents to come out. Astra and Christel had climbed out of the van, and so had Karl and Josef. Only the driver had remained behind the wheel, in anticipation of the gate being opened.

I saw my mother coming out of the hut and, seeing a number of people by the gate and the van, she called my father, then both of them came along the path towards the gate. I think my mother recognized me, or maybe Christel or Astra because, all of a sudden, she started to run towards the gate. She opened the small door and stared at us.

I felt the lump in my throat. I was happy to be back, and to have succeeded in bringing back my two sisters. My mother pushed me to the side and ran to the van, saying out of breath:

'Where is the boy, where is the boy?'

I stopped smiling. I felt as if somebody had hit me. All my mother was interested in was the boy, my brother Hans, whom I had not brought with me. Tears came into my eyes. I did not want anybody to see this, so I turned away. But somebody had noticed. My father put his arms around me and hugged and kissed me.

'You wonderful, wonderful brave girl', he whispered. 'You are back, you are back. I have worried such a lot about you.'

He then let go of me and hugged and kissed Christel and Astra. By now, my mother had realized that Hans was missing. She said:

'You did not find him then, did you?'

'No, Mama, but I brought Astra and Christel, and also two friends, who helped me to get here, Karl and Josef. I hope that they can stay here for a few days in one of the huts.'

'Of course they can,' said my father. 'Anybody who helped you is welcome here.'

Of course we all had a lot to tell. On top of that, we had to find somewhere for Karl and Josef to sleep. My mother only had one spare palliasse, which she allocated to Astra. I said that Christel could sleep with me, but there was no bedding for Karl and Josef. It was much too late to get anything in the village, so my two friends had to make do with the two blankets which they had brought with them.

Karl produced some tins of food from his case and my mother soon made something to eat for us all. It was very late when, at last, we got to sleep and, even then, we had not finished our stories.

The next day, Karl and Josef went off to explore the district, to get some ration cards and bedding. Astra and my mother suddenly seemed to have a secret. My father was informed, and then Christel and at dinner time the bombshell dropped. Karl and Josef had not returned, so we sat down to our meal - cabbage soup, with two potatoes - which we had to share. Suddenly my mother said:

'Astra is expecting a baby.'

I stared at them all. I realized that this was probably also the only reason why she had come with me to Hamburg. Why ever didn't she tell me about it, or even mention it to Christel? I could not understand my sister. And then I thought:

How is she going to cope with it? A baby on the radio station, with no comfort, no running water, no beds, no heating and, on top of that, nobody had any money.

I looked at my mother, then at my father, and then turned to Christel. They were all watching me. None of them looked very happy.

'I don't know why you are all looking at me,' I said. 'I am not having the baby. If Astra is happy about it, then congratulations. It won't be easy to have a baby here, but I am glad, Astra, that you have come here, so that Mama can help you. When is the baby due?'

'At the beginning of January,' said my mother.

'That was the reason why I didn't want to come with you,' said Astra. 'I wanted to wait for Otto. He doesn't know about it. I didn't know myself until he had been taken away or, at least, I wasn't sure.'

My father never said anything. It was most unusual for him to be so quiet. I think he was just shocked. We were so terribly poor, and now there was Astra and that new life growing in her, another responsibility, an extra little being to be added to the family. How were we all going to cope?

'We will have to go to Kaltenkirchen, and see a doctor', said my mother to Astra. 'You will also have to have extra rations and, particularly, good milk. There are some cows in the next field. Helga, you know how to milk, so you could go every night, and get a little milk for Astra.'

'But that is stealing,' I said.

'Call it what you like,' said my mother. 'We are desperate. We only want a little bit.'

After that my mother made sure Astra got good food. She pampered and spoilt her. I had hoped that my mother would not mention the cows in the next field again, but she did, and even had a talk to Karl. He thought it would be fun. So, one night, Karl and I climbed over the fence with a bucket.

A popular name for a cow in East Prussia was Liesschen, so I decided to whisper this name. One of them seemed to like my whisper and trotted slowly towards me. I stroked her neck, and whispered Liesschen. Gently I moved my hand down to her udder, and then started milking her. She stood quite still. I didn't take much milk, maybe half a litre, and was soon back at the fence, where Karl took the bucket, whilst I climbed over. After that, I went every night, getting half a litre of milk from Liesschen, until the herd was moved.

# CHAPTER EIGHT

## Surprise Arrivals - Second Trip South

Karl and Josef led their own lives. Both spent quite a bit of time in Hamburg, sometimes not even returning at night. Often Karl would come back on his own, and stay for a few days. He had supplied us with a number of extra ration cards, and I did the shopping, using the bike, in the surrounding villages. I think Karl dealt quite a lot in the black market. He always had plenty of money and food, and gradually brought a few things back, which he asked us to keep for him. The radio station was probably his secret address. Here he could hoard things, and hide them. We never went into his room which was in one of the other huts. He shared it with Josef and, when he went to Hamburg, he would close the shutters on the window. I did look through the window once or twice when he was there, and saw that he had quite a number of boxes. He was a proper wheeler dealer, and enjoyed what he was doing. My parents didn't object, because they benefited from it.

Our first big surprise arrived on the 24th of August, only six days after we returned from Habach. It was my brother Hans who banged the bucket bell. I had gone shopping and when I returned, I found my brother sitting outside the hut on the bench with my mother next to him holding his hands.

'Mama nearly fainted when she saw Hans,' said Christel. 'She kept on touching and feeling him, as if he was a ghost, and I think that she thought that he might disappear again, because she kept on holding his hand. She can't believe that he isn't hurt.'

'Hans has found us all on his own,' said my mother. 'He has been to the Red Cross in Hamburg, who gave him our address.'

Hans embraced me. We always had been good friends and, being his elder sister, he had often come to me for help or advice.

We had no lunch that day, because we were all listening to Hans's story. He had been evacuated with his school from Königsberg into the country in October 1944. They did not stay in one place, but were moved around. Eventually they occupied a village school near Braunsberg. At first, we received letters from Hans, particularly my mother but by the end of November the letters stopped.

'In the second week of December, a notice was put up, asking for volunteers for the army,' said Hans. 'Most of us were sixteen years old, some fifteen. A few volunteers were collected in a van. We never saw them again.

Mr Fieber, our form master, was an old man. He had been an officer in the First World War, and had been shot in the chest. He only had one lung left, and was, therefore, never called up. Times had become very desperate, and suddenly he, too, was asked to do war duty. Our class had shrunk to sixteen boys, when Mr Fieber was informed that he and the boys in his charge had to report for training at the Flak Unit in Braunsberg. Mr Fieber didn't say very much; he just told us to pack our things and be ready in the morning, when we would be collected. I went to see Mr Fieber and explained about my being Swiss and not wanting to join the German army. He told me that I had a choice, either I kept my mouth shut and came with him, or take my bag and try and get back to Königsberg, where the Russians would soon arrive. I decided to stick with Mr Fieber and my school friends.

In Braunsberg, we had two days training, and then were put on anti-aircraft guns. We had no uniforms. Most times we didn't even know what we had to do on the guns. Even Mr Fieber was unsure, not having had any training in this type of unit before. He got his old rank of lieutenant back and, with that, also power over his subordinates. He discovered a store room full of winter uniforms. He ordered the sergeant in charge of the store to fit us all out with clothes. This was an excellent idea, and good foresight; it probably saved our lives later.

We all received not only the ordinary uniform, but also fur lined boots, fur jackets with hoods, gloves, rucksacks and emergency rations, including First Aid Kits. Lieutenant Fieber discovered bikes in another store room, and everybody was allocated a bike. At the time we thought it rather stupid to have a bike, as we were not living far from our anti-aircraft gun, but Lieutenant Fieber had planned ahead.

We didn't have a bad Christmas. Lieutenant Fieber had organised some extra food, but we all felt a bit pessimistic on New Year's Day, and wondered what the next year would bring.

Our gun went wrong in the first week of January. Nobody knew how to repair it, and I had the feeling that Lieutenant Fieber didn't want it to be repaired either. He had always mumbled under his breath that he didn't like children to fight. So now we had nothing to do, except to keep ourselves warm. Food started to get short. At one time, we had one tin of corned beef each, now, two boys had to share one.

Headquarters ordered us to join a fighting unit, and Lieutenant Fieber got out the maps to see where we had to march to. I could see he didn't like it. The news on the radio, and the messages which we got were always good, but soldiers started to arrive in the town telling a different tale. It was bitterly cold, and there seemed to be unending snowfalls. Refugees had poured through Braunsberg for weeks, and now, suddenly, there was talk that one could only get away across the frozen Haff and on to the Nehrung, as Russian tanks would be with us any day. The stream of refugees suddenly stopped. The Russians must have broken through somewhere. The only way left, was over the Haff. Lieutenant Fieber just told us one day to be ready by the next morning. We were ordered to put on all our warm clothes. We were each allowed a rucksack and two blankets on the carriers of our bicycles, and a satchel attached to the handlebars. We were supplied with tins of food and a loaf of bread, and had to make sure that we had our First Aid Kits and our Iron Rations. Most of our private belongings had to be left behind. Lieutenant Fieber was very strict about this, and anybody trying to take more had his things taken away.

We assembled, and then marched off. We had no idea where to, because we had not been told whether it was to the new unit, or to the Haff. We soon realized that Lieutenant Fieber had decided to take us across the frozen waters to the Nehrung. We joined a column of refugees, but we passed them, as we were walking faster.

There is no point in going into too many details, if Helga crossed the Haff in the same way, she knows all about it and has probably told you what it was like. I must say, we were glad of our warm clothes, and of our bicycles. We couldn't ride them, but at least they carried our luggage.

We marched along the Nehrung, and then along the coast, finishing up in Danzig. By now, Lieutenant Fieber was very ill. He had been very good, the way he kept us together and looked after us, but the cold played havoc with his lung.

In Danzig, Lieutenant Fieber was able to get medical help and after that he seemed better. Of course, we realized that he had disobeyed orders when he took us across the Haff. He never discussed anything with us, just gave the orders, and expected us to do what we were told. He only made one concession, from now on, somebody always had to accompany him wherever he went. I think that he realized that he was a very sick man, and might collapse somewhere and then not be able to return to us.

Some of the boys said it might be better to split up, as it would be difficult to find a place for all of us on a ship. Lieutenant Fieber said that everybody was free to go if they wanted to. Three of the boys disappeared and we never saw them again. We got bored, hanging around with nothing to do, and also not being allowed to go off in case Lieutenant Fieber returned from one of his trips to the authorities, where he hoped to get a place on a ship for us.

And then one day Lieutenant Fieber's escort returned very excited. We had a place on a ship and had to be ready in half an hour. The ship was a *Lazarettschiff* (hospital ship), full of stretcher cases and wounded, and we were allocated as helpers. We quickly got our things together. Not all the boys were there, only ten of us, so we left a note.

The ship was guarded by soldiers with guns, keeping the refugees at bay. Only stretcher cases and wounded were allowed on board, and our small column of ten boys. We piled our luggage into a corner on the ship, and got on with carrying the stretcher cases on board. I thought my arms would drop from carrying so many people, some of them quite heavy. No wonder they permitted us to go with the transport. The loading was done in haste, not walking, but running up and down the plank to the ship, and then it was full up, and we were off.

I don't know what happened to all the boys, I like to think that they were all on the ship, but it was so crowded, that we could not walk about and try and find one another. We couldn't even find our luggage at first. I was in a group of four, and we decided we would not part.

The passage was rough, cold, and frightening at times. There was no hot drink anywhere, and even the wounded were short of food.

On the third day out from the harbour we heard that a number of wounded had died, and that they would be buried at sea. This was a terrible day. They lined the dead up at the side of the ship. The parson said a short prayer, two sailors rested the first body on to a board, covered it with the Swastika flag, lifted it up, and slid the dead man overboard, whilst a third sailor held on to the flag. They only had one flag, so it had to be used again for the next body, and the next body. The dead were not even rolled into a blanket, they were clothed, that was all. There were no spare blankets.'

Hans suddenly got up from the bench. My mother tried to hold on to him, but he pulled his arm away.

'Lieutenant Fieber was also buried there. I don't like to talk about it.' He walked off.

My mother wanted to follow him, but I stopped her.

'Leave him alone,' I said. 'He is not a child any more. He has become a man, don't pamper him, he doesn't want that.'

My mother looked at me crossly, but my father added:

'She is right. Leave him alone, he will tell you the rest later.'

Hans never talked about the boat journey again, but we gradually heard the rest of his story. Sometimes I felt he had left things out because, like me, he couldn't talk about them yet, and maybe never.

His ship arrived in Swinemünde, and everybody poured off the vessel. There was some kind of organisation in the harbour. There was a Red Cross station, a soup kitchen, and a makeshift hospital. Again, the boys helped with the stretcher cases. They met some of the other boys, but Hans didn't know how many had come in the ship.

With their leader now gone, there was no unity any more and they split up. Hans stuck with his small group, and the four of them helped each other. They never had had guns, they were very young, but they were in uniform, and it was therefore assumed that they were soldiers. The refugees stared at them and felt that the four boys should not join them, and the army units didn't know what to do with them as they were not trained and also not equipped for any fighting.

Hans decided to make his way south to Astra's address. The other three came with him for part of the way. Their main aim was to reach either the British or the American forces, because then they would be safe. As long as they were in the unconquered part of the country, they didn't know which enemy force would reach it first.

The boys mostly drifted amongst the civilian refugees. It was the end of March now and not so cold any more, but food was short, and farmers not always willing to let them sleep in their barns. Eventually they came to Braunschweig. Near the town, they surrendered to the British forces, and were put into a P.O.W. camp, with a lot of other soldiers and officers.

'We had a good time in prison,' said Hans. 'We were looked after. We had accommodation in wooden huts, which we had to help to build, and we had regular food. We were interviewed, and all four of us decided to stick to the truth. We said that we had been schoolboys, and suddenly had trained for two days in the use of the Flak. We had never done any fighting, and really should not be imprisoned. Because we were in uniform, our story was only half believed. I think that they realized that we were very young, but they also knew that some of the young Hitler Youth groups had fought fiercely and loyally for Hitler.

The war finished, but we were not released. On the contrary, more prisoners arrived, and the camp was pretty full. We played football, we played cards, we scrubbed floors and tables and latrines. We cleaned windows, we swept the camp, we ate, we slept, and we were bored. A lot of soldiers wanted to go home.

One day, two boys disappeared. Nobody seemed to worry. The guards shrugged their shoulders. They always had felt sorry for us. Everybody knew that they had gone home.

I had made friends with a boy, Martin, who came from Hamburg. He was a year younger than I and, like us, had been taken to the Flak, through his Hitler Youth association. His father was a *Reeder* (ship owner) in Hamburg, and quite well off, so Martin told me. He wanted to go home. He thought his parents would still be somewhere in Hamburg. He did not have the courage to escape on his own. He wanted me to accompany him and guaranteed me a home with his parents.

We made our plan on how to get out. There was a fence around the camp, but it was easy to dig a hole and squeeze under it. Actually, that's how the other two boys had done it. We could not do it during the day in case we were seen, so we started to dig at night. We had no spade or shovel, only pieces of wood. We scraped the earth away for a few nights, returning it loosely again, before going back to our hut. In the end, there was just a loose heap of earth there, which wouldn't take long to scrape away when we had decided to leave.

One night, we just pushed the loose earth away, then lifted the fence a little, and Martin slipped through. I pushed our bags through and then crawled under the fence to the other side. We made quite a noise with the scraping of the earth, and the fence squeaked a little, but we never heard or saw a guard near our part of the fence. And then we just walked off, away from the camp.

The first two nights we avoided villages and people, sleeping rough in the fields, because Martin was afraid somebody might look for us but, after that, we asked farmers whether we could sleep in their barns. We reached Hamburg in a week. Martin found his parents; part of their house was still standing. His parents were overjoyed to see him, as they had already lost a daughter in a bombing attack just before the end of the war. They made me very welcome. They gave me civilian clothes and assured me that I could stay with them as long as I liked.

I knew, Mama, that you had an aunt in Hamburg, but I didn't know her name, or her address, because you only called her Auntie Dora, so I couldn't contact her. Then, one day, Martin's mother told me about the Red Cross, who had started a Missing Persons File, and I went there to register. The woman in charge was very nice. She said that they had quite a lot of missing persons cards beginning with "Z" and, if I liked, I could put my card into the right alphabetical spot myself, which would be a great help for her because she was very busy. And then, Mama, going through "Z", and then "i", and then "r", I came to the card which you had all filled out with the name "Zirkel", and the address as the radio station in Kisdorf. I couldn't believe it when I saw it. I had always thought that everybody would make their way south, to Astra, and here it was in black and white, that you were not far from Hamburg. And that's how I found you, and now I am here. If you have no room for me, I can always go back to Martin and his family.'

Of course there was room for Hans. We still had a spare room between the kitchen and the room in the back, where Christel and I slept. Hans stayed with us for a few days, then my mother decided that he really ought to go back to school. He was only seventeen, and it had always been planned that he would do his matriculation and go to university, to study engineering.

My mother and Hans went to Hamburg to see Auntie Dora and her husband. This time, my mother took some extra food with her, which Karl had provided. She stayed one night in Hamburg, and returned without Hans. She told us that her uncle, an ex policeman, was now a night watchman, and that Auntie Dora was quite willing to have Hans lodging with her during term time. I think that the extra rations which my mother took along, finally persuaded them to take Hans in. After that, my mother went to Hamburg a few times, taking extra food, also some bottled meat and vegetables, which Auntie Dora promised to keep for her in her cellar as it was cooler there.

Another big surprise was our second visitor, Hermann. I must admit that I had at times forgotten about him. I remembered Wolfgang and his sweet shyness, his fondness of me and his kindness. I even thought of Sam sometimes, but I always felt that was a happy dream for a few days, and I knew that I would never see him again.

Hermann had never struck me as a man with a lot of feelings. He was a scientist who, once he had worked out something, had to put his project into practice - nothing else mattered then. He was not important to me any more. It had been my mother who had pushed me towards him, in the belief that this was a man who could give me a secure future.

So, when Hermann rang our bucket bell at the radio station - it was the middle of September by now - I was shocked to see him. He thought I was stunned with happiness! Poor Hermann, he never realized what an excellent actress I was. He kissed me, and hugged me, and told me he was pleased to see me. He had got my address from his sister Lotti in Starnberg, whom he had gone to see. My mother, of course, was thrilled to see him. Here she was with three girls, one of them expecting a baby but with a lost husband, and there, suddenly, was an eligible bachelor, who genuinely seemed to be in love with me. At least one daughter would now have a decent husband. She kept on whispering to me:

'Be kind to him, don't spoil your chances.'

Hermann lived in Hannover now, and from having been a scientist with Wernher von Braun's team, worked in an accumulator factory in a menial job. He felt it would not be long before things would change. Of course, we all hoped that the different occupied zones would soon be given back to Germany. Once the Russians had left their zone, Hermann felt he could return to Greifswald to his parents and probably his old job as lecturer at the university. That was the moment we would get married. I was not asked, I was told that that was his plan.

Hermann stayed with us for three days. He slept in the room which we had allocated for Hans. We went for walks, we talked and all the time I felt like saying:

'Please, don't waste your time on me, find somebody else, and quickly, because I don't love you,' but I never said it, because my mother stopped me. She was the one who came to my room at night and told me to try and persuade Hermann to accept a contract for America with von Braun, and then follow him to that country and start a new life. Not only would there be a future for me, but probably a future for all of us because in time they all could come to this new, vast and modern country.

'Mama,' I said. 'I don't love him and, at times, I don't even like him. He is cold, he is selfish, he is calculating, and he looks different in civilian clothes. When I met him first, he was a dashing officer, with an open car. We had fun, we could show off, we enjoyed ourselves, but there was no depth in Hermann. It is finished now, it was already finished when I met his family in Greifswald. It is not fair to play with him. There are a lot of things that I don't like about him, but he is a decent, honest man and, if his principles do not permit him to go to America so that that country can benefit from his scientific knowledge, I respect him for it, and will not persuade him to change his mind. Tomorrow Hermann will go back to Hannover.'

'Promise me you will not finish with him yet', begged my mother.

I did not promise, but I did not finish with Hermann either. I walked with him to the other side of Kisdorf and promised to write as soon as the postal service was in operation. I kissed and hugged him, and I was glad when he walked away.


Life on the radio station gradually became boring. I wanted something else to do. The weather was quite good that summer, and I did a bit of gardening, tidying up the rose beds in front of our main hut. My main job was to go shopping to the different villages in the district, and gradually I got to know the places, and often also the short cuts across the fields, when I had to push my bike. This was sometimes quicker than cycling round the main road, and the bike took the weight of the shopping. We were very isolated so, wherever we went, we had to allow a lot of time.

For weeks I had gone to do my shopping from the same butcher in a neighbouring village. At first he was quite nice to me. I had the meat coupons, he had the meat and the sausages. As we were short of money, I always had to take the cheaper cuts of meat, and the cheaper sausages. The butcher did not like this after a time because, having such a large meat allowance, I sometimes cleaned him completely out of his cheaper cuts of meat and sausages. He started to ask questions about where I lived, where the camp was, or the group of people I was living with, because that's what I had told him at first. I didn't like to be questioned, I had difficulties in thinking up vague answers so, in the end, I didn't go there any more.

The new butcher I found lived further away. This was as well, but it took more time to travel there, particularly as I never cycled directly to a place, but always made a detour, in case somebody followed me, or saw me. The roads were not crowded. I met a farmer occasionally, with a horse and cart. There were very few cars about, and sometimes a jeep or lorry from the British occupation forces passed me. But there were a number of vagrants about. I called them that, because these were people without roots, and no interest in settling down anywhere. A number of them were like Karl and Josef, released from concentration camps, and young Poles, who spoke broken German, and didn't want to go home. They now felt that they were the masters. They were very outspoken, greedy, rude, and demanding.

Once or twice, whilst cycling along the road, I had met some of them. They shouted:

'Where are you going, pretty maiden? Give us a kiss!'

They tried to grab me, but I was a fast cyclist and soon pedalled away. As a rule I was not frightened of anything, but I was frightened of these people, if there were more than two of them. I mentioned it to my parents, and my mother said that I had to be careful, whilst my father looked at me thoughtfully.

'If you feel unsafe, don't go any more. Mama, I think we will have to manage with our own rations which we can get locally. Helga is right, I have seen these people about, and I don't trust them either. I am afraid our daughter might be molested one day, and neither of us would like that.'

'Helga knows how to look after herself,' said my mother. 'Somebody who can safely travel all alone to Mainburg and back is not going to be molested by some Poles walking along the road. In any case, we need the food, you too, Papa, are eating it. The rations for one person are very very small. We also have to think of Astra, who is expecting a baby.'

My father just looked at my mother, and then walked out. My mother kept on mentioning Astra's pregnancy. Astra was pampered and spoilt. She had to have the best food, she had to have the only sheets we had on her bed, she had to have two chairs in her room (we had none in ours), she had a rug in front of her bed and now my father had to chop wood every day, because the *Bürgermeister* had promised my mother an iron stove for Astra's room so that it could be heated when the winter came, and she would have a warm place for herself and her child.

My father gradually got fed up with Astra and, whenever her name was mentioned, particularly about the future baby, he didn't say anything, but just walked away. It had become quite obvious that he didn't agree with the way my mother protected Astra, and how we all were expected to do our share towards her comfort and well-being.

Astra did not contribute anything. She mostly kept to her room, or sat outside if the weather was fine. She had her walk every day and, to keep herself occupied, she had started to knit baby clothes. My mother had been able to get some wool in the village, and now Astra made some lovely little garments. She was good at it, and seemed to enjoy it.

My fears about the vagrants became reality. I only went to the butcher once a week, because I didn't like the journey. On this particular day, I was pushing my bike up a hill when I saw five men by the side of the road. As soon as I saw them, I got frightened, because I knew there would be trouble. I looked around. There was nobody else on the road. I had pushed my bike, because of the hill. It was not a very steep hill, but it was hard to ride my bike uphill with a shopping bag on the back.

The five men spread out across the road. It was much too late for me to try and cycle through them, so I just stopped. They came towards me. I realized by their broken German that they were Poles. One of them got hold of my bike and pulled it away. Before I knew what had happened, the others were on top of me.

A hand tore the front of my blouse, another pulled my head back, pulling my hair. Somebody tried to pull my skirt, but I had still got my arms free. I had not fought with boys for nothing in my younger days. My fists started to fly and I hit hard. I kicked two of them below the belt where it hurts, and somehow got free. The Pole who had taken my bike just stood there surprised. I knew I couldn't get the bike back, but I had to have my shopping bag with the food. I grabbed this quickly from the carrier. It pulled off easily, and I swung it round in a circle, hitting one or two of the Poles.

I was a strong and tough girl and being frightened gave me even more strength. I think the only one who didn't get hurt was the Pole who took my bike. I had no time to hit him. I had surprised them all with my fierce defence. I had hurt some of them, but I was also not waiting for anybody to come at me again. I ran off as fast as I could across the field, with my shopping bag. I did not look round, but I could hear them following me; I could hear their short, puffing breaths. It was hard going, because the field had been ploughed recently, and the earth was sticky, lumpy and wet.

After a while, there seemed to be only one left behind me. I, too, started to get out of breath. He was right behind me, when I jumped to the side like a hare, which he had not expected. He must have been on the point of throwing himself on to me, because he fell down. I took a big lump of wet earth and pressed it into his face. I looked back, and saw two of them coming towards me again, and then there was the Pole on the ground. The rest were still on the road. I did not wait, but ran off, because I could see a small wood on the other side of the field. This time I could not run so fast; I was still out of breath.

I reached the wood and, hiding behind a tree, I looked back. The two Poles were helping the third one to get up, cleaning his clothes, and helping him to clean his face.

I should have kicked him, I thought crossly. It was not enough only to push wet earth into his face.

I had tears in my eyes because I had lost my bike. I was glad nobody could see me crying. I looked again to see what the Poles were doing. The three of them started to walk back across the field towards the road and I made my way through the wood. I tried to tidy myself up, but there was nothing I could do about the torn blouse, and the skirt, too, had a tear in the front. The only way to hide it was to carry the shopping bag in front, pressing it against my tummy and breast. This is what I did when I came near houses, which I avoided as long as I could.

I knew the different short cuts to the radio station and also how to miss out villages, even if the journey took me longer. I was afraid to get to the road in case I met the Poles again. I knew that if they saw me I would get no mercy from them. I would not only be raped but also beaten up.

Only once did I have to cross the road. Before doing so, I crawled into the ditch, then eased my head up and looked along the road both ways, making sure nobody was there. I ran across the road, and carried on walking along the cornfield on the other side.

It was supper time when I reached the radio station. They were all sitting in the kitchen having something to eat, Mama, Papa, Astra and Christel, and even Karl was there. When I walked in, they all stared at me. I probably looked a sight, with my torn blouse and skirt, my legs and shoes full of earth, and the rest of me was probably dirty too, because I had crawled along the ditch, and lay in a field.

'Oh my God, my God, Helga, what happened to you?' called out my mother. My father jumped up, and put his arms around me, and hugged me quietly. I gently pushed him away, I was grateful for his kindness.

'I have been attacked by five Poles,' I said. 'I am sorry I have lost the bike, they took it away. I saved the shopping bag with the food, so Astra had better have one jolly good meal now because I will never again go so far to the butcher any more.'

With that, I laid the bag on to the table, and walked out.

The next thing that happened was that we suddenly had mice again. Not in Christel's and my bedroom, but in Astra's room. The first we heard of it was when Astra screamed. It was night time and we had all gone to bed, when there was suddenly a scream from Astra's bedroom. We all jumped out of bed and ran to her room. Christel was afraid, so she hid behind me. We found Astra huddled up at the bottom of her bed, looking very frightened and upset.

'There are mice in the room!' she kept on screaming.

My mother went to her straight away, trying to calm her down, telling her that in her condition it was wrong to get too excited, and that mice really were harmless, and more afraid of human beings than the other way round.

'Hans,' said my mother, 'you will have to do something about it. We had mice before in Helga's room, but we put poison under the skirting boards and they stopped coming.'

'I will see to it in the morning, my dear,' said my father sarcastically. 'We must not upset the expectant mother, must we?'

I looked at Christel. We both smiled a little, and then we disappeared back into our room.

My father still had some poison from before, and asked me to come and help him, as he wanted to pull everything away from the wall and push the poison under the skirting boards, where there was quite a space. We pulled the bed out and pushed the suitcases away from the wall. When my father pulled Astra's big box away, we saw two mice coming from underneath it and diving under the skirting boards. My father suddenly stopped what he was doing and said to Astra:

'What have you got in that box?'

'They are all my things, and nobody is going to touch them,' she replied.

'I still would like to see what you have got in your box. The mice seem to be rather interested in it.' He tried to open the lid. Astra practically threw herself at him, pushing him away, and shouting for my mother to come and help her.

My mother came running in, followed by Christel, who had heard the commotion. By now, Astra was sitting on the box, and my father was trying to lift her off it.

'Stop it!' called out my mother. 'Stop it, tell me what happened. Surely we can sort this out without fighting.'

'Papa wants to open my box. It is mine, I don't want anybody to touch it,' said Astra.

My father took a deep breath to calm himself, and then said very controlled, but firmly: 'We are going to have a look to see what is inside this box. Mice have come out of it and if there is a nest we will have to destroy it. Astra, you are going to sit on the bed with your mother. Christel, you can go and sit on Astra's chair, and Helga, you can help me. You can all be witnesses, to see that I will not steal anything from Astra.'

My mother took Astra to the bed, and sat down with her. She realized that this time Astra would have to obey. Christel and I also did what we were told. My father opened the lid of the box, which was not locked, and started to take out the things.

There were some of Astra's winter clothes on the top, and then my father took out some tablecloths, sheets and pillowcases. We stared at them. None of us slept in sheets. The only pair my mother had, taken from Hermann's flat in Greifswald, was given to Astra, because she was the expectant mother! Then came towels, blankets and cushions, a bit of china. But the biggest surprises were at the bottom of the box:

Chocolates, half eaten by mice, with the paper torn, sugar, flour and semolina, with maggots crawling in them. There was mouse dirt everywhere. The bags of food were half eaten away so when my father lifted them up they split and spilled on to the floor and the bottom of the box. There was even milk and egg powder, most of it mouldy or full of maggots.

I felt sick, I was so furious. There was all this food, and I had to go and steal milk, travel to the villages in the district to get extra food, and we had to go without even necessary things, whilst Astra had all this in her box all the time.

'You selfish, selfish, devil!' I shouted and, lifting my fists, I ran towards her. All I wanted to do was to hit her, to make her feel how unfair, how demanding, how egocentric she had been, and still was. My father stopped me.

'I know how you feel,' he said. 'We all feel like that, and we all would like to do what you want to do now, but you are not going to hit her. To me, it is no surprise, at least not the food part of it, because when Astra shouted 'mice', I knew there was food in the box. I didn't realize there was so much, and that it had gone bad.'

Turning to Astra, he said furiously: 'How long have you been hoarding that food?'

'Otto used to bring extra food home, so that I could start putting it by. I didn't know it had gone bad. We had enough food here, so I kept it in case I got hungry, or for the baby later.'

I looked at my mother, who had been holding my sister's hands. Now she let go of Astra, and moved a little away from her. Tears were running down her face and she whispered:

'How could you do this, Astra, how could you do this?'

Until Karl gave us some more plates and cups and cutlery, we had to share everything, not being able to eat at the same time, and there was all that china in Astra's box. But to have food go bad, that was a crime. We all knew what it was like to starve. Astra, I am sure, had never known hunger.

'You can clear up all this mess,' said my father.

'I hope the mice eat you in the night,' I said furiously.

My father took my hand: 'Let's go for a walk, and get some fresh and clean air into our lungs, after this sensation here.'

He did not say another word, but pulled me along until we got outside the radio station boundary; then he let go of my hand, and walked briskly along the road, with me following him. I think he had been afraid that I might harm Astra.

The walk did us good; we both felt better after a time. Just before we got back to the radio station, my father said: 'Always remember, she is your sister. Don't harm her, it is often better to be quiet, and to just walk away. She has always been so different from you all.'

When we returned, we didn't see Astra, she didn't leave her room for the rest of the day. My mother didn't mention the incident at all. When Christel and I went to bed, we found a towel and a pair of sheets under our blanket. I knew my mother had put them there. The next day, some of Karl's china and cutlery was packed away, and Astra's arrived in the kitchen. My sister joined us sulkily for meals again. She did not talk to anybody for days. A great silence prevailed over the *Funkstation*, with nobody mentioning Astra's box, or its contents.


We heard that trains had started to run, mostly goods trains, but there was an occasional passenger train going. Astra informed us one morning that she thought she would like to go back to Mainburg to ask about Otto, and also do something about her furniture. By now she was seven months pregnant and quite big.

We all stared at her. None of us believed for a moment that she meant it except maybe my mother. She looked a bit worried, whilst my father laughed loudly and walked out. He thought it was a great joke. But Astra was not joking. She packed a bag, asked my mother for some food and her ration book, also for some money, and set off, walking towards Kisdorf. My father told my mother to let her go, he was sure she wouldn't go far, but come back.

'I don't know what she is up to this time,' he said, 'but you will see, when she gets tired, she will come back.'

Unfortunately, my mother was not waiting for that. She went after Astra and, after a little while, they both came back. From now on, Astra kept on talking about Otto, and that one ought to find out what had happened to him.

Karl suddenly arrived, he had a bag full of tinned food, and quite a lot of cigarettes. Josef had left some time ago, and Karl said he had lost contact with him. Karl listened to Astra's moaning about Otto and her furniture and, when we were alone, he said:

'Shall we both travel south, and see what we can find out? I wouldn't mind disappearing for a bit. I have to keep away from Hamburg for a time. There are some trains. Usually the passenger trains are packed full of people, but one can get on to the goods trains.

'Are you in trouble?' I asked.

'Not yet, but I will be soon. The *Funkstation* has always been my little haven. Nobody knows about it, only Josef, and he won't tell.'

'I will think about it,' I replied.

I liked the idea of going to Mainburg with Karl. At least it would not be so boring and, maybe, we could find out something about Otto. I informed the family that Karl and I had decided to go south together.

'I thought I could also call and see Hermann in Hannover,' I told my mother. She was very pleased about this, thinking that at last I had relented and would marry Hermann. Astra was very pleased. She said that, if there was no news about Otto, I should sell her furniture. My father was concerned, but felt that if Karl was with me I would be alright. Only Christel was disappointed.

'I will miss you,' she said. 'I don't like sleeping alone, and also I am worried about you, that you might not come back.'

I promised her that I would return, whatever happened.

Karl and I started off at the beginning of November. It had already begun to get cold, and we had to dress warmly. Karl still wore his leather jacket with the big pockets, and his leather cap. He had a small suitcase for his belongings, whilst I had a rucksack, and I also took a rug with me, tied to my back pack. This time, we travelled light, thinking also that it would not be long before we would return.

At the main station in Hamburg, where we hoped to get a train, we discovered that this was quite a nightmare. People queued up at the ticket offices, not for hours, but for days, often sleeping in the queue. Even if you did buy a ticket, this didn't mean you could get on to the train. The platforms were packed with people and luggage. They stood there, like sardines in a tin. As soon as a train came in, and the doors opened, people pushed, shoved, and even hit one another to get in. There were several guards on duty, but they were powerless against this mass of people.

Karl and I mixed with the waiting people for the rest of the day. In the evening, Karl deposited me with my rucksack and his case in a corner of the big station, and went off. It was pretty late when he returned and sat down next to me. The station was full of people, sitting, or lying on the floor, waiting for transport.

'We will never get a ticket,' he whispered. 'And, even if we do get one we might have to try for days to get on to a train. I have found out that there are goods trains, some full, some empty, but they run more frequently than passenger trains. One can jump on to them at certain places, where they are going slowly.'

He produced some bread and two small hard sausages from under his jacket. 'Have something to eat. There is probably a train at 4 o'clock in the morning, so let's have a little sleep before that.'

I ate my bread, chewed the sausage, and nodded off to sleep. From time to time I woke up and looked at my watch. Karl seemed to do the same. At 3.30 am, we got up quietly and, climbing over stretched-out people, and luggage, made our way to the toilets.

Karl knew exactly where to go, through the station, around the building, to the goods yard, and then he followed the railway line to a small hut. Here, several railway lines branched off, and Karl chose one to follow. He seemed to know which one.

'I bribed the guard,' he said. 'He told me which is the line to Hannover. He also said there was a train at 4 o'clock, if there is enough coal. We will have to wait by the next points, because that's where the driver will slow down.'

We heard the sh, sh, sh, of the train and the wheels clanking over the points before we saw it. There were only two lights on at the front of the engine, the rest of the train was in darkness. The train slowed down, going gently over the big points near us. As soon as the engine had passed us, we jumped up. I could recognize the shape of the wagons. They seemed to be closed. Then came some piled high with coal and after that some open ones, which looked empty, but were too high for us to jump on to.

'We will have to get in from the back of the wagon, where the buffers are. Come on, come on!' shouted Karl.

He threw his case and my rucksack into one of them, and then jumped on to the buffer and pulled himself up on the wall of the wagon, over it, and disappeared inside. The train was travelling quite slowly and I ran next to it. When I saw that Karl was successful, I, too, jumped on to the buffer, holding on to the sides of the wagon, and Karl helped me over the top. The sides of the wagon reached up to our shoulders, and it was dirty inside but, crouching down, we were sheltered from the wind. Two more people had made it, and the four of us settled down for the journey, hoping nobody would evict us.

The wagons rolled fast, they rolled slow, they stopped, they started again and, from time to time, we went through a station, but didn't know where we were, because we didn't know the places. Often we seemed to be on a side line. Being a goods train, there was no need to go through a station. Although it was not such a long journey to Hannover, it was afternoon before we got there, because of the holdups along the way. We were shunted into a siding, and quickly climbed out and hid amongst the other wagons.

I found a toilet in the station, where I could wash my face and hands. My clothes were only dusty, which I could brush off. I decided it was not too late to go and visit Hermann. It was only going to be a short visit, and I would meet Karl again later in the evening at an arranged spot.

Karl said: 'I will pretend not to know you if Hermann comes with you to the station. There is a train early in the morning to Hildesheim and Kassel, but there is also one at midnight, so I will leave it to you to tell him which one you are taking. In the meantime, whilst I wait for you, I will find out whether we can get tickets.'

I enquired where the road was where Hermann lived, and was pleased to be told that a tram went near there. I still had to walk ten minutes from the tram stop. Hermann had told me that he was lodging with a widow with two children so, when I rang the bell, and a young pretty woman opened the door, I was surprised when she said she was Mrs Senner. I had always thought of widows as old but, of course, the war had widowed many young women.

I told Mrs Senner who I was, and that I had come to see Hermann. She smiled straight away, and asked me to come in. She knew all about me, as Hermann had told her about his visit to the radio station. She said that Hermann was still at work, but wouldn't be long, and she asked me whether I would like some supper with him, as she always cooked him his evening meal. I said that I did not like to take her rations, but she said she had enough, and she would like me to have a meal with Hermann. She made me wait in the living room, which was furnished quite elegantly, whilst she got on with the meal.

There were some pictures on a side table, one a photograph of a very good looking young officer, presumably her dead husband, one of two young children, a boy and a girl, probably six and eight years old, and one of an elderly couple, the woman looking a bit like Mrs Senner.

Maybe her parents, I thought.

There was also a small pile of photographs laying on the table. The top one was a picture of the two children under a tree in a wood. They looked very happy and, without thinking, I picked up the pictures, and looked through them. I suddenly realized Mrs Senner must have had these pictures only recently developed, and they were an eye opener to me. There were pictures of Hermann in the wood with the children, laughing, hidden half behind a tree, pictures of Mrs Senner and the children, and one very happy picture of Mrs Senner and Hermann looking laughingly and happily into one another's eyes.

Suddenly I felt fine. I had been a little apprehensive, not knowing what to say to Hermann but, seeing these pictures, which I quietly put back again, I realised that this woman could probably give Hermann the happiness which he was looking for.

I waited about half an hour, then I heard the bell ring, then voices. Hermann came in alone, he looked a little embarrassed, but he smiled, said how pleased he was to see me, kissed me, made me sit down, and told me that Mrs Senner would bring in some supper for us in a minute. He seemed to talk more than usual, asking questions, but not waiting for the answers, changing the subjects, and then coming back to them. Hermann was nervous, I had never seen him like that. Gradually he calmed down, and I was able to tell him that I was on a trip to Mainburg for my sister Astra, who wanted me to see whether I could get any information about Otto.

I think Hermann was relieved when I said that I had to catch a train at midnight. Mrs Senner served a very nice meal. She was charming to me. When she heard that I had to catch a late train, she reminded Hermann that the last tram to the station went at 10.30 pm.

Time went very quickly, and I had to leave to catch the last tram. I thanked Mrs Senner for the meal, she asked me to come again, and said that if I didn't mind sleeping on the settee in the living room, I could even stay the night. I could see that she didn't want me to think that she was stealing Hermann from me. I never thought she was, things had just developed in that way and, as it happened, I didn't mind. Neither Mrs Senner nor Hermann knew my thoughts, or that I had seen the pictures. Hermann accompanied me to the tram, but told me that he could not come to the station, because there was no tram back for him, which meant a half hour walk, which he could not do, as he had to go to work in the morning.

He was certainly not in love with me!

The tram came and, in all the hurry, I forgot to kiss Hermann, so I blew him some kisses, and smiled and waved from the moving tram.

I found Karl at the station, who proudly informed me that he had got railway tickets for us both to Kassel on the train at midnight. When I wanted to know how he got them, he said he stole them. This was usually his reply when he didn't want to tell me how he had done something, and I had learnt not to question him any further, when he replied like that.

Again the platform was packed with people, not quite as many as in Hamburg probably but, even so, most of them wouldn't get on to the train. This time Karl had a plan of how to get into the train.

When the train arrived, it was already occupied. The doors opened and some people got out. Karl pushed through like an arrow, leaving his suitcase with me. He got into the train, squeezed into the first compartment he could reach and opened the window. I gave him his suitcase and my rucksack, then he helped me to climb through the window into the train. I could have never got through the door. Karl was only successful because he had no luggage.

This was a very good plan, which we used after that again and again. Karl and I also realized that no ticket collector could squeeze through the train so many times we didn't even have a ticket.

From Kassel, we travelled through Fulda to Schweinfurt, and then Nürnberg. Here we had to have a goods train again. This time we didn't even have to jump on to it, as it was an empty train, starting from Nürnberg, and going to Ingolstadt. From there, we hitchhiked to Mainburg, getting a lift on a lorry.

There was a small hotel in Mainburg, and Karl was able to get two single rooms, with the help of some cigarettes. Things had changed very little in the town. Most of the Americans had moved out, leaving behind a small unit, with an office in the *Rathaus*. The *Bürgermeister* was now in charge again.

The poor man was quite shocked when he saw me. He recognised me at once, and wanted to know where my sister was. I told him that Astra was near Hamburg, with my parents. He seemed relieved. Then I told him why I had come. He had no news for me regarding Otto, but agreed that it might be a good idea to approach the Americans.

I went to the official office in the *Rathaus*, and met the captain on duty. I told him my story. He spoke quite a bit of German, and he said he had heard about the disappearance of the men. He didn't think that anything had happened to them locally, because somebody would have seen or heard something, and would have talked about it by now. He, too, felt the men were dead, otherwise they would have returned. Only high Nazis were kept as prisoners, and the Russians had not released all their prisoners either. Otto was not a Nazi, neither was he a soldier. The captain said that after a certain time Otto could be declared dead. My sister would then officially be a widow, and would probably be entitled to a German or Austrian widow's pension. I could get no more news about Otto.

After that, I went to see Astra's old landlady. She was willing to buy Astra's furniture, and I took what she offered me for it, already knowing that Astra would not be satisfied.

Karl and I stayed four days in Mainburg, and left again on a lorry on our way to Ingolstadt. I felt that it had been an absolute waste of time and money to come again to this town. Everything I had done could have been achieved by writing a few letters.

I imagined Astra, as pregnant as she was, jumping on to goods trains, climbing through train windows, sleeping on railway stations, and using dirty toilets, and I had a little laugh.

We went back the same way as we had come, as far as Fulda. First we got a train to Nürnberg, then Schweinfurt, and then Fulda. There we got stuck. It was the first time that our plan didn't work.

When the train to Kassel came into Fulda station, Karl again pushed his way through and opened the carriage window. I handed his suitcase in, and the rucksack but, when he tried to help me climb inside, somebody threw the case and rucksack back on to the platform. I pushed through the people to retrieve the luggage. This was very difficult and, by the time I got hold of it and pushed back again towards the carriage window the train started to move. I couldn't see Karl, so I just stood there and stared and the train rolled away. The people started to move off the platform, so I sat down on to Karl's suitcase. We had never talked about what would happen if we got separated; we had always stuck together, shared our food and our money, and assumed that it would carry on like that, at least until we returned to the radio station. I wondered whether Karl would return on the next train but, when I looked up, I suddenly saw him walking towards me. He looked a bit untidy, with his cap pushed to the side, and I noticed he had a swollen eye.

'I had a fight,' he said, not looking at me. 'The other one looks worse than me. I had a job to get out of the train. Let's see whether we can get another one.' He took his suitcase and walked off. I picked up my rucksack, and followed him.

We got on to a train to Kassel the next morning but from there we took a slightly different route, taking a train to Braunschweig rather than to Hannover as it came into the station first. In Braunschweig, we were told that we had to catch a train to Hannover, in order to get to Hamburg; the other line was through Celle and Munster, but there were only a few trains going on this less popular line. Somehow, Karl and I didn't like the idea of going through Hannover again so, when Karl heard about a goods train going to Celle, we decided to go for that one.

The goods train consisted of a number of closed wagons, we used to call them *Viehwagen* (cattle trucks). The doors were open, and we were allowed to climb in, and shut the doors when the train started. In Celle, Karl thought it might be a good idea to get some transport by road, so we walked into the town. Unfortunately, I had an accident there.

I still don't know how it happened. Karl and I were walking along in the town, wanting to get to the other side of it, where the main road to the north was. Suddenly Karl saw a tram and ran after it, shouting to me to follow him. We had always been very good at jumping on and off moving things and, having my rucksack on my back, I was usually quite quick and mobile. This time, I was not alert enough. Karl was already on the tram, which was moving slowly, and I was still on the pavement. Without looking, I jumped into the road to get on to the tram. I twisted my ankle and fell. At the same time, I heard a screech of brakes and something hit me on my head. Everything went black, and I shut my eyes.

The first thing I remembered was shouting - voices - they spoke German and they spoke English, and I heard the word "hurt" and "hospital" in English. I felt very tired, so I just kept my eyes closed.

I have had an accident, I thought. But, never mind, they seem to be able to cope with it, I am too tired, in any case, to get up and walk away.

I also realized that my right foot and my head hurt.

I was lifted very gently and carried by two people. Two soldiers from the British Occupation forces, one a sergeant, the other a corporal, were carrying me to a jeep and they laid me on to the back seat. They saw that I had opened my eyes, so one of them said in broken German that I should not worry, but I was hurt, and they would take me to the hospital.

Soon I was installed in a clean bed, dressed in a hospital nightgown, with my leg bandaged and raised, and lying flat, without a pillow, because of the so-called concussion. I must have hit my head when I fell, but I didn't think I was all that bad. I had the feeling that all this only happened because the British jeep had brought me, thinking it was their fault.

I wondered what had happened to Karl, and whether he would be able to find out what had happened to me, and where I was. Late in the afternoon, a man arrived from the *Verkehrsamt* (transport office), and wanted to know whether I intended to put in a claim to the British Authorities, as they were responsible for my accident. When I said 'no', he tried to persuade me. I just said 'no' again. I did not explain that I felt that they were not to blame.

Two things happened the next day. Firstly, I received a parcel in the morning, which a nurse brought in, smiling all over her face. When I opened it, I found some chocolates and cigarettes in it, the highest paid commodities on the black market, and a note in bad German. It was from the sergeant and the corporal who were involved in the accident. They hoped I would get better soon, and thanked me for not putting in a claim.

The second thing was that Karl visited me. He had tried to spruce himself up. He looked freshly shaved, his trousers seemed to have had a brush down, but his old leather jacket with the shiny marks still looked dirty. He appeared a very run-down figure in the tidy and clean hospital, and he knew it, which made him shy and uncomfortable. He didn't know what to say, and just stood there, twisting his cap, and looking down on to his worn-out shoes. Karl was alright in a crowd, amongst the refugees, when jumping on and off trains, outside in the street, where most people walked about like that, because they had lost everything through the war, and were poor, but here, in the hospital, he stuck out, being so different, and everybody stared at him.

I told him what had happened. He said he knew, he saw it, because he jumped off the tram, but he didn't interfere because he felt that it was a good idea to get me into hospital. He wanted to know how long I would have to be in bed. I said a few days, and he said he would wait and come again, but, if not, he might even return to the *Funkstation*.

I said that that would be a good idea, because I wanted my family to know what had happened. We talked a little more, he didn't stay long, and when he left, he said it would maybe be better if he returned to the radio station, as I might have to stay longer in the hospital than I thought, and he didn't like to hang around. - He left, and didn't come again.

After a week I was allowed to get up and after another week I was allowed to leave. I was able to get a train from Celle to Munster, and then Hamburg, but it took me two days and by the time I started walking from the underground station to make my way to Kisdorf, my ankle was quite painful and swollen again. Usually I would not have taken a lift from a farmer, because their horses and carts moved too slowly for my liking, but this time I did because I wanted to rest my leg. The weather was cold, it had even started to snow, but the snow did not lie on the road for long, only on the fields, and the trees in the forest.

It is nearly Christmas, I thought, only another week. I had been away over a month, with two weeks in hospital.


When I arrived at the *Funkstation*, I was wet from the snow and the slush on the road, and my foot hurt. They were all there, Mama, Papa, Christel, Astra, and even Hans, but not Karl. They all stared at me. Then Christel jumped up, and threw her arms around my neck:

'You are back, you are back!' she cried. 'We thought you would never come. What happened? Are you alright?'

'Didn't Karl come and tell you what happened?'

'No, we have had no news from you or Karl since you both left in November', said my father.

He, too, got up and hugged me. They all did in the end, even Astra, who was very big with the baby now.

I sat in front of the warm stove, with my bad leg in Christel's lap.

I had a hot drink, and started to get warm and dry. I told my story, starting at the beginning, when we travelled on the goods train.

I described some of the good, bad and dangerous happenings, and once or twice said to Astra:

'However you could have thought of doing this journey, is unbelievable'.

Everybody was glad I was home. Nobody had heard anything from Karl, which was very surprising. Christel and I talked about him later on when we were alone, and we both felt that he probably had got caught by the authorities, as he was deeply involved in the black market underground organisations. He had wanted to disappear from Hamburg for a while so maybe when he returned, he got caught.

I gave Astra the money for the furniture and, as expected, she thought it was not enough. She took the money, and we never saw any of it again. She expected to live free, because she was with her parents. She disappeared into her room after that, and Christel said that she did this most of the time.

Suddenly there was a shout from Astra: *'Eimer'* (bucket). A door had opened and shut. I looked questioningly at everybody. Hans and Christel looked a little uncomfortably at me. My father didn't stir. My mother, who looked worn out and very frail, got up, took a cardigan from behind the door, put it on, and left the kitchen. After that, I heard the front door opening and shutting and footsteps outside. I could not see through the window, because the shutters were closed to keep the warmth in and, in any case, it was getting dark earlier now, at the end of the year.

'Mama is emptying the bucket for Astra,' said Christel. 'It is too cold for her now to go outside to the toilet. Every time she uses the bucket, she puts a cloth over it and puts it on to the landing, and calls out *Eimer*. Mama has arranged this. She is the only one who empties it. Astra has a stove in her room, and spends nearly all day in it to keep warm.'

I looked at my father. He just stared at me, and I could hear what he said to me when we went for the walk after we had opened Astra's box: 'It is often better to be quiet, and just walk away.' I looked at Hans, who said quickly:

'Mama said it is not my job, and she won't let Christel do it, because she has just had a cold.'

This life is gradually going to kill my mother, I thought. It has already destroyed the unity of our family.

Mama informed us that we were short of food. The spare ration cards from Karl were used up, and now she had to feed two more people, Hans and me. Hans had brought his card with him, but some of the things which we got allocated monthly had been taken by Auntie Dora. It had been better whilst I was away, because I had not taken my card and, therefore, there was a little extra food. Christmas was coming and, as my mother had taken food to Hamburg to store in Auntie Dora's cellar, she intended to go with Christel for a day to Hamburg and collect some of it.

The night before she left, she asked me whether I would empty the bucket for Astra if it was necessary, and fill her stove up with coal, so that it wouldn't go out. I felt very sorry for my mother and hugged her. She had a lot of courage and she kept on persevering, but I also felt that she did a number of things wrong. I couldn't discuss it with her, she only got upset, so I, too, kept quiet, but I helped her.

The next day, the hut seemed empty without Mama and Christel, and I was glad when they returned in the evening, rather later than expected. Mama looked awful and went straight into her bedroom. Papa followed her, and I could hear my mother crying. I took Christel into the kitchen, the only warm place, and asked her to tell me what had happened.

'Auntie Dora was very surprised when we turned up,' said Christel. 'With Hans having returned for the Christmas holiday to us here, she didn't expect anybody to come until the New Year. Uncle and Auntie seemed very nervous. Auntie Dora said that Uncle had to go out to buy something, and she wanted to give him some money. She took Uncle into the bedroom and we heard them arguing. After that, Uncle went out and Auntie Dora wanted to know about Astra, about Papa, about the radio station, and so on. She kept on asking questions, and Mama had no chance to explain why we had come. Uncle came back and joined us. He must have done the shopping in the meantime. At last, Mama mentioned why we had come. Auntie Dora went to get the keys for the cellar, and asked Uncle to come with us.

When we got downstairs, we found Auntie's cellar partition broken in. People only have thin pieces of wood dividing off certain spaces for the occupiers of the flats. It is not difficult to smash them in. Anyway, as I said, the partition was broken and, would you believe it, all our food had gone. All the jars with the meat and gravy and the vegetables had disappeared. Auntie Dora had a few jars too, but they were in the back, and had not been touched. Ours stood in the front, and could easily be reached after the partition was broken. Mama was speechless, Auntie Dora threw her arms in the air, and shouted:

'Thieves, thieves, they have broken into our cellar, oh dear, oh dear. Erna, I am sorry, I am sorry, they took all your food. I didn't know. I have not been in the cellar for over a week.'

Uncle just stood there and never said a word. One could see where the jars had stood, because the shelves were dusty and there were clean ring marks. Mama said sarcastically:

'They must have stolen everything this morning, because one can still see the clean places where the jars have stood. I am sorry, too, to have lost all the food. There won't be anything for us for Christmas, and there won't be anything for you, because I had hoped to give you something to help you to celebrate the festive season.'

'Mama then turned to me,' continued Christel, 'and said, "Let's go home". Auntie Dora tried to persuade us to have a hot drink, but Mama just pulled me outside, and we walked to the underground station. It was snowing again, and I was cold. I would have liked a drink, but I didn't say anything. At the station, we sat down, and Mama produced a sandwich for me. She didn't eat anything, but she exploded. 'What a cheek, what a cheek,' she said. 'There were no thieves, Auntie Dora was the thief. She made Uncle go down into the cellar, break the partition, and remove the jars, whilst she was asking me all those questions. I wondered why she wouldn't let me say a word. She doesn't usually enquire so much about everybody. All that food gone, and the jars also. It will not only be a poor Christmas, but a hungry winter for all of us. Why did I let Auntie Dora persuade me to use her cool cellar in the summer. I should have kept the food on the *Funkstation*.' Christel said she asked Mama why she didn't accuse Auntie Dora openly, but my mother said:

'How could I say anything to her? I want her to look after Hans again in January when he goes back to school. This time, she won't get any extra food for him, because we haven't got any. It's a good thing that we didn't mention that Karl has disappeared. She knew that that's where we get the extra food from. We will have to tell Hans not to mention anything about Karl when he goes back, so that she carries on thinking there will be some extra food soon, otherwise she might not even keep Hans.'

'After all that,' said Christel, 'we came home. Mama was silent all the way, and never even ate anything. Maybe we ought to give her some soup, or something to eat.'

Hans had joined us in the kitchen and had also heard the story.

'I don't know whether I want to go back after all this,' he said.

'Don't be silly,' I replied. 'Of course you will go back, you have to go to school. Just pretend you don't know anything. If Auntie Dora asks about Karl, just say he keeps on going to Hamburg, and only spends a little time with us. That reminds me, I think I will go and have a look in Karl's room. Maybe he has got something which we can use as a bribe to get extra food for Christmas.'

I walked off and went to the other hut where Karl and Josef used to sleep. Nobody had been in that room since Karl had left over a month ago and, when I turned the light on, a mouse ran across the bare floor. There were two palliasses on the floor, a small rug, and some boxes. In one box were some plates and mugs and a few kitchen utensils. In another box was some underwear, towels, shaving and washing things. There was no food, but I found half a bottle of brandy, and a few packets of cigarettes.

One of the palliasses looked as if Karl had mended it. The stitching must have gone, because somebody had sewn the seam again with crude stitches. I looked at it, and suddenly it occurred to me that maybe Karl had hidden something in there. I cut it open, using a kitchen knife from the box. I put my hand through the opening, but felt only straw at first.

Then I thought I could feel paper. I eased it through the hole, and saw that it was money. There was quite a bit of it. Although it would be useful, it didn't belong to me and Karl might come back for it. I put it back into the palliasse, but I did not sew up the hole.

If Karl has not returned by the Spring, I can take it, I thought. In the meantime, I took the cigarettes and the brandy.

When I returned to our hut, my father was in the kitchen. He, too, looked old and worn out. He had finished taking one of the huts to pieces, and had it all piled up in a large heap, but now, with the cold and snowy weather, he could not work outside any more. I told him about the cigarettes. He was pleased about them, and said that he would take some and bribe a farmer; maybe we could get a boiling fowl for Christmas.

'Go and see your mother,' he said to me. 'Give her some of your strength. You always seem to come up on top again, you are so young.'

He looked at me and smiled. 'In the New Year, I will go to the embassy again. They should have the proof that we are Swiss by now, and then we are entitled to some help.'

I went to see my mother, who had gone to bed. It was cold in the room, after the warm kitchen. My mother was shivering, so I climbed under her thin blankets and we hugged one another. There was no need to discuss anything, Christel had told me the story.

When Mama was warm, I got up and fetched her one of my blankets, and got Karl's blankets for myself. There was no need to have blankets on an empty bed. Josef had taken all his things. I knew he would never return. Karl, I was convinced, had been caught, during his shady dealings, and was imprisoned.

# CHAPTER NINE

## Christmas 1945 - The New Baby - Moving to Hamburg

The winter of 1945/46 was not as cold as the year before. It started snowing at the beginning of December. Even to go down the hill to Kisdorf and back up again for our shopping was quite an effort, particularly on a nearly empty stomach.

As promised, my father visited some of the farmers in the district, with Karl's cigarettes, and was successful in obtaining an old chicken. We had to pluck it and my mother cooked it for a long time to get it soft. The local bus driver, who had always been very kind to me, gave me some potatoes, and I had also got the half bottle of brandy from Karl. This was our food for Christmas. There were six of us, and we stretched the chicken over two days. My mother made plenty of soup, using a lot of water, but it did at least taste a little like chicken. We even tried to eat the bones but, because it was such an old fowl, the bones were brittle, and splintered when one bit on them.

My mother hardly ate anything; she gave it all to Astra, who was now quite big with the child. None of us were allowed any butter, my mother gave it all to Astra. My father never ate margarine, he insisted on his butter ration, or ate dry bread.

Christmas day was terrible. We talked about our old Christmases at home, when Papa used to play the piano and often made mistakes. We tried to remember some of the Christmas poems we had learnt and we recited them again. We could not sing because when we tried *Stille Nacht* and looked at the little bare green tree which my father had stolen in the night from the wood, my mother cried, my father seemed to have something in his eye, Christel put her arms around me, and I could feel a lump in my throat. Astra left the kitchen, and went into her room, and Hans, too, was fighting tears.

'Let's stop this,' said my father. 'We will all go outside, and get a few lungs-full of fresh air.'

My mother got up to fetch Astra. When she returned, she had put on her beautiful Persian lamb coat, and even her Persian lamb hat. She smiled suddenly:

'Happy Christmas,' she said.

Astra was covered with a rug. as we could not afford maternity clothes. We walked to the deserted road and never met anybody either. Just before it started to snow again, we returned.

We all huddled together in the kitchen, where the cooking stove kept us warm. We were short of fuel, so Astra's iron stove in her bedroom was kept low.

We decided that there would be no point in staying up for New Year; we had nothing to celebrate. We went to bed like every other night, and the next day, we all said 'Happy New Year', and hoped 1946 would be better than 1945.


What we all needed most, of course, was food. In April 1945, at the end of the war, the rations for one week were:

1,700g bread, 125g sugar, 250g meat, 125g fat, 33g *Ersatzkaffee* (no real coffee was available in the shops), 75g *Nährmittel* (cereal products).

Potatoes were the main nutrition. Bread was the next main food, but this was always short. All other food was a luxury. Per month now there was 300g - 400g of meat. Another thing that hardly existed was fat. The ration per month was 200 - 300g. Butter was often only allocated to children and the sick, everybody else only got oil, margarine, and *Sparfett* (low fat).

Hunger was a constant companion. Suddenly people arrived with goods from their homes, and bargained for food. They came on the underground, as far as it went, then walked, or caught the bus, and some of them even arrived in Kisdorf, and our district.

My mother, having grown up in the country, remembered that the farmers in her district had *Mieten* (clamps) in the fields, where they buried animal food for the winter. She told me to see whether I could find some. Any field I searched, I had to approach from the road, because of the snow. I might leave footmarks, which could be traced to the radio station.

Eventually I found a large clamp, where a kind of turnip was buried. It was pinkish-red, and was used for animal fodder in the early Spring. I remembered it being grown in East Prussia when I worked on the farm there. I dug some out, and took them home. My mother cooked them in salt water. They didn't taste all that nice, but they filled up the stomach.

We ate them hot, we ate them cold, we had big or small pieces, or we had them mashed. My mother even served them raw, in grated form. She became quite an expert in the preparation of this animal turnip, and I became quite an expert in the collecting of them.

Astra came nearer to her confinement. She had been taken to the hospital for checkups in October, and in the first week of December. The nice lady doctor in the Kaltenkirchen hospital had arranged for her to be fetched by ambulance. She also suggested that Astra should come to the hospital in the first week of January, as she thought the baby would be due then any time. She felt it would not be a bad idea for Astra to be a few days in hospital before the birth. She was concerned that we lived so isolated and primitively, and afraid that by the time we got an ambulance, the baby might be born before Astra arrived at the hospital.

In the first week of January, I called in at the *Bürgermeister*, and asked him to arrange for an ambulance to take my sister to Kaltenkirchen. My mother went with her. She returned late in the afternoon, looking very tired and wet. She had walked over the fields, as this was a shorter way but, even so, it was a long walk. She said that Astra was quite happy, and was in a lovely room, with two more women who had just had their babies.

Christel and I went to see Astra two days later; the baby had not arrived yet. Astra complained because Mama didn't come. I told her that it was cold and frosty and too far for Mama to walk. I reassured her that Mama would come, once the baby was born, although it was a trip of 10 km there and back.

Astra's baby was born on January 13th, a little girl, which she called Monika Christel. We got the news through the postman. The hospital had phoned the *Bürgermeister*, who told the postman to pass on the news the next morning, when he came to deliver letters to the next farm. He also brought me a letter from Hermann, who wrote that he hoped to come and see me, as soon as the weather got better.

My mother was very thrilled about the baby and, although it was snowing, she got herself ready to walk to Kaltenkirchen to see Astra in hospital, as promised. She returned again, completely exhausted, but happy about how Astra was being looked after, and very excited about something else.

I didn't hear about it until the next morning. Hans was back at school in Hamburg and my father was busy with something, when my mother took Christel and me into the kitchen.

'There is something I want you to do for me, Helga,' said my mother, 'and maybe Christel can help you. - When I returned from the hospital, I saw, just on the outskirts of Kaltenkirchen, that there are some houses with small gardens in the front and a little back yard. The last house has a small tin tub hanging on the wall. This is just the thing we need to bath baby Monika. We have got nothing here, only a bucket or two, and I have been worrying about how we are going to manage. To get it, you will have to walk along the garden path to the back door, but Christel could hold the gate open, so that you can run away quickly.'

I looked at my mother. Then I said: 'You want me to steal it.'

'Yes,' she replied. 'We are doing it all the time, - with the ration cards, with the turnips and, before that, with the milking of the cows. We are trying to survive, we are desperate. The best time to take it would be late in the afternoon. It gets dark early. You already know your way back from Kaltenkirchen over the fields to us here, so you should be able to find your way even in the dark.'

I stared at my mother; she had never spoken so firmly when she had asked me to do something wrong. I didn't like to do it, this was something really big, and dangerous, and I could be caught. It was also something which I had to do for Astra and, after the opening of her box, I had made up my mind not to do anything for her again.

'What happens if I get caught?'

'You won't. You can run fast and if anybody follows you just drop the tub and keep on running.'

'No,' I said. 'I will not do it, not for Astra, not after the incident with the box. She never does anything for anybody and I am supposed to commit a crime for her. This is much too dangerous. Anyway, Christel cannot run as fast as myself.'

'You are using big words,' replied my mother. 'You are right, Astra does not deserve it. But what about that innocent little baby? How are we going to keep her clean? We will only be able to let Monika have a wash, and she will never have the enjoyment of splashing in a little bath, like all of you did when you were young.'

She suddenly sank down into herself, and all strength seemed to have gone out of her. Then she said quietly and softly:

'You are right, I am sorry, it is wrong of me to make you go and commit a crime like that. I thought about it all the way back from Kaltenkirchen. Somehow, I never saw the seriousness of it all, or the danger and that it might go wrong. The consequences would be terrible.

Let's just forget it, but please, could you both go and see Astra tomorrow, I don't think that I have got the strength to do that trip again.'

We promised and Christel and I started off to Kaltenkirchen in the morning, each taking a piece of dry bread with us, as we knew we would not be back until the afternoon.

It was hard going, the walk over the fields, as the snow was very deep at times. We could not see the ditches. They were covered with snow, and often we sank in up to our knees. The sun was shining and the white of the snow hurt our eyes. We had no gloves, so our hands were red and cold. Several times we stumbled and fell. I remembered the time when I had to flee over the Haff, and comforted myself with the thought that this was only a short trip.

It took us three hours to get to the outskirts of Kaltenkirchen, and we were pleased to see it, as we had thought once or twice that we had lost our way. It was easier to walk along the roads in the small town, because the snow was trodden down there. We had passed the first two houses in Kaltenkirchen, when Christel suddenly held my arm:

'There is the tub, on the wall.'

Sure enough, there was a small, silver-looking tub with two handles, hanging on the wall; an ideal little bath for a baby. I looked at the gate and the path leading up to the back door and the wall with the tub. It was not all that far and if Christel held the gate the tub could be unhooked easily. One could get away quite quickly. But no, I was not going to do it, this time I was going to be firm.

Astra was not at all pleased to see us. She had expected my mother, because she had had no visitors the day before. I told her that it had taken us three hours to get there, and that it was impossible for Mama to do this trip as she was much too weak.

'Mama should have come. She promised she would come again. I have difficulties in feeding the baby and I am sure she wants to know about this.'

'Well, I can tell her this news,' I replied. 'You will just have to tell the doctor or the nurses about it. Grow up, you are a mother now. It is about time you stood on your own feet, and did things for yourself. What would you have done had you stayed in Mainburg?'

Little Monika was a beautiful baby. I fell in love with her when I saw her and so did Christel. I could suddenly understand why my mother wanted to do so much for her. It flashed through my mind that my mother had wanted me to see the baby so that I, too, would like the little creature, and would be more prepared to help. As usual, she was right.

We left in the late afternoon and I told Christel that I was going to try and get that little bath from the wall.

We waited until it was nearly dark, then returned quietly to the house. There was nobody about, not even on the road. It was bitterly cold but it didn't snow. Christel held the gate open whilst I quietly ran up the path. I had pulled the sleeves over my bare hands, in case the metal of the bath would cling to my skin.

We had not reckoned with a dog, which suddenly started barking. A man shouted something from inside the house, then there was a woman's voice. I grabbed the tub and ran along the path towards the gate. Christel had got frightened, and had run off, which shut the gate. Unfortunately, the gate closed and opened towards the garden side, which meant I had to stop, and pull the gate towards me, losing valuable time.

I heard shouting from the house, but took no notice. Instead, I ran along the road, pulling the tub behind me. I soon caught up with Christel, and we climbed through an opening in the hedge and ran along the other side of it. We stopped after a little while and hid the bath in the hedge, covering it with snow.

The hedge ran along the side of a field and the road. We followed it until the end, then stepped back into the road. There was nobody there and it was dark now. We returned along the road to Kaltenkirchen again.

I felt that as I had not got the bath with me, we should be alright, but Christel was afraid to go back, so I told her to wait for me near the hedge whilst I went back alone.

When I got near the house, I saw a few people standing outside talking.

I limped a little, pulled my collar up, and tied my scarf over my head, all of which I hoped would make me look different. Nobody took much notice of me.

I walked as far as the hospital, then turned round and walked back, passing the house on the other side of the road this time. By now, the people had gone. It was much too cold to stand outside for long. I climbed through the hedge retrieved the bath, and carried it in front of me, not wanting to leave a mark in the snow from sliding it along. The bath was quite heavy and I was glad to come to the end of the hedge, where Christel was. She was glad to see me. We both got hold of the tub and, making sure all marks in the snow were wiped out, we carried it together.

The journey back was very difficult. It was dark by now, not pitch dark, but it would have been easier if we had had a full moon. We tried to follow the footmarks from the morning. Other people had used our new trodden path but sometimes we didn't know which one was ours. Again we sank into the snow where there were ditches. Whenever we did this it left a mark from the bath where it rested on the snow, and had to be wiped out. We were cold, hungry, tired and worried, but we stumbled along. I do not remember how many hours it took us but, when we reached the radio station and stumbled into the warm kitchen, absolutely exhausted, I said:

'I will never visit Astra again in the hospital. It is too far to walk.'

'Neither will I,' said Christel, and sank, exhausted, on to the floor.

We took our wet clothes off, my mother gave us something to eat and a hot drink. I collected our palliasses, and pulled them into the kitchen, where the stove was always burning (very low at night). I said:

'We deserve to sleep here tonight,' and we went to sleep.

I could hear my mother raking the stove in the morning. We got up and, of course, told our story from the day before, and how we got the tub. My mother was most grateful, my father shook my shoulder, and said I had been lucky, but had also been quite clever about it.


Astra stayed three weeks in hospital, because she had a breast infection and also difficulties in breast feeding. She came back by ambulance. My mother made sure Astra's bedroom was warm for her and the baby. Monika slept in a pram, which the hospital had been able to get for her. Astra never thanked us for the tub, just accepted that the small bath was there. From now on everything revolved around Astra and her child.

We all had our jobs. Mine was to collect the food and particularly the milk every day from Kisdorf. My father had to see to the fuel for Astra's stove, and the kitchen one, and Christel took the baby for a walk, if the weather was not too cold, so that Astra could have an afternoon rest. She also helped my mother when needed. My mother saw to the meals, helped to bathe and change the baby, often washed the nappies and, of course, emptied the bucket for Astra. Because of the cold weather, Astra still did not use the outside toilet, which I had to clean when necessary.


My father had been to Hamburg, and came back with the good news that at last proof had arrived that we were Swiss and we all could expect a Swiss passport or identity card soon. He said that he had also told the embassy that he would be interested in repatriation. But the best thing was, that he had also brought a food parcel back, and said that we could collect more. We were entitled to one every two weeks.

He had visited his old friend, Mr Maierhofer who, because he had been a big Nazi before, was going to lose his flat. He told my father that he would be very interested in buying one of the wooden huts from the *Funkstation* from him. He could put it next to his allotment hut. This would then be enough to accommodate his whole family.

My father asked my mother and Astra whether they had any spare money to pay for the transport, saying that they would get it back. Both said they had nothing. I knew it was not true. Astra had money. I had given her the money for the sold furniture. I think my father, too, remembered this, because he kept on looking at her silently. He never queried her reply.

I went to Karl's room, and took some money out of his palliasse - I was only borrowing it - and gave it to my father. He looked at it, very surprised, but he asked no questions. Eventually he gave me the money back and I returned it to Karl's palliasse.

Hans visited us for his birthday and shortly afterwards I developed a terrible cold. I was allowed to have my palliasse in the kitchen in the corner, because my bedroom was much too cold. Astra never came into the kitchen, so that she wouldn't catch my cold, and all the others kept well away from me. Nobody else caught my cold, so maybe I had something else. At times I felt so bad that I thought I would never reach the outside toilet, but I always did in the end. Christel said that I ought to use the bucket and she would take it outside, but I couldn't let her do it, thinking how awful it was that Astra still called for my mother every day when she had used the bucket. I felt it was so degrading and unnecessary and my mother should stop it.

Gradually I got better, but felt very weak. Because I was so ill, my mother and Christel took it in turns to go to Kisdorf to collect the milk and any necessary shopping.

One day it was rather late before my mother went off to Kisdorf for the milk. Astra suggested that Christel could take Monika for a walk in her pram, which she did. It was the first time that I had got up and dressed, and I sat by the window, looking out. My father came in, bringing some wood and coal for the kitchen stove. He smiled at me and wanted to know how I felt. I told him I was very weak and I kept on shivering. He said I didn't look too good, and maybe I ought to go back to bed. Before I could reply, Astra came into the kitchen, and asked me to take her bucket outside as Mama was still not back from Kisdorf. She said it was rather smelly, and she didn't think it ought to remain too long in the hallway.

I stared at Astra, I just couldn't believe that she really meant what she said. There was nothing wrong with her; it was my mother's idea that she shouldn't use the outside toilet, because it was too cold, because she had just had a baby, and because she was a nursing mother (Monika was six weeks old by then). I had only just got up from my sick bed and, even whilst ill, I had still used the outside toilet.

'You can take your own bucket out,' said my father sternly.

'Mama said I must not use the outside toilet, I might catch a chill, and then I won't have any milk for Monika.'

'Rubbish, get that bucket, and empty it outside. And, in future, you are going to use the outside toilet like everybody else or, if you use the bucket, you are going to empty it yourself. There is nothing wrong with you. I will not have Mama being your slave all the time.'

With that, my father took Astra roughly by the shoulder, and tried to push her towards the door.

'Leave me alone,' shouted Astra. 'I will not go outside with the bucket. It will just have to smell and stink in the passage until Mama gets back.'

Astra looked wild. I suddenly saw that she had the same temper as my father. He did not let go of her shoulder; he looked white, too, with fury. He tried to twist and push her towards the door.

After that, things happened very quickly. There was shouting, there was pushing, arms were flying, and then, suddenly, my sister slapped my father's face. I held my breath.

He is going to kill her, I thought and got up to interfere, when the door opened and my mother walked in. She must have heard the shouting. My father, in his fury, had got hold of Astra again, but my mother pushed herself between the two, and got hurt by both of them.

'You make Astra go and empty her bucket,' shouted my father, 'or, by God, I will walk out of this place. You are not her servant. I will not look on any more, and see her lording it over everybody, only because she had a child by a . . .'

My father didn't get any further, because my mother put her hand over his mouth, and said:

'Be quiet, Hans, that is enough.' Then she turned to Astra and said: 'Go into your room. I met Christel, she will be back with Monika in a few minutes.'

Astra quickly went to her bedroom. When I heard the front door banging, I knew that my mother had gone to empty the bucket. My father stood a few minutes by the door, then came to me, and asked in a husky voice filled with suppressed emotion:

'Where is my food ration card.'

My mother had put the shopping on to the table and I knew that the cards would be in her bag. I went and opened the bag, took out my father's food card and gave it to him. He took the card and left the kitchen. I heard him go into his bedroom.

My mother came indoors and when she came into the kitchen she wanted to know what had happened. I told her, but she never said a word, not even when I said that Astra had slapped Papa's face.

I could hear Christel bumping the pram over the front door ridge. My mother left the kitchen to help Christel, and I heard Astra's door opening and closing. Christel went into our bedroom to take off her outer clothes.

My father came into the kitchen. He was dressed warmly, and had a bag in his hand, bulging with things.

'If you want to know where I am, ask Mr Maierhofer at the allotments', said my father. Then he hugged me hard, and whispered: 'I just cannot take any more. Take care of yourself. I am sure you will be alright. Don't forget your food parcels from the Swiss embassy.'

I felt like crying, but I didn't. My father left, and I knew he hadn't said goodbye to anybody else.

My mother came late into the kitchen to prepare the evening meal. I realized that she didn't know that Papa had left because when Christel laid the table and left one place setting out, she assumed that Christel thought Astra would not come into the kitchen. She said:

'Astra is eating with us. She won't be able to avoid your father for ever; she might as well start now.'

Astra came in, quite brazenly, and sat down. Christel looked at me, and then I said it:

'Papa has gone. He said he had had enough. He just couldn't take any more.' I felt cross. I still wasn't well and, even if it didn't sink in to Astra that her behaviour was wrong and selfish, somebody would have to say it. I carried on, not looking at my mother, but watching Astra:

'You shouldn't have slapped his face. There is nothing wrong with you. You can use the outside toilet, the same as we all do. Papa tried to protect Mama, who works like a slave for you. She has spoilt you all your life and you take advantage of it. If you were an ordinary married woman with a husband, you would have to run your home, clean it and cook for him, even do the washing, and still look after your baby. We all have jobs here. You have none and always get the best food. Your mother is your permanent servant, and that is what our father resented. He is not the only one. I, too, feel the same and, I am sure, so does Christel, except that she has not got the courage to say it.'

Astra just looked at me, then at my mother for help. My mother had turned her back to us. Her shoulders were shaking, as if she was crying quietly. I got up and hugged her. I felt sorry for her. She probably didn't know what to do at times and now she was left to cope on her own. When I looked at Astra again she, too, was crying, but I knew it wasn't because she was sorry. She cried to get out of an awkward situation.

'Stop crying,' I said to her. 'You can turn the tap off. I am not going to take the slightest bit of notice of it.'

Astra immediately stopped crying. She could see that there was no help forthcoming from my mother. After that, we had our menial supper in silence.

We did not hear anything from my father. The weather got warmer, and the snow started to melt, which made our path to the road wet, sticky and muddy. I had recovered from my cold and went shopping again.

Astra had been told by my mother to use the outside toilet. She had no more help in washing the nappies, and my mother even made her responsible for keeping the passageway in the hut clean which, in the muddy weather, was quite a job. She had to scrub the boards from time to time, and we were told off by her for bringing in the mud, so there were occasional eruptions!

I had told my mother that as soon as the weather was better, I would try and get a job in Hamburg. We were short of money. I had been to Karl's palliasse twice. My mother was surprised when I suddenly gave her some money, but she didn't ask any questions; she didn't want to know.

At the beginning of March, Hermann suddenly arrived. He was doing well at his job, and felt a date for "Our" wedding could be set. This time, my mother did not say anything. I lied to Hermann, saying that I already had a job in an office promised to me in Hamburg, which I had to take up on March 15th. I tried to make him understand that I could not let the family down; they needed my wages and the help they got from me. My father was not there, and I explained this by saying that he was at the embassy in Hamburg. My parents hoped to go back to Switzerland, and start a new life there.

Hermann could not understand all this. He, too, wanted to get on with his life. If my family had applied for repatriation, then we could just get married and they would leave for Switzerland when the time was right. I told him that I would not make any decisions until we had heard from the embassy.

Hermann stayed only one night. Our relationship was strained, and when he left, he did not ask me to write or to reconsider my decision just gave me a cold peck on the cheek, and walked off. I knew this was the end.

He is a cold man, I thought. I am glad he is going. I hope he will be happy with Mrs Senner.

A week later, I received a letter from Hermann, telling me that he would not come again to see me on the *Funkstation*. He just said:

'You know where Hannover is.'

It was a short note, quite polite, non-committal and cold. I did not reply, neither did he write any more. I never saw Hermann again and I always felt that it was a rather peculiar finish to somebody who was nearly my husband.


I went to Hamburg and stayed a night with Auntie Dora. For two days I queued at the labour exchange and finished up with two or three addresses for possible places to work. On the second day, late in the afternoon, I introduced myself at a little office called Roku, *Werbezentrale* (advertising agency).

I couldn't believe it when they offered me a job with the princely salary of 140 RM (Reichs Mark) per month. (The DM or Deutsche Mark came after devaluation). I had to start on March 15th, the date which I had given Hermann as my starting date.

Because Auntie Dora had no accommodation for me I had to get up at 4.30 every morning as it was a walk of over two hours to the Underground station, then by U-train into Hamburg, where I had to start at 8 o'clock. In the evening, my friendly bus driver was able to give me a lift from the Underground station to Ulzburg, but I had to walk from there, which took another three-quarters of an hour. I usually went to bed at 9 o'clock.

The main thing was that I had a job in Hamburg, I earned money, and now I could apply for accommodation at the *Wohnungsamt* (Housing Office). There, I was put on to the waiting list. I visited the embassy and discovered that my father had been there and filled in an application for a Swiss passport, so I did the same. Foreigners, Jewish people, ex-concentration camp inmates all got privileges, and I felt that once I got my Swiss passport I would be able to get some accommodation, and also be able always to go to the front of any queue.

There was very little employment available, but to have a liaison with a soldier from the occupation forces, meant food, chocolates for the children, and cigarettes, which were the essential currency for the black market. There were also the centres of exchange, where anything imaginable could be bartered. Roku, the firm for which I worked had a different idea. People did not bring their goods to be exchanged to the office, but they advertised through Roku. All over the town, Roku had large billboards, full of small typed notices, advertising articles for exchange.

Walli, who managed my office, gave me half a day off, so that I could try and find my father in the allotments. I was shocked when I found him. He looked embarrassed, unhappy, cold, thin and hungry. He had made himself a kind of shelter, with the wood from our dismantled hut. He had an overall on and a thick torn cardigan. He had not shaved for days and looked unkempt. He told me proudly that, at last, he had a job. He had only just got it, but it gave him some money, so that he could buy the food that he was entitled to on his ration card. He had joined the league of people who were employed to clear away the debris of the war with their bare hands. They dug out the corpses and buried them, and turned the rubble into building material.

I told my father about my new job, and how hard it was to get up so early every morning. I said that I had hopes of getting some accommodation in town soon. My father suggested trying an old couple he knew who lived near the Lattenkamp.

'They need the money,' said my father. 'I am sure they will find you a place to sleep, if you can pay. I would have taken it up myself but I haven't got the money. The little I have started to earn is just enough for my food. Mama still has a little money, but she needs it, as I cannot give her any more at the moment.'

I felt very sorry for my father. I had nothing much I could give him, except a little money. I pushed a note into his cardigan pocket. He knew what I did but pretended not to notice it. He was a proud man, and it hurt him to take money from his daughter. I said I would try the old people and promised to come and see him again.

He wanted to know about the rest of the family and was pleased to hear that Astra had been given some jobs and was using the outside toilet. He hugged me hard when I left and I could feel his deep emotions and terrible loneliness.

I went to see the old people at the Lattenkamp, and they offered me a small settee in their living room. My staying the night there had to be unofficial because I did not have permission to live in Hamburg, so I just had to say that I was a visitor. I was most grateful; it saved the journey by bus, underground and the long walk, and also the getting up so early in the morning. Every other day I went to the *Wohnungsamt* in my dinner hour to ask about accommodation. I hoped that if I went often enough they would, in the end, find something for me. - On Saturday I went back to the *Funkstation*, and spent the Sunday with the family.

One day when I came back from work, I met the old couple quite excitedly telling me that my father had been and left me a note. My father wrote saying that I should inform everybody in the family that we could go to the embassy and fill in our forms for our passports. He asked me to tell Mama that he would come to see us all on Sunday. He didn't realize that I had already filled in my form.

My father arrived on Sunday morning and brought my brother with him. Although still painfully thin, he looked clean, tidy, and had even had a shave. He looked happier too and we were all pleased to see him. He kissed Mama and Christel, and then looked at Astra. We all held our breath, and waited. Astra had Monika in her arms and played with her, pretending not to notice my father looking at her.

'Are you going to apologize?' asked my father.

'If you want me to, I will say sorry. Alright, I am sorry.' She looked defiantly at him.

My father left it at that. He did not take it any further. He told us that the embassy were prepared to give us Swiss passports. He had already filled in a form for repatriation, and had brought the forms for the passports along. I told him that I had already filled in a form, but he said that I had not given the embassy a photograph of myself and would still have to do this as soon as possible.

'I have come back,' said Papa, 'and brought Hans with me, because we have to discuss the future, particularly the future of Astra and Monika. If Astra is married to an Austrian citizen, she has lost her Swiss nationality and she will not be able to come with us. She can apply for repatriation as a widow, but this will take longer, and might not even be given yet.'

'I won't go to Switzerland without Astra,' said my mother. 'We cannot leave her behind. How is she going to live, and how is she going to manage?'

'I thought that would be your answer,' said my father. 'So we will have to think of another way. If Astra hadn't been married, there would be no difficulties, even with Monika. The thing for her to do is to take her maiden name again and apply for a passport. I want you all to think about this before you give me an answer. I have brought a food parcel from the embassy, so let's have something to eat first.'

He unpacked some tins, and also produced a loaf of bread and some jam. This was going to be a feast day! Christel, Hans and I had a talk. We felt it would be a good idea to go to Switzerland. Hans wanted to have a normal life again. He didn't like to live in Hamburg on his own, with Auntie Dora and Uncle; he missed us. He thought that in Switzerland we could, at least, all live together. There would be food, and there would be accommodation. He could carry on at school. We all felt that was important and after that we hoped for a grant for him to go to university.

'I might be able to carry on with my medical studies,' I said. 'Although I have forgotten a lot. It will mean a good bit of extra learning, but I don't mind. Life here is not life, it is trying to exist, and there seems to be no future.'

Christel, too, was in favour of going to Switzerland. She had no idea what she was going to do but was willing to work, so it should be possible for her to get a job.

My father, of course, thought that anything was better than the life he had been leading on the allotments. I had seen his hands; they were rough and torn from the work he did. The elegant, refined gentleman had become a labourer, which was demoralising for him. Switzerland was the silver star, the light, the bright future.

We were all in favour of going back to Switzerland, except for Astra and, because of her, my mother refused to go. Astra had no idea how and where she was going to live. She knew that my mother would not go if she refused to come with us, and I think that's what helped her to be so stubborn.

Suddenly my father got up, and told my mother to come for a little walk with him. In the meantime, I told Astra off, telling her how unfair she was, because she prevented our mother from coming with us to Switzerland. She just shrugged her shoulders, and said she was not stopping my mother from going.

My parents returned. My mother glanced at Astra, and then quietly sat down. Astra looked a little uneasy, she had probably expected my mother to say something encouraging to her. We all waited for my father to speak.

'Astra, ever since you have joined us at the *Funkstation* there have been eruptions. The unity of the family has gone. We have all pulled together to help you, to protect you, to shield you and your child. You have put a rift between Mama and me and in the end I left, because I couldn't take any more. You are not stupid; you must realize that if we all go to Switzerland you couldn't cope. You would have to go to one of the refugee camps and hope for help from the authorities there. Mama is not going to stay behind alone with you. This would kill her in a short time. There is hardly anything left of her after all the hard work here, and the poor and little food she is consuming. Either we all go to Switzerland, or we all stay here. Can you take the responsibility of having ruined a brighter future for your parents, your sisters, your brother and even your child? You have not given us one valid reason why you don't want to come with us because if it is Otto you are worried about, he is either dead or gone, otherwise you would have heard from him. Should he turn up later on, you can always return to Germany, if you want. We can tell the people in Mainburg to contact the Swiss embassy for your address. For once in your life, think of your family, not only of yourself.'

My father stopped talking, and we all looked at Astra. I was surprised that my father also wanted to stay behind, if Astra wouldn't come, and he had made that decision for us. He had never thought much of Otto and not having met him made it even worse. I knew he thought that a man with two teenage children wasn't worth much, if he left them and his wife, and then got himself involved with a young innocent girl. My father had never said it to Astra, but I had heard him talking to my mother. He had always been very tactful about this subject and avoided talking to Astra about it.

To my great surprise, Astra just said: 'Alright, I will come, if I can take all my things.'

'Good,' said my father. 'I cannot promise whether you can take all your things, but I will try and see what can be arranged.'

The family filled in the forms and Papa, Hans and I returned to Hamburg. We needed photographs, which the three of us could get in Hamburg, whilst Mama, Astra and Christel had to take it in turns to travel to Segeberg for them. Christel stayed with Monika when Mama went with Astra on the bus, and then she went on her own the next day. Because of all this, it took a week before the forms were taken to the embassy. Astra's form was accepted under her maiden name, and Monika added to it. We received our passports and from that moment things changed for the better for us.

From one day to the next we had become foreigners and had privileges in a number of places, the same as the Jewish people, the Poles and the people from the concentration camps. My father came with me to the

*Wohnungsamt*. We went straight to the front of the queue, showing our passports. This time we were asked to come into the interviewing room. Before that, I always had to talk to an official through a glass partition after waiting nearly an hour in the queue, and often longer. We were told that if we could find accommodation, we would get the *Zuzugsgenehmigung* (permission to move) to Hamburg but, even so, we would now be on top of the list of people waiting for accommodation.

Then my father got some money from the embassy. He had to sign a statement that he would pay the money back if he ever got his money out of East Prussia, or got compensation for his lost property. My father had no hesitation in signing this statement. He had been a very rich man and would have been only too willing to return the money, if he got back what he had lost. My father could now give up his job of clearing the rubble away, but he still stayed in his shelter in the allotments on and off, to save himself the long and tiring journey to the *Funkstation*. He kept on going to the *Wohnungsamt* and the embassy, and also looked for accommodation himself.

Things also changed for me. Once Walli discovered I had a Swiss passport, she decided to make use of it. Nothing could be bought in the town without a permit, unless it was on the black market, because everything was so scarce. The Permit Office was staffed by the British Occupation forces, and there were long queues everywhere. With my Swiss passport, I could get to the front of the queue and, with my limited English, I could explain what I wanted. There were different departments for furniture, office equipment, tools, machinery, etc. The first permit I had to get, was for two extra chairs for the office, then a permit for a typewriter, then a permit for writing and typing paper. Writing paper was very short, some shops would not let you have any, unless you brought old paper in return. It was different if you had a permit, and it was for office use.

My job at Roku was now very easy, as nobody could really check up how much time I needed to go and get a permit. I could call in at the *Wohnungsamt*, enquiring whether anything had turned up for us. We now needed quite a big flat for all of us, not just one room. I could also call at the embassy, and I even had time for a quick visit to Auntie Dora to see Hans. I still had to spend time in the office, where I would attend to customers, or take over the switchboard. I lived with the elderly couple at the Lattenkamp, and we got on well together. I told them that I had received my Swiss passport, and now they were not worried any more that I stayed with them.

I started to make friends at the Permit Office, and was invited to the British Club. No Germans were allowed in the club but, with my Swiss passport, I had an entrance ticket. Everybody liked me at the club, and some of them wanted me to be their *Fräulein*. They spoilt me, by giving me cigarettes, food, coffee, and tea, which I could pass on to my family, or sell on the black market.

I started to know a number of soldiers, and my English improved. I never let anybody take me home and I never went out with anybody either. They called me the "ice maiden", but I didn't mind.

The club was the only social life I had. I worked during the day for Roku and, at the weekend, I went to Kisdorf, to see my mother and my sisters, and take some of the extra food which I could get, to help them with their rations.

I got introduced to the black market through Franz, who was the *Ausläufer* (delivery man) for Roku. We went to St. Pauli, near the Reeperbahn. There were a few small roads, most of them full of people who just walked about. There was no traffic. People walked and talked, stopped and talked to one another, parted again, carried on talking and mumbling. It was very noisy, and it took me a time before I got used to the noise, and gradually understood what was going on. The people walked about, mumbling what they had to offer, and what they wanted in return.

Everything was very expensive, always based on the value of cigarettes - 100 RM for a packet of 20. One could buy anything with them.

I went several times to the black market, usually with Franz. I felt safer with him. I changed cigarettes for food for my family. I never got caught, although there were several "razzias". These were quite frightening. Suddenly the small road would be blocked off at both ends by a number of British military police, who arrived in several vans. The back doors were opened, and they just pushed the people inside, and took them away.

One day, I had a tummy ache. The pain came and went all day, and Walli said I ought to go and see a doctor. The next morning I was really bad, but I went to work. I felt very hot and, when Walli saw me, and felt my forehead, she thought I had a temperature. Franz said it wasn't a doctor I wanted, but a hospital. He had a quiet chat with Walli and, after that, informed me that he knew a nurse at the *Stadtkrankenhaus*, and he would take me there.

After that, everything went very quickly. Franz accompanied me to the hospital. There he found his nurse, who took my pulse and temperature and then called a doctor. He examined me and told me that he thought I had a grumbling appendix. He insisted that I stayed in the hospital and if it wasn't any better in a day or two I would have to have an operation. Franz went back to the office with the news and I finished up in a bed in a large ward. Nurse gave me some painkillers and I went to sleep. I hardly woke up for lunch as I didn't want anything to eat, but I woke late in the afternoon. I felt better, but the nurse said I still had a temperature. She had come to tidy the ward, because the big Chief was coming to make his rounds. She helped me to sit up in bed and had just finished, when I saw a group of people in white coats entering the ward.

Sister was flapping around the big, tall, grey haired man, whose face I could not see. This was probably the professor, I thought. It reminded me of my days in the military hospital in Königsberg. There were a number of students, young doctors, and a middle-aged man, probably the professor's assistant. The group gradually made their way along the ward. They did not stop at every bed. Only when Sister picked up the temperature chart from the bottom of the bed and gave it to the professor did the group stop, and the big man said a word or two to the patient.

I watched them and suddenly I saw the old man's face. My heart nearly stopped. It was Professor Strauss, from my hospital in Königsberg. The one who had made me come to the operating theatre to watch some operations, because I had the same name as his killed daughter, and was a medical student. The group was going to pass my bed, but I just had to have the courage to speak up:

'Professor Strauss,' I said loudly.

He stopped and looked at me.

'I wonder whether you remember me. I was with you in the military hospital in Königsberg. I was working there as a medical student. They called me nurse Helga, and you said I reminded you of your daughter.'

For a moment or two he looked at me unbelievingly, then he suddenly pushed the people around him to the side and came to me and took my hand.

'Of course I remember. I had just lost my daughter - the same name, the same age, also a medical student.' Whilst talking like that, he was holding my hand. 'You helped me, although you didn't know it. I liked you in the operating theatre.' He patted my hand and smiled. 'I am glad you were able to get out of East Prussia. Are you living in Hamburg with your family?'

'No, we are like so many other refugees, living in very primitive circumstances in a wooden hut near Segeberg.' I felt it was better to mention Segeberg, because Kisdorf was such a small village, he would not have heard of it.

'How did you get out of East Prussia? Was it in good time?'

'Not really, I had to flee over the frozen Haff.'

'You poor thing, you poor thing,' he said. A faraway look came into his face, as if he was thinking back and remembering something. Sister coughed. She was getting impatient. The professor was wasting everybody's time but, being the chief, she couldn't very well say anything.

Professor Strauss looked at Sister. 'May I have the chart, please.' He studied it, felt my forehead, then my pulse, and then gently examined my tummy.

'You know what you have got, and what you will have to have?' he asked me.

'Appendicectomy,' I said.

Professor Strauss looked at the middle-aged man in the white coat and said: 'I am going to do it.' Then he turned to Sister: 'Make a note on the chart, Miss Zirkel is my patient.' He then turned to me again: 'I am going to do the operation, and I am going to give you the smallest possible cut, so that, in later years, when you look at the little scar, you can say Professor Strauss did that, and I am proud of it.'

He stroked my cheek, smiled encouragingly and, because Sister was coughing again discreetly, he turned round to her and said quite firmly:

'I know you are in a hurry, Sister, but you must permit an old man to feel sympathy for a former student, and put out a helping hand to her, who was a comfort to me in my hour of need.'

It was late in the evening when I felt very hot indeed, so I called the night nurse and asked her for a drink. She took my temperature, but she didn't give me a drink. She must have called the houseman, because a young doctor came to see me, and examined my tummy, looked at the chart, and had a whispered conversation with the Night Sister. I heard her stress the point: 'She is Professor Strauss's patient. He will want to know.'

They walked off and I dozed, not quite going to sleep. Sister glided in and out of the ward, coming several times to me, then suddenly whispered:

'I am going to give you an injection. They are going to come and fetch you. Professor Strauss is going to operate. He does a lot of operations at night. He just sent word that you are on the list.'

I had my injection. I was rolled along the ward to the lift, and down to the operating theatre. I only heard later that this was a very well-equipped theatre in the cellar, which had functioned during the war, day and night, as it had its own power supply, and could carry on even during the bombing.

I woke up very thirsty. It was daylight, and I was in a comfortable bed in a small room, with another bed on the other side, which was occupied by a young woman.

'How are you?' she said. 'You had a good sleep, I have been waiting for you to wake up.'

'I am very thirsty,' I replied.

'I will ring for the nurse.'

Nurse came and gave me a drink, and gradually I became more alert. I discovered that I had been put into a private room - instructions from Professor Strauss. Everybody was very intrigued by the sudden favouritism which I received. I felt a little embarrassed, because the nurses were so kind to me.

Professor Strauss came to see me in the afternoon but this time he only brought the Sister with him. He had a little chat with the young woman in the other bed, who was also his patient, and then he told me that it had been high time to take out the appendix; it might have burst in a day or two. Even so, he hoped I would be pleased with the scar, when I saw it.

Things had happened rather quickly and I had not told my family where I was, and what had happened to me. I had been told that I would have to stay in the hospital approximately seven to ten days. Walli, my only visitor, came to see me on the third day, so I asked her whether she could get me some writing paper from the office, because nobody had any in the hospital as paper was so short. Walli promised to bring me some, but she didn't come again until the day before I left. Even so, I wrote to my mother and told her about my operation and Professor Strauss, but I also stressed that there was no need for her to come to Hamburg as I was leaving the hospital the following day. After that, I was supposed to have two weeks recuperation but, because I could not possibly walk from Ulzburg to Kisdorf, and to the *Funkstation*, I decided to stay in Hamburg. I found out later that my mother received the letter but, because she had no paper, she never replied.

Professor Strauss came to see me every day. He told me that the operation and my stay in hospital, were free. He kept me ten days and when I left it was already the beginning of June. He said he hoped I would be able to carry on studying medicine once I returned to Switzerland. If ever I needed a recommendation or help, I was to contact him. It was quite a sad farewell and I think we both knew that we would never meet again.

My father came to see me when I was back at work. He had been to the *Funkstation*, and had heard that I had been in hospital. He brought good news. We had a big flat in town, and we could now all move together.

My father organised a lorry to collect all our belongings from the *Funkstation*. We were surprised how much we had collected. I went and got the things from Karl's room, and I even took the money out of the palliasse, but did not tell my parents or Astra about it. I knew Karl wouldn't come back any more; it was now the end of June.

It was a happy, but also a sad day, when we left Kisdorf. The *Funkstation* had been a home to us for over a year and, although the life there was primitive, at least we always had our privacy.

We had no keys to any of the doors. So we just shut the shutters and the door, closed the gate, and left.

We soon settled down in Hamburg, but found the flat very noisy. Our rooms were situated in a large block of flats, and many people with children used the common staircase. The *Funkstation* had been very quiet because of its isolation. Shopping in the town was more difficult because the queues were longer. My mother sent Astra shopping from time to time; she could take Monika with her, and carry everything in the pram. As we were all living together, there was now more to buy; even Hans had returned.

Mr Robertson was very pleased with my work and I got a rise, starting from July 1st. I was now earning 160 RM a month. When one considered that 20 English cigarettes fetched 100 RM on the black market, it was hardly worth while going to work. I had opened a bank account, and deposited Karl's money. I also occasionally sold some English cigarettes and put the money into my account. We were alright for food, as we still received the food parcels from the embassy.

All through July and August we lived quietly in our flat. Hans had his summer holiday from school, and got himself odd jobs to earn a little money. There were not many permits needed any more, so my trips to the Authorities gradually stopped. I recovered well from my appendicectomy. Professor Strauss was right, I only had a tiny scar which over the years faded, so that today it is hardly visible.

We waited for the repatriation to Switzerland, which came at the beginning of September. My father brought the news that in two weeks time we would be on a transport to the "Homeland". I gave notice at Roku. Everybody was sorry to see me go, particularly Walli, who had grown very fond of me. I promised to write, and told Walli to come and have a holiday in Switzerland.

We were only allowed to take one suitcase each because of the limited space on the lorries and coaches, which were supplied by the Swiss embassy for the *Rückwanderer* (returning emigrants). My mother sold everything which we could not take, not for money, that would have been worthless in Switzerland, but in exchange for goods we needed. We got suitcases, a little pushchair for Monika, clothes for everybody, also baby things. My mother did very well. She got suits for my father and brother and a coat each for us three girls. Astra again had insisted on taking her box, but my mother made sure it was full up with useful things. She said it must be possible to take it as it contained the baby clothes and Monika had no suitcase.

The transport consisted of two coaches and three lorries. The places in the coaches were allocated to elderly people and mothers with small children. Anybody not receiving a coach seat had to find a place in the lorries amongst the luggage. A few benches were fixed to the sides of the lorries.

Astra got a seat in the coach because she had a baby. It was the middle of September and Monika was eight months old. There was no seat for Monika; Astra had to have her on her lap. My parents were not considered old people, and Hans, Christel and I were young, so we were told that we would have to find a place in one of the lorries.

I hardly slept the last night in the flat. There were many thoughts going through my head. We had been told that, because of the children in our transport, the journey would be spread over two days, but night accommodation would be provided. I realized that I would only have one more night in Germany.

It was not often that I thought back to the time when we lived in Königsberg. Thoughts about that period were painful. I avoided them, blocked them out. If pictures of the past came into my mind, I quickly thought of something else, or kept myself busy. But that night I faced the past again. I thought of all the things I had lost, my sports certificates, my trophies, my souvenirs, my photos, my books and my papers, my clothes, and all my little personal things. I remembered my box with the letters and photographs of all my friends who were killed in the war. What did they fight for? They had given their young lives for a defeated and ruined Germany.

I had not only lost material things, but the contact with anybody I had ever known in my young days. Once I had left Germany, that would be the end; that would be the moment my past was finished. Switzerland was the new beginning. Where were all my school friends? My dancing partners? My friends and neighbours from the Metgetherstrasse? Where was Wolfgang? Was he killed in Russia, or did he get out of East Prussia and into the west? Was anybody looking for me in the same way as I was looking for them? I had been to the Red Cross and filled out cards that I was looking for several people and, in particular, for Wolfgang. I had given the address of the embassy, who had promised to contact me if there was any news, but I felt that now that I was leaving Germany I would never again meet anybody whom I had known before. I thought of Hermann, the only one who had found me. He had never written again, neither had I contacted him. Once I had left, that would be the finish with him also. Even that made me sad, because I remembered the happy times in Tuchel and I felt guilty for not having been honest with him. I thought of Sam, who so much wanted me to contact him, but I knew that I would never do it. A year had passed, the time in Gerabronn was like a dream, and Sam was now probably back in the USA. I thought of Karl, and wondered where he was. He had been good to us, and even helped us indirectly when he had disappeared.

I tossed and turned on my palliasse, I dozed, and then saw pictures from my past again, happy ones and sad ones. I must have gone to sleep in the end because, suddenly, I was back on the Haff, and there were the frozen dead bodies of women and children lying on the ice, and I got colder and colder, until I started to shiver and shake. I woke up in a cold sweat. I hadn't dreamt about those horrors for a long time.

Christel, with whom I shared the room, was still asleep. It had just started to get light, so I got up. I knew I wouldn't sleep any more. I packed my sheets into my suitcase and tied my blanket to the top of the case. Christel must have heard me moving about, because she woke up. I told her I was going for a quick walk, I wanted some fresh air, and then I left the flat. My father had always done this. Whenever something troubled him, he would go for a walk, partly to think about things whilst alone and partly to make himself tired. I had a brisk walk and gave myself a good talking to. I was not going to hanker after the past, and I was not going to think again about my flight from East Prussia and the horrors I had seen then. Today was the day of my New Beginning, the day my family would start the trip to Switzerland, to a New Life.

# EPILOGUE

Switzerland, the silver star, the light, the bright future. That's how we all had thought of our homeland. We could see it from the back of our lorry after crossing the border and were struck by its beauty, colour and cleanliness. The houses were painted and had colourful flower boxes, and the people wore gay summer dresses and talked and laughed. Nothing was destroyed and the shops were full of goods and there was even chocolate! We had not eaten any for years. Everybody got terribly excited and we pointed things out to one another and chatted, until we passed through a large gate which closed after us, and we realized we had arrived.

There was silence, bewilderment, uneasiness and surprise. We were in a camp, a quarantine camp. It was a rude awakening when men, women and children had to separate. We had to strip, we got disinfected, de-loused and examined naked by a doctor. Nobody had informed us that this would happen.

So that was the beginning of our new life. More disappointments were to follow. The Swiss government saw to it that we had food and accommodation, but we all had to try and find a job as soon as possible. None of us had a finished education, except Astra, and she had a child and could not go out to work. My mother with her knowledge of shorthand and typing became the main breadwinner. My father found it very difficult to get any employment as certificates of achievements were asked for everywhere, and he had none. In any case there were plenty of people about who knew how to make butter and cheese - one of the reasons why my grandfather emigrated.

As *Rückwanderer* we were not popular either. We did not speak the Swiss dialect, so our language gave us away. Again we felt like foreigners, this time in our home country.

My mother saw to it that Monika had a good home with foster parents as Astra just could not cope. She died three years later, aged fifty, thin, worn out, ill and disillusioned. My father followed her a few years later, just after he had started quite a thriving business in Germany, which my brother was able to take over and sell later.

None of us had an easy life. We were desperately poor for years, but all of us eventually got on well. Astra, the only one who never wanted to go to Switzerland remained in our homeland. She learnt the Swiss dialect. Her daughter, Monika, married a proper Swiss citizen and they have two grown-up sons. Christel, her husband and three grown-up children live in Italy. I found new roots in England and have my own family now, two sons and grandchildren, a kind and understanding husband, and I am happy.

The family unit was destroyed when we lost our home. Poverty and suffering had made us hard. Swiss people who never experienced war could not understand us and that is the reason why we left again. Four children, each living in a different country. Even my parents are not buried together; my mother in Switzerland and my father in Germany.

The past was brought back to me again very vividly about ten years ago when I met some of my schoolfriends and even heard from one of them what had happened to Königsberg because she stayed behind - a terrible tale.

My life was never dull, it was full of happenings, joyful and sad, but that is another story.

# ABBREVIATIONS

| | |
|---|---|
| BDM | Bund Deutscher Mädchen (Band of German Girls) |
| DM | Deutsche Mark |
| Flak | Flugzeugabwehrkanone (anti-aircraft or ack ack) |
| FS | Frauenschaft (Women's organisation) |
| H.G.W. | Hermann Goering Werke (Factory) |
| HJ | Hitler Jugend (Hitler Youth) |
| IMT | International Military Tribunal (Nuremberg) |
| KTC | Königsberger Turn Club (Königsberger Sports Club) |
| N.C.O. | Non-Commissioned Officer |
| NSDAP | Nationale Socialistische Deutsche Arbeiter Partei: NAZI |
| OKW | Ober-Kommando der Wehrmacht (German Supreme Command) |
| RAD | Reichsarbeitsdienst (State Labour Service) |
| RM | Reichs Mark |
| SA | Socialistische Arbeiterpartei (Socialistic Worker's Party) Later they were called Sturm Abteilung (storm troops) which were paramilitaries and wore brown shirts. |
| SS | Schutzstaffel (military formation of the Nazi party) This was the elite black uniformed corps which was Hitler's principal instrument of control. The Waffen SS wore grey uniforms, had the same role as the SS, but as an army command. |
| TCP | A disinfectant |